Los Angeles
Line
Line
ine
NORTH HOLLYWOOD
Hollyw
Highland
Hollywood/
Vine
HOLLYWOOD
Vermont/Santa Monica/
LA City College
Vermont/Beverly
Whilshire/
Normandie
WILSHIRE/
WESTERN
Whilshire/
Vermont
Westlake/
MacArthur
Park
UNION
STATION
Civic Center
Pershing Square
7th St./Metro Center
Pico
Grand
San Pedro
Washington
DOWNTOWN
Vernon
VERNON
Slauson
HUNTINGTON
PARK
Florence
Firestone
SOUTH
GATE
103rd St.
Hawthorne/
1-105
Aviation/
1-105
Vermont/
1-105
Avalon/
1-105
ROSA PARKS
Long Beach/
1-105
I-605/
I-105
Crenshaw/
1-105
Harbor/
1-105
Mariposa/
Nash
El Segundo/
Nash
Lakewood
1-105
Compton
LYNWOOD
Douglas/
Rosecrans
COMPTON
Artesia
MARINE/
REDONDO
Del Amo
CARSON
Wardlow
Pacific
Ocean
Willow
Pacific Coast Hwy.
Anaheim
Pacific
5th St.
Transit Mall
1st St.
LONG
BEACH
Travel better, enjoy more
ULYSSES
Travel Guides

The Los Angeles County Museum of Art houses a large, impressive collection. This museum showcases a variety of art from the world's major cultures, from ancient times to the modern era. - *LACVB*

The Central Library, which features visual arts as well as literature, has been a significant part of the L.A. landscape since 1922. This building has undergone several renovations, and now occupies several floors and many different wings. - *Michele & Tom Grimm/LACVB*

Los Angeles

Authors
Eric Hamovich
Olivier Jacques
Clayton Anderson

Editor
Caroline Béliveau

Publisher
Pascale Couture

Copy Editing
Eileen Connolly
Anne Joyce

Computer Graphics
Stéphanie Routhier

Translation
Danielle Gauthier
Renata Isajlovic
Cindy Garayt
Coordination
JacquelineGrekins

Page Layout
Typesetting
Anne Joyce
Visuals
Caroline Béliveau

Cartographers
André Duchesne
Bradley Fenton
Yanik Landreville
Patrick Thivierge

Artistic Director
Patrick Farei (Atoll)

Illustrations
Richard Serrao
Lorette Pierson
Myriam Gagné

Photography
Cover Page
Gunnar Kullenberg/SuperStock

Inside Pages:
LACVB
Richard Serrao

OFFICES
Canada: Ulysses Travel Guides, 4176 St-Denis, Montréal, Québec, H2W 2M5, ☎ (514) 843-9447 or 1-877-542-7247, ≠(514) 843-9448, info@ulysses.ca, www.ulyssesguides.com

Europe: Les Guides de Voyage Ulysse SARL, BP 159, 75523 Paris Cedex 11, France, ☎ 01 43 38 89 50, ≠01 43 38 89 52, voyage@ulysse.ca, www.ulyssesguides.com

U.S.A.: Ulysses Travel Guides, 305 Madison Avenue, Suite 1166, New York, NY 10165, ☎ 1-877-542-7247, info@ulysses.ca, www.ulyssesguides.com

DISTRIBUTORS
Canada: Ulysses Books & Maps, 4176 Saint-Denis, Montréal, Québec, H2W 2M5, ☎ (514) 843-9882, ext.2232, 800-748-9171, Fax: 514-843-9448, info@ulysses.ca, www.ulyssesguides.com

Great Britain and Ireland: World Leisure Marketing, Unit 11, Newmarket Court, Newmartket Drive, Derby DE24 8NW, ☎ 1 332 57 37 37, Fax: 1 332 57 33 99 office@wlmsales.co.uk

Scandinavia: Scanvik, Esplanaden 8B, 1263 Copenhagen K, DK, ☎ (45) 33.12.77.66, Fax: (45) 33.91.28.82

Spain: Altaïr, Balmes 69, E-08007 Barcelona, ☎ 454 29 66, Fax: 451 25 59, altair@globalcom.es

Switzerland: OLF, P.O. Box 1061, CH-1701 Fribourg, ☎ (026) 467.51.11, Fax: (026) 467.54.66

U.S.A.: The Globe Pequot Press, 246 Goose Lane, Guilford, CT 06437 - 0480, ☎1-800-243-0495, Fax: 800-820-2329, sales@globe-pequot.com

Other countries, contact Ulysses Books & Maps, 4176 Saint-Denis, Montréal, Québec, H2W 2M5, ☎ (514) 843-9882, ext.2232, 800-748-9171, Fax: 514-843-9448, info@ulysses.ca, www.ulyssesguides.com

Canadian Cataloguing in Publication Data (see page 6)

ISBN 2-89464-385-3

I went from room to room
from city to city,
hiding, looking, waiting ...
for what?
for nothing but the
irresponsible and negative
desire
to at least
not be like
them.

From the poetry collection *Bone Palace Ballet*
by Charles Bukowski

Table of Contents

Write to Us

The information contained in this guide was correct at press time. However, mistakes can slip in, omissions are always possible, places can disappear, etc. The authors and publisher hereby disclaim any liability for loss or damage resulting from omissions or errors.

We value your comments, corrections and suggestions, as they allow us to keep each guide up to date. The best contributions will be rewarded with a free book from Ulysses Travel Guides. All you have to do is write us at the following address and indicate which title you would be interested in receiving (see the list at the end of guide).

Ulysses Travel Guides
4176 Saint-Denis
Montréal, Québec
Canada H2W 2M5
E-mail: text@ulysses.ca

Cataloguing

Canadian Cataloguing-in-Publication Data

Los Angeles

(Ulysses travel guide)
Includes index.

ISBN 2-89464-385-3
1. Los Angeles (Calif.) - Guidebooks. I. Series

F869.L83L67 2001 917.94'940454 C2001-940015-2

Thanks

Thanks to: Mathieu Landry; Carol Martinez and Stacey Litz of the Los Angeles Convention & Visitors Bureau; Bonnie Tregaskis; Melissa Centano; Special thanks to Vida Smart of Los Angeles for hospitality and support.

We acknowledge the financial support of the Government of Canada through the Book Publishing Industry Development Program (BPIDP) for our publishing activities.

We would also like to thank SODEC (Québec) for its financial support.

Symbols

(ship logo)	Ulysses's Favourite
♿	Wheelchair Access
☎	Telephone Number
⇄	Fax Number
≡	Air Conditioning
⊗	Fan
≈	Pool
ℜ	Restaurant
⊛	Whirlpool
ℝ	Refrigerator
K	Kitchenette
⌂	Sauna
⊘	Fitness Center
tv	Television
sb	Shared Bathroom
fb	Full Board (Lodging + 3 Meals)
½ b	Half Board (Lodging + 2 Meals)
bkfst incl.	Breakfast Included
♠	Casino

ATTRACTION CLASSIFICATION

★	Interesting
★★	Worth a visit
★★★	Not to be missed

The prices listed in this guide are for the admission of one adult.

HOTEL CLASSIFICATION

$	$40 or less
$$	$40 to $80
$$$	$80 to $130
$$$$	$130 to 200
$$$$$	$200 and more

The prices in the guide are for one standard room, double occupancy in high season.

RESTAURANT CLASSIFICATION

$	$10 or less
$$	$10 to $20
$$$	$20 to $30
$$$$	$30 and more

List of Maps

Table of Symbols

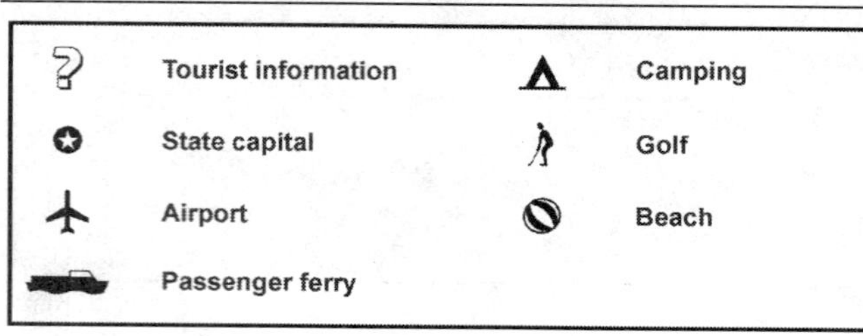

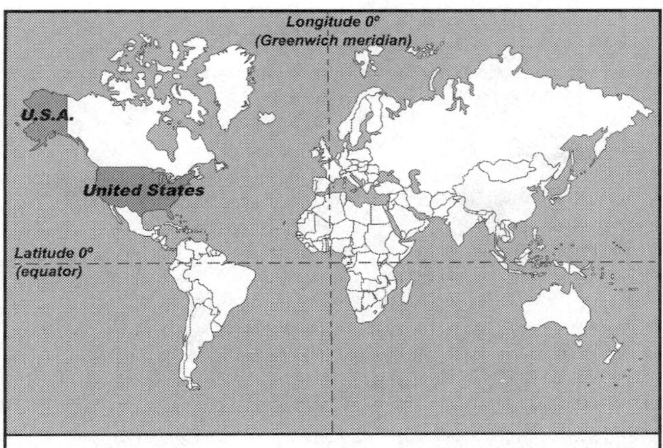

Where is Los Angeles?

California
Capital: Sacramento Population: 29,760,025 inhab. Currency : US dollar Area : 411,000 km²
Los Angeles
Population: 3,700,000 inhab. Surroundings: 9,700,000 inhab.

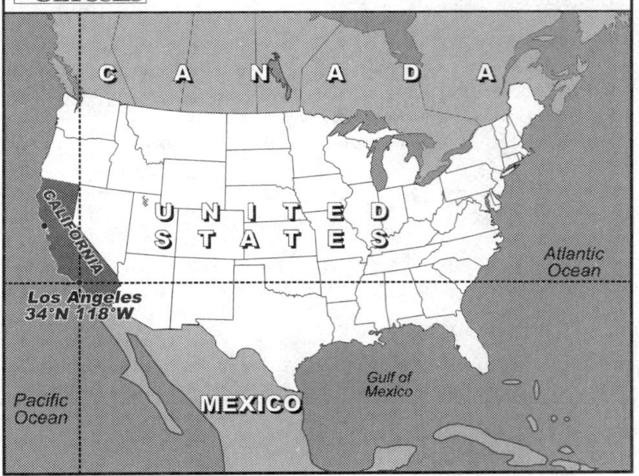

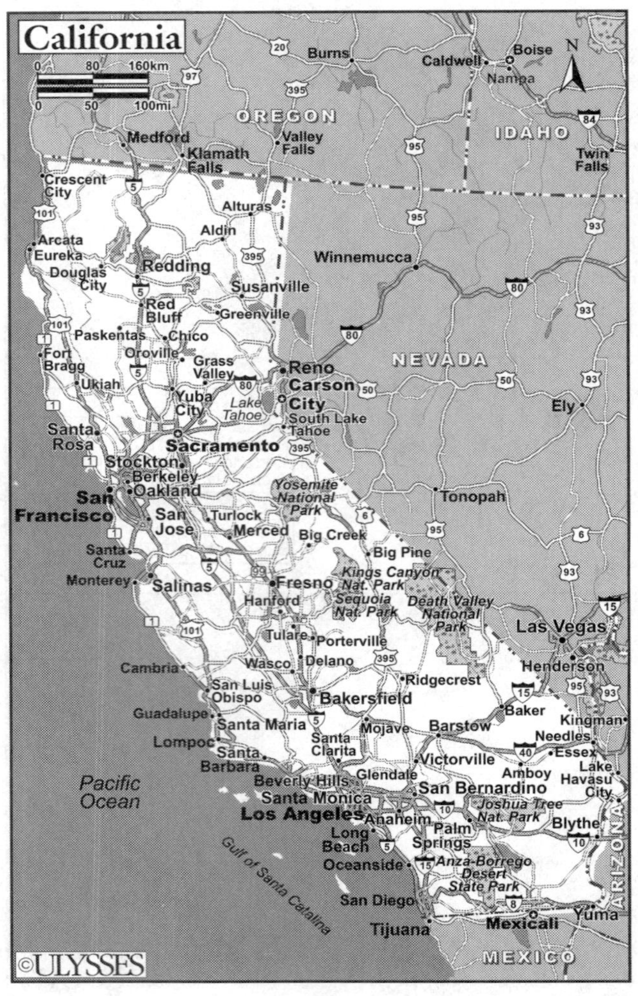
California
0 80 160km
0 50 100mi
OREGON
IDAHO
NEVADA
ARIZONA
MEXICO
Burns
Caldwell
Boise
Nampa
Medford
Klamath Falls
Valley Falls
Twin Falls
Crescent City
Alturas
Aldin
Arcata
Eureka
Douglas City
Redding
Winnemucca
Susanville
Red Bluff
Greenville
Paskentas
Chico
Fort Bragg
Oroville
Grass Valley
Reno
Carson City
Ukiah
Yuba City
Lake Tahoe
South Lake Tahoe
Ely
Santa Rosa
Sacramento
Stockton
Berkeley
Oakland
San Francisco
Yosemite National Park
Tonopah
San Jose
Turlock
Merced
Big Creek
Santa Cruz
Big Pine
Monterey
Salinas
Fresno
Kings Canyon Nat. Park
Hanford
Sequoia Nat. Park
Death Valley National Park
Las Vegas
Tulare
Porterville
Cambria
Wasco
Delano
Henderson
Ridgecrest
San Luis Obispo
Bakersfield
Baker
Guadalupe
Santa Maria
Kingman
Mojave
Barstow
Needles
Lompoc
Santa Clarita
Santa Barbara
Essex
Victorville
Amboy
Lake Havasu City
Pacific Ocean
Beverly Hills
Glendale
San Bernardino
Santa Monica
Joshua Tree Nat. Park
Los Angeles
Anaheim
Blythe
Long Beach
Palm Springs
Gulf of Santa Catalina
Oceanside
Anza-Borrego Desert State Park
San Diego
Tijuana
Mexicali
Yuma
©ULYSSES

Portrait

Los Angeles is the megalopolis of cars, the capital of illusion.

Permeated with smog, it stretches southward between the Santa Ana, Santa Monica and San Gabriel mountains. Some consider this mythical, excessive and sprawling city to be monstrous, while others simply adore it.

Los Angeles is complete chaos: no reference points exist in what seems to be a centreless and boundless expanse. Save for the giant downtown towers where people work (but don't live), the city is a huge suburb of 16.3 million residents. Some say Los Angeles is unliveable because of its traffic, earthquakes, fires, floods and crime. This, however, is neither completely true, nor completely false.

The remarkably intertwined network of highways forms a bona fide spider web that envelops the city, where the car is indisputably king. Intended to link districts, Los Angeles's freeways also serve as invisible borders between districts. The city nevertheless remains the symbol of success for U.S. citizens, like stumbling

Smog: At Least You Can See What You're Breathing!

Smog is one of the curses of life in Los Angeles. The city's millions of motor vehicles and thousands of industrial establishments spew a noxious stew of gases that cannot disperse easily because of the city's walled-in saucer shape, creating a dull brown haze that varies in intensity from day to day. Smog alerts are issued on certain days, during which people with respiratory problems are urged to stay indoors. Exhaust gases and moisture (the word smog signifies smoke plus fog) are often held in place by layers of cooler air above and cooked to an unappealing consistency by hours of relentless sunshine. On certain days, the result is highly visible to anyone approaching the city by air.

The South Coast Air Quality Management District, whose job it is to enforce regulations set by various levels of government, has clamped tighter controls on factories and ordered changes in the design of vehicle exhaust systems. These efforts have achieved modest success, and the number of smog alerts has declined. Lifestyle-infringing measures, such as the restriction of private vehicle, use appear to be unthinkable, however. Public policy seems aimed less at eliminating the problem than at keeping it from getting worse. To be sure, air pollution in L.A. is less severe than in many Third World cities, and even within the U.S. it has been eclipsed by Houston, under the Texas government's very lax environmental standards. Smog is an element of local identity in L.A. that seems to be worn almost proudly as a badge of self-deprecation.

upon an oasis after crossing the desert. Imposing villas, fast cars, extravagant clothes, classy restaurants and the latest fashionable drugs are perhaps elements of the American Dream incarnated in the paroxysm of L.A. Seduced by these powerful symbols, many travellers and immigrants continue to flock to this Promised Land. The slightest mention of Sunset Boulevard, Beverly Hills and Rodeo Drive evokes captivating images which continuously draw people to California's metropolis.

You'll best appreciate L.A. by exploring. This city of a thousand faces is both rugged and refined, tumultuous, yet pleasant, and multicultural, though very American.

Geography

Los Angeles is the second most populated city in the United States and is nestled deep between five mountain chains and an ocean. Its heart reveals sandy beaches, as well as untamed hills and deserts swept by wind. At night, from up above, the city resembles a lit up checkerboard that stretches from the ink-blue Pacific to the obscure outskirts of the mountains.

Los Angeles (within its strict administrative boundaries) stretches over 467sq mi (1,210 km²), which makes it the second largest city in the United States. However, the greater metropolitan area (including the counties of L.A., Ventura, Orange, Riverside and San Bernardino) comprises a much greater area of 21,230sq mi (55,000km²). The dimensions of this huge metropolis extend 50mi (80km) from east to west, between Malibu to Euclid Avenue, and 37mi (60km) from north to south between the San Fernando Valley and the port of L.A.

Geological Foundations

The western United States was created, and is still greatly affected by, the counter-movement of two plates, which form rigid and gigantic sheets of the earth's crust. Around 400 million years ago, its edge, then part of the Pacific plate that almost reached Asia, slid under the western edge of the North American plate during a process known as "subduction." As the dominating edge of the North American plate continued to shift westward, thus covering the Pacific plate, parts of the earth's crust along the contact area were compressed and pleated, creating mountain chains, while smaller peripheral land masses joined the North American plate. The Pacific plate changed direction and began to pivot 25 million years ago. Today, it mainly slides northwestward, while the North American plate continues to regularly shift westward.

The Californian region most affected by this tectonic instability lies along the San Andreas fault. This fault stretches from the Imperial Valley in the southeast to Cape Mendocino on the northern coast, and runs less than 34mi (54km) from downtown L.A. More than a dozen other faults cut through the metropolitan area, likening the city to a cracked eggshell. Like other faults, the San Andreas fault was created by the movement of the Pacific and North American plates, that move toward each other at an average rate of 2in (5cm) per year.

Imperceptible plate movements often occur along faults, but such shifting may sometimes be impeded by rigid materials such as granite, which places greater strain on the fault when plates move. When the obstructions finally give way, the suppressed pressure causes an earthquake, a violent, sudden and destructive tremor that shakes the earth along the fault. In the 1850s, two violent tremors (estimated at 7.1 on the Richter scale) destroyed nearly every building in the young city of Los Angeles, and no earthquake of such magnitude has shaken the city since. In 1971, an earthquake in the San Fernando Valley killed 64 people and caused over $1 billion in damages. On January 17, 1994, another earthquake measuring 6.7 on the Richter scale shook the entire metropolitan basin. Its epicenter was once again located in the San Fernando Valley, this time in Northridge, and caused the death of 72 people and over $10 billion in damages. The last earthquake occured in October 1999, and measured 7 on the Richter scale. It rattled the city, with its epicenter located in the Mojave Desert. Fortunately, the tremor caused little damage. However, Los Angeles residents constantly live in fear that the "Big One" could happen anytime.

Regional Scenery

Greater L.A. covers a vast coastal plain that is bordered to the west and south by the Pacific Ocean, to the north by the San Gabriel Mountains, and to the east by a smaller mountain chain that stretches to the Mojave Desert. The Santa Monica Mountains separate Hollywood and Beverly Hills from the San Fernando Valley in the north.

The hot and dry summers increase the risk of forest fires in the area. Strong winds often fuel huge forest fires. From August to November, the Santa Ana winds sweep through the city, bringing with them clear and pleasant weather. During this same period, however, the forests of the Santa Monica and San Gabriel mountains and the Laguna Hills, are constantly at risk of breaking out in flames. In 1993, more than 1,000 homes in Altadena (near Pasadena), Laguna Beach and Malibu were completely destroyed by fire; 148sq mi (384km^2) of forest suffered the same fate.

Water Resources

Since its founding, Los Angeles, which is located in a semi-desert region, has had to continuously deal with the problem of main-

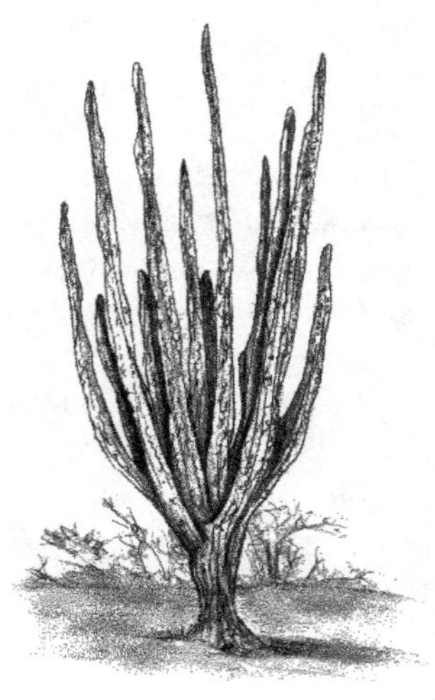

Water: an Ongoing Struggle

A bone of contention between agricultural, environmental and urban groups, managing the water supply was and continues to be a major challenge for California's government. Subject to periodic dry spells, the state has had to adopt an efficient management plan that involves ecological groups, suppliers and government agencies. Through awareness-raising campaigns, officials have more or less succeeded in conserving water and creating reserves that can be drawn on during heat waves. Increasingly, cities are recycling used water, and several have initiated desalination programs.

There is no denying that California's development flies in the face of its limited water resources. About 75% of the state's precipitation falls north of Sacramento, while 75% of the demand for water comes from the coastal region. During the 1930s, a network of reservoirs, dams and aqueducts had to be built to maintain the Central Valley's productivity and to develop the urban centres of Southern California. Major challenges remain to this day, since the southern areas are experiencing rapid population growth, due to immigration from retired Anglos as well as Latinos from Mexico.

taining an adequate water supply to support its growth and development. When the city's population reached 200,000 people at the start of the 20th century, it became evident that the ground water level was clearly insufficient to meet the city's needs. A plan was thus devised to import water by aqueduct and solve the problem once and for all.

Along with a recent aqueduct completed in 1970, the Los Angeles Aqueduct, which was built by William Mulholland and Fred Eaton in 1908, still provides 75% of Los Angeles's water. As the largest aqueduct network in all of California, this system runs 240mi (386km) through the Owens Valley from the Sierra Nevada in the east, to deliver water to the city. Another 10% of L.A.'s water supply comes from the Colorado River Aqueduct, which transports water over a similar distance from Lake Havasu, located near the state's southeastern border.

A Little History

Around 10,000 years ago, well before Los Angeles became one of the world's media capitals, and long before the arrival of Spanish colonizers, America consisted of fields inhabited by some 30,000 Aboriginal people, who had come from Asia by the Bering Strait. The Gabrieleño and Chumash people arrived in the region some 5,000 to 6,000 years BC. While the Gabrieleños populated the hinterland, the Chumash settled on the coast between what was to become Malibu and Santa Barbara. Like the Sierra Nevada peoples, these two Aboriginal nations hunted and lived off the land, and the Chumash also survived by fishing. Their cultures were highly developed technically and economically. The Chumash especially excelled at building canoes for sea navigation; wooden boards were assembled, then coated with tar to make them watertight. The quality of the handicrafts (dominated by pottery) created by these two Aboriginal peoples greatly impressed the Spanish, as did their grass-woven huts. The latter were assembled by using curved wooden sticks, which formed a type

Star of India

Important Dates in California's History

1542
Serving in the Spanish navy, Portuguese explorer Juan Rodríguez Cabrillo lands on the shores of San Diego Bay.

1579
English explorer Sir Francis Drake first sets foot on the shores of San Francisco Bay.

1602
Spanish explorer Sebastián Vizcaíno presses on a little further, following the Pacific Coast.

1769
With the help of Gaspar de Portolá, the Spanish Fransiscan priest Juníperro Serra founds the Catholic mission of San Diego de Alcala, the first on Californian soil.

1770
The first *presidio* is erected in Monterey.

1776
Founding of San Francisco de Asis.

1781
Founding of Los Angeles de Porciuncula.

1821
Mexico becomes independent. California is under the jurisdiction of the new nation.

1826
Jedediah Strong Smith leaves Saint Louis, Missouri and crosses the Sierra Nevada, becoming the first person to reach California by land.

1833
Franciscan missions are disbanded and secularized.

1846
Beginning of the territorial war between Mexico and the United States.

1848
Mexico is defeated. Under the Treaty of Guadalupe Hidalgo, New Mexico, Arizona and California fall to the United States.

James Marshall, an employee of John Sutter, discovers the first gold nuggets in the American River.

1849
The gold rush begins. Arrival of more than 55,000 prospectors, known as the "Forty-niners."

1850
California becomes the 31st state to join the Union.

1869
The transcontinental railroad is inaugurated.

1876
The coastal line of the Southern Pacific railroad is built.

1885
The coastal line of the Santa Fe railroad is built.

1906
The great San Francisco earthquake practically destroys the city.

1915
San Francisco's Panama Pacific International Exhibition marks the city's reconstruction, as well as the opening of the famous Panamá Canal several months earlier.

1920
This is the decade marking the beginning of the great era of Hollywood film.

1965
Racial riots break out in Los Angeles's Watts district.

1967
San Fransisco's hippie movement proclaims this year the "Summer of Love."

1992
Fifty people lose their lives in the Los Angeles race riots.

1998
The election of Governor Gray David marks the Democrats' return to power after a 12-year interval.

of dome at their peak. Unlike most North American aboriginal peoples, the Gabrieleños and Chumash burried their dead.

In 1542, Juan Rodríguez Cabrillo, a Portuguese explorer that served under King Charles I of Spain, became the first European to visti the Los Angeles basin and come into contact with Native Americans. In the two centuries that followed, L.A.'s future site was merely a simple supply stop on the trans-Pacific route, where Spanish galleons from the Philippines heading to Mexico stocked up on goods. It was only when other nations set their sights on California that Spain decided to colonize this region to reinforce its hold on America.

In the Name of Christ

The Spanish returned in 1769 dressed in monk's robes with a rope tied around their waists and sandals on their feet. To contain the advance of the British, and especially that of the Russians, who were already well settled in Fort Cross, Charles III of Spain, the sovereign of a weakened kingdom, sent missionaries to evangelize (and colonize) Alta California (Upper California), which he deemed a strategic and economic interest. Colonizers, led by Father Junípero Serra, a 55-year-old Franciscan priest, and Captain Don Gaspar de Portolá, ventured north of Mexico to establish no fewer than 21 missions in California. In 1771, the San Gabriel Arcángel mission was founded 9mi (15km) from today's downtown core. The founding of these missions allowed the Spanish to consolidate colonial territories, expand borders and convert Native Americans to Christianity. Unfortunately, Natives could not adapt to the new lifestyle, due to the diseases introduced by the colonizers. Several thousands died in the years that followed, so many, in fact, that the Aboriginal population never recovered.

In the years that followed, Felipe De Neve, California's commanding officer, decided that the region needed a *pueblo* and began drawing up plans. In 1781, a group from Mexico consisting of 12 men, 11 women and their 21 children, arrived at the mission. On September 4, they founded the new city: El Pueblo de Nuestra Señora la Reina de Los Angeles de Porciúncula, literally "the village of Our Lady the Queen of Angels of Porciúncula." These first colonizers were a mix of Spaniards, Native Americans, *mestizos* and African-Americans. Los Angeles, as the village was to be called shortly thereafter, developed into a large, prosperous town. Given the abundance of sunshine and the scarcity of water, colonizers concentrated on developing orange, olive and wheat crops, as well as cattle, sheep and horse farms.

Ranchos

Felipe De Neve's successor passed new laws authorising him to grant vast areas and grazing rights to colonizers. He thus distributed thousands of acres, mainly to his friends. In no time, a dozen *patrones* (land owners) took possession of nearly the entire coast of Los Angeles County, with the exception of land held by missionaries and farms surrounding the *pueblo*. As colonial powers that controlled all commerce on their territories, Mexico and Spain benefited from the riches of the *ranchos* (farms) and missions in California. The U.S. East coast, however, quickly became aware of the lucrative production of the Californian colonies. Opposed by only a handful of Spanish ships and militia that were powerless in enforcing colonial commerce regulations, Yankee ships began exploiting this profitable new market. Mexico gained independence in 1821 and annexed Alta California the following year. Bostonian Joseph Chapman became the first Yankee to settle in Los Angeles, in 1818. Fifteen years later, the city only counted 29 U.S. residents. This small cluster of settlers nevertheless bustled with activity and showed great initiative by developing farms and workshops. By developing a credit formula for *ranchos*, they created the first U.S. banking system.

Following Mexico's Independence, Spanish priests were soon expelled from California, and the missions' social organization followed suit. Towards 1830, commissioners were named to distribute nearly 7.5 million acres (three million hectares) held by missionaries, mostly to families and to the most powerful *ranchos*. Reduced to slavery, Native Americans helped make these *ranchos* prosperous.

In 1846, U.S. colonizers, backed by the government of the Union states, stirred up the Bear Flag Revolt. That summer Captain John C. Fremont and Captain

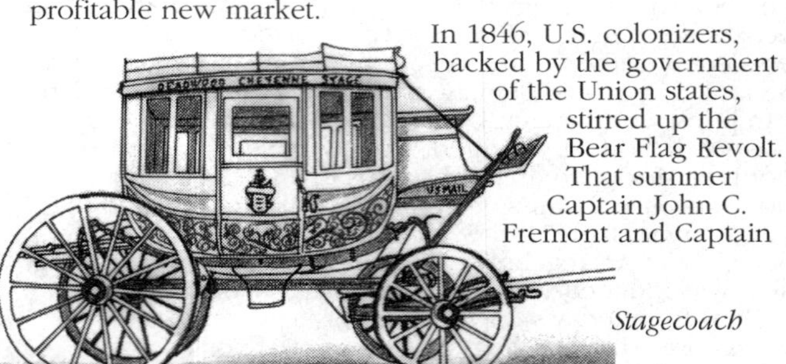

Stagecoach

Stockton pursued Governor Pío Pico from Los Angeles to San Juan Capistrano in the south, and forced the Mexican dignitary to take refuge on the other side of the border. Mexican combatants put up a valiant fight, often resisting forces that were several times greater in number. But their efforts were ultimately in vain, and the conflict came to an end as the Treaty of Guadalupe Hidalgo was signed in a San Fernando Valley residence in February 1848. After this the U.S. flag was raised over California, New Mexico and Texas. At the same time, nearly half of Mexico's territory was annexed to the United States of America.

Gold Rush

That same year, the discovery of gold in Northern California radically changed the entire state. Many Los Angeles residents rushed to the gold mines, but those who stayed behind took advantage of the lucrative market to provide supplies and materials to miners. Meat production was substituted for that of leather and tallow, and became the ranches' primary industry. Cattle were transported northward, where they could be sold for 10 times the prices in effect.

From Boom to Boom

On April 4, 1850, the city of Los Angeles was established and declared the administrative heart of the county with which it shared its name. Its first newspaper, *The Star*, appeared that same year and was published in both Spanish and English. The city was but a small town whose dirt roads were lined by adobe buildings that housed brothels and gambling clubs. Towards 1854, when the gold mines in Northern California had been picked clean, waves of unemployed miners flocked to the region, as banks and mining companies closed their doors.

In 1876, after several more or less illegal dealings, a railway reached Los Angeles by cutting through the San Joaquin Valley. In 1885, the Atchison, Topeka & Santa Fe Railroad directly linked L.A. and the east coast, by crossing the Arizona Desert. Due to the fierce competition that ensued between this railroad and its rival the Southern Pacific, the cross-country trip cost next to nothing. In 1887, trains transported more than 80,000 travellers to Los Angeles, whereas the city itself counted only 35,000 residents. Many of these travellers were immigrants who had come to permanently settle in the area, thus unleashing the biggest real estate boom in the country's history.

Oranges

At that same time, orange growing was flourishing in Southern California, especially in Riverside and Anaheim, thanks to agricultural irrigation. Around 1873, the federal Department of Agriculture had introduced three Brazilian orange trees that were the origin of this new resource. California oranges made their way to New York grocery stores. Their promotion rested on an intensive ad campaign by the Chamber of Commerce. This California orange craze later gave L.A. its nickname of "the Big Orange," in jest of New York's "the Big Apple."

At a time when everyone had California on their minds, Easterners were further enticed by the incentive of newspaper editor Horace Greeley, who wrote "Go West, Young Man." L.A.'s charms were already becoming renowned: the city looked nothing like the business world of New York and Chicago, and its climate, beautiful scenery and the lifestyles of its residents were greatly appealing to Easterners. Its population thus jumped from 2,300 in 1860 to more than 50,000 in 1890, and hit the 100,000-mark in 1900.

Due to rapid population growth, lots were quickly snatched up. So many new communities were founded, that at the end of 1887, 25 satellite cities had sprung up along railway lines. One such city, founded by Horace and Daeida Wilcox following the division of their 247,100-acre (100,000 ha) orchard, was named Hollywood.

The boom in the real estate industry ended three years later, in 1890. However, a new campaign geared towards Midwest farmers re-

Important Dates in Los Angeles's History

1771	Founding of the San Gabriel Arcángel Mission.
1781	Founding of El Pueblo de Nuestra Señora la Reina de Los Angeles de Porciúncula.
1825	California is annexed to Mexico.
1848	The Treaty of Guadalupe Hidalgo brings an end to the war between Mexico and the United States. California becomes part of the United States.
1850	California becomes a state.
1853	Don Matteo Keeler plants the first orange trees.
1876	The Southern Pacific, the first transcontinental railway line, arrives in Los Angeles.
1880	Founding of the University of Southern California.
1881	The *Los Angeles Times* publishes its first edition.
1892	Discovery of oil in Long Beach.
1909	Construction of the jetty in Santa Monica.
1913	Cecil B. De Mille directs *The Squaw Man*, the first feature-length film in movie history.

1923	Construction of the giant Hollywood sign.
1927	Opening of the Chinese Theater (today Mann's), a theatre designed by Graumann. Founding of the Academy of Motion Picture Arts and Sciences.
1928	Opening of L.A.'s first airport, Mines Field, located on the site of the LAX.
1932	The Olympic Games are held in L.A.
1947	Hollywood's highway links downtown to the San Fernando Valley.
1955	Opening of Disneyland in Anaheim.
1961	Launching of the Hollywood Walk of Fame.
1969	Charles Manson is guilty of the death of actor Sharon Tate.
1984	The XXIII Olympiad is held in L.A.
1992	The Rodney King riots.
1994	The Northridge earthquake. Massive damage.
1995	The O.J. Simpson trial captures the world's attention.

vived immigration. The touting of California's exceptional produce attracted a wave of farmers. As of 1880, immigration essentially consisted of Anglo-Americans, even though the arrival of populations from

Asia, Mexico and the southern United States provided the workforce to complete large infrastructure projects. Despite their diverse backgrounds, immigrants adapted with incomparable vigour.

The discovery of oil in 1892 in Long Beach signalled that industrialisation was thriving and added more names to the list of wealthy residents. The first oil well, drilled by Edward Doheny and Charles Canfield, produced 45 barrels per day. In five years, nearly 2,500 wells had been bored within the urban perimeter, and the industry was flourishing. Oil gushed out of wells in the vicinity of Huntington Beach, Long Beach and San Pedro, enriching the coffers of coastal municipalities and destroying coastal scenery. At the end of the century, California was producing a quarter of the world's oil supply.

In 1899, construction of an artificial port began in San Pedro, 23mi (37km) south of Los Angeles, and it was inaugurated in 1914. The ports of San Pedro and Long Beach grew exponentially, and transformed Los Angeles into an important coastal centre, the largest on the West Coast.

The 20th Century

Having become a dynamic city only 50 years after its founding, Los Angeles continued to grow at a rapid pace. Following a new ad campaign featuring the slogan "Oranges for Health, California for Wealth," its population trippled in the first decade of the 20th century to reach 300,000 residents. Henry Huntington, the nephew of railway tycoon Collis P. Huntington, founded the Pacific Electric Railway Company and caused a succession of real estate investments by deploying tramway lines in all directions.

A major obstacle curbed expansion, however: the lack of water. As the population was booming, the Los Angeles River (formerly known as Río Porciúncula), the city's only source of water, could no longer meet the city's needs. In 1904, William Mulholland, then chief engineer of the Municipal Water Department, developed a system to import water from the Owens River, which was fed by snow melting in the Sierra Nevada Mountains. It was thus decided to build a huge canal, but the project was costly and the city of Los Angeles could not finance it alone. It therefore contacted neighbouring agglomerations; some accepted and joined the city, which took on the strange and extremely jagged shape for which it is now known. This aqueduct, a pure engineering marvel that criss-crossed through nearly 250mi (400km) of desert, provided Los Angeles with enough water to annex the entire San Fernando Valley. A hydroelectric power station was also completed along the aqueduct in 1917, thus instigating a new wave of industrial expansion. This project was not without opposition, and even today the system is still contested, notably by farmers in the Owens Valley and residents of Northern California, who are deprived of their water; however, it provides more than 75% of Southern California's water supply. The rest is provided by dams on the Colorado River, 310mi (500km) eastward.

For a good part of the 19th century, San Francisco enjoyed a dominant position in California thanks to the gold rush and the exceptionally favourable agricultural conditions in neighbouring areas. It thus became the undisputed financial and transportation centre. However, when entire neighbourhoods were destroyed by the 1906 earthquake, San Francisco began to lose ground to its rival, Los Angeles. Thousands of San Francisco residents were suddenly homeless and moved towards L.A. This stage marked the rise of L.A. as the most powerful metropolis in the western United States. After the First World War, its population was the largest in the country. With 12 additional cities, the metropolis now stretched from the port of San Pedro in the south, to the San Fernando Valley in the north. L.A. had become the wealthiest and most diverse region in North America.

Large oil refineries were built, and the arrival of Firestone and Goodyear turned L.A. into a major tire manufacturing centre, with the car already playing a central role in the lives of residents. In 1925, Los Angeles was the world's most motorized city. The Pacific Highway was completed in the 1930s, and campgrounds for motorists and car drivers sprung up like never before in Southern California.

The Lockheed brothers and Donald Douglas established airplane factories in the area, which paved the way for a major aeronautics industry. Production was facilitated by a climate that guaranteed ideal conditions for test flights. However, no activity would replace the movie-making industry: in 1919, Los Angeles was already producing 80% of the world's movies and this industry was one of the top 10 biggest employers in the United States. During this period, establishments required by the flourishing city were built, such as the Bilmore Hotel, the Central Library, city hall and the University of Southern California (1880).

In 1929, Los Angeles, like the rest of North America, suffered through the Great Depression, a serious economic crisis whose origin is traced to the New York Stock Market crash. Southern California's growth took a downturn, while financially-ruined farmers from the Dust Bowl (mid-south United States) and a wave of not-so-welcome migrants (swindlers, adventurers, outlaws and artists) headed West. Many travelled north to the San Joaquin Valley, a farming area 298mi (480km) long, and a true cornucopia that has today become the world's most productive agricultural region. However, many dreamed of fame and glory, and stayed in Los Angeles, begging for any jobs available, somehow managing to find work one way or another in the movie industry. In 1935, the economy took off again and L.A. County ranked fifth among the country's industrial counties.

The Second World War

Los Angeles almost became a major industrial centre overnight during the Second World War. Aircraft, missiles and ships for the war against Japan had to be built near the Pacific. Within 18 months, L.A. had become one of the country's most imposing aviation production sites, a gigantic hive of activity where all kinds of war equipment was being manufactured. Workers flocked to the city to work in the numerous ship-building yards or aircraft factories. Close to 200,000 African-Americans settled in the industrial neighbourhood of South Central. Mexicans, who had been looked down upon since the end of Mexican rule, were hired en masse. The problems of overpopulation, and the effects of prejudice and social status, which continued to be a source of tensions well after the war, can be traced back to this period.

Towards the end of the Second World War, billions of dollars in military contracts were injected into Southern California. The thriving aeronautics industry was accompanied by an urban explosion; cities sprung up at a phenomenal rate in the south, notably Lakewood, north of Long Beach, which was built overnight to house McDonnell-Douglas employees. Freeways criss-crossed new suburbs, establishing the car as the only means of transportation. The city was thereby organized according to its road network, not vice-versa. This highway expansion was made even more essential by the dismantling of the tramway lines, which was orchestrated by their new owner, a company controlled by General Motors. Everything was now built with respect to the car, notably the well-known Disneyland, inaugurated in 1955 and built along Orange County highways.

Television made its debut and was such a giant success, that the production of fiction in the city's studios increased considerably. This new medium stifled the movie industry at first, but the situation stabilized in the early 1960s; the television and movie industries became extremely powerful and required an army of actors, make-up artists and scriptwriters.

At the same time, important migratory changes gave the city a new face, as L.A. continued to greet many newcomers. When economic conditions worsened in Mexico due to the collapse of oil prices, waves of Mexicans crossed the border, both legally and illegally. Following the lead of their northern neighbours, many Guatemalans, Salvadorians and other Latin-Americans helped transform the character of the city, where a quarter of the population's mother tongue was Spanish. In the late 1960s, after the disaster in Vietnam, many Laotians and Vietnamese people settled here. Iranians, who were fleeing the Islamic revolution in Teheran, brought with them great wealth they had amassed under the Shah's rule. Russians of Jewish descent did likewise; though less wealthy, they were ready to merge into the feverish life of Los Angeles. These new immigrants included reputable talents such as writers Thomas Mann and Bertolt Brecht, as well as composers Kurt Weill, Arnold Schoenberg, Béla Bartók and Igor Stravinsky.

New Challenges

Other events were less joyful. Rapid population growth caused water-supply problems, cuts in services and rising racial tension. In 1963, California became North America's most populated state. In the summer of 1965, riots broke out in the Watts ghetto, in the South Central neighbourhood, when an African-American motorist was charged for driving under the influence. Six days marked by vandalism, pillaging and fires caused the deaths of 34 people and $40 million in damages. History repeated itself in the spring of 1992, following the Rodney King affair (see p 41), which provoked riots that were particularly brutal. These troubles revealed new tensions created by police radicalism in poor neighbourhoods, which are often perceived as occupied territories. Even though efforts were made to rectify the situation, notably through renewing the police corps and by having the Los Angeles Police Department adopt a new approach, the problem is far from being solved. In 1999, an anti-gang brigade was dismantled after certain agents were found guilty of using excessive force against gang members they were attempting to restrain.

Many other tragedies, such as the O.J. Simpson trial, fires, floods and killer earthquakes, marked the period from 1971 to 1994 (see p 42). Of course, these events made the front pages of newspapers around the world, which did not tell the whole story. In particular, press coverage of interracial tensions has been extremely negative, but marriage statistics in the last few years in L.A. County paint a more positive picture: the number of interracial marriages is constantly on the rise. Despite what is said, the bonds between residents in the different communities of the "City of Angels" do tend to blend together.

The city of Los Angeles today has 3.7 million inhabitants, but more than 9 million people live in L.A. County. The area is constantly challenged by a myriad of social problems. Its strong economy and the restoration work visible throughout the city, however, have created new optimism with the arrival of the new millennium.

Political Life

The city of Los Angeles is governed by a mayor (executive power) and a city council consisting of 15 members (legislative power), all of which are elected by universal suffrage for a four-year mandate. The district attorney and auditor are also elected. On July 1, 1993, Republican Richard Riordan succeeded outgoing mayor Tom Bradley, a Democrat. Riordan, a millionaire lawyer and entrepreneur, was re-elected in 1997 for another four-year term. One of the mayor's main responsibilities is to present the city's annual budget and have it approved by city council. He or she must also approve decrees, regulations and the nominations of local officials and commissioners, in addition to greeting dignitaries passing through Los Angeles.

The city council decrees new regulations, determines taxation laws, authorizes investments, calls elections and regulates commerce. City council members are currently representative of L.A.'s cultural mosaic: African-Americans, Latinos, Asians, Whites and gays sit side-by-side to manage the city's business. L.A. County, which consists of 88 independent cities including Los Angeles, is governed by the Board of Supervisors. The Board's five members, who are also elected for a four-year term, have extensive executive and legislative powers over the entire metropolitan area. As a general rule, the liberal and democratic values of L.A. County favour the election of Democratic candidates, while other counties, especially that of Orange, are more conservative and often elect Republican representatives. Although many Republicans view the Holloywood élite and stars as Democrat activists, the reality is that the movie capital also has its share of pro-Republicanism.

Residents of the Los Angeles metropolitan area play an important role in the State of California's political scene, as they make up 40% of the state's voters. Like the country's other 49 states, California elects its governor, senate (39 members) and house of representatives (79 members) by universal suffrage. This three-branched government enjoys jurisdiction over a great number of sectors. As a champion of individualism, California has developed the concept of "direct democracy" more than anywhere else in the United States. During various elections, the population is often called upon to vote in a referendum on a multitude of questions, ranging from dog collars to dam construction projects. This procedure was inscribed in the state's constitution in 1911. With the support of 5% of the population, any citizen may propose a law that will be put to a referendum in a subsequent election. Therefore, voting in California often entails marking a check in 30 different boxes.

Under pressure by residents, California has always

played a leading role in protecting the environment. It has contributed to the creation of several parks and nature reserves, and, more recently, to controlling smog in cities, coastal development, and especially water management. The latter is a sensitive issue that has given rise to unprecedented co-operation between state and federal governments.

The Economy

Los Angeles's great economic diversity makes it a leader in areas such the aeronautics, entertainment and tourism industries.

The aeronautics industry was already well established in this area prior to the Second World War, thanks to regional investors who had no qualms about taking risks, as well as a temperate climate that allowed for test flights all year-round. In addition to airplanes, missiles and related equipment were also manufactured here. After the war, rocket motors and guidance systems were added to the industry's product lines. The end of the Cold War, however, hit the industry hard, resulting in significant layoffs and requiring companies to adjust their production to the civilian market. Boeing is the sector's largest employer and today employs 28,000 people, which makes it the largest single employer in any sector, in L.A.

Once a peaceful suburb, Hollywood became the country's biggest movie production centre in the 1920s, when major movie studios left Chicago and New York for Los Angeles. In the 1950s, the arrival of television affected box-office ticket sales, but the movie industry dealt with this in several ways: by filming fewer, though bigger-budget movies for theatres; by producing feature-length movies for the small screen; and even

Downtown Los Angeles

Myths about Los Angeles

Myth #1: Los Angeles is a city of glitz and glamour.

Reality: Los Angeles is largely a gritty, blue-collar industrial town with North America's heaviest concentration of manufacturing jobs, ranging from low-wage clothing production to advanced military aircraft assembly to cutting-edge ventures in various high-tech realms. The city is surrounded by a vast sprawl of white-collar, white-bread suburbs, many with their own share of industrial establishments. To the west and to the north are a few glitzy or quirky enclaves on which the city's rarified image has been built. Although this image is not totally unfounded, it bears no closer resemblance to total reality than do the products of Hollywood's film and television studios. Visitors who remain firmly ensconced on the west side of the metropolitan area may escape exposure to the more plebeian reality beyond, but it's definitely out there, along street after street of humble bungalows, bleak gas stations, and ubiquitous mini-malls. More than 16 million people live in the Los Angeles area. Only an infinitesimal fraction are movie stars. Many people work at jobs that pay little more than minimum wage. As in any other wealthy part of the world, the majority of the population lead humdrum, middle-class lives. In fact, most of the L.A. area has a startlingly "middle America" character, which surprises some travellers who come expecting to find a city with a zanier disposition. Its very ordinariness can come as a shock.

Myth #2: Los Angeles has no real downtown area.

Reality: Los Angeles has sometimes been characterized more as a cluster of villages than as a coherent city, but it does indeed have an area that is instantly recognizable as downtown, with office towers, public buildings, cultural attractions, shopping streets and an extensive skid road. Many first-time visitors are surprised to discover that downtown L.A. is nowhere near the coast. In fact, it lies 12.4mi (20km) inland, near the site where an early Spanish outpost was established in 1781. Because of the region's very decentralized character, downtown L.A. doesn't form as strong a central focus as do the downtown areas in more traditional cities, though it does lay claim to Southern California's highest concentration of office space. (When referring to downtown, it is useful to specify "downtown L.A." since several suburban municipalities have their own, more modest, downtown areas.) Large parts of downtown L.A. are far from pretty and things can turn quite spooky at night. But downtown is for real and it's definitely worth visiting.

Myth #3: It's impossible to get around without a car.

Reality: L.A.'s extensive freeway network is more than myth, and it's true many Angelenos wouldn't dream of going beyond the next corner without jumping in the car. Alternatives do exist, however. Getting around car-obsessed L.A. by public transit requires patience, but it's still quite possible. The author of a travel guidebook from a well-known New York publisher sneers: "I've heard rumors about visitors to Los Angeles who have toured the city entirely by public transportation, but they can't be more than that—rumors." The Los Angeles County Metropolitan Transportation Authority (mercifully abbreviated as MTA) is the butt of countless jokes: in fact, it is under court order to add more buses to relieve overcrowding on certain routes. But the MTA and other operators do offer a fairly comprehensive service. The mostly bus-based transit system is augmented by a small subway and light-rail network and by suburban trains. With a little planning, visitors wishing to avoid car expenses and freeway madness can reach most points of interest by bus, though late-

-evening service is spotty. An unusual and very un-L.A. note: the Getty Center, a top cultural attraction in a remote hilltop setting, actually favours transit users. Visitors arriving by car require advance parking reservations, which may be hard to get at certain times. Bus passengers can arrive whenever they choose.

Myth #4: Culture in Los Angeles is all candy floss and superficiality.

Reality: There's substantially more to culture in L.A. than what emerges from the Hollywood studios and their amusement park adjuncts. Let's start with museums. By one count, the L.A. area has nearly 300 museums, historic buildings, libraries with special collections, botanical gardens, and other sites with exhibits or collections open to public view. (Many, though not all of them, are explored in this chapter.) The Getty Center and the Los Angeles County Museum of Art both house extensive collections covering numerous periods and backgrounds. Together with the Museum of Contemporary Art, they reveal L.A. to be much more than an upstart in the world of art. In the domain of public performance, Los Angeles provides a broad array of venues offering many forms of music and theatre. While popular music tends to overshadow what esthetes may regard as more sophisticated forms like jazz and classical, variety is the key. A glance at the listings in weekly entertainment guides will amaze and delight culture lovers who come expecting little more than the one-dimensional scene that L.A.'s commercial image-builders have mischievously succeeded in conveying. Yes, there's life beyond Universal Studios and Disneyland.

by associating itself with television, the record industry and the advertising world to form huge media and entertainment conglomerates. Between 1990 and 1996, employment in the movie industry jumped from 143,300 to 224,300 employees, and generated $26 billion in economic spin-offs.

The millions of people who visit Los Angeles each year for business or pleasure have made the city one of the most popular tourist destinations in the United States. Drawn by the myriad of tourist attractions, and recreational and leisure activities, residents and visitors injected $12.3 billion into the local economy in 1999. This influx of cash boosted many industries, notably the accommodations, food and retail sales industries, travel agencies, transportation companies, entertainment production companies, and also helped create and preserve close to 253,000 jobs.

As in other industrialized countries, the services sector has become the strong point of the metropolis's economy. More than 32% of jobs are related to services concerning finance, administration, commerce, personnalized services, the high-tech industry and liberal arts professions. The real estate industry developed alongside the construction industry. The manufacturing sector employs 663,400 workers and the fashion industry employs 122,000.

The recession in the early 1990s and government budget cuts in the Defence Department were detrimental to the defence industry and caused significant unemployment and serious economic setbacks. However, the major restructuring of the economy in the last few years coupled with the end of the recession has finally allowed L.A. to resume its economic growth.

Population

The agglomeration of Los Angeles (L.A. County) counted around 9.1 million people in 2000, who lived in 88 different cities such as Santa Monica, Beverly Hills, West Hollywood and, of course, Los Angeles proper with its 3.7 million residents. For its part, the population of the greater metropolitan area (including the counties of L.A., Ventura, Orange, Riverside and San Bernardino) has 16.3 million people. L.A. ranks second among U.S. cities in terms of population, behind New York and before Chicago. Many consider the Californian metropolis to be an ideal place to live due to its low urban density. Contrary to what many believe, Angelinos do not live on top of one another, but enjoy a lot of space. While New York's population density is 23,494 residents

The Evolution of Los Angeles's Population

1781	44
1800	315
1840	1,250
1850	1,600
1860	2,300
1870	5,614
1880	11,000
1890	50,000
1900	100,000
1910	300,000
1920	1 million
1930	2 million
2000	9.1 million

per square mile, Los Angeles's is only 6,830.

The city was shaped by the various waves of immigrants that made their way to the continent, and to the United States in particular, in the 19th and 20th centuries. It continues to constantly attract large numbers of hopeful immigrants from across the country and around the world. For example, an average of 85 New Yorkers leave the Big Apple every day to move to the Big Orange. The city today features great cultural and ethnic diversity.

Anglo-Americans

White communities, including European descendants, form the city's largest ethnic group (48%). Between 1990 and 1996, its representation in the cultural mosaic dropped by 6%. However, this group still enjoys the most economic, political and social success, which no doubt explains why many live in wealthy suburbs and the city's most affluent neighbourhoods.

Spanish-Speakers

Members of the Hispanic community make up the city's second largest ethnic group, accounting for 27% of the population. Latinos are originally from Latin America and Chicanos are from Mexico. The Latin-American district, if it can be considered as such, is located downtown around Olvera Street, which is also the city's Hispanic cradle. Most of the community, however, lives in inner-suburbs east of L.A. With its four million residents (not including the 500,000 illegal immigrants), L.A.'s Hispanic community forms the third largest Spanish-speaking city in North America, after

A Common Identity

Despite their ethnic diversity, all Angelinos share the feeling of having been drawn to the city by its reputation as a place where anything is possible and anyone can start a new life. L.A. pioneers, like those in the rest of California, jumped at the chance of creating a new society, whose most important characteristics were independence, infinite resources and the ability to tolerate individual differences. This spirit of generosity and tolerance has continued to attract immigrants throughout the 20th century, as different beliefs can be expressed freely.

This diversity and tolerance may surprise and catch foreigners and newcomers off guard, when they first encounter bikini-clad in-line skaters on the Venice Beach oceanfront or Gay Pride (a homosexual movement) members parading in the street. Individual liberty is extremely important here, and visitors who think this freedom is translated only as liberalism should remember that not only is California the cradle of the freedom of expression crusade, but that of the John Birch Society, an extreme-right movement in Orange County. Its diversity is therefore represented in many forms. Even though the city's splendid reputation seems to be an illusion when considering the terrible poverty that reigns in the South Central neighbourhood, its legendary beaches and elegant Beverly Hills boutiques tell a different story. Los Angeles is a city of political, cultural and social contrasts that claims its true identity by not allowing itself to be pigeonholed.

Mexico City and Guadalajara, Mexico.

African-Americans

African-Americans now make up nearly 12% of the city's population. Even though their presence in Los Angeles can be traced back to the founding of the *pueblo*, it was not until the influx of migrants from the South in 1910 that the first ghetto developed. Today, the poorest live in the neighbourhoods of South Central and Watts, which are extremely dangerous.

Asians

Asians account for 11% of L.A.'s population, with Chinese people being California's oldest Asian community. The extremely lively Chinatown is located north of downtown. Many Japanese live in Little Tokyo, a Japanese neighbourhood south of the city that is bordered by First Street, Alameda Street, Third Street and Los Angeles Street. This district consists of the largest Japanese community living outside of Japan. Koreantown, where many Koreans live, lies between Hollywood and the downtown core. Little Saigon is a neighbourhood almost exclusively inhabited by Vietnamese people, who came to the United States as political refugees after the Vietnam War and Vietnam's reunification by the communists in 1976. This neighbourhood is located in the south, in Orange County, in the district of Westminster.

Finally, the Jewish people number close to half a million in the metropolis. No more than 27,300 Native Americans, who were once the only inhabitants here, live in L.A.; they now account for less than one percent of the population.

Languages and Religions

English is the State of California's official language and is still the most spoken language in the metropolis, even if it is estimated that 30% of Los Angeles residents do not understand it. Spanish is almost as common as Shakespeare's language, since 80% of non-English speakers are Hispanic. Korean, Vietnamese, Hmong and Cantonese are also widely spoken, as the signs and billboards in their respective neighbourhoods can attest. In fact, 86 different languages are spoken in L.A. In 1981, bilingual education was introduced in schools in non-English speaking neighbourhoods to offer children an education in their mother tongue.

This law was abolished in 1998, however, when California residents voted against it in a referendum. The linguistic issue has remained controversial ever since.

Like the great variety of languages spoken in the metropolis, many religions are practised by its residents, as well. The spiritual monopoly of Protestantism is a thing of the past. To this date, more than 600 different religious groups have been listed, even more than in London or New York. Christianity is the most common religion, and Catholicism is the most prominent denomination in the city, with 2.5 million followers. Protestantism is nevertheless practised by a good number of individuals, grouped under different congregations: Methodist, Presbyterian, Episcopalian, Lutheran, The Church of Latter Day Saints, Reformist and Baptist. Buddhism is also practised by many Angelinos.

Racial Tension

With its various cultural groups, Los Angeles is constantly subject to inner tension. Despite the fact that ethnic tension continued to grow during the first half of the 20th century, politicians chose to ignore this social problem. In 1943, clashes broke out between Latin-Americans and Anglo-Americans. In the 1960s, tensions rose in the South Central neighbourhood, which was principally inhabited by poor African- and Latin-Americans, and came to a head with the August 1965 riots in the Watts district: 34 people were killed and 1,000 more were injured during six days of fires and pillaging.

The city experienced serious trouble in 1992, following the Rodney King affair. The African-American motorist was stopped and beaten by four police officers, and the entire event was captured on videotape by an amateur. The videotape, which was broadcast around the world, revealed the perpetual racist behaviour of the police and gave the affair unprecedented significance. On April 29, 1992, a jury acquitted the white police officers, and a serious uprising broke out. South Central's angry mob attacked all the symbols of a consumer society by pillaging and setting fires. The riot lasted two days; 51 people were killed and material damage was estimated at $1 billion. The most brutal attacks were suffered by Korean merchants, newcomers who seemed to have established their businesses with the utmost ease, in nearby districts and Koreantown. The controversial acquittal of O.J. Simpson, the former African-American U.S. football star accused of murdering his (white) wife and her friend, illustrated that racial tension was far from being appeased. The abolition of welfare programs, the racism of a number of police officers, the high unemployment rate in the ghettos and the increasing gap between the wealthy and the poor continue to undermine the fragile peace between the various ethnic communities living side by side.

Culture

L.A., a microcosm of the country's values, dominates the world's cultural scene in the age of communications, serving as a vehicle for U.S. culture throughout the world. The distinction between art and culture, and business and finance, is often difficult to make. We are, of course, referring to the movie industry, even if Hollywood has produced several movie classics. The absence of a model in this new society has allowed artists to express their ideas without restraint, thus making L.A. a real cultural laboratory. Since the end of the Second World War, this city has drawn producers from around the world, like a magnet. In addition to being receptive to new ideas and having a taste for risk, its residents have the necessary capital to put their most original ideas into practice. For a long time Angelenos have had a complex towards Europeans and people from the East Coast, and have taken great pains to catch up to, and then surpass these perceived competitors, thus engendering the notion of research and continuous progress. Living with the constant threat of the next major earthquake destroying the city, has also created a sense of spontaneity that is best defined by living each minute to the fullest.

Literature

English-language accounts of voyages and life in Hispanic California constitute the state's first literature, the most remarkable work being Richard Henry Dana's *Two Years Before the Mast* (published in the 1840s), which tells of life along the California coast. It was not until the end of the 19th century, however, that Los Angeles's own literature was born. Helen Hunt Jackson gave us a memorable chronicle on everyday life in the City of Angels. With *Ramona* (1884), a fictionalized history of life during the era of the missions, the author enjoyed much popular success.

A number of renowned writers, including William Faulkner, F. Scott Fitzgerald and Aldous Huxley, lived in Los Angeles in the 20th century, and German writers Bertolt Brecht and Thomas Mann made L.A. their home during the Second World War.

The City of Angels has been a favourite subject of novelists since the 1920s. Several have criticized L.A. on a political note, such as Upton Sinclair's *Oil!* (1927), a novel that denounces the city's excessive capitalism. The dark side of Hollywood's studios is explored by scriptwriter Nathaniel West (1903-1940) in his apocalyptic novel *The Day of the Locust* (1939). *The Last Tycoon* (1940) by F. Scott Fitzgerald and *What Makes Sammy Run?* (1940) by Budd Schulberg followed in the same vein by further criticizing the movie-industry capital. More recent examples of novels set in L.A. were published in the 1970s: Terry Southern's *Blue Movie* depicts Hollywood's decline; Joan Didion employs a biting tone to describe Angelinos in *Play It as It Lays; Chicano*, by Richard Vasquez, is devoted to the dramatic study of life in the Latin district of East L.A. Today, a new generation of writers addresses all subjects in all styles, ranging from the bestsellers of Maxine Hong Kinston and Amy Tan, who write epic tales of relations between Asia and California, to the original fables on life in Los Angeles by T. Coraghessan Boyle, a novelist living in the San Fernando Valley. However, among all literary styles, the detective novel has had the most success in capturing Los Angeles, and author Raymond Chandler (1888-1959) is surely the most influential of his genre. He distinguished himself from traditional whodunnit authors in his four novels that feature a certain Philip Marlowe, a tough-guy private investigator in Los Angeles. Others have also left their mark on this genre: James M. Cain, Steve Fisher, Charles Willeford, Jim Thompson. Detective novels have recently gotten their second wind of populartity with the public, with intrigues set in L.A.; Elmore Leonard, Walter Mosley and James Ellroy are among those authors who have garnered the most success.

The Stage

Angelinos play an extremely influential role when it comes to theatre in

Musicals

Musicals have enjoyed great success in Los Angeles. Here are some of the most memorable:

1936	*Show Boat* by James Whale. Music by Jerome Kern. With Paul Robeson, Irene Dunne, Allan Jones and Helen Morgan.
1940	*Dancing Broadway* by Norman Taurog. Music by Cole Porter. With Fred Astaire, Eleanor Powell.
1951	*Singin' in the Rain* by Stanley Donen and Gene Kelly. Music by Nacio Herb Brown. With Gene Kelly, Donald O'Connor and Debbie Reynolds.
1961	*West Side Story* by Robert Wise and Jerome Robbins. Music by Leonard Bernstein. With Nathalie Wood, Richard Beymer, Russ Tomblyn and Rita Moreno.
1964	*My Fair Lady* by George Cukor. Music by Frederick Loewe. With Audrey Hepburn and Rex Harrison.

the United States, making L.A. the most important theatre hub after New York. In the 1960s, the city earned an enviable reputation nationally as its number of theatres increased. Drawn by a sunny climate that inspires creativity and the lure of Hollywood, many actors and writers set out to practise their art on the city's stages, breathing remarkable life into the theatre scene. The Music Center holds two of the biggest theatres: Ahmanson Theater (2,100 seats), where Broadway productions are staged, and the Mark Taper Forum (750 seats), which offers experimental theatre. Plays from the classical repertoire and original works recognized at the national level are also presented in L.A.

Classical music

Classical music is performed throughout the city, and prestigious concerts are regularly given at the Los Angeles Music Center Opera, among other places. Several European composers have contributed to the vitality of this type of music. In the 1930s and 1940s, Otto Klemperer settled in the area and went on to conduct the L.A. Philharmonic; Kurt Weill and Arnold Schoenberg composed their *Fourth Quartet* here; and Igor Stravinsky composed his *Symphony in C* and *Rake's Progress* opera in Hollywood, where he settled in 1940.

Popular Music

Los Angeles became the hub of musical talent in the 20th century.

Jazz

In the 1920s, a distinctive style of music appeared on the scene: jazz. Several orchestras consisting of black musicians sprang up throughout the city. In the 1940s, clubs on Central Avenue, the commercial artery of the African-American district, attracted the best jazz musicians in the United States. Jazz on the West Coast was influenced by homegrown Angelinos such as Dexter Gordon and Art Pepper, and adopted sons like Buddy Collette, Gerry Mullingan, Charles Mingus and Chet Baker. Today, this musical genre enjoys new vitality in the metropolis, and the number of public concert halls and jazz bars is continually increasing, as is the extreme popularity of the Playboy Jazz Festival.

Blues

Like jazz, the blues made its debut in California in the South Central neighbourhood. The leadership of Watts, an extremely influential producer, helped popularize this style, along with artists such as T-Bone

Walker, Amos Milburn, Charles Brown and the Penguins. In the 1950s and 1960s, the record companies of Johnny Otis and Sam Cook also attracted several talented soul and gospel performers to L.A.

Rock

Los Angeles continues to be recognized as one of the birthplaces of rock n'roll, a musical genre that appeared in the 1950s and was popularized by such bands as the Beach Boys and the Doors. Other groups, including X and Black Flag, also contributed to the development of an alternative form of rock, known as punk. In the 1980s, L.A. witnessed the birth of the Latin rock of Los Lobos, Dave and Alvin, as well as The Blasters. Since then, several local talents have left their mark on the national and international scene, notably the Red Hot Chili Peppers, with their alternative rock.

Rap and Hip-Hop

The district between South Central and Long Beach is the cradle of rap artists. Rappers Easy E, Ice Cube and Dr. Dre from the group NWA are all from this hood. The great popularity of rap and its contemporary, hip-hop, has led to the discovery of Kid Frost, Bone Thugs-n-Harmony, Coolio, Brandy and Usher. Today, L.A. is the backbone of hip-hop, a style of music that has become one of California's flagship cultural exports.

Visual Arts

The legendary brightness and climate of California's metropolis, as well as the influences of myriad cultures, have contributed to the strong development of visual arts in the city, making L.A. one of the international capitals of art.

In the 19th century, fine art began to flourish in the City of Angels. The influx of people and wealth in the wake of the gold rush allowed for the the massive importation of art into California. The vast fortunes of railway tycoons and other "economy kings" were the foundations of major private collections (including the Huntington Art Collections in Pasadena). These wealthy collectors introduced art from Europe and the Eastern United States, thus allowing Impressionism and genre paintings to influence art in the metropolis. In 1880, the first art school was founded, which included the L.A. School of Art and Design and the fine arts college of the University of

Southern California. As of the late 19th century, artists were coming to settle in Pasadena, Topanga Canyon and Laguna Beach (Orange County). Hence the birth of the Eucalyptus School, in which Southern Californian impressionists created sparkling sceneries, inspired by the region's exceptional natural environment and radiance.

With the growth of Los Angeles in the late 1910s and the development of the entertainment industry, art in Southern California adopted a more modern and more abstract look. This is especially obvious in the work of Stanton Macdonald-Wright, who was inspired by cubist shapes and created a style he named Synchromist. Oskar Fishinger, Albert King, Man Ray, Charles White and Jackson Pollock are other artists who belonged to the same movement. In the 1930s, abstraction, Surrealism and Socialist Realism marked the works of painters and muralists, including such masters as Orozco and Siqueiros. Their first works inspired the murals that now adorn many Latino districts.

Following the Second World War, artists such as Richard Diebenkorn launched a new figurative painting movement that was named Bay Area Figuration. Popular culture inspired pop artists in the 1960s, including Ed Rusha. During this period, art museums greatly expanded, notably the Los Angeles County Museum of Art. Regional painters explored absolute abstraction (John McLaughlin, Lorser Feitelson), accenting a "perfect finish" of the surface and light, which is an obvious detail in the works of Roberts Irwin and James Turrel. Accepted as an authority, the artistic scene developed in the 1950s around the Ferus Gallery, which launched the careers of painters Edward Kienholz and Ed Moses. In the decades that followed, several new museums and galleries sprung up in the region, notably the Getty Center, the Armand Hammer Museum and the Museum of Contemporary Art, which would make the city an important international art centre. Renowned painters such as David Hockney, Jonathan Borofsky and Guillermo Gomez-Pena, worked here and attracted the art world's attention to Los Angeles. Largely under represented, woman artists have had little opportunity to leave their mark on the city's artistic scene. Muralist Judith Baca is perhaps the sole exception to the rule, as her works still adorn

Hollywood: the Stuff of Legend

The origins of U.S. cinema date back to the first decade of the 20th century. Independent directors in New York produced the first works in this medium, which was just taking its first tentative steps. All films were shot outside at the time, so production was forced to stop in winter because of the weather. Determined to gain control of this new industry, which was already raking in healthy profits, the mafia began to harass small producers so they could buy out their businesses and take over. As a result, some producers left the East Coast in search of a more favourable climate, where they would be safely out of the grasp of organized crime, and where the weather would allow them to shoot year-round. In 1911, David Horsley rented (for $30 a month) the Blondeau Tavern, located at the corner of Sunset Boulevard and Gower Street, set in the peaceful rural suburb of Hollywood. Here he produced *The Law of the Range*, the first Hollywood film to be shot in a studio. Other entrepreneurs recognized the possibilities and founded production studios on Sunset Boulevard. Hollywood's legendary reputation was born.

several walls in the metropolis.

Today, L.A.'s fast-paced art scene features avant-garde artists, both local and international, who continue to attract attention in the many museums and private galleries of Beverly Hills, West Hollywood and Santa Monica.

Hollywood Movies

The *cinématographe* (a motion-picture camera and projector in one), invented by the Lumière brothers and perfected by Edison, revolutionized the way we view the world. The U.S. movie industry originally centred around New York, then moved to the Californian metropolis. As of 1908, independent producers flocked to Los Angeles. The sunny climate and the various natural environments of the surrounding area allowed them to film seaside, desert and alpine scenes outdoors. The proximity of the Mexican border also allowed them to quickly dispose of their equipment to keep it out of the hands of New York agents responsible for enforcing the exclusive rights of the cinematographic process. These rights were held by a company (the MPPC) that brought together Edison and Eastman, the founder of Kodak. L.A. thus helped producers get around the draconian patent law that plagued New York.

Studios were established in Culver City and Universal City, but Hollywood, an L.A. suburb, emerged as the movie capital. Its growth was favoured by the decline in European production, due to the First World War. Directors such as D.W. Griffith and Cecil B. De Mille marked the golden age of silent film. The comedy, which was initially based on pursuits that featured a succession of gags, became, with Charlie Chaplin, Buster Keaton or Harry Langdon, an extremely popular genre.

It typically focussed on the adventures of endearing characters grappling with the ups and downs of everyday life. The western, with its unmistakable star Tom Mix, was also a favourite with audiences.

Bound to Hollywood cinema, the star system was instilled right from the start. Producers launched actors on the market like products. Not all actors, however, were puppets. In 1919, Charlie Chaplin, Mary Pickford, Douglas Fairbanks and D.W. Griffith founded United Artists, a firm responsible for the marketing of their movies.

In 1927, *Jazz Singer*, a mediocre film accompanied by sound, tolled the death-bell for silent movies. A generation of actors and directors arose alongside veterans who had successfully adjusted to this new format, to renew production and revive the star system. *Gone With The Wind*, in 1939, was the height of pre-war Hollywood, in every respect.

Following the global conflict, during which the movie industry entirely served the war effort, a witch hunt began to undermine the foundations of Hollywood's influence: Senator McCarthy and his like hunted down anyone who was the least bit suspected of being a communist sympathizer, right down to Charlie Chaplin, who was forced into exile in Europe. Finally, the rise of the television industry hastened the decline of the movie capital. It wasn't until the 1980s, and the formidable (commercial) success of Steven Spielberg and George Lucas, that Hollywood returned to the forefront in world film. Japanese financiers expressed a growing interest to invest in major Hollywood studios in the 1990s, but have not changed the face of the California movie industry.

Architecture and Urbanism

Greater Los Angeles is a fertile land for architectural experimentation. The pleasant climate, the variety of natural environments and the prominent artistic community benefiting from exceptional financial resources, have given rise to some original architecture.

The 18th Century: Spanish and Mexican Architecture

The first imported architectural traditions were those of the Spanish colonizers and priests, who established farming communities (*pueb-*

los) and religious buildings (missions). Inspired by Spanish monasteries, but more specifically based on the Mexican monastery model, a mission complex was generally built around a large, square courtyard and included a narrow church and structures featuring arcades that held the priests' quarters (*convento*), huts, workshops, an infirmary and buildings reserved for single Native Americans and children. The Franciscans made adobe, an extremely abundant black-clay brick, which served as their main construction material. To make adobe bricks, straw was mixed with clay, and molds were filled and set out to dry in the sun.

The 19th Century: Toward an American Style

Mexicans gave architecture a new look. The typical construction of Mexican colonizers consisted of a rectangular, adobe, street-level building, with a dirt floor and flat rooves covered with tar. The wealthiest homes opened onto a courtyard that was accessed by an open porch or *corredor*.

The first British architectural influences appeared in Los Angeles late in the 19th century. The Victorian style was the first, truly British style to take hold in California. Wooden homes became fashionable, and though deemed Victorian, they featured a hodgepodge of indefinable architectural styles. These residences reflected the rapid evolution of industrial procedures, U.S. preferences and commercial techniques. A few examples are still standing, notably on Carroll Avenue, in Echo Park, which features several.

The Italian style, most prominent in the 1870s, based itself on the construction of homes that featured overhanging flat-face windows adorned with relatively simple and classic details such as keystones. In fact, these homes are the wooden version of the rows of brick or brown sandstone houses that were extremely popular in eastern cities. The shingle style, a less ornamental structure considered an alternative to the traditional shingle style, appeared in the 1880s. The famous Queen Anne style was revealed in a few of the more picturesque Victorian homes between 1880 and 1890; they featured irregular roof levels and countless towers and turrets, high chimneys, bay windows, set-back balconies and pediments.

The 20th Century

Fine-art Classicism became fashionable in California, as in the rest of the country, after having been popularized at the World's Fair in Chicago, in 1893. With the invention of metal frameworks, downtown commercial buildings rose 10 storeys high and more. A precursor of the technological possibilities to come, the glass atrium of the Bradbury Building, constructed by George Wyman, revolutionized architecture.

At the turn of the 20th century, the great ideas of the Arts and Crafts Movement had already made their way to the western United States and began to flourish in the work of local architects such as Charles Green (1868-1957) and Henry Green (1870-1954). Graduates of the Massachussetts Institute of Technology, the Green brothers moved to L.A. in 1893. They combined home and nature by building their signature Gamble House in Pasadena and designed the first exportable architectural element: the bungalow.

A more sculpted and radical approach to the home appeared in the 1910s, when, inspired by Southern California's heavenly environment, renowned architect Frank Lloyd Wright (1867-1959) moved to L.A. in 1917. Wright, recognized as one of the most prolific and influential U.S. architects, came here to create a few of his more inventive designs, such as the Hollyhock House and Miniatura in Pasadena. Built in a Californian romanticism style, these works of reinforced-concrete blocks were inspired by pre-Columbian Mexican architecture.

The early 1920s saw the emergence of the Spanish colonial style. This developed in response to the complexity of the Queen Anne style, and was stimulated by the public's enthusiasm for the romanticism inspired by buildings constructed for the Panamá-California Exhibit in San Diego, in 1925. On this occasion, New York architect Bertham Goodhue was directly inspired by the Spanish colonial architecture of Mexico, which featured an abundance of elaborate decorations, cupolas and stained glass. This architectural renaissance was also illustrated by the use of stucco, a coating consisting of fine plaster, slaked lime and chalk, as a construction material. Irving Gill, the great architect of the 1920s, was even successful in integrating Spanish influences in his concept of modern architecture.

Unorthodox architecture also appeared during this era, and is attributable to both the Angelinos' desire to create a past for themselves and the growing influence of movie sets on the real world. In 1905, an industrialist had already created Venice, a replica of the Italian city, in the port of Los Angeles. In the 1920s, the Chinese Theatre (a traditional-style Chinese movie theatre), was also built in Hollywood, and became world famous for its Hollywood movie premieres, where stars arrive in limousines under blinding spotlights that sweep the sky.

Towards the late 1920s, the increasingly industrialized society of the United States was pushing architects to look for means to express modernity without resorting to historical references. Art Deco thus became the style of choice for designers of public buildings and office towers. With its vertical and symmetrical lines, Art Deco was also willingly adopted by the car and movie industries, which were thus able to convey their prestigious image. This architectural style features particularly heavy floral, cubist and zigzag motifs above windows and doors. The Eastern Columbia Building, located downtown, the Witern Theater and the Bullocks

The Bungalow

This street-level house model is constructed of wood with a vast covered veranda, sometimes linked around a backyard patio. The effect of the transition between interior and exterior space is particularly minimized, and the garden is seen as part of the house. Countless variations of the Californian bungalow were mass produced throughout the entire country in the first 20 years of the 20th century. Several examples of this type of architecture can still be seen in Pasadena.

Wilshire department store are excellent examples of this style in L.A.

Other architectural approaches eliminated the superfluous to allow structures to express their basic function. This philosophy was the basis of the international style, which made its Californian debut with the homes of architects such as Rudolph Schindler (1888-1953) and Richard Neutra

(1892-1970), who immigrated from Vienna in the 1920s. As the apparent successors of Frank Lloyd Wright, these two men went on to work for the same client, the extravagant Dr. Lovell, a few years apart. Schindler's beachhouse and Lovell's home, which was designed by Neutra, were each respectfully completed in 1926 and 1929. These two avant-garde architectural creations explore new domains: cement or metal structures, free plans** and strict geometry.

By pushing the limits of audacious designs, several roadside restaurants featuring the particular local architecture took the shape of objects as unlikely as a zeppelin or a hat. The most famous example was the Brown Derby restaurant (no longer standing). These structures were the basis of the California Crazy architectural style, which has most recently been featured in the Chiat-Day-Mojo Building (1991, Frank O. Gehry) in Venice, built in the shape of binoculars.

Post-Second World War

As industries such as aeronautics expanded, and newcomers arrived in droves, the construction industry flourished. The city was like an experimental laboratory in terms of residential architecture, where architects perfected the gracious, open, modern home.

The downtown core had been transformed several times since the 1960s, such as when the city abolished the 164ft (50m) height limit for buildings, which was intended to prevent catastrophes when earthquakes hit. New technologies helped pave the way for the construction of increasingly higher buildings that were able to withstand major earthquakes, as well as buildings of various styles ranging from the international style to post-modernism.

It is in this nostalgic vein, indifferent to the dawn of the 1970s, that one of the most original and enigmatic figures of contemporary architecture emerged in Los Angeles: like artists of his time, Frank O. Gehry (born in 1929) discovered the savage beauty of cities. He explored new avenues, tossed around generally accepted ideas and revealed the anxiety and contradictions of architecture in a U.S. society looking for its second wind. He used ordinary materials such as plywood and chicken wire in an innovative and often sculptural manner.

Like Gehry, Richard Meier (born in 1934) aimed to perfect and transcend the visions of modernism developed early in the 20th century by such architects as Schindler and Neutra. His masterpiece, the new Getty Center, which was built at a cost of $1 billion and covers 110 acres (45ha), shows to which point L.A.'s architecture can still be renewed.

Area Development

As a western city par excellence, Los Angeles has expanded horizontally to vast areas rather than simply grow vertically within a restricted perimeter. Starting as a collection of suburbs seeking a common identity, it broke all the rules, to the point that urbanists describe the city as an assembly of constellations forming a metropolitan galaxy. L.A. has a thousand urban faces; 88 municipalities make up L.A. County, not counting its 1,490mi (2,400km) of highway and 6,585mi (10,600km) of road.

The city's urban fabric stretches endlessly and offers a symmetrical network accented by a checkerboard pattern. Any visitor approaching L.A. by air is immediately struck by the scale of the systematically aligned network of roads that form right angles. This geometric division of the area into even blocks corresponds to Thomas Jefferson's (1785) township system, which is found throughout the United States. The block plays a central role in this meshing, which consists of a juxtaposition of checkerboard patterns that correspond to the different stages of urban development. These blocks essentially consist of houses.

The pattern of neighbouring residential units is interrupted, from time to time, by a greater density of buildings corresponding to complexes holding office towers and shopping centres, as well as community centres, theatres or movie theatres, like in Century City, in the southwest. The downtown core, which established itself in the last 15 years, is distinguished by its many mini-centres. A highway network runs above this vast urban fabric connecting the different areas. Pedestrians are not part of Los Angeles's scenery, except on the beach and in a few specific areas.

The Car Cult

The L.A. of today is a megalopolis linked by a network of tangled highways, a real maze of interchanges, viaducts and rapid eight-lane arteries travelling in both directions. Given the size of the region and the endless labyrinth of freeways, it isn't surprising that the car is king. The 10 most used freeways in the country are located in the areas surrounding L.A. Half a million cars use Highway 101, the most popular freeway of all, every day. This does not come as a shock, since 6,370,000 cars are registered, or one car per 1.4 person.

The metropolis became the car capital at the same time as the oil boom accompanied the "car revolution." Almost overnight, 1,243mi (2,000km) of railway were replaced by roads and highways. From this point on, people relied on cars to get around. Drive-ins sprung up everywhere, making it possible for people to watch a movie, enjoy a hamburger or cozy up with someone without ever leaving their beloved car.

Here, driving is an experience in itself. You are what you drive, which explains the impressive number of Ferraris, BMWs, Mercedes and Range Rovers. People don't let traffic affect their jobs; many motorists are glued to their cellular phones. Finding your way from one place to another is a challenge every time. Because many attractions are scattered between Malibu and Disneyland, you can end up spending a lot of time in your car. To really understand this place, you have to go with the flow of motorists. To the car!

Practical Information

This chapter contains all the information you need to plan your trip to Los Angeles, and to make the most of your visit to the city.

You will find helpful addresses and phone numbers, as well as other information that will be useful to you. Have an excellent trip to Los Angeles!

Entrance Formalities

Travellers from Canada, the majority of western European countries, Australia and New Zealand do not need visas to enter the United States. A valid passport is sufficient for stays of up to three months. A return ticket and proof of sufficient funds to cover your stay may be required. For stays of more than three months, all travellers, except Canadians and citizens of the British Commonwealth, must obtain a visa (*$120*) from the U.S. embassy in their country.

N.B.: as medical expenses can be very high in the United States, travel health insurance is highly recommended. For more information, see the section entitled "Insurance" on p 85.

Customs

Foreigners may enter the United States with 200 cigarettes (or 100 cigars) and duty-free purchases under US$400, including personal gifts and 33.8fl oz (1l) of alcohol (the legal drinking age is 21). There is no limit on the amount of cash you can carry, although you must fill out a form if you are travelling with more than US$10,000.

Prescription medication must be placed in clearly marked containers (you may have to present a prescription or a written statement from your doctor to customs officials). Meat and meat by-products, all kinds of food, grains, plants, fruit and narcotics cannot be brought into the United States.

If you are travelling with your cat or dog, you will have to show a health certificate (provided by your veterinarian), as well as certification of rabies vaccination. Note that the vaccine must be administered at least 30 days before the date of departure and cannot be over one year old.

For more information, contact:

United States Customs Service
1301 Constitution Ave. NW
Washington, DC 20229
☎ *(202) 566-8195*

Getting to Los Angeles

By Plane

The Los Angeles area is served by five airports offering scheduled commercial flights. (Several smaller airports in the region handle only private or military flights.)

The biggest and busiest by far is the **Los Angeles International Airport**, often referred to by its three-letter international code, **LAX**. This gargantuan facility, located in the southwestern part of the city near the Pacific shoreline (most departing eastbound flights circle briefly over the ocean before turning inland), handles nearly all international flights destined for Southern California and a great many domestic flights as well. LAX's terminal buildings laid out in a horseshoe shape and are numbered from 1 to 7. An eighth building, the newer Tom Bradley International Terminal (named after a former mayor), is located between Terminals 3 and 4.

LAX is served by a very impressive roster of international carriers. Nearly all of the world's major trans-Atlantic and trans-Pacific airlines offer scheduled service here on a daily basis. It is among the busiest airports in the western hemisphere for international traffic and *the* busiest by far for trans-Pacific traffic. It is also served by an impressive array of carriers from Latin America and Canada. A long list of cities on five continents are linked to LAX by non-stop flights.

Most non-U.S. carriers, but by no means all of them, operate from the bright, spacious Tom Bradley International Terminal. Some operate from other terminals. For example, Air Canada, KLM, Virgin Atlantic and Air New Zealand are among the airlines using Terminal 2. With a new wave of alliances and consolidations sweeping the world airline industry, it would be hazardous to guess, even a few months after these words are written, which terminal any given carrier is operating from. When arranging to have someone meet an arriving flight, or when catching a departing flight, it is essential for travellers to check their printed itineraries to avoid mixups. If the information is not clear, they should consult their airline company or travel agent. For connections between terminals, free buses, marked by the letter A and running every few minutes, circle the airport in a counter-clockwise direction, stopping near the lower level of each terminal building at stops marked "LAX Shuttle."

LAX is also served by a vast number of domestic flights. All major U.S. airlines, and some minor ones as well, provide frequent service to Los Angeles from their respective hub cities, as well as from additional points including the larger east coast cities. The most frequent service on short-haul routes, including the very busy corridor to the San Francisco area, is operated by rivals United Airlines and Southwest.

Although amenities such as food and shopping at LAX have improved somewhat in recent years, the choice remains slim in comparison to many other major airports around the world. One retailer holds a monopoly on duty-free goods, and prices are not cheap.

The other commercial airports serving the Los Angeles area are:

• **Ontario International Airport**, in the far eastern suburbs, with domestic flights

Getting to or from LAX

There's often no way around it. Countless travelers each day must confront the muddle and confusion involved in getting to or from Los Angeles International Airport. Travelers armed with a few bits of information have the battle half won. Following are the main options:

• **By private car:** A broad bi-level ring road circles the terminal buildings, with departure areas at the upper level and arrivals at the lower level. At peak holiday periods traffic moves very slowly. Motorists waiting outside the terminal buildings must remain in their vehicles. Unattended vehicles are often ticketed or towed. Huge long-term parking lots are situated near the airport, while short-term (very expensive) parking is available right on the airport grounds, within easy walking distance of each terminal building. Free buses, marked by the letters B, C or D, serve the three largest off-site parking lots. Running every few minutes, they circle the airport in a counter-clockwise direction, stopping near the lower level of each terminal building at the stops marked LAX Shuttle. After arriving at the respective parking lots, they run in a fixed circuit to drop off or pick up passengers at clearly marked stops.

• **By rental car:** Most of the major car rental companies have their offices and drop-off points clustered in a small area just northeast of the airport. Each company operates buses (referred to, for some bizarre reason, as "courtesy trams" even though they are clearly buses and not trams) that fetch passengers from fixed stops near the lower level of each terminal building. Next to illuminated panels in the baggage claim areas, free phones are provided to contact the various car rental companies.

• **By hotel bus or van:** Some hotels located near the airport provide free pickups for guests. It is wise to check with the hotel in advance.

• **By taxi:** Taxis are easy to find near the lower level of each terminal building. Fares are high and are augmented by a $2.50 airport surcharge (applying to trips from the airport but not *going to* the airport). To downtown L.A. or Hollywood, the total fare (without tip) comes to about $30; to the mid-Wilshire district or West Hollywood about $25; to Santa Monica about $20.

• **By shared-ride van:** Several companies, among them Super Shuttle *(☎800-554-3146, 323-775-6600 or 782-6600; www.supershuttle.com)* and Xpress Shuttle *(☎800-474-8885; www.xpressshuttle.com)*, operate vans that provide door-to-door service with set fares to specific parts of the metropolitan area. Normally, vans carry several passengers going to the same general area, meaning there may be intermediate stops along the way and an indirect routing. On the other hand, fares for single passengers are typically about one-third less than the corresponding taxi fare, with discounts for additional passengers going to the same destination. For three or more people travelling together, taxis may often cost less, however. Van services can be arranged in advance or upon arrival at the airport by using a pay phone or the free phones in baggage claim areas attached to the illuminated panels advertising hotels and car rentals. Some van companies compete on price, and it may not hurt to compare. Vans can also be flagged at the appropriately marked stops near the lower level of each terminal building, and are identified by signs on each vehicle showing the area served. There is no central collection point. Shared-ride van services are available for travel *to* the airport as well but require reservations many hours in advance.

• **By scheduled bus:** Several points in Southern California, among them Disneyland, Van Nuys and Santa Barbara, are served by direct scheduled bus services from LAX. Information and tickets are available from the Ground Transportation kiosks located outside some of the terminal buildings at the lower level.

• **By public transit:** There is no direct rail or local bus service from Los Angeles International Airport, although both are available nearby.

The geniuses who planned the Green Line, part of L.A.'s rail transit system, chose a routing that serves areas near the airport but manages to skirt the airport entirely. The Green Line's Aviation station and the airport are linked by a free bus, marked by the letter G, that runs at intervals of 10 to 15min, stopping at the LAX Shuttle stops near the lower level of each terminal building. The trip normally takes about 10min, but can be slower in heavy traffic. Green Line tickets are sold at vending machines near station entrances, with change provided. The Green Line itself runs from nowhere to nowhere, mostly along a highway median, but it does connect with the Blue Line running between Downtown L.A. and Long Beach.

The bus situation is somewhat better. Numerous local bus routes radiate from the LAX Transit Center, located adjacent to Parking Lot C a short distance from the airport. Free buses marked by the letter C stop near the lower level of each terminal building at the stops marked "LAX Shuttle,"and after circling the airport run in a long loop through the parking lot before stopping next to the transit centre. To save time, passengers can disembark at the first stop after leaving the airport and walk the block-and-a-half to the transit centre. (Going back to the airport, buses leave directly from a point next to the transit centre.) Scheduled departure times for each bus route are displayed on a large panel at the transit centre. Some routes are run by the MTA, the region's main transit operator, and other routes by suburban systems. Passengers must have the exact fare. Among routes most likely to be useful to visitors are the MTA 42 local to downtown L.A.; MTA 439 express (premium fare) northeast to downtown L.A.; MTA 439 south to Manhattan Beach, Hermosa Beach and Redondo Beach; MTA 561 express (premium fare) north to the San Fernando Valley, stopping en route at the U.C.L.A. campus and the Getty Center; Santa Monica (blue bus) No. 3 northwest to Venice and Santa Monica, and Culver City (green bus) No. 6 north to U.C.L.A. with useful transfer connections along the way to various MTA east-west bus routes.

serving points in the western U.S. plus some key midwestern and eastern airline hubs, as well as a small handful of international flights from Mexico and Canada.

• **John Wayne Airport** (named after the Hollywood cowboy), in Orange County southeast of Los Angeles, with a fairly heavy schedule of flights to points in the western U.S. and some airline hubs further east.

• **Burbank Airport**, in the northern part of the metropolitan area, close to Hollywood and Pasadena, served by a handful of airlines offering busy schedules of mostly short-haul domestic flights.

• **Long Beach Municipal Airport**, near the southern tip of Los Angeles County and the quietest of the five main airports, with a small array (this is relative, of course) of domestic flights.

By Car

Motorists approaching Los Angeles from the north (or heading north) have three main alternatives. Interstate Hghway 5 (or I-5) provides the fastest link to or from the San Francisco area through the rather dull scenery of the San Joaquín Valley deep in the interior. The same highway continues north to Oregon, Washington state, and the Canadian border near Vancouver. A slower but more interesting route is U.S. Highway 101, also known as the 101 Freeway, that hugs the coast in some spots near San Luis Obispo and Santa Barbara. Slowest but most scenic is the Pacific Coast Highway, designated Highway 1, a narrow, curvy road that clings to the coast most of the way (but is prone to fog and occasional washouts).

South to San Diego and Tijuana, Interstate 5 is really the only direct route. Interstate 405, running along the west side of Los Angeles and then turning east past Long Beach, meets the I-5 in the southern part of Orange County. Going east from L.A., Interstate 10 runs through southern Arizona, New Mexico and Texas all the way to Florida. To reach Las Vegas, the I-10 connects with the I-15 near San Bernardino. Because much of the territory north and east of Los Angeles is uninhabited mountain or desert, there are fewer road links than might otherwise be expected given the city's size. Sunday evening traffic into L.A. can often be very slow.

To get to Inland Orange County

The inland Orange County area is reached by way of the I-5 Freeway from either the north or south. The exit for Disneyland is very clearly marked and leads to the centre of Anaheim.

To get to the Beaches of Orange County

The Pacific Coast Highway makes for a wonderful drive down the coast, passing through each of the beach cities in this tour. The PCH as it is known locally, can be reached via Highway 55 from inland Orange County or via Highway I-710 out of Los Angeles.

To get to Palm Springs

To get to Palm Springs, take Highway 10 from Los Angeles. The trip takes about 1hr, depending on the traffic.

Hitchhiking

Hitchhiking is not recommended.

By Train

Amtrak *(☎800-872-7245; www.amtrak.com)* operates regional services as well as long-distance trains from the beautiful and ornate Union Station at the edge of downtown Los Angeles. (Union Station is worth a visit even if rail travel is not in your plans: see page 105) The station is served by Metrolink suburban trains, by the Metro Red Line (subway), and by numerous local bus routes. Long-haul trains, offering coach, sleeping-car and dining-car service, include the *Coast Starlight* to Seattle via Oakland and Portland, the *Southwest Chief* to Chicago via Flagstaff (near Arizona's Grand Canyon), Albuquerque and Kansas City, and the *Sunset Limited* to Tucson, Houston, New Orleans and Orlando. Regional service from San Diego to Los Angeles (trip time: 2hrs, 40min) operates 11 times daily along a scenic route with many intermediate stops in San Diego County and Orange County. Four of these trains continue north to Santa Barbara, with one going as far as San Luis Obispo. Daily service between Los Angeles and Las Vegas was set to begin operation in 2001. Amtrak also runs buses from Union Station to Bakersfield connecting there with its four daily trains to the San Francisco Bay area via the San Joaquín Valley.

By Bus

Scheduled inter-city bus service to and from Los Angeles is dominated by **Greyhound Lines** *(☎800-231-2222; www.greyhound.com)*. The main Los Angeles terminal is located along Sixth Street about 1mi (2km) east of the downtown area (served by MTA bus route 60) in a bleak industrial zone. The surrounding streets are not safe at night, and taxis are scarce. The terminal, although built recently, is cramped and uncomfortable—not the best way to begin or end a journey. Greyhound seems determined to pursue its sad and relentless downmarket thrust. That said, hourly service is provided to San Diego and across the border to Tijuana. Greyhound also runs several buses a day to San Francisco and serves Las Vegas, as well as points as near as Santa Barbara or Palm Springs and as distant as Boston or Miami. A Mexican company operating under the names Crucero and Golden State *(☎213-627-2940)* operates from the same terminal, offering competing service to Tijuana and to certain points in the California interior. Another Mexican company called Americanos *(☎213-688-0044)* operates to points in Mexico and Texas from an even more unpleasant terminal directly across the street.

Embassies and Consulates

U.S. Embassies and Consulates Abroad

AUSTRALIA
Moonah Place, Canberra, ACT 2600
☎ ***(6) 214-5600***

BELGIUM
27 Boulevard du Régent
B-1000 Brussels
☎ ***(02) 512-2210***
⇄ ***(02) 511-9652***

CANADA
2 Wellington St.,
Ottawa, Ontario, K1P 5T1
☎ ***(613) 238-5335***
⇄ ***(613) 238-5720***

Consulate:
Place Félix-Martin,
1155 Rue Saint-Alexandre,
Montréal, Québec, H2Z 1Z2
☎ ***(514) 398-9695***
⇄ ***(514) 398-9748***

Consulate:
360 University Ave., Toronto
Ontario, M5G 1S4
☎ ***(416) 595-1700***
⇄ ***(416) 595-0051***

Consulate:
1095 West Pender,Vancouver,
British Columbia, V6E 2M6
☎ ***(604) 685-4311***

DENMARK
Dag Hammarskjölds Allé 24
2100 Copenhagen Ø
☎ ***(35) 55 31 44***
⇄ ***(35) 43 02 23***

FINLAND
Itaïnen Puistotie 14B
FIN-00140, Helsinki, Finland
☎ ***358-9-171-931***

GERMANY
Clayallee 170, 14195 Berlin
☎ ***(30) 832-2933***
⇄ ***(30) 8305-1215***

GREAT BRITAIN
24 Grosvenor Square
London W1A 1AE
☎ ***(171) 499-9000***
⇄ ***(171) 491-2485***

ITALY
Via Veneto 119-a
00187 Roma
☎ ***(06) 467-41***
⇄ ***(06) 467-42217***

NETHERLANDS
Lange Voorhout 102
2514 EJ, Den Haag
☎ ***(70) -9209***
⇄ ***(70) 361-4688***

NORWAY
Drammensveien 18
0244 Oslo
☎ ***22448550***

PORTUGAL
Avenida Das Forças Armadas
1600 Lisboa Apartado 4258
1507 Lisboa Codex
☎ ***(351) (1) 727-3300***
⇄ ***(351) (1) 727-2354***

SPAIN
C. Serrano 75
Madrid 28006
☎ *(1) 577-4000*
⇄ *(1) 564-1652*
Telex (1) 277-63

SWEDEN
Strandvägen 101
11589 Stockholm
☎ *(08) 783 53 00*
⇄ *(08) 661 19 64*

SWITZERLAND
93 Jubilam Strasse
3005 Berne
☎ *31-43-70-11*
⇄ *31-357-73-98*

Foreign Consulates in Los Angeles

AUTRALIA
Century Plaza Towers
2049 Century Pk., E., 19th floor
Los Angeles, CA 90067
☎ *229-4800*

BELGIUM
6600 Wilshire Blvd., Suite 1200
Los Angeles, CA 90048
☎ *(213) 857-1244*
⇄ *(213) 936-2564*

CANADA
550 S. Hope St., 9th floor
Los Angeles, CA 90071-2627
☎ *(213) 346-2700*
⇄ *(213) 620-8827*
lngls@dfait-maeci.gc.ca

DENMARK
10877 Wilshire Blvd., Suite 1105
Los Angeles, CA 90024
☎ *443 2090*
⇄ *443 2099*

FINLAND
1900 Ave. of the Stars, Suite 1025
Los Angeles, CA 90067
☎ *203-9903*
⇄ *203-9186*

GERMANY
6222 Wilshire Blvd., Suite 500
Los Angeles, CA 90048
☎ *(323) 930-2703*
⇄ *(323) 930 2805*

GREAT BRITAIN
11766 Wilshire Blvd., Suite 400
Los Angeles, CA 90025
☎ *477-3322*
⇄ *575-1450*

ITALY
12400 Wilshire Blvd., Suite 300
Los Angeles, CA 90025
☎ *820-0622*
⇄ *820-0727*

NETHERLANDS
11766 Wilshire Blvd., Suite 1150
Los Angeles, CA 90025
☎ *268 1598*
⇄ *312 0989*

NORWAY
Honourary Consulate
1840 Century Park E.,
Suite 1050
Los Angeles, CA 90067
☎ *277-1293*
⇄ *788-0858*

Portugal
There is no Portugese consulate in L.A. Inquiries should be addressed to:
3298 Washington St.
San Francisco, CA
(415) 364-3400

Spain
5055 Wilshire Blvd.
Suite 960
Los Angeles, CA 90036
☎(323) 938-0158 or 938-0166
⇄(323) 938-2502

Sweden
10940 Wilshire Blvd., Suite 700
Los Angeles, CA 90024
☎ 445-4008
⇄ 473-2229

Switzerland
11766 Wilshire Blvd., Suite 1400
Los Angeles, CA 90025
☎(480) 945-0000
⇄(480) 947-0020

Tourist Information

Tourist Information Offices

The **Los Angeles Convention & Visitors Bureau** *(☎213-689-8822 or 800-228-2452)* provides assistance by telephone and also operates two visitor information centres. One is located downtown at 685 South Figueroa Street between Wilshire Boulevard and Seventh Street *(Mon to Fri 8am to 5pm, Sat 8:30am to 5pm)*. The other is in Hollywood at 6541 Hollywood Boulevard near Cahuenga Boulevard *(Mon to Sat 9am to 1pm and 2pm to 5pm)*. Both these centres offer a wide range of leaflets (including transit information) and multilingual staff to help with inquiries.

Other visitor centres include those run by the **Santa Monica Convention and Visitors Bureau** *(every day 10am to 4pm, in the park along Ocean Ave. between Santa Monica Blvd. and Broadway)*, the **Beverly Hills Visitors Bureau** *(239 S. Beverly Dr., ☎-248-1015)*, and the **Pasadena Convention and Visitors Bureau** *(171 S. Los Robles Ave., ☎626-795-9311)*.

The **Catalina Island Visitor's Bureau** *(1 Green Pleasure Pier, ☎510-1520, www.catalina.com)* offers a warm welcome and precise information to help you plan your stay on the island.

Inland Orange County

Anaheim / Orange County Visitor & Convention Bureau
800 W. Katella Ave., Box 4270
Anaheim, CA 92803
☎888-598-3200
☎(714) 765-8888
⇄(714) 991-8963
www.anaheimoc.org

The Beaches of Orange County

Seal Beach

Seal Beach Chamber of Commerce
311 Main St., Suite 14A
Seal Beach, CA 90740
☎ ***(562) 799-0179***
www.sealbeachchamber. com

Huntington Beach

Huntington Beach Conference and Visitors Bureau
417 Main St.
Huntington Beach, CA 92648
☎ ***(714) 969-3492***
☎ ***800-729-6232***
www.hbvisit.com

Newport Beach

Newport Beach Conference and Visitors Bureau
3300 W. Coast Hwy.
Newport Beach, CA 92663
☎ ***(949) 722-1611***
☎ ***800-942-6778***
⇄ ***(949) 722-1612***
www.newportbeach-cvb.com

Laguna Beach

Laguna Beach Visitors Bureau
252 Broadway, Box 221
Laguna Beach, CA 92652
☎ ***800-877-1115***
⇄ ***(949) 376-0558***
www.lagunabeachinfo.org

Dana Point

Dana Point Chamber of Commerce
24681 La Plaza, Dana Point, CA 92629
☎ ***800-290-3262***
www.danapoint-chamber. com

San Clemente

San Clemente Chamber of Commerce
1100 N. El. Camino Real
San Clemente, CA 92672
☎ ***(714) 492-1131***
www.scchamber.com

San Juan Capistrano

San Juan Capistrano Chamber of Commerce
31781 Camino Capistrano
Franciscan Plaza, Suite 306
San Juan Capistrano
CA 92693-1878
☎ ***(949) 493-4700***
⇄ ***(949) 489-2695***
www.sanjuanchamber.com

Oceanside

Oceanside Chamber of Commerce
928 N. Coast Hwy.
Oceanside, CA 92054
☎ ***800-350-7873***
www.oceansidechamber. com

Palm Springs

Palm Springs Visitor Information Center
2781 N. Palm Canyon Dr.
☎ ***778-8418***
☎ ***800-347-7746***
www.palmsprings.com

A Recent History of Public Transit in L.A.

Until just after the Second World War, the Los Angeles area had one of the world's most extensive networks of streetcars and electric railways connecting the city with its far-flung suburbs. Starting soon after the war, the system was totally dismantled under pressure from the automobile industry, which was able to influence local and state politicians to direct massive public investment into developing a major urban freeway network. This established a prototype that was subsequently imitated in other American cities.

For several decades, transit users in the U.S.'s second-largest metropolitan area relied on a totally bus-based system that operated on a shoestring budget. Then in the 1980s, along came federal funds aimed at promoting public transit development. The MTA, picking up where a predecessor agency left off, devised expensive plans for new rail systems that appeared to place the interests of consultants and contractors above those of the eventual users. The result is a very limited urban rail network that nonetheless developed huge cost overruns and long construction delays.

Nor did it escape notice that heavy subsidies were being directed to comfortable suburban trains serving affluent commuters while buses serving urban working-class areas were becoming increasingly decrepit and overcrowded. Legal action by a public interest group led to federal court orders calling for a rapid expansion of the bus fleet. Despite some foot-dragging by the MTA, service has slowly been improving. It is less common now to see crowded buses having to skip stops and strand passengers waiting to board, although this does still happen sometimes.

Table of Distances (km/mi)

Via the shortest route

©ULYSSES

1 mile = 1.62 kilometres
1 kilometre = 0.62 mile

	Bakersfield	Eureka	Fresno	Las Vegas (Nev.)	Los Angeles	Monterey	Palm Springs	Redding	Reno (Nev.)	Sacramento	San Diego	San Francisco	San Luis Obispo
Bakersfield													
Eureka	889/549												
Fresno	175/108	738/456											
Las Vegas (Nev.)	466/288	1368/844	638/394										
Los Angeles	179/110	1060/654	351/217	444/274									
Monterey	401/248	632/390	245/151	859/530	543/335								
Palm Springs	369/228	1237/764	532/328	457/282	184/114	731/451							
Redding	711/439	253/156	534/330	1170/722	890/549	513/317	1072/662						
Reno (Nev.)	659/407	687/424	488/301	721/445	838/517	526/325	1031/636	477/294					
Sacramento	438/270	483/298	261/161	908/560	628/388	301/186	810/500	268/165	219/135				
San Diego	384/237	1258/777	547/338	543/335	200/123	750/463	232/143	1086/670	1045/645	829/512			
San Francisco	459/283	449/277	289/178	921/569	616/380	178/110	800/494	353/218	366/226	146/90	819/506		
San Luis Obispo	198/122	824/509	206/127	762/470	310/191	234/144	506/312	700/432	712/440	495/306	517/319	372/230	
Tijuana (Mex.)	399/246	1283/792	573/354	566/349	225/189	773/477	255/157	1111/686	1070/660	857/529	28/17	845/522	546/337

Example: the distance between Los Angeles and San Francisco is 616km or 380mi.

Getting Around Los Angeles

By Car

Los Angeles has a worldwide reputation for its extensive freeway network. Indeed, the city and its suburbs became the prototype soon after the Second World War for the car-dependent U.S. model where hardly anyone would dream of going anywhere without hopping into an automobile, and distant places could be reached swiftly and effortlessly along multi-lane ribbons of controlled-access highway. This began in 1940 with the opening of the Pasadena Freeway (initially known as the Arroyo Seco Parkway and now designated a historical monument—you take your history where you can find it), snaking through the hills northeast of downtown L.A. The network later expanded throughout the metropolitan area and beyond.

L.A.'s urban freeway network is probably the most extensive anywhere, although there are not quite as many freeways as some first-time visitors may imagine. Indeed, in parts of the city it's possible to travel fairly long distances without encountering a freeway. Some other U.S. cities have denser networks, at least in relation to population. In L.A., the early dream has turned into a nightmare for many motorists, who have to put up with ever-lower speeds and massive traffic jams on a daily basis, and not just at rush hours. Some radio stations devote a significant part of their programming to traffic reports. Often, it's possible to avoid the freeway system altogether. But when entering Los Angeles, or when going long distances within the metropolitan area, chances are that anyone going by car will spend at least part of the trip on a freeway.

The freeways are identified both by name and by highway number. Some, but not all, are officially designated as part of the interstate highway network. Several freeways change names along the way. For example, Interstate Highway 10 (I-10 for short) is an east-west highway that is named the Santa Monica Freeway west of downtown L.A. but the San Bernardino Freeway east of downtown. The north-south I-5 is called the Hollywood Freeway north of downtown L.A. but becomes the Santa Ana Freeway south of downtown.

Other major freeways include the San Diego Freeway (I-405) that branches off from the I-5, following a more westerly route through the L.A. area (and passing near the airport) before rejoining the I-5; the Pomona Freeway (California 60) running east from downtown L.A. parallel to the I-10 but along a more southerly route; the Harbor Freeway (I-110) from downtown L.A. south to San Pedro; the Pasadena Freeway (California 110) northeast to Pasadena; the Long Beach Freeway (I-710) south to Long Beach from areas east of downtown L.A.; the Hollywood Freeway (U.S. 101, changing to California 170 in North Hollywood) from downtown L.A. northwest through Hollywood and the San Fernando Valley); and the Ventura Freeway (U.S. 101), picking up where the Hollywood Freeway leaves off in North Hollywood and running west to Ventura county. Keep in mind that this list is by no means comprehensive.

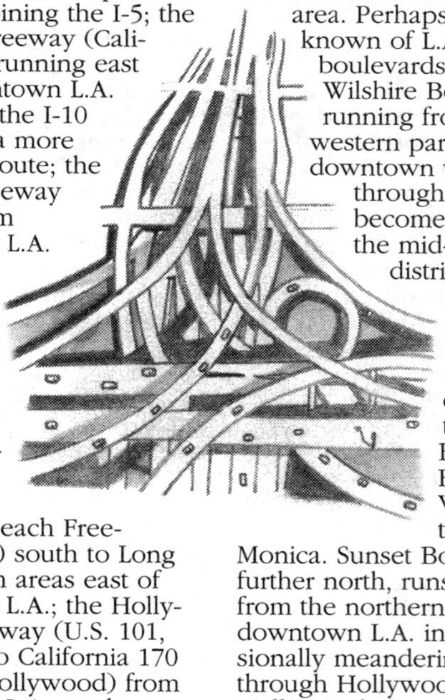

Of course, there's a lot more to the road network than just freeways. Some of the main roads run for very long distances, forming a solid rectangular grid across much of the metropolitan area. Perhaps the best known of L.A.'s urban boulevards is Wilshire Boulevard, running from the western part of downtown west through what has become known as the mid-Wilshire district (home to several museums), and then on through Beverly Hills and Westwood to Santa Monica. Sunset Bouelvard, further north, runs west from the northern edge of downtown L.A. in an occasionally meandering route through Hollywood, West Hollywood, Westwood, Brentwood (passing near the Getty Center), and then through the hills of Pacific Palisades before reaching the coast.

To get between Los Angeles International Airport and Hollywood or downtown L.A., Fairfax Avenue and La Brea Avenue, parallel north-south arteries, can be handy time-savers, with short freeway-like stretches over part of their length south of the Santa Monica Freeway. They run through a hilly area with working oil wells clearly visible near the roadsides.

Parking is not often a problem in most of L.A. This is a city built for cars, and an astounding portion of the landscape is covered with parking lots. Many of the more expensive restaurants and hotels, and even a few of the medium-priced ones, offer valet parking. Parking can be more difficult in downtown L.A. and downtown Santa Monica, as well as near Venice Beach and parts of Hollywood or Beverly Hills. What this usually means, however, isn't that it's impossible to find any sort of parking but that visitors have to use paying parking lots rather than being able to count on free street parking. This may even mean having to walk a couple of blocks, something that could horrify some Angelenos but that most visitors will take in stride.

Things to Consider

Driver's License:
As a general rule, foreign driver's licenses are valid in the United States. Take note that certain states are linked by computer to provincial police services in Canada, and that a ticket issued in the United States is therefore automatically transferred to your file in Canada.

Driving and the Highway Code:
Signs marked "Stop" in white against a red background must always be respected. Some stop signs are accompanied by a small sign indicating "4-way." This means that all vehicles must stop at the intersection. Come to a complete stop even if there is no apparent danger. If two vehicles arrive at the same time, the one to the right has the right of way. Otherwise, the first car to the intersection has the right of way.

Traffic lights are often located on the opposite side of the intersection, so make sure to stop at the stop line, a white line on the pavement before the intersection.

Turning right on a red light after a full stop is permitted, unless otherwise indicated.

When a school bus (usually yellow) has stopped and its signals are flashing, **you must come to a complete stop, no matter what direction you are travelling in**. Failing to stop at the flashing signals is considered a serious offense, and carries a heavy penalty.

Seat belts must be worn at all times.

There are no tolls on the highways, except on most Interstate highways that are indicated by the letter "I" followed by a number. Interstate highways are also indicated by a blue crest on a white background. The highway number and the state are written on the sign. "Interstate" is written on a red background at the top of the sign.

The speed limit is 55mph (88km/h) on most highways. These signs are rectangular with a black border, white background and black writing.

The speed limit on Interstate highways is 65mph (104km/h).

Red and white triangular signs with the word "Yield" under them indicate that vehicles crossing your path have the right of way.

A round, yellow sign with a black X and two Rs indicates a railroad crossing.

Gas Stations: Since the United States produces its own crude oil, gasoline prices are less expensive than in Europe; gas is also less expensive than in Canada due to hidden taxes north of the border. Self-serve stations will often ask for payment in advance as a security measure.

Warning: Criminals looking to rob tourists have adopted a strategy to get you out of your car. Whether in moving traffic or not, these miscreants will start bumping you from behind. Don't fall for this trick, and make sure you **do not** stop to argue with the other driver.

Do not stop for hitchhikers, always lock your doors and be careful.

Car Rentals

Most of the companies listed below have rental locations at Los Angeles International Airport and in other parts of the L.A. area.

Avis
☎800-331-1212
☎(213) 977-1450
☎ 646-5600

Beverly Hills Rent A Car
☎ 337-1400

Bob Leech's Auto Rental
☎800-635-1240
☎ 673-2727

Budget
☎800-221-1203

Dollar
☎*800-800-4000*
☎ *645-9333*

Enterprise
☎*800-736-8222*

Fox Car Rental
☎*800-225-4369*
☎ *641-3838*

Hertz
☎*800-654-3131*

Los Angeles Rent-A-Car
☎ *670-9945*

Lucky
☎*800-400-4736*
☎ *641-2323*

Midway
☎*800-824-5260*
☎ *445-4355*

National
☎*800-227-7368*

Payless
☎ *645-2100*

Shooshani's Avon Car Rental
☎*(323) 650-2631*

Thrifty
☎ *645-1880*

Motorcycle Rentals

EagleRider
☎*800-501-8687*
☎ *320-4008*

By Taxi

As a general rule, taxis are used not by motorists but by those who do not own their own car. Since most people in L.A. who have enough money to take taxis are rarely far from their own vehicles, there is little demand for taxis and hence not many taxis for a city this size. Although there is no rule against flagging taxis on the street, it is rare to see unoccupied taxis cruising by. There are stands with waiting taxis in a handful of places, for example at the airports, the main railway station, outside some (but not all) of the bigger hotels, especially downtown, and near several spots with heavy pedestrian traffic downtown and in Hollywood or Santa Monica. Otherwise, passengers must phone a taxi company and hope the dispatcher can locate a vehicle not too far away. Sometimes the wait can be quite long. Among the companies with citywide fleets are **Yellow Cab** *(☎800-808-1000)*, **L.A. Taxi** *(☎800-652-8294)* and **Independent Taxi** *(☎323-462-1088)*. Fares start at $1.90 and rise by $1.60/ mi ($1.00/km). Since the distances to be covered are sometimes considerable, taxis can be an expensive proposition. There is a surcharge of $2.50 on trips

A Glimpse at Metro Rail and Metrolink

Metro Rail, with hefty construction costs and controversial route planning, provided an inauspicious start to the era of modern mass transit in Los Angeles. But parts of the system are now being used quite heavily. Its biggest drawback is that it doesn't cover more territory. Metro Rail consists of three lines: the Red Line subway, with trains running underground, and two light rail lines, the Blue Line and Green Line, running mostly at surface level or along elevated track.

The **Red Line** runs west from Union Station across downtown L.A. and then northwest to Hollywood and North Hollywood. A shorter branch runs west to Wilshire and Western. Trains from downtown alternate between these two branches: pay attention when boarding. The **Blue Line** runs south from downtown L.A. to Long Beach, connecting with the Red Line downtown at 7th Street and with the Green Line at Rosa Parks station in the Watts district, about halfway to Long Beach. The **Green Line** looks more than anything else like an afterthought to accompany the new east-west Century Freeway in the southern part of the city, running mostly along the median of this freeway (station platforms are not protected from noise or fumes). It runs essentially from nowhere to nowhere, passing near LAX airport (but not going to the airport) and then turning south to the municipality of Manhattan Beach (without going anywhere near the beach).

While station design on the Blue and Green lines is very ordinary, each Red Line station features large-scale works of art, some of them quite imaginative. These works, each by a local artist, form part of the decor at the mezzanine level and are not visible from track level, but they offer pleasant surprises to passengers entering or leaving stations. Unlike many public installations in Los Angeles, Metro Rail stations are kept spotlessly clean and free of graffiti.

Metrolink is the name given to the suburban rail network. Six lines radiate from Union Station in downtown L.A., serving points as distant as Oxnard, Lancaster, San Bernardino and Oceanside. A seventh line provides a direct link between distant suburbs in Orange, Riverside and San Bernardino counties. Rolling stock consists of modern double-deck coaches. Some lines operate only at rush hours. Saturday service is very limited, and there is no service at all on Sundays or holidays. Tickets are sold from vending machines at each station, and all passengers must hold tickets or passes before boarding.

originating at Los Angeles International Airport.

By Public Transit

Despite its well deserved reputation as a car-obsessed city that seems to spread out endlessly, Los Angeles does have a fairly comprehensive public transit system. Hundreds of bus routes link various parts of the city and the surrounding suburbs, augmented by a small network of subway and light rail lines called Metro Rail and a commuter rail system called Metrolink.

Few people brag about L.A.'s public transit system except in a pejorative sense. Some trips by bus seem to take forever, with long waits and long travel times. But things aren't as bad as they are often portrayed, and visitors who aren't in a huge hurry will find the transit system to be an economical and entirely feasible way of getting around. Most points of interest to visitors (with the notable exception of Dodger Stadium) are reasonably well served, although reliability is sometimes a problem, and service on most routes drops to infrequent intervals by mid-evening. A few bus routes operate 24hrs a day. Most others run from about 5am to midnight, seven days a week. Some do not operate in the late evening or on weekends, while some others run only at rush hours. Most buses, and the entire rail network, are accessible to passengers in wheelchairs.

L.A.'s dominant transit operator is the Los Angeles County Metropolitan Transportation Authority, thankfully abbreviated as MTA. Several suburban municipalities have their own bus operations that serve as part of a coordinated network in conjunction with the MTA. Service within downtown Los Angeles and in several other parts of the city is supplemented by short and sometimes circuitous bus routes forming the separate DASH system.

Here are a few pointers on getting around by public transit. Remember that a little advance planning can save plenty of time. The route network is quite complex, and some routes offer faster or more frequent service than others. Once you've decided where you want to go, consult (if you have Internet access) the MTA website at ***www.mta.net***. This site provides a customized trip planning service, with detailed route and schedule information. It also provides links to the websites of other transit operators in the region.

Of course, not everyone has easy Internet access away from home. Another solution is the information service provided by telephone, reached by dialing ***☎800-COMMUTE*** *(☎800-266-6883)*. Voice prompts (in English or Spanish) direct callers to the pertinent transit operator and route number or service. Bus routes serving many points of interest are indicated in the "Exploring" section of this chapter. Printed information is also available. Tourist information offices and MTA customer centres sometimes have route maps available and can usually provide printed timetables for specific routes. MTA customer centres are located at Union Station (east portal); downstairs in the Arco Plaza building at Fifth and Flower streets downtown; in the mid-Wilshire district at the corner of Wilshire and La Brea; and in several other locations. With a few rare exceptions, schedules are *not* posted at MTA bus stops.

The standard MTA fare (at press time) for bus or Metro Rail is $1.35 per trip anywhere within Los Angeles County. From 9pm to 5am the fare is $0.75. Tokens, sold in bags of 10, cost $0.90 each. Weekly passes, valid for unlimited travel on the MTA system from Sunday until the following Saturday, cost $11 and have become very popular. Monthly and semi-monthly passes are also available. Children under five travel free.

Transfers for connections between buses or between bus and rail cost $0.25 per use and are valid until the time marked on them. Express buses with route numbers in the 400s or 500s require fare supplements of $0.50 or $1, or sometimes higher, depending on the distance travelled on express portions of the route. No supplement is required for portions of these routes providing local service. Exact change is required when boarding any bus: drivers are not allowed to provide change. (Obviously, it's important to keep a good supply of 25-cent coins and $1 bills or coins.) Pass holders do not require transfers but do have to pay express supplements.

At Metro Rail stations, tickets for individual trips are sold by vending machines, which provide change. Bills, coins and tokens are all accepted. Passengers with valid transfers or passes can proceed directly to the boarding area. Fare collection on Metro Rail works on the honour system, subject to occasional inspections: passengers caught without a valid ticket, transfer or pass are subject to heavy fines. Tokens and passes are sold at MTA customer centres, at some food stores and pharmacies, and at the ubiquitous cheque cashing shops that dot the L.A. landscape. Tokens and passes are *not* available at Metro Rail stations!

As if this weren't complicated enough, the MTA isn't the only show in town. A parallel system called DASH operates some short-distance local routes within downtown L.A. and in certain other areas, including Hollywood. The fare is only $0.25, though downtown DASH buses do not accept MTA transfers or passes. The DASH system can be a useful way of getting around the downtown area, within a perimeter extending from Chinatown in the north to Exposition Park in the south. Service on most routes is frequent, with buses at 5min intervals.

In addition, some municipalities in L.A. County have

their own bus systems. The system most likely to be of use to visitors is Santa Monica Municipal Bus Lines, with a base fare of $0.50 (or $1.25 for the No. 10 express bus between Santa Monica and downtown L.A.). The Culver City system has a base fare of $0.60. Both companies accept MTA transfers but not MTA tokens or passes. Transfers valid for connections to the MTA cost $0.25.

Tour buses can be a way of getting around certain parts of the city. Limited information on bus tours is provided in the "Exploring" section of this chapter.

To get to Orange County

The **Metrolink** *(☎800-371-LINK, www.octa.net)* is a commuter service that runs from Oceanside to Anaheim. This service will take you to Union Station in Los Angeles. Stops are made in Oceanside, San Clemente, San Juan Capistrano, Irvine, Santa Ana, Orange and Anaheim. A full-day unlimited pass is just $2.50. Contact Metrolink for detailed times and fares.

By Bicycle

Getting around the sprawling L.A. area by bicycle is no longer as preposterous an idea as it once was. Many MTA buses now have front-end racks carrying up to two bicycles each, available for use at no additional fare. Leaflets describing procedures and listing the bus routes providing this service are available from MTA customer centres or by Internet at www.mta.net. This enables passengers to enjoy the flexibility of cycling at either end of their journey while using the bus for the longer hauls and to avoid areas of heavy traffic. Bicycles are accepted outside rush hours on the Metro Rail subway and light rail lines, but only to holders of special permits, making this less practical for visitors.

Los Angeles has a network of what are described as bike routes, although only a small part of this network consists of true cycling paths separated from motor traffic. In many cases, the so-called bike routes consist of little more than signage alongside busy streets. One notable exception is the coastal bike path extending from the northwestern tip of Santa Monica all the way south to Redondo Beach (see page 161).

Bicycle rentals are available at several easy-to-spot locations along or near the beach in Venice and Santa Monica.

On Foot

Among the joys of travel is being able to walk to where you're going or finding places that are conducive to a pleasant stroll. In many parts of Los Angeles, people have developed a heavy physical and psychological dependance on automobiles, making pedestrians notable by their scarcity. In certain places, walking is regarded as a sign of eccentricity. But fear not: pedestrians are far from extinct even in this stronghold of automobile culture.

Much of downtown L.A. is eminently walkable, with a vibrant pedestrian scene along Broadway Avenue and the streets immediately to its west. In Santa Monica, a very lively three-block stretch of Third Avenue is closed to motor traffic and provides one of the world's great pedestrian experiences by day and by night (see page 150). And, of course, several long stretches of beach offer ideal opportunities for a leisurely stroll, with Venice Beach providing a particularly interesting scene. This list is far from exhaustive: parts of Hollywood, Beverly Hills and Westwood draw large numbers of people on foot, as do some other spots.

Motorists generally tend to yield to pedestrians at intersections and at designated crossings, although care is still advised. Police enforce traffic laws regarding pedestrians and will issue tickets to jaywalkers who cross against the signal or to motorists who fail to yield the right of way. One minor annoyance: at some intersections, pedestrians actually need to ask permission to cross; they are required to push a button before the pedestrian signals can be activated. This is not a serious inconvenience, but it does reinforce the second-class status of people without vehicles.

Ferry to Catalina Island

Catalina Island lies 22mi (35km) off Long Beach and is easily reached by ferry. **Catalina Express** *($38 return; reservations required in summer and on weekends; take Hwy. 710 toward the* Queen Mary *and follow the signs, ☎519-1212 or 800-995-4386)* offers ferry service from Long Beach or San Pedro *(take Hwy. 110, Harbour Blvd. Exit toward the Catalina Terminal)* to Avalon in 60min. **Catalina Cruises** *($25 return; ☎800-228-2546)* offers more affordable passenger service to the island from Long Beach, San Pedro or Redondo Beach. Those with deep pockets can also get here by helicopter with **Island Express** *($121 return; ☎510-2535).*

Money and Banking

Money

The monetary unit is the dollar ($), which is divided into cents (¢).
One dollar = 100 cents.

Bills come in one, five, 10, 20, 50 and 100 dollar denominations; and coins come in one- (penny), five- (nickel), 10- (dime) and 25-cent (quarter) pieces.

Dollar and fifty-cent coins exist, as does a two-dollar bill, but they are very rarely used. Virtually all purchases must be paid in U.S. dollars in the United States. Be sure to get your traveller's cheques in U.S. dollars. You can also use any credit card affiliated with a U.S. institution, like Visa, MasterCard, American Express, Interbank, Barclay Bank, Diners' Club and Discovery.

Please note that all prices in this guide are in US dollars.

Exchange Rates*

$1 US = $1.53 CAN		$1 CAN	= $0.65 US
$1 US = £0.70		£ 1	= $1.44 US
$1 US = $1.84 AUS		$1 AUS	= $0.54 US
$1 US = $2.37 NZ		$1 NZ	= $0.42 US
$1 US = 1.71 SF		1 SF	= $0.59 US
$1 US = 1.13 € (Euro)		1 € (Euro)	= $0.88 US
$1 US = 45.59 BF		10 BF	= $0.22 US
$1 US = 2.21 DM		1 DM	= $0.45 US
$1 US = 188.03 PTA		100 PTA	= $0.53 US
$1 US = 2,188.12 ITL		1000 ITL	= $0.46 US
$1 US = 2.49 fl		1 fl	= $0.40 US

*Samples only—rates fluctuate

Banks

Banks are open from Monday to Friday, 9am to 3pm.

There are many banks in the city, and tourists can take advantage of most services. Those who choose to stay for an extended period of time should note that a **non-resident** cannot open a bank account. To obtain cash, your best bet is always traveller's cheques. Withdrawing from your own account outside your home country can be costly since commission fees are high. However, most banks have ATMs which accept Canadian and European bank cards, allowing you to make a withdrawal. What'S more, ATMs are often accessible 24hrs a day. Those who have resident status, permanent or non-permanent (immigrants, students), can open a bank account. To do so, all you need is your passport and a proof of your resident status.

Exchanging Money

Several banks readily exchange foreign currency, but almost all charge a **commission**. While there are exchange offices that do not charge commission, their rates can be less competitive. These offices often have longer opening hours. It is a good idea to **shop around**.

Traveller's Cheques

It is always best to keep a certain amount of money in traveller's cheques, which are accepted in some restaurants, hotels and shops (those in U.S. dollars are most widely accepted). They are also easy to cash in at banks and exchange offices. Always keep a copy of the serial numbers of your cheques in a separate place; that way, if the cheques are lost, the company can replace them quickly and easily. Do not rely solely on traveller's cheques, however, as you should always carry some cash.

Credit Cards

Most credit cards, especially Visa, MasterCard, and American Express (in that order) are accepted in many businesses, including hotels and restaurants. While the main advantage of credit cards is that they allow you to avoid carrying large sums of money, using a credit card also makes leaving a deposit for a rental car much easier. In addition, the exchange rate with a credit card is usually better.

Credit cards also let you avoid service charges when exchanging money. By overpaying your credit card (to avoid interest charges), you can then withdraw against it. You can thus avoid carrying large amounts of money or traveller's cheques.

Withdrawals can be made directly from an automated teller if you have a personal identification number (PIN) for your card.

Taxes and Tipping

Taxes

A total tax (city and state) of 12% is applicable on accommodations, while the goods and services tax is 8.5%.

Tipping

In general, tips are applicable to all table services, that is, in restaurants and other places where you are served at the table (fast-food establishments do not fit this category). According to the quality of service, you should leave approximately 15% of the amount before taxes. Contrary to Europe, the tip is not included in the bill, so it is up to the customer to figure out how much to give the server. Airport baggage-handlers usually get $1. It is also proper to tip in bars and nightclubs, as well as bellhops, chambermaids and taxi drivers.

Insurance

Cancellation

Your travel agent will usually offer you cancellation insurance upon purchase of your airline ticket or vacation package. This insurance allows you to be reimbursed for the ticket or package deal if your trip must be cancelled due to serious illness or death.

Health

This is the most useful kind of insurance for travellers and should be purchased before your departure. Your insurance plan should be as complete as possible because health care costs add up quickly. When buying insurance, make sure it covers all types of medical costs, such as hospitalization, nursing services and doctor's fees. Make sure your limit is high enough, as these expenses can be costly. A repatriation clause is also vital in case the required care is not available on site. Furthermore, since you may have to pay on the spot, check your policy to see what provisions it includes for such situations. To avoid any problems during your vacation, always keep proof of your insurance policy with you.

Theft

Most residential insurance policies protect some of your goods from theft, even if the theft occurs in a foreign country. To make a claim, you are required to fill out a police report. It may not be necessary to take out further insurance depending on the amount covered by your current home policy. As policies vary considerably, you are advised to check with your insurance company. European visitors should take out baggage insurance.

Health

Vaccinations are not necessary for people coming from Europe or Canada. On the other hand, it is strongly suggested, particularly for medium or long-term stays, that visitors take out health and accident insurance (see above). There are different types, so it is best to shop around. Bring along all medication, especially prescription medicine. Unless otherwise stated, the water is potable throughout California.

The Sun

Despite its benefits, the sun also causes numerous problems. It is needless to say that the rising occurrence of skin cancer is due to overexposure to the sun's harmful rays. It is important to keep well protected and avoid prolonged exposure, especially during the first few days of your trip, as it takes a while to get used to the sun's strength. Overexposure to the sun can also cause sunstroke, symptoms of which include dizziness, vomiting and fever. Always use sunblock to protect yourself from the sun's harmful rays. Many of the sunscreens on the market do not provide adequate protection. Before setting off on your trip, ask your pharmacist which ones are truly effective against the UVA and UVB rays. For the best results, apply the cream at least 20min before going out in the sun. Even after a few days, moderate exposure is best. A hat and pair of sunglasses are indispensable accessories in this part of the U.S.

Safety and Security

Unfortunately, the United States is still a rather violent country. That said, there is no need to panic and hide in your hotel room! If something does happen to you though, remember to dial ***911*** for help, or ***0*** for the operator.

Crime rates in Los Angeles are pretty close to the U.S. average, which is to say somewhere along a continuum between the relative security found elsewhere in the industrialized world and the higher levels of danger that characterize parts of the Third World. As in much of the U.S., rates of violent crime have been falling in recent years, but it is still a good idea to take certain precautions. People on vacation often want to embrace a carefree attitude, and this can make them more vulnerable to criminal attack. Remember to keep valuables well hidden in public areas. When taking cash from an automated banking machine, do so only in a well-lit, well-trafficked area.

Bear in mind that some parts of Los Angeles are more dangerous than others. Generally speaking, the west side is fairly safe, while many areas to the south or east of downtown L.A. are much less secure, plagued by some of the city's notorious youth gangs. Certain streets that feel entirely safe by day may turn quite frightening at night. This is especially true in much of downtown L.A. and certain parts of Hollywood. Visitors on foot after dark should use common sense and avoid unfamiliar areas where there are few other pedestrians. L.A. has a substantial number of homeless people, some of whom suffer from mental illness or drug problems. Usually they are more deranged than truly dangerous, but they can still throw a scare into unsuspecting passersby. Clusters of them may be found on the east side of the downtown area and in parts of Hollywood and Santa Monica.

Motorists also should take extra precautions and, when travelling late at night, be quite sure they know where they're going and keep their doors locked. The scandal-wracked Los Angeles Police

Department is not as ineffective as some critics suggest, but it is stretched rather thinly over a very large territory. The emergency phone number (free from public phones) is 911.

Climate

Packing

No matter what type of trip you choose, you will only need Bermuda shorts, light shirts and T-shirts, casual pants, one or two bathing suits, a sweater or light jacket, and a casual or dressy outfit if you plan on going out.

Don't forget books and other essential items.

If you visit Los Angeles in winter, bring a jacket, as it can get quite cool, especially at night. Comfortable, light shoes are also a must for your visit.

Don't leave your camera behind (sunsets on the Pacific are breathtaking) and enough film to capture those memories.

Mail and Telecommunications

The telephone system in the United States is extremely well designed. You will have no trouble finding pay phones using change ($0.35) or telephone cards.

The area code for Los Angeles and Catalina island is 310. Unless indicated otherwise in the L.A. chapters of this guide, assume that all phone numbers have this area code.

San Fernando Valley: ***818***

Area Codes for Orange County and Palm Springs

Seal Beach: ***562***

Anaheim, Orange, Buena Park, Santa Ana, Costa Mesa, Huntington Beach : ***714***

Newport Beach, Laguna Beach, Dana Point, San Clemente, San Juan Capistrano: ***949***

Oceanside, Palm Springs: ***760***

To reach Los Angeles from Canada, dial ***1-310,*** then the number.

From Europe, dial ***00-1-310***, then the number.

By calling at specific times, you can also take advantage of substantial discounts. Inquire with your long-distance company.

To reach Canada Direct from Los Angeles, dial ***1-800-555-1111***. For long-distance calls outside North America, dial ***011*** + the country code

Pay attention to those new phone codes!

It seems to be a matter of dogma in North America that all local telephone numbers must have seven digits, regardless of how big or small the locality may be. For decades, this worked quite well. More recently, however, an explosion in the use of cellphones, pagers, fax machines and computer modems has caused most large metropolitan areas to run out of numbers.

Rather than switch to eight-digit local numbers, as telecom authorities have done in several parts of the world, the private-sector agency that decides on such matters in North America opted instead to chop up local calling areas and add new three-digit area codes. This means that many local calls, even if no toll charge applies, have to be treated as long-distance calls, prefixed by the numeral 1 and the three-digit code.

All numbers shown in this chapter are prefixed by the area code, except those in the 310 area. When calling another number starting with the same code, only the last seven digits have to be entered.

The old 213 area code that once covered all of Los Angeles County now applies only in downtown L.A. and areas within a radius of 5km (3m) of downtown. Surrounding this zone like a doughnut is the new 323 code, covering much of the inner city, including Hollywood, and some of the nearby suburbs. A few years ago the 310 area code was created to cover the west side, including Santa Monica, Beverly Hills and LAX airport. This zone later started running out of numbers, and the new 424 code was superimposed, meaning that some people have to enter 11 digits to call their next-door neighbours.

+ the area code + the number.

In addition, most hotels are equipped with a fax machine and offer access to the Internet. However, it will cost you more to call from your hotel than from a pay phone, however.

Internet

Thanks to the Internet, keeping in touch with the folks back home has never been so easy. Indeed, the growing popularity of this means of communication is almost making postcards a thing of the past. All you need to do is get an e-mail address before you leave.

Some hotels offer e-mail service, but usually charge higher fees than Internet cafés.

Several Internet sites provide useful information for visitors and up-to-the-minute listings of events and attractions. The Los Angeles Convention & Visitors Bureau provides a wide range of information on its site at ***www.lacvb.com***. *The Los Angeles Times* newspaper has a very useful site for cultural listings of all sorts at ***www.calendarlive.com***. Another good source of listings and other information is ***www.at-la.com***.

Post Offices

Post offices are generally open Monday to Friday from 9:30am to 5:30pm (sometimes until 8pm on Thu), and Saturday from 10am to 2pm.

Business Hours

Stores are generally open Monday to Wednesday from 9:30am to 5:30pm, Thursday and Friday from 10am to 9pm, and Sunday from noon to 5pm. Supermarkets close later or, in some cases, are open 24hrs a day, seven days a week.

Public Holidays

The following is a list of public holidays in the United States. Note that most stores, government offices and banks are closed on these days.

New Year's Day
January 1

Martin Luther King Jr. Day
Third Monday of January

President's Day
Third Monday of February

Memorial Day
Last Monday of May

Independence Day (American National Holiday)
July 4

Labor Day
First Monday of September

Columbus Day
Second Monday of October

Veterans Day
November 11

Thanksgiving Day
Fourth Thursday of November

Christmas Day
December 25

Seniors

In Los Angeles, people aged 65 and over can take advantage of discounts on admission fees to museums and other attractions, as well as hotels and restaurants. These reductions are not necessarily publicized, so you should always inquire.

Also, be particularly vigilant when it comes to your health. In addition to your medication, bring along your prescription in case you need to renew it. You may also want to bring your medical chart, as well as your physician's name, address and phone number. Lastly, make sure your insurance covers you when travelling abroad.

American Association of Retired Persons
601 E. St.
Washington, D.C. 20049
☎ *(202) 434-227*
The American Association of Retired Persons offers many advantages, such as discounts on organized trips for a number of agencies.

Travellers with Disabilities

Los Angeles is making great efforts to make more and more destinations accessible to those with disabilities. Most tourist attractions should not pose a problem.

Children

It can be quite easy to travel with children, even young ones. Of course, a few precautions and plenty of preparation will make your trip even more pleasant.

In Hotels

Many hotels are well equipped for children, and there is usually no extra fee for travelling with an infant. Many hotels and bed and breakfasts have cribs; ask for one when reserving your room. You may have to pay extra for children, however, but the supplement is generally low.

Car Rentals

Most car rental agencies rent car seats for children. They are usually not very expensive. Ask for one when making your reservation.

The Sun

Needless to say, a child's skin requires strong protection against the sun; in fact, it is actually preferable not to expose toddlers to its harsh rays. Before going to the beach, remember to apply sunscreen (SPF 25 for children, 35 for infants). If you think your child will spend a long time in the sun, you should consider purchasing a sunscreen with SPF 60.

Children of all ages should wear a hat that provides adequate protection for the head, not just during the sun's peak hours in the afternoon, but all throughout the day.

Swimming

Children usually get quite excited about playing in the waves and can do so for hours on end. However, parents must be very careful and watch them constantly; accidents can happen in a matter of seconds. Ideally, an adult should accompany children into the water, especially the younger ones, and stand farther out so that the kids can play between the beach and the supervising adult. This way, he or she can quickly intervene in case of an emergency.

For infants and toddlers, some diapers are especially designed for swimming, such as "Little Swimmers" by Huggies. These are quite useful when having fun in the water!

Women Travellers

Women alone should not encounter any problems as long as they follow all the necessary precautions (see "Security", p 87). Keep in mind that it is dangerous to hitchhike and that it is better to avoid staying at accommodations located on the edge of town. Bed and breakfasts, youth hostels and YMCAs generally offer a more secure environment, as well as one that is conducive to meeting other travellers.

Miscellaneous

Time Difference

When it's noon in Montréal or Toronto, for example, it's 9am in Los Angeles. The time difference for the U.K., Belgium or Switzerland is nine hours. Don't forget that several time zones exist in the U.S.: Los Angeles is therefore three hours behind New York and five behind Hawaii.

Drugs

Recreational drugs are against the law and not tolerated (even "soft" drugs). Anyone caught with drugs in their possession risks severe consequences.

Alcohol

You can purchase alcohol 24hrs a day. Liquor stores are the best places to find a wide selection of products, but you can also buy wine and beer in grocery stores. You must be at least 21 years old to drink.

Electricity

Voltage in the United States is 110 volts and 60 cycles, the same as in Canada; to use European appliances, you must have a transformer/converter.

Electrical plugs are two-pinned and flat; you can

Note to Smokers

It is strictly forbidden to smoke in public places in the state of California, and the law is rigorously applied and carries heavy sanctions. As a result, you will notice, first with surprise and then with a touch of amusement, that smokers light up in front of restaurants, bars and hotels. They find secluded spots, as though they were a little ashamed of themselves... It is true that smoking cigarettes in California is not really trendy. Strict measures and advertising campaigns seem to have worked since very few people have taken up the habit and consequently, there is little tolerance towards smokers. If you absolutely have to smoke, note that cigars are a little more fashionable.

Weights and Measures

Weights
1 pound (lb) = 454 grams (g)
1 kilogram (kg) = 2.2 pounds (lbs)

Linear Measure
1 inch = 2.54 centimetres (cm)
1 foot (ft) = 30 centimetres (cm)
1 mile = 1.6 kilometres (km)
1 kilometres (km) = 0.63 miles (mi)
1 metre (m) = 39.37 inches (in)

Land Measure
1 acre = 0.4 hectare (ha)
1 hectare (ha) = 2.471 acres

Volume Measure
1 U.S. gallon (gal) = 3.79 litres
1 U.S. gallon (gal) = 0.8 imperial gallons

Temperature
To convert °F into °C: subtract 32, divide by 9, multiply by 5.
To convert °C into °F: multiply by 9, divide by 5, add 32.

find adapters in Los Angeles, or purchase them at a travel boutique or bookshop before your departure.

Media

Newspapers

The city's dominant newspaper is *Los Angeles Times*, by far the most distinguished daily newspaper in

Organized Tours

Sometimes the hassle of getting around on your own in an unfamiliar city may seem a bit much. Organized tours can provide an introduction to parts of the city and, if this sort of thing interests you, a chance to glimpse the mansions of certain Hollywood celebrities and pick up bits of gossip from chatty tour guides. The most popular tour programs are the half-day "City Tour and Movie Stars' Homes" offerings—the names vary slightly from one company to the next—typically priced at $40 to $45. Some tour companies provide visits to various theme parks or to the Getty Center, but in reality this is little more than a transportation service. Shopping tours, nightlife tours and full-day tours to out-of-town destinations like San Diego are also available.

Companies operating these tours include **Starline Tours of Hollywood** (*☎800-959-3131*), **Guideline Sightseeing Tours** (*☎800-604-8433* or *323-465-3004*), **Go West Adventures** (*☎216-2522, www.gowestadventures.com*), **Euro Pacific Tours** (*☎574-0595 or 800-303-3005*), **Hollywood Sightseeing** (*☎323-469-8184*) and **L.A. Tours** (*☎323-937-3361*). The bell captains at some hotels have arrangements with particular tour companies.

the western U.S., with many news bureaus across the country and abroad, as well as comprehensive local coverage. Its main local competition comes from the Spanish-language daily *La Opinión* and a number of very locally oriented suburban dailies, the most important of which is the *Daily News*, published at Van Nuys in the San Fernando Valley.

The *L.A. Times* publishes movie and cultural listings in its daily Calendar section, as well as thorough listings for the coming week in its

Sunday edition and for the following weekend in its Wednesday edition. Other excellent sources of listings and suggestions are two weekly papers, the *L.A. Weekly* and the slimmer but more informative *New Times*. Both are distributed free from racks near the entrances to various stores, restaurants and public buildings as well as from some street boxes.

Large selections of magazines, as well as some foreign newspapers, are available at certain newsstands in Hollywood and Santa Monica as well as from bookstore chains such as Borders and Barnes & Noble.

Radio and Television

Los Angeles offers an interesting variety of radio stations. Many stations stick to the Top 40 or "adult contemporary" formulas, but other tastes are also catered to. There are two all-news stations, found at 980 and 1070 on the AM dial. On the FM dial, jazz and blues may be heard at 88.1 and classical music at 91.5 or 105.1. Programs of National Public Radio can be picked up at 89.9.

L.A. has television stations affiliated with all the major networks (including PBS at Channel 28, or Channel 3 on some cable systems), in addition to several unaffiliated local channels. CNN and a vast variety of other cable channels are available at most hotels.

Exploring

Los Angeles has sometimes been described as more of a cluster of villages than a coherent city.

In many urban areas around the world, the main attractions tend to be grouped in or around the city centre, with remaining points of interest easily accessible by a short trip to the suburbs. In Los Angeles it's the other way around: the downtown area offers its share of curiosities, but visitors are likely to spend most of their time elsewhere.

Far-flung parts of the metropolitan area offer their own special charms. Getting a varied taste of Los Angeles means not only a fair bit of moving around, but also some careful planning. Because of the distances involved, touring can't really be done haphazardly. Congested freeways and slow public transit can make for long travel times. You can't just hop from Pasadena over to Santa Monica, for instance, because even in light traffic it could take close to an hour. Many points of interest are clustered in a few small areas, but these areas are widely scattered.

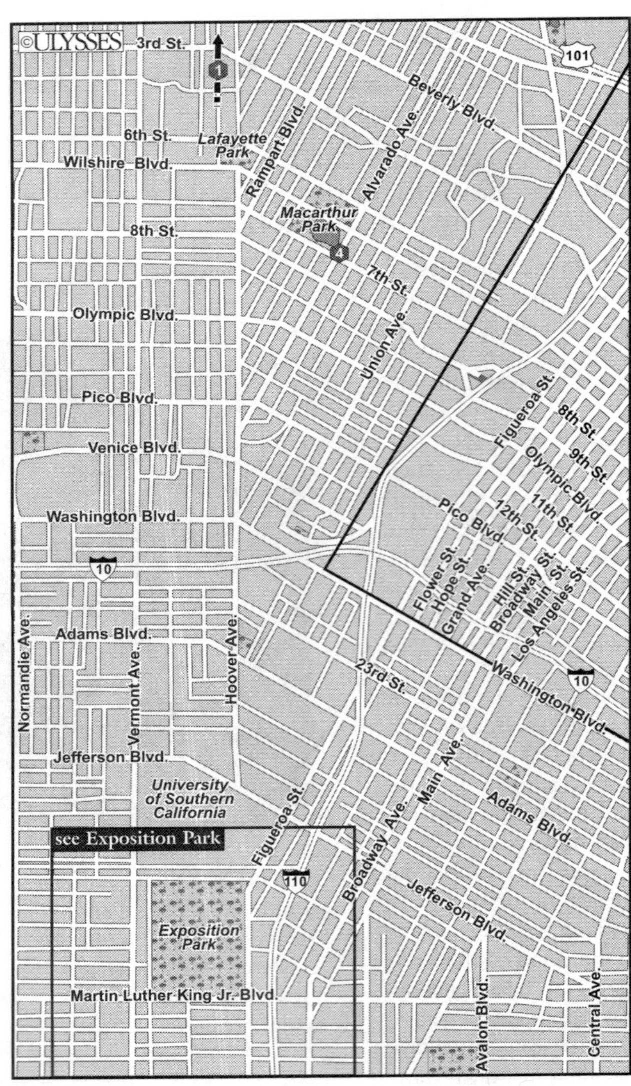
©ULYSSES
3rd St.
6th St.
Lafayette Park
Wilshire Blvd.
Rampart Blvd.
Alvarado Ave.
Beverly Blvd.
101
Macarthur Park
8th St.
7th St.
Olympic Blvd.
Union Ave.
Pico Blvd.
Venice Blvd.
Figueroa St.
8th St.
9th St.
Olympic Blvd.
11th St.
12th St.
Pico Blvd.
Washington Blvd.
10
Flower St.
Hope St.
Grand Ave.
Hill St.
Broadway St.
Main St.
Los Angeles St.
Normandie Ave.
Adams Blvd.
Vermont Ave.
Hoover Ave.
23rd St.
Washington Blvd.
Jefferson Blvd.
University of Southern California
Main Ave.
Adams Blvd.
see Exposition Park
Figueroa St.
Broadway Ave.
110
Jefferson Blvd.
Exposition Park
Martin Luther King Jr. Blvd.
Avalon Blvd.
Central Ave.

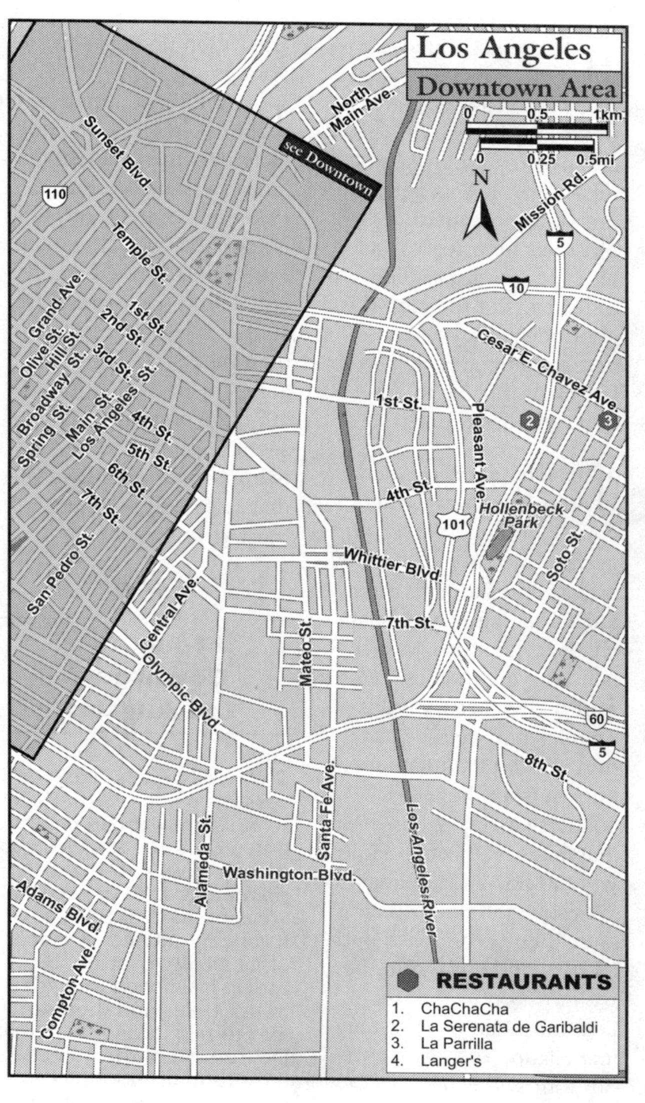

Los Angeles
Downtown Area
0
0.5
1km
0
0.25
0.5mi
N
see Downtown
North Main Ave.
Mission Rd.
Sunset Blvd.
110
Temple St.
Grand Ave.
1st St.
2nd St.
Olive St.
Hill St.
3rd St.
Broadway
St.
Spring St.
Main St.
Los Angeles
4th St.
5th St.
6th St.
7th St.
San Pedro St.
Central Ave.
Olympic Blvd.
5
10
Cesar E. Chavez Ave.
1st St.
Pleasant Ave.
4th St.
101
Hollenbeck Park
Soto St.
Whittier Blvd.
7th St.
Mateo St.
60
5
8th St.
Santa Fe Ave.
Los Angeles River
Alameda St.
Washington Blvd.
Adams Blvd.
Compton Ave.
RESTAURANTS
1. ChaChaCha
2. La Serenata de Garibaldi
3. La Parrilla
4. Langer's

Because accommodations in the downtown area often tend toward extremes of lavish expense or desperate gloom, and because downtown L.A. is generally not very pleasant after dark, most leisure travellers are likely to end up staying in other parts of the city. It is a good idea to try to coordinate lodging and sightseeing plans, if only to cut down on travel time.

This chapter is divided into 12 sections, each corresponding to a specific geographic zone of the city and its surrounding areas. Each area has a particular character that provides certain unifying themes. We start with downtown Los Angeles and then proceed northeast to Pasadena, continuing from there in a counter-clockwise direction that takes us through Hollywood, Mid-Wilshire and Westside, the South Bay area, then Long Beach and its surroundings. From there we move on to the San Fernando Valley, then Catalina Island. The last leg of our tour will take us to Orange County and its beaches, then finally to Palm Springs.

If you look at a map of the entire region, it immediately becomes evident that large swaths of territory receive no mention in this guidebook. Not all parts of Los Angeles are created equal, and some areas are simply more interesting than others. As in cities almost everywhere, there are large areas that may seem important to people living or working there but that offer little to entice most visitors.

Tour A: Downtown Los Angeles

To travellers who have experienced some of the world's great urban centres, downtown Los Angeles may come across as a big disappointment. Like the central areas of many U.S. cities, it has been drained of much of its vitality over the decades. It enjoyed a heyday in the 1920s and then sank into torpor during the Great Depression of the 1930s. As the suburban boom took hold and gained momentum in the decades following the Second World War, downtown L.A. fell into in a long era of relative decline, interrupted by brief periods of revival and stabilization. These periods included a massive bout of office construction in the 1980s, although several of the glittering new towers remained half-empty for years afterwards until they were rescued by strong economic growth in the mid- and late-1990s.

Downtown L.A. has a decidedly schizophrenic character. On its western side are groups of office towers and high-rise hotels, hemmed in by a busy expressway. This area, part of which is known as the financial district, is not without its attractions; however, activity at street level is minimal except at noon hour or immediately after work. Part of downtown L.A. is set on a high promontory known as Bunker Hill.

In the middle of the downtown area is the traditional retail district, with Broadway Avenue as its spine and Seventh Street, perpendicular to Broadway as a major cross street. This latter is the former home of several big department stores. Decades ago, business trickled away to the suburbs, leaving behind rows of empty storefronts. New waves of Mexican and Central American immigration later revived the Broadway retail district. Listening to people talk and seeing the range of merchandise displayed in store windows and entrances over a bustling multi-block stretch, it's easy to imagine yourself on the main shopping street of a prosperous provincial centre in Mexico. (Much of Seventh Street, on the other hand, remains boarded up.)

Further east, downtown L.A. takes on an almost otherworldly persona. This is home to an extensive garment-manufacturing and wholesaling district. (It is no secret that some of the labourers hidden away from public view are undocumented immigrants paid at less than minimum wage.) Several of the streets north of the garment district form a massive skid row area with several seedy hotels and bands of homeless people visible at most hours of the day and night, many of them looking drunk or dazed or just plain unwell. This is definitely *not* Beverly Hills. A little beyond is the small but prim Little Tokyo district.

Some first-time visitors are surprised to discover that downtown L.A. is nowhere near the beaches of the Pacific. It lies about 12mi (20km) inland, closer to the

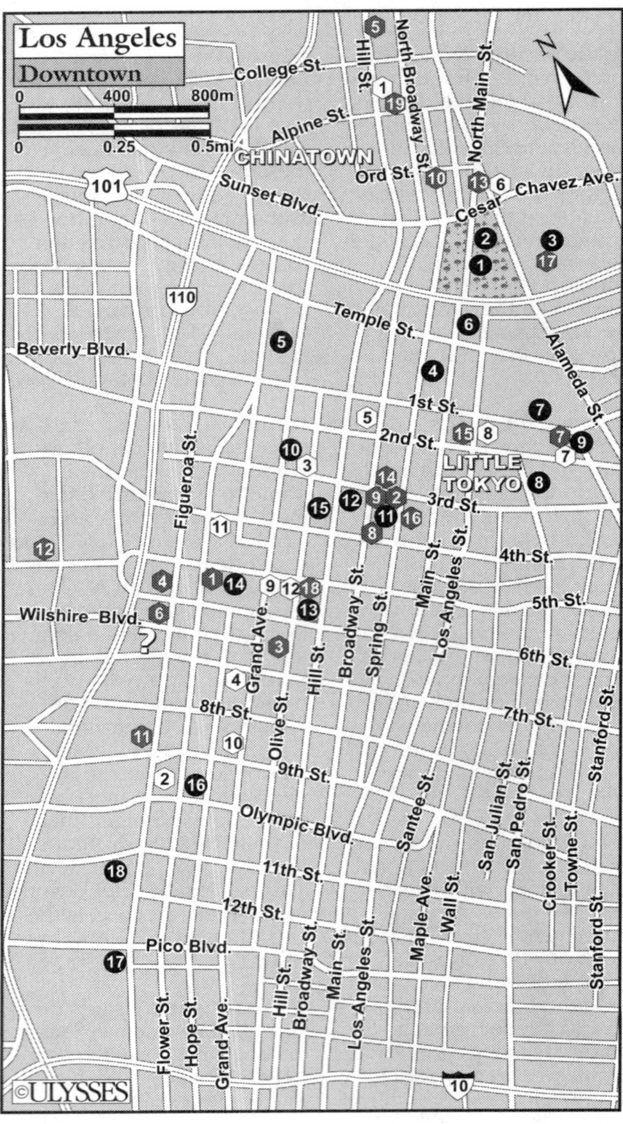

Los Angeles
Downtown
0
400
800m
0
0.25
0.5mi
CHINATOWN
LITTLE TOKYO
College St.
Alpine St.
Ord St.
Sunset Blvd.
Cesar Chavez Ave.
Hill St.
North Broadway St.
North Main St.
101
110
10
Temple St.
Beverly Blvd.
1st St.
2nd St.
3rd St.
4th St.
5th St.
6th St.
7th St.
8th St.
9th St.
Olympic Blvd.
11th St.
12th St.
Pico Blvd.
Wilshire Blvd.
Alameda St.
Figueroa St.
Grand Ave.
Olive St.
Hill St.
Broadway St.
Spring St.
Main St.
Los Angeles St.
Santee St.
Maple Ave.
Wall St.
San Julian St.
San Pedro St.
Crooker St.
Towne St.
Stanford St.
Flower St.
Hope St.
Main St.
©ULYSSES

geographic centre of the sprawling metropolitan area. Downtown is bound on the north by the Civic Centre, comprised of a rather sterile and lifeless collection of public buildings, including city hall and the federal courthouse. The friendlier Chinatown district lies just beyond, several blocks further north. On the southern fringe of downtown are the gleaming new Staples Center arena and the recently expanded convention center, although the surrounding streets are rather desolate, despite some rush landscaping that was done to greet delegates to the national Democratic Convention held several months prior to the controversial 2000 presidential election. About 2mi (3km) south of downtown lies the campus of the University of

ATTRACTIONS

1. El Pueblo de Los Angeles Historic Monument
2. Olvera Street
3. Union Station
4. City Hall
5. Music Center
6. Los Angeles Children's Museum
7. Japanese American National Museum
8. Japanese American Cultural and Community Center
9. Geffen Contemporary at MOCA
10. Museum of Contemporary Art
11. Grand Central Market
12. Angels Flight
13. Pershing Square
14. Central Library
15. Wells Fargo History Museum
16. Museum of Neon Art
17. Convention Center
18. Staples Center

ACCOMMODATIONS

1. Best Western Dragon Gate Inn
2. Figueroa Hotel
3. Hotel Inter-Continental Los Angeles
4. Hyatt Regency Los Angeles
5. Kawada Hotel
6. Metro Plaza Hotel
7. Miyako Inn
8. New Otani Hotel
9. Regal Biltmore Hotel
10. Stillwell Hotel
11. Westin Bonaventure Hotel
12. Wyndham Checkers Hotel

RESTAURANTS

1. Café Pinot
2. China Cafe
3. Cicada
4. Ciudad
5. Empress Pavilion
6. Engine Company No. 28
7. Frying Fish
8. Grand Central Market
9. Maria's Pescado Frito
10. Mon Kee
11. Original Pantry Café
12. Pacific Dining Car
13. Philippe the Original
14. Roast to Go
15. Shabu Shabu House
16. The City Pier
17. Traxx
18. Water Grill
19. Yang Chow

Southern California and, immediately adjacent, Exposition Park, home to a couple of interesting museums (though the area is not especially safe after dark).

The preceding description probably makes downtown L.A. sound less appealing than it really is. This is a little unfair. It is true that downtown is shunned and even despised by many people living in other parts of Los Angeles, perhaps influenced in part by race or class prejudice. But there is also plenty to admire downtown. Readers should not hesitate to visit this area, since it is full of character and quite walkable, at least by L.A. standards. It is also home to several architectural gems and numerous cultural attractions.

A good place to begin a tour is where the city began, not far from the banks of the diminutive Los Angeles River (except after heavy rains, this "river" forms just a tiny trickle, channeled through a massive concrete-walled ditch skirting the eastern fringe of the downtown area). This is where Spanish explorers arriving from central Mexico discovered a small Native American settlement and where they established one of their own a few years later, in 1781. The oldest surviving structure, built in 1818, now forms part of **El Pueblo de Los Angeles Historic Monument** ★, a small cluster of buildings and plazas occupying a 44 acre (18ha) site bisected by Main Street in the northeastern part of downtown L.A. between Union Station and the Civic Center. Designated a state park, the site includes a **visitors centre** *(Mon to Sat 10am to 3pm, 622 N. Main St., ☎213-628-1274)* located in the Sepulveda House at the entrance to the Old Plaza. Brochures and general information are available, as are exhibits depicting the area's history and culture, including a 20min video. It is the departure point for free guided tours of the park offered hourly from 10am to 1pm from Tuesday to Saturday. Nearby is the **Avila Adobe** ★ *(free admission; Mon to Sat 10am to 5pm)*, the oldest building in L.A. This thick-walled structure was home to a wealthy family during much of the 19th century, and visitors can see several rooms furnished in the style of that period, as well as a leafy courtyard. Other buildings of note include **Firehouse No. 1**, built in 1884 and displaying historic fire-fighting equipment *(free admission; every day 10am to 3pm, Sat to Sun until 4:30pm)*, as well as the stylish Pico House (a former hotel) and the former Merced Theatre. The two latter buildings, both erected in 1870, lie vacant while they await new uses.

By far the liveliest part of the historic park is **Olvera Street ★★**, a short pedestrian-only street that attempts to recapture some undefined period in Mexican history. It is lined with numerous Mexican handicrafts stalls and several restaurants. It is popular not only with tourists but also, perhaps surprisingly in view of its unauthentic character, with members of L.A.'s sizable Mexican community, some of whom are drawn to the area by the 19th-century **Iglesia de Nuestra Señora la Reina de Los Angeles** (Church of Our Lady Queen of Angels), on the other side of Main Street. Besides numerous masses celebrated in Spanish, this church is a favoured spot for weddings and baptisms. Family celebrations often spill into nearby public areas. Olvera Street, along with the church and the Old Plaza, is a central venue for the Cinco de Mayo celebrations that bring many Mexicans together on May 5, as the festival's Spanish name suggests. At the top of Olvera Street is the **Instituto Cultural Mexicano ★** that includes a bilingual (Spanish and English) bookshop, a consulting library, and a famous mural depicting the blessing of the animals. It is located in the historic Biscailuz Building that once housed the Mexican consulate.

One block east, on the other side of Alameda Avenue, lies **Union Station ★★**, which opened in 1939 and is the last of the truly grand railway stations constructed in the United States. Currently served by Amtrak intercity trains and Metrolink suburban trains, this magnificent structure is well worth a short visit even if rail travel is not part of your plans. With its bell tower and soaring arched windows, it imitates the early California-mission style on an enormous scale, also incorporating Moderne elements. Inside, it features tiled floors in earth tones, wood-beamed ceilings nearly 52ft (16m) high, massive chandeliers and, in the waiting area, most of the original heavy wooden furniture. Hidden away (but freely accessible to the public) are two spacious and pleasant patios with gardens, shade trees and comfortable seating—a minor treasure that few people seem to have discovered. The north patio is partly occupied by a small café and restaurant with outdoor tables. The pedestrian tunnel providing passenger access to the trains also leads to the Patsaouras Transit Plaza, served by many city bus routes. This is more a showplace than a bus terminal, covered in marble and granite and featuring trees, fountains and artwork that includes several large murals.

To the north, past Cesar A. Chavez Avenue (named after a Mexican-American farm union leader who achieved world fame in the 1960s after calling for grape boycotts to protest dismal working conditions), lies the **Chinatown ★** district. This covers an area roughly four blocks wide and four blocks long, and centred on North Broadway Avenue. This area is not nearly as picturesque as its San Francisco counterpart, and it is home to only a minuscule portion of L.A.'s large Chinese population (most live in the suburbs), but its countless food stores, restaurants and souvenir shops serve as a magnet, especially on weekends, for many people of Chinese and other origins. The Chinese New Year, which falls in late January or early February, is a time of celebration, with the Golden Dragon Parade as a special highlight.

South of Chinatown and southwest of El Pueblo de Los Angeles historic district, the **Civic Center** occupies a multi-block area centred around Temple Street, an east-west artery running across the northern part of downtown L.A. It is occupied mostly by undistinguished government office buildings and courthouses fulfilling various functions at the city, county, state and federal levels. The key word here is bland. The only true landmark is the 28-storey **City Hall** *(200 N. Spring St. near Temple St.)*. Opened in 1928, the building will be familiar to some film buffs: it has often been used as a backdrop. Recently, it was undergoing a massive and costly facelift.

The **Music Center**, along Grand Avenue between First and Temple streets, lies at the western edge of the Civic Center and comprises three halls set around a plaza adorned by a large Jacques Lipschitz sculpture and a massive fountain. The largest of the halls, the Dorothy Chandler Pavilion, seats 3,200 (see page 321). The two smaller halls are the Ahmanson Theater and the Mark Taper Forum. They will be joined at some point by the on-again, off-again Walt Disney Concert Hall.

The **Los Angeles Children's Museum ★** *($5; year-round Sat and Sun 10am to 5pm; late Jun to early Sep Mon to Fri 11:30am to 4pm; rest of the year by special arrangement only; 310 N. Main St. near*

Temple St., ☎213-687-8800), around the corner from City Hall and not far from El Pueblo de Los Angeles Historic Monument, was intended as a temporary facility when it opened in 1979 and has hopes of moving to larger quarters once the politically sensitive issue of location is settled. This is a hands-on sort of place where children are encouraged to touch the exhibits, many of which have an educational theme in addition to being entertaining. They range from the Cave of the Dinosaurs to Sticky City with its large velco forms, and Club Eco, which teaches about recycling. The museum also has a performance space with story-tellers, musicians or dancers.

Little Tokyo

The **Little Tokyo** ★ district, southeast of the Civic Center, occupies much of the area bounded by Temple, Los Angeles, Fourth and Alameda streets. Like Chinatown, it has only a tiny residential population and serves more as a meeting place for shopping, eating and certain cultural pursuits. With the exception of a handful of buildings, the area is not especially attractive, and there is little that people from the real Tokyo would find familiar. The district contains several shopping malls, the biggest of which is the Japanese Village Plaza (see page 345), in the form of a winding pedestrian-only zone meant to resemble a village street in Japan. The **Japanese American National Museum** ★★ *($4; Tue to Sun 10am to 5pm, Thu until 8pm; 369 E. First St. at Central Ave., ☎213-625-0414)* occupies two buildings, one a former temple and the other a much bigger annex opened in 1998 and acclaimed for its design. The museum features a rotating series of exhibitions depicting the Japanese immigrant experience in the United States as well as certain home communities in Japan. One of the saddest chapters in U.S. history was the Second World War internment of approximately 100,000 U.S. citizens for no reason except their Japanese ethnic background. This facet of history is presented in certain exhibits and in the interactive

A Taste of History: Walking Tours Presented by the Los Angeles Conservatory

To most Europeans and even to many North Americans, Los Angeles comes across as a thoroughly modern city with only faint reminders of the past. Because the city's history doesn't go back very far, with the area not emerging as a major metropolis until early in the 20th century, historical consciousness is not firmly rooted among local inhabitants. As a result, historical buildings, such as they are, have been vulnerable to abandonment or demolition. A volunteer organization that calls itself Los Angeles Conservancy has fought, often successfully, to preserve older buildings with architectural or symbolic value. Some of its demands have stirred controversy, including a campaign to save the earthquake-damaged Saint Vibiana cathedral (closed since 1994) against the wishes of the Catholic archbishop. (A new cathedral is under construction.)

No one, however can object to the extensive program of walking tours the Conservancy offers each Saturday morning *($8; most tours start at 10am; reservations required: Mon to Fri 9am to 5pm, 523 W. Sixth St., Suite 1216, ☎213-623-2489).* Most tours last from 2 to 2.5hrs and depart from the entrance to the Biltmore Hotel *(515 S. Olive St. facing Pershing Square)*, with group size usually limited to 15 people. Tours are led by trained docents, some of whom are very effective at conveying their knowledge of local architectural history. Several different tours operate on any given Saturday. The most popular tour visits the spectacular old movie palaces along Broadway Avenue, some of them still in operation (it is useful to reserve places for this tour well in advance). Another popular tour, which also runs each week, visits some of the impressive Art Deco office buildings that dot downtown L.A., each displaying fine ornamental detail. Some tours operate only one or two Saturdays each month: these include tours of Union Station, Little Tokyo and the former financial district along Spring Street. For further information, please consult Los Angeles Conservancy at the address or phone number above.

Legacy Center, where visitors can trace family internment files through a computer link. The **Japanese American Cultural and Community Center** ★ *(244 S. San Pedro St. between Second and Third sts., ☎213-628-2725)* is built around a plaza and a rock garden at the lower level that make for a pleasant stroll *(every day 9am to 6pm)*. The centre is a focal point for cultural and educational activities. Its 841-seat theatre serves as a venue for both Japanese and non-Japanese music, dance and theatre presentations.

The **Geffen Contemporary at MOCA** ★★★ and the **Museum of Contemporary Art (MOCA)** ★★★ form a single museum housed in two buildings that are situated eight blocks apart *($6 valid at both sites on the date of purchase; Tue to Sun 11am to 5pm, Thu until 8pm; Geffen Contemporary: 152 N. Central Ave. near First St. in Little Tokyo; MOCA at California Plaza: 250 S. Grand Ave. between Second and Third sts. in the financial district; ☎213-626-6222, www.moca-la.org)*. Named for David Geffen, a music producer and benefactor of the arts, the Geffen Contemporary occupies a former warehouse adapted to exhibition space by Los Angeles architect Frank Gehry. When it opened in 1983, it was dubbed the "Temporary Contemporary" because it was expected to close following the completion in 1986 of the new building on Grand Avenue designed by Japanese architect Arata Isozaki and consisting of two red sandstone pavilions in highly original shapes straddling an open plaza. Because of its size, the Geffen is well suited to large-scale installations, and a decision was thus made to keep it open. Together, the two buildings house a very impressive permanent collection, augmented in recent years by numerous acquisitions and bequests. They also showcase many temporary exhibits. (The two sites are connected by DASH bus route A.)

If only minor vestiges remain of 19th-century Los Angeles, the same cannot be said of the early decades of the 20th century. Spring Street and Broadway, two parallel streets a block apart, contain many architectural reminders of downtown L.A's heyday. In the 1920s, **Spring Street** ★ was the centre of finance and proudly bore the title of Wall Street of the West. Nowadays the street conveys a rather seedy, bedraggled air, although it remains lined with many handsome buildings, some of them boarded up but others restored to their former glory or rumoured as candidates for restoration. At 300 South Spring Street, at the corner of Third Street, is an office building recently converted for use by the State of California (and named after former governor and president Ronald Reagan), which has a very exuberant large-scale mural in the lobby by artists Carlos Almaraz and Elsa Flores. Other buildings of note along Spring Street include the Title Insurance Building at No. 433 with its attractive Art Deco lobby and the somewhat rundown Alexandra Hotel at the corner of Fifth Street with its old-fashioned interior palm court.

Broadway ★★, one block west, finds itself in better circumstances, with a very vibrant Mexican-accented retail trade bringing life to the street, especially between Third and Ninth streets. It too has many handsome buildings from the early 20th century, although some of the interiors behind the impressive facades have been gutted. Some of the grand old movie palaces along this stretch of the street (more than a dozen of these structures survive) have been converted to retail stores or evangelical churches, but others continue to operate as cinemas, mostly showing films in Spanish. The best way to catch a glimpse of their very ornate interiors is to take a Los Angeles Conservancy tour. Several office buildings along Broadway have noteworthy architectural features. These include the Bradbury Building *(No. 304, corner of Third St.)*, with its five-storey glass-roofed atrium, and the gorgeous Art Deco Eastern Columbia Building *(No. 849, between Eighth and Ninth sts.)* with its distinctive turquoise exterior topped by large clock faces.

One of the most fascinating sights in downtown L.A. is **Grand Central Market ★**, covering the block bound by Broadway, Third, Hill and Fourth streets. This public market has been a beehive of activity since it opened in 1917, with dozens of stalls selling fresh produce, meats, fish, dairy products and other types of food that reflect the city's ethnic diversity. It also includes several restaurants and snack counters.

Behind the market, on the Hill Street side, is the lower station of the **Angels Flight ★** funicular railway *($0.25; every day 6:30am to 10pm; ☎213-626-1901)* that climbs one steep block at a 33-degree angle to Olive Street atop Bunker Hill. When service was inaugurated in 1901, Bunker Hill was regarded as a very desirable residential neighbourhood, and people living there used the railway to reach their homes from the commercial district below. Service provided by the railway's very distinctive bright red carriages was halted in 1969 and resumed in 1996. Today, this beloved anachronism is used mostly, but not exclusively, by tourists. It runs every few minutes.

One of downtown's focal points is **Pershing Square**, a park (set atop an underground parking garage) covering the block bound by Hill, Fifth, Olive and Sixth Streets. (Hill is one block west of Broadway.) A public park since 1886, it was remodeled at great cost in 1994. Although not as heavily crime-ridden as it once was, Pershing Square (named after a First World War general) is not especially appealing despite the resources that went into fountains and public art, some of it in the form of whimsically coloured geometric shapes. With its absence of shade trees or comfortable seating, it is more a place to traverse than to linger in.

The **Central Library** ★★ *(Mon, Thu to Sat 10am to 5:30pm; Tue to Wed noon to 8pm; Sun 1pm to 5pm; 630 W. Fifth St. between Grand and Flower sts., ☎213-228-7000)* is the hub of L.A.'s extensive public library system and a major reference library, with close to three million books and other documents. Most of the books are accessible in open stacks. Designed in 1922, the building was extensively renovated and expanded following two disastrous fires in 1986; it reopened in 1993. The addition of a new wing and new underground levels doubled the library's capacity, and the creation of a skylit atrium added to the aesthetic appeal of the building, with its vaguely Egyptian motifs. Built-up grime actually saved the library's precious murals from heavy fire damage; these include tableaus in the main rotunda dating from 1933 that depict four eras in California history. One section of the library is devoted to children. The library grounds include the **Maguire Gardens** ★, named after a major benefactor, with abundant shade trees and seating (unlike Pershing Square). On the other side of Fifth Street are the **Bunker Hill Steps**, with a broad stairway and watercourse winding around a modern office tower, flanked by sculptures and outdoor cafés, and providing a shortcut to the Museum of Contemporary Art. Local boosters say this is L.A.'s answer to Rome's Spanish Steps.

There are two small downtown museums that perhaps

deserve more attention than they receive. The **Wells Fargo History Museum** ★ *(free admission, Mon to Fri 9am to 5pm; 333 S. Grand Ave. between Third and Fourth sts., ☎213-253-7166)*, sponsored by the bank of the same name, depicts elements of mid-19th-century California history, including stagecoaches used to cross the western U.S. Secondly, the **Museum of Neon Art** ★★ *($3.50; Tue to Sat 11am to 6pm; 501 W. Olympic Blvd. at Hope St., ☎213-489-9918)* is a weird and wonderful place where the only lighting comes from the art itself, part of a collection of old neon commercial signs rescued by artist Lili Lakich, as well as some contemporary creations using the same medium.

In the following section are several museums that lie outside the downtown area, but are still not far from downtown.

The **Southwest Museum** ★★★ *($5; Tue to Sun 10am to 5pm; 234 Museum Dr. in Highland Park northeast of downtown L.A.; by car, Pasadena Fwy. to the 43rd Ave. exit, turning right onto Figueroa and up the hill; by bus from downtown L.A., MTA routes 81 or 83, about 15min; ☎323-221-2164, www.southwestmuseum.org)*, founded in 1907, is the oldest museum in Los Angeles. Perched on a remote hillside in a mostly residential area, it holds one of the world's most extensive collections of Native American artifacts, with an emphasis on the cultures of California and other parts of the U.S. Southwest. Indigenous cultures of the Great Plains, the U.S. Northwest, Mexico and Central America are also represented, ranging from prehistoric to contemporary periods. The exhibits of Navaho textiles are especially impressive. Pottery, clothing, baskets and teepees help round out the collection. Unfortunately, exhibition space is very limited, and only a tiny part of the collection can be showcased at any time. (A satellite location in the Wilshire corridor near the Los Angeles Country Museum of Art allows some additional items to be displayed.

Exposition Park, south of downtown L.A. (connected by DASH bus route F) and facing the campus of the University of Southern California, is home to four museums. One of these, the Aerospace Museum, is closed for the time being pending decisions on renovations, although some of the outdoor exhibits remain in place, including a four-engine Douglas DC-8 jetliner painted in United Airlines colours clearly visible

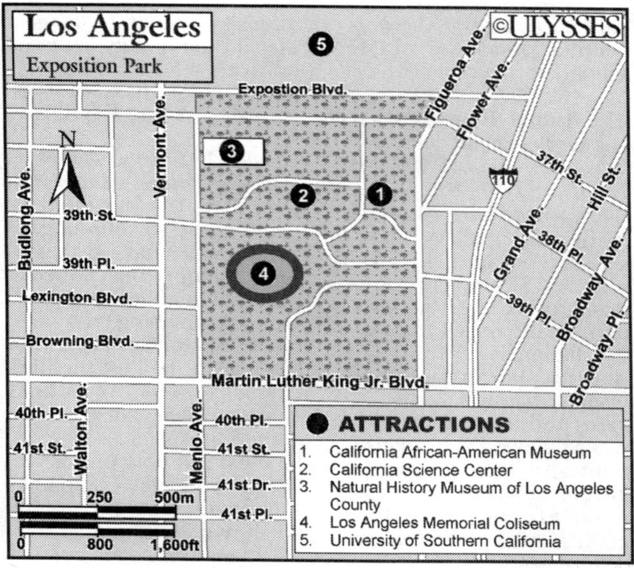

at the southwest corner of Exposition Boulevard and Figueroa Avenue. Exposition Park also encompasses the mammoth 106,000-seat Los Angeles Memorial Coliseum (the site of major events at the 1932 and 1984 Olympic Games) and the adjacent sports arena.

The **California African-American Museum** ★★ *(voluntary contribution; Tue to Sun 10am to 5pm; 600 State Dr., Exposition Park, ☎213-744-7432)* presents mostly temporary exhibitions portraying various aspects of African and African-American culture and historical experiences, including historical artifacts and contemporary art.

The **California Science Center** ★★ *(free admission; every day 10am to 5pm; 700 State Dr., Exposition Park, ☎213-744-7400, www.casciencectr.org)* is a family favourite that invites participation by children at its many interactive displays exploring physics and biology as well as certain aspects of human technology. Among the more popular areas of the museum are an earthquake simulator and the Bodyworks theatre, which enables visitors to see the inside of a 50ft (15m) human-shaped creature named Tess. The museum also includes an IMAX cinema *(admission charge).*

The **Natural History Museum of Los Angeles County** ★ *($6; Tue to Sun 10am to 5pm; 900 Exposition Blvd., ☎213-763-3466, www.nhm.org)* attracts many visitors who come to see its dinosaur hall, which includes a complete tyrannosaurus skull. Other sections of the museum present mammals of North America and Africa, birds, insects, marine life, and gems and minerals. Elsewhere, there are displays of Native American cultures, including Navaho textiles. At the lower level, California history is portrayed in detail.

Tour B: Pasadena and Surroundings

Every New Year's Day, Pasadena plays host to the Tournament of Roses Parade, an extravagant affair featuring hundreds of lavishly flower-adorned floats whose stately progress is transmitted live to millions of television viewers across the United States. This is followed by the Rose Bowl college football championship game held at the namesake stadium. Then the crowds depart and Pasadena can revert to its usual elegant tranquillity, so close and yet so far from the smog-choked metropolis on the other side of the hills.

Nestled in the San Gabriel Valley northeast of downtown L.A., Pasadena and some of the surrounding communities have managed to retain an old-fashioned, small-town atmosphere without forsaking cultural and commercial amenities that match the best the big city has to offer. As far as some residents are concerned, this is close to idyllic. First promoted in the 1880s by railway companies as a winter retreat for wealthy midwesterners, Pasadena has never quite abandoned its semi-aristocratic roots. Many of the old mansions have been lovingly maintained, several of which are open to the public.

Cultural attractions include two institutions that have achieved worldwide fame: the Norton Simon Museum in Pasadena and the Huntington Library, Art Collections and Botanical Gardens in nearby San Marino. Several smaller museums add to the scene, such as Pasadena's Pacific Asia Museum. But what probably draws the greatest number of visitors is pedestrian-friendly Colorado Boulevard, as well as some of the neighbouring streets in gentrified Old Pasadena with their Victorian ambiance and many original shops and restaurants. In addition to some of the more obvious attractions, the Pasadena Convention and Visitors Bureau offers several suggestions for walking tours.

Colorado Boulevard is the main east-west avenue crossing downtown Pasadena. It forms an inverted *L* with South Lake Avenue—another shop-lined street—toward the eastern edge of downtown Pasadena. Numerous parking lots dot the area, particularly along the streets behind South Lake Avenue and behind Colorado Boulevard in the Old Pasadena area between Arroyo Parkway and Pasadena Avenue. A free bus service (look for the stops marked ARTS) operates at intervals of 15 to 20min along this L-shaped loop, running west along Colorado Boulevard as far as Orange Grove Boulevard near the Norton Simon Museum, then east along Green Street one block to the south, and down South Lake Avenue. Further north along Orange Grove Boulevard lie the Pasadena Historical Museum, the Gamble House and the Rose Bowl.

To reach Pasadena by car from downtown Los Angeles, the most obvious route is the Pasadena Freeway, numbered California Highway 110 and also known as the **Arroyo Seco Parkway**. Opened in 1940, this 10km (6mi) stretch of highway was the first freeway in the L.A. area and has been designated a historical monument! With its meandering path through the hills of the San Gabriel range and the pleasant greenery beyond its shoulders, it bears little resemblance to newer parts of the urban-freeway network.

By bus, MTA express route No. 401 runs north along Olive Street in downtown L.A., taking about 25min to reach the corner of Colorado Boulevard and Los Robles Avenue in downtown Pasadena. Service is twice an hour on weekdays, more frequent at rush hours and once an hour on evenings and weekends. From Hollywood, MTA routes 180 and 181 run along Hollywood Boulevard, through Los Feliz and Glendale, and then along Colorado Boulevard. Several other bus routes also serve the area.

The very helpful **Pasadena Convention and Visitors Bureau** *(Mon to Fri 9am to 5pm, Sat 10am to 4pm, 171 S. Los Robles Ave. between Green and Cordova sts., ☎626-795-9311)* offers many useful leaflets and maps as well as

ATTRACTIONS	
1. Pasadena Convention and Visitors Bureau	5. Rose Bowl
2. Norton Simon Museum of Art	6. City Hall
3. Pasadena Historical Museum	7. Pacific Asia Museum
4. Gamble House	8. Huntington Library, Art Collections and Botanical Gardens

ACCOMMODATIONS	
1. Bissell House	5. Ritz-Carlton Huntington Hotel & Spa
2. Doubletree Hotel	6. Saga Motor Hotel
3. Pasadena Hotel Bed & Breakfast	7. Westway Inn
4. Pasadena Hilton	

RESTAURANTS	
1. All India Café	7. Shiro
2. Goldstein's Bagel Bakery	8. The Raymond
3. Kuala Lumpur	9. Twin Palms
4. Mi Piace	10. Yujean Kang's Gourmet Chinese Cuisine
5. Old Town Bakery and Restaurant	
6. Rack Shack	

information and suggestions. The leaflets include suggested self-guided **walking tours** of historic residential areas featuring architectural designs that have had a significant impact in California and beyond.

One place to begin your visit is the **Old Pasadena** district, centred around Colorado Boulevard between Arroyo Parkway on the east and Pasadena Avenue on the west, also extending south along Fair Oaks Avenue to Central Park and north along Raymond Avenue to Memorial Park. This was the main business district a century ago, and its many shops and former warehouses have been revived to create a quaint sense of traditional small-town U.S.A. (not often found in the western part of the country) that many people find appealing for shopping, dining out, moviegoing, or simply strolling along the broad, café-lined sidewalks. Several of the buildings display whimsical architectural features, particularly along Raymond Avenue near Green Street.

A little further west along Colorado Boulevard, beyond Freeway 210 but before Orange Grove Boulevard, is the **Norton Simon Museum of Art** ★★★ *($6; Wed to Sun noon to 6pm, Fri until 9pm; 411 W. Colorado Blvd., ☎626-449-6840, www.nortonsimon.org)*. This museum is named for a food-processing magnate and arts benefactor whose personal collection of works by Degas, Renoir, Gauguin, Cézanne and several of the Old Masters now forms an important part of the museum's permanent collection. The Norton Simon occupies an airy, at-

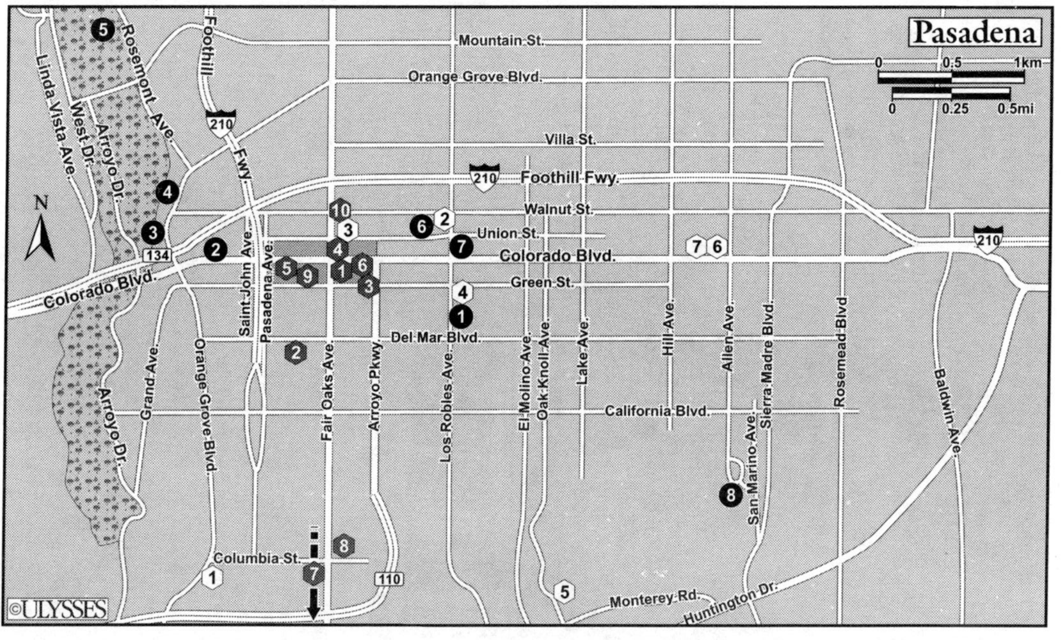

Pasadena
0
0.5
1km
0
0.25
0.5mi
N
Mountain St.
Orange Grove Blvd.
Villa St.
Foothill Fwy.
Foothill
Fwy.
210
Walnut St.
Union St.
Colorado Blvd.
Green St.
Del Mar Blvd.
California Blvd.
Columbia St.
Monterey Rd.
Huntington Dr.
Rosemont Ave.
Linda Vista Ave.
West Dr.
Arroyo Dr.
134
Grand Ave.
Orange Grove Blvd.
Saint John Ave.
Pasadena Ave.
Fair Oaks Ave.
Arroyo Pkwy.
110
Los Robles Ave.
El Molino Ave.
Oak Knoll Ave.
Lake Ave.
Hill Ave.
Allen Ave.
San Marino Ave.
Sierra Madre Blvd.
Rosemead Blvd
Baldwin Ave.
©ULYSSES

Pasadena City Hall

tractive building with uncluttered lines and a sensible layout flanked by a sculpture museum and garden café. The collections of European art, covering most major periods from Renaissance to modern, are supplemented by substantial selections of East-Indian and Southeast-Asian art. The museum shop offers a vast array of art books, cards, maps and gift items.

A couple of blocks north along Orange Grove Boulevard, at the corner of Walnut Street, is the small **Pasadena Historical Museum** ★ *($4; Thu to Sun 1pm to 4pm; 470 W. Walnut St., ☎626-577-1660).* Far more interesting to many visitors than the collections of photographs and assorted period mementos is the 1906 mansion, called the Feynes House, that houses the museum and forms part of Pasadena's original Millionaire's Row. Features include mahogany pillars at the entrance, oriental rugs and silk damask wall coverings. A small building in the mansion's lavish gardens contains, of all things, a collection of Finnish folk art.

A block further north, just off Orange Grove Boulevard is the **Gamble House** ★★ *($5; Thu to Sun noon to 3pm, group tours offered at other times with advance notice; 4 Westmoreland Pl., ☎626-793-3334, www.gamblehouse.org).* Designed by architects Charles Sumner Greene, and Henry Mather Greene and built in 1908 for one of the founding families of the Procter and Gamble Company, it is widely regarded as a masterpiece of the Arts and Crafts movement. Visitors are taken on 1hr guided tours that run every 15min. Although the design relies heavily on traditions of wooden architecture using a blend of many exotic and native species, it also has a strongly Southern California character, with wide terraces and open sleeping porches to bring the indoors and outdoors together. Broad overhanging eaves and a studied effort to capture cross-ventilation adapt to the climate rather than attempt to conquer it. What is perhaps most impressive is the architects' attention to detail in the articulated joinery, built-in cabinetry and panelling, stained-glass doors, and careful integration of lighting, rugs and various furnishings. The site includes a bookstore and museum shop.

Just northwest of the Gamble House is Brookside Park, home to the famous 98,000-seat **Rose Bowl** football stadium.

Back in downtown Pasadena, one of the most striking public buildings in all of California is the red-tile-domed 1927 **City Hall ★** *(Garfield Ave. at Union St.)*, which blends Spanish, Moorish and Italian Renaissance influences. Two blocks behind, on Walnut Street, is Pasadena's Central Library.

The **Pacific Asia Museum ★★** *($4; Wed to Sun 10am to 5pm; 46. N. Los Robles Ave. between Union St. and Colorado Blvd., ☎626-449-2742)* is housed in a jewel of a building designed in the 1920s in Chinese imperial-palace style, with an enticing courtyard garden and pond. Its very limited exhibition space allows for only small rotating displays from its own permanent collection of mostly Chinese and Japanese art from various periods, though other countries are also represented. It makes for a brief but interesting visit.

The **Playhouse District**, named for the famed Pasadena Playhouse (see page 322), is a shopping and entertainment area centred along Colorado Boulevard between Los Robles Avenue on the west and **South Lake Avenue** of the east. The latter avenue features several blocks of shops, restaurants and cafés, some of them located in European-style arcades in the block between Cordova Street and Del Mar Avenue.

San Marino, directly south of Pasadena, is home to the fabulous **Huntington Library, Art Collections and Botanical**

Gardens ★★★ *($8.50; free first Thu of each month; late May to early Sep Tue to Sun 10:30am to 4:30pm, early Sep to late May Tue to Fri noon to 4:30pm, Sat to Sun 10:30am to 4:30pm; 1151 Oxford Rd. near Huntington Dr., ☎626-405-2100, www.huntington.org).* A bookshop, tea room and restaurant serving light meals are located on the premises.

As the name suggests, this sprawling cultural institution comprises three entities, each of which can be described in superlative tones. It is set on an 207-acre (84ha) former ranch once owned by railway magnate Henry E. Huntington, who collected books and art with the same fervour with which he built his numerous businesses.

Today, the **library** holds about four million items, including half a million rare books, as well as many maps, prints, drawings and photographs. The collection is noted for its many early quartos and folios of Shakespeare plays, as well as early editions of many later British and U.S. writers, and documents penned by several leading U.S. historical figures. A continuous series of rotating exhibitions presented in the library's Exhibition Hall draws upon the extensive archives, going back to the Middle Ages and including illustrated Books of Hours and Bibles.

The **art collections** are housed in a former Huntington family residence that was later augmented by an extensive gallery wing. The earliest collection amassed by Huntington, who died in 1927, and his second wife, Arabella, centred around Old Masters. To this they later added collections of 18th-century British and French paintings, as well as sets of Beauvais tapestries and Savonnerie carpets. The British paintings include many full-length portraits, among them famous works by Thomas Gainsborough. Nor is American art neglected: one wing of the gallery focuses on the Arts and Crafts movement of the early 20th century.

The extensive grounds are shaded by more than 1,000 mature oaks and numerous specimens of other trees. A carefully planned series of **gardens**, some of them formal in the European tradition, others more bucolic, provide a graceful setting for the buildings and a thoroughly delightful area for visitors to stroll or rest. Winding pathways are lined with various species of flowers. Other areas include a desert garden and conservatory, as well as Japanese,

Australian, subtropical and jungle gardens.

Getting here can sometimes be tricky, though parking is rarely a problem. By car from downtown L.A., take Highway 110 (the Pasadena Freeway), exit at California Street and turn east. By bus from downtown L.A., MTA route 79 runs north along Olive Street and takes about 35min to reach Huntington Drive and San Marino Avenue, several minutes' walk from the main entrance. Buses run 30min apart (40min on Sun). By bus from downtown Pasadena, the relatively short hop actually takes longer because there is no direct link: MTA bus 260 southbound along Los Robles Avenue connects with the No. 79 at Huntington Drive.

Tour C: Hollywood and Surroundings

No name evokes the magic of the movies the way Hollywood does. Mention Hollywood to people almost anywhere on earth, and what comes to mind is the glamour of the silver screen and the romantic lives of movie stars. Hollywood isn't the only place in the world where movies are made, but its prodigious production and its heavily hyped stars have dwarfed everything else, in box office receipts if not always in quality. This has been the case since "the industry" (in L.A., this is shorthand for the entertainment industry) set roots early in the 20th century in what had been a semi-rural suburb northwest of downtown L.A. It was drawn here by the mild California climate and the variety of scenic backdrops nearby. Later, Hollywood also became the world's top production centre for popular music and television programming.

What visitors to Hollywood will now see is a far cry from what existed in the glory days. The Hollywood name sticks to the entertainment industry even though all but one of the major studios have relocated to more spacious facilities in other parts of the L.A. area. Much of the Hollywood urban area has fallen on hard times, and Hollywood Boulevard, its fabled thoroughfare, is only beginning to re-emerge from the decades of neglect that gave it a decidedly seedy character. In the last several years, redevelopment efforts have switched into higher gear. The aim—as with the clean-up of New York's Times Square—is once again to make Hollywood safe for suburbanites. Abandoned theatres are being rebuilt,

ATTRACTIONS	
1. Hollywood Bowl	4. Schindler House
2. Universal Studios	5. Barnsdall Art Park
3. Pacific Design Center	
ACCOMMODATIONS	
1. Argyle Hotel	4. Park Sunset Hotel
2. Best Western Sunset Plaza Hotel	5. Saharan Motor Hotel
3. Mondrian	6. Universal City Inn
RESTAURANTS	
1. Atch-Kotch	7. Jitlada
2. Birds	8. La Poubelle
3. Figaro	9. Le Petit Bistro
4. Fred 62	10. Patina
5. Hugo's	11. Pinot Hollywood
6. Ita-Cho	

office buildings are being spruced up, and several down-at-the-heels apartment buildings are being resuscitated. In addition, a large luxury hotel is under construction, one or two landmark restaurants are being restored, and some of the porn shops and tacky souvenir emporiums are beginning to give way to more presentable retailers. A modern and suitably glitzy new home for the Academy Awards is set to open in 2002 near the legendary corner of Hollywood and Vine. Hollywood Boulevard could again become the throbbing heart of entertainment in the region. It still has a long way to go, however, and getting rid of the accumulated grime (both literally and figuratively) will not be accomplished overnight. Visitors in search of glamour may have to wait a while longer. But the signs are hopeful.

Meanwhile, Hollywood continues to trade on its image and star-studded past. Some of the attractions are decidedly kitsch, like the names of long-ago denizens of the silver screen cast in tiny terrazzo and bronze plaques planted in neat rows at pavement level. Other attractions aim a little higher, though nearly always with entertainment as the central theme. Some visitors may find that, apart from walking around and soaking up a little atmosphere, there isn't really very much to see or do in Hollywood.

This tour covers not only central Hollywood and the Hollywood Hills (which form the eastern part of the Santa Monica range), giving some sense of identity to

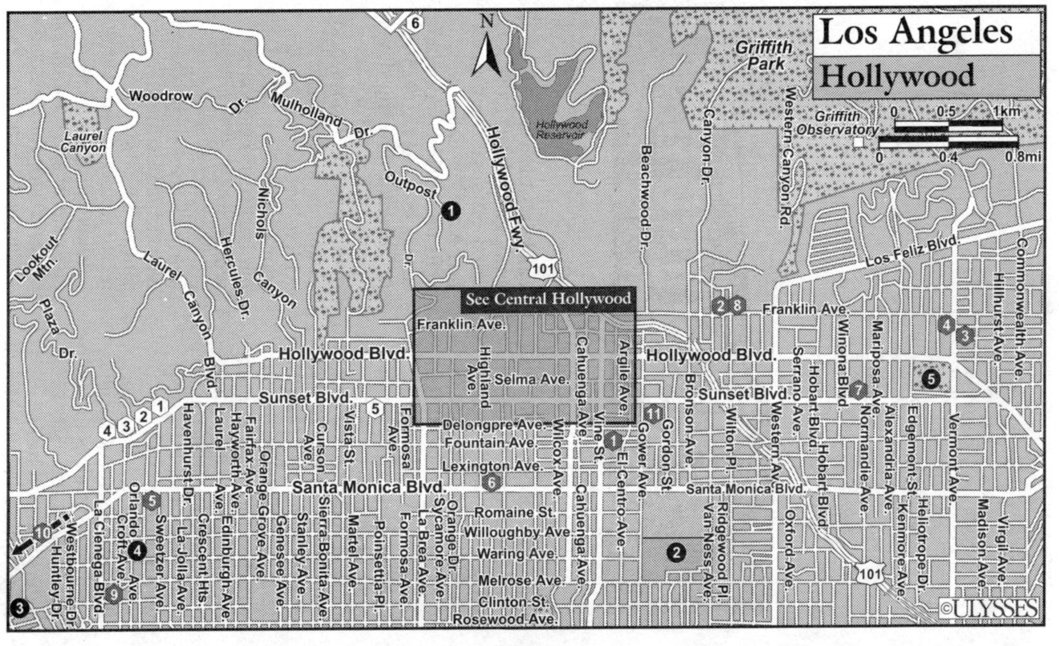
Los Angeles
Hollywood
0 0.5 1km
0 0.4 0.8mi
N
Griffith Park
Griffith Observatory
Western Canyon Rd.
Canyon Dr.
Beachwood Dr.
Hollywood Reservoir
Hollywood Fwy.
101
Woodrow Dr.
Mulholland Dr.
Laurel Canyon
Outpost Dr.
Nichols Canyon
Hercules Dr.
Laurel Canyon Blvd.
Lookout Mtn.
Plaza Dr.
See Central Hollywood
Franklin Ave.
Highland Ave.
Selma Ave.
Cahuenga Ave.
Argile Ave.
Hollywood Blvd.
Sunset Blvd.
Los Feliz Blvd.
Commonwealth Ave.
Hillhurst Ave.
Vermont Ave.
Winona Blvd.
Mariposa Ave.
Normandie Ave.
Alexandria Ave.
Edgemont St.
Heliotrope Dr.
Kenmore Ave.
Madison Ave.
Virgil Ave.
Serrano Ave.
Hobart Blvd.
Western Av.
Oxford Ave.
Wilton Pl.
Ridgewood Pl.
Van Ness Ave.
Bronson Ave.
Gordon St.
Gower Ave.
El Centro Ave.
Vine St.
Wilcox Ave.
Delongpre Ave.
Fountain Ave.
Lexington Ave.
Santa Monica Blvd.
Romaine St.
Willoughby Ave.
Waring Ave.
Melrose Ave.
Clinton St.
Rosewood Ave.
Orange Dr.
Sycamore Ave.
La Brea Ave.
Formosa Ave.
Poinsettia Pl.
Martel Ave.
Vista St.
Curson Ave.
Sierra Bonita Ave.
Stanley Ave.
Genesee Ave.
Orange Grove Ave.
Fairfax Ave.
Hayworth Ave.
Laurel Ave.
Edinburgh Ave.
Havenhurst Dr.
Crescent Hts.
La Jolla Ave.
Sweetzer Ave.
Orlando Ave.
Croft Ave.
La Cienega Blvd.
Westbourne Dr.
Huntley Dr.
©ULYSSES

Hollywood sign

local topography, but also to neighbouring areas—West Hollywood, Los Feliz, Griffith Park and, just beyond the hills, North Hollywood. The Los Angeles Convention & Visitors Bureau operates a visitor information centre in Hollywood *(Mon to Sat 9am to 1pm and 2pm to 5pm, 6541 Hollywood Blvd. near Cahuenga Blvd.)*, which offers a wide range of pamphlets (including transit information) and multilingual staff to help with inquiries.

Perhaps the most familiar landmark of all is the **Hollywood sign** whose 50ft (15m) letters are perched on 1,640ft-high (500m) Mount Lee in an off-limits section of Griffith Park. This sign is easily visible (except on the smoggiest days) from a great distance over much of Los Angeles. Originally, the sign read "Hollywoodland." It was erected in 1923 to publicize a housing development. In 1945 it was deeded to the Hollywood Chamber of Commerce, which lopped off the last four letters. As it was decaying badly, the sign was rebuilt in 1978.

Many visitors come to Hollywood expecting to see film or TV studios. As already noted, most of the studios are now located elsewhere. see the box on page 128 for information on studio tours. And yes, bus tours with guides spouting corny remarks about the stars and their lavish abodes really do exist.

First, we take a look at Hollywood Boulevard, beginning at the corner of Vine Street, where passengers emerging from the gleaming new Metro Red Line station are greeted by the sight of the **Pantages Theater ★** across the street. Following extensive restoration work carried out by the Walt Disney Company, this 2,700-seat landmark reopened in September 2000 with a stage production of *The Lion King* that appears set to run for years.

Want to see your favourite Hollywood star from the past? His or her name just might be embedded in the sidewalk along the **Hollywood Walk of Fame ★**. More than 2,000 actors and musicians have been commemorated in this way since the program began in 1960. The tiny black-and-gold, star-shaped monuments decorate the sidewalks along Hollywood Boulevard from Gower Street all the way west to La Brea Avenue (a distance of more than 15 blocks), and along three blocks of Vine Street between Sunset Boulevard and Yucca Street. A leaflet published by the Hollywood Chamber of Commerce *(7018 Hollywood Blvd., ☎323-469-8311)* and also available from the tourism office *(6541 Hollywood Blvd.)* provides a complete list with exact locations.

On Vine Street, a half-block north of Hollywood Boulevard, is the **Capitol Records Tower ★**, a circular building erected in 1956 in the shape of a stack of vinyl records with a stylus on top. (Like most vinyl albums, the Capitol label has faded from view.) Another distinctively shaped Hollywood landmark from that period is the **Cinerama Dome**, a couple of blocks south on Sunset Boulevard between Vine and Ivar streets, built in 1963 as a futuristic movie theatre and still the world's only geodesic dome built entirely of concrete.

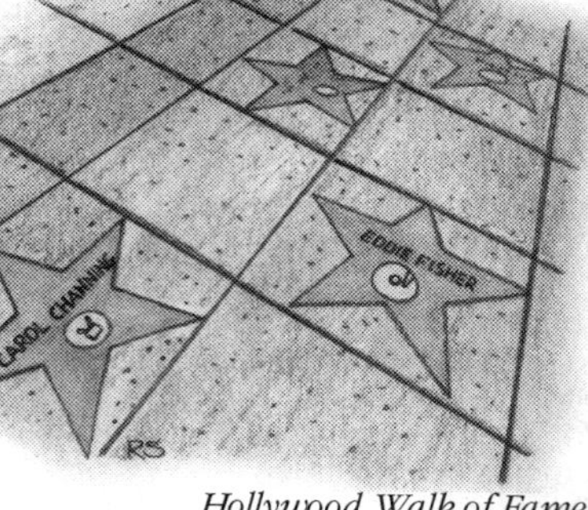

Hollywood Walk of Fame

Mann's Chinese Theater

Back on Hollywood Boulevard, three of the truly grand old movie palaces have made stirring comebacks. These are the **Egyptian Theater** ★ *(6712 Hollywood Blvd. at Las Palmas Ave.)*, **El Capitan** ★ *(6838 Hollywood Blvd. at Highland Ave.)* and **Mann's Chinese Theater** ★ *(6925 Hollywood Blvd. near Orange Dr.)*, all located within two blocks of each other. The Egyptian, built in 1922, reopened in 1998 following extensive restoration work that maintained the original kitschy elements such as hieroglyphs and sphinx heads while dramatically improving sight lines and technical equipment. It is now home to the non-profit American Cinematheque, which presents retrospective series. El Capitan, built in 1926 with an ornate Spanish colonial exterior and opulent interior decor, has been restored by the Disney organization and is now showing first-run films. Mann's Chinese Theater, probably the most famous of all with its giant pagoda-shaped exterior, not only shows films but also displays the cement foot-

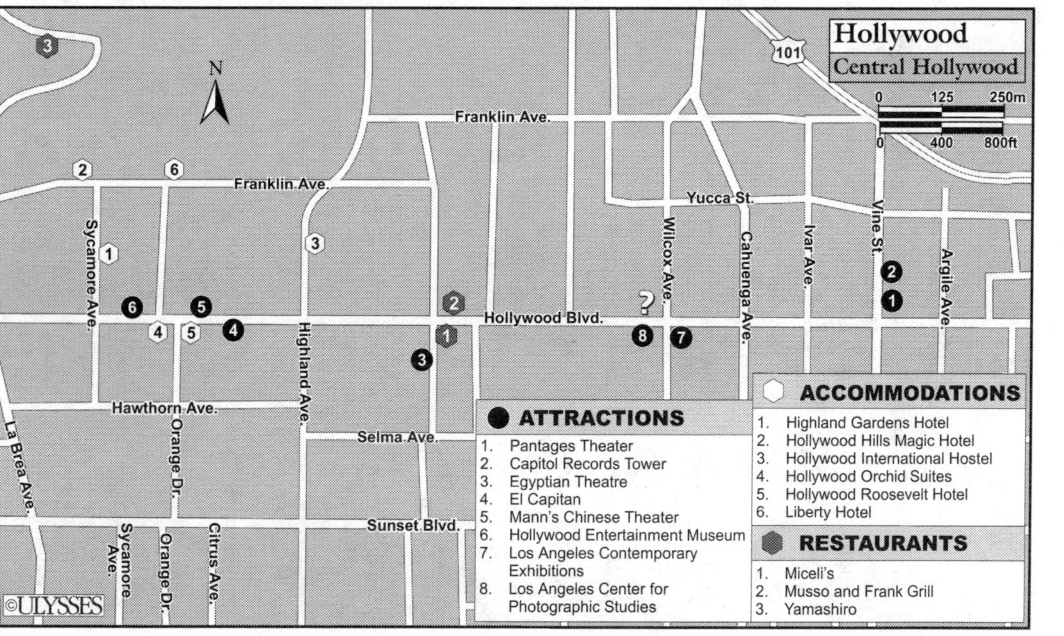

Hollywood
Central Hollywood
0 125 250m
0 400 800ft
N
101
Franklin Ave.
Franklin Ave.
Yucca St.
Hollywood Blvd.
Hawthorn Ave.
Selma Ave.
Sunset Blvd.
La Brea Ave.
Sycamore Ave.
Orange Dr.
Highland Ave.
Wilcox Ave.
Cahuenga Ave.
Ivar Ave.
Vine St.
Argile Ave.
Sycamore Ave.
Orange Dr.
Citrus Ave.
ATTRACTIONS
1. Pantages Theater
2. Capitol Records Tower
3. Egyptian Theatre
4. El Capitan
5. Mann's Chinese Theater
6. Hollywood Entertainment Museum
7. Los Angeles Contemporary Exhibitions
8. Los Angeles Center for Photographic Studies
ACCOMMODATIONS
1. Highland Gardens Hotel
2. Hollywood Hills Magic Hotel
3. Hollywood International Hostel
4. Hollywood Orchid Suites
5. Hollywood Roosevelt Hotel
6. Liberty Hotel
RESTAURANTS
1. Miceli's
2. Musso and Frank Grill
3. Yamashiro
©ULYSSES

Studio Tours

Publicity-conscious "Hollywood" studios (most of them located outside Hollywood) are always happy to peddle their wares and to squeeze a little extra cash out of their adoring fans in the process. All cynicism aside, studio tours enable visitors to get behind-the-scenes glimpses of the daily operations of major film and television facilities. Because of a continuously changing mix of productions, no two tours are exactly alike. It may be possible on occasion to see a well-known film or TV personality, though visitors are not always taken to areas where filming is underway. Reservations are always recommended, and good walking shoes are often suggested.

Paramount Studios *($15; Mon to Fri, every hour from 9am to 2pm; 5555 Melrose Ave. near Gower St., parking entrance on Bronson St., south of Melrose, ☎323-956-1777)* is the only major Hollywood studio actually located in Hollywood, though it is in the quiet southeast corner of Hollywood far from much of the action. This lends the 2hr tour a sense of history that may be less apparent in some of the other studios. Children under 10 are not admitted. (By bus: MTA routes 10 or 11 from downtown L.A. or West Hollywood, or MTA route 210 along Vine Street from Hollywood Boulevard or Crenshaw Boulevard, get off at Melrose and walk east.)

Sony Pictures Studios *($20; tours start Mon to Fri at 9:30am, 11am, 12:30pm and 2pm; 10202 W. Washington Blvd., east of Overland Ave., Culver City, ☎323-520-8687)* offers 2hr walking tours (children under 12 not admitted) that provide glimpses of historic sound stages, current film and TV productions, and future advances in production technology. Among the TV shows filmed here is Jeopardy. Tours leave from the Sony Pictures shopping plaza. Culver City lies in the western part of the L.A. area, southwest of Hollywood and east of Venice. (By car: Overland Avenue exit from the Santa Monica Freeway, or Venice Boulevard exit from the 405 Freeway. By bus: Culver

City Route 1 along Washington Boulevard from Venice or the West L.A. Transit Center, or MTA Route 33 along Venice Boulevard from downtown L.A. or Santa Monica, get off at Madison Avenue and walk two blocks south.)

Warner Bros. Studios *($30; tours Mon to Fri only, Jun to Sep every 30min 9am to 4pm, Oct to May every hour 9am to 3pm; 4000 Warner Blvd., near Hollywood Way and Olive Ave., Burbank, ☎818-972-8687)* is considered by some connoisseurs to offer the best of the studio tours, with the least amount of gimmickry and the most realism, as well as the greatest chance of witnessing a live filming. The tour runs 2hrs 15min, partly on foot, partly by electric cart. It begins with a 15min film and continues with a visit to the Warner Bros. Museum, which features archival material celebrating the stars. Visitors are then taken around the vast backlot with its many sound stages, with stops at some of the technical departments. Warner Bros. and NBC Studios (below) are located in Burbank, at the southern edge of the San Fernando Valley. Children under eight are not admitted. (By car from downtown L.A.: 101 Freeway, Burbank Boulevard exit. By public transit from downtown L.A. or Hollywood: Metro Red Line to Universal City station, connect to MTA bus 96 or 152 eastbound.)

NBC Studios Tour *($7; tours depart at regular intervals Mon to Fri 9am to 3pm, open later and on weekends during the summer; 3000 W. Alameda Ave., Burbank, entry via California St. south of Olive Ave., ☎818-840-3537)* provides a 1hr 15min tour starting with a brief history of NBC radio and television. This is now strictly a television studio, but it has sound stages and technical departments similar to many of those at the film studios. Visitors can request tickets to be part of the studio audience at tapings of popular programs such as The Tonight Show with Jay Leno. (By car from downtown L.A.: 101 Freeway, Burbank Boulevard exit. By public transit from downtown L.A. or Hollywood: Metro Red Line to Universal City station, connect to MTA bus 96 or 152 eastbound.)

Universal Studios Hollywood is more of a theme park than a true studio tour and is covered separately on page 135.

For a list of film shoots around town and the opportunity to sneak a peek and maybe get an autograph, visitors may request the free "shoot sheet" from the **Motion Picture Coordination Office** *(Mon to Fri 8am to 6pm, 7083 Hollywood Blvd., Fifth floor, ☎323-957-1000).*

For tickets to TV show tapings, sources include **CBS** *(☎323-852-2458)*, **NBC** *(☎818-840-3537)*, **Audiences Unlimited** *(preferred distributor for ABC, ☎818-506-0043)*, or **Television Tickets** *(☎323-467-4697).* Requests for popular shows should be made well in advance, although tickets are sometimes available the day of the taping. Sometimes several episodes are shot back to back, requiring extra audience stamina.

prints of about 150 stars from Hollywood's golden era.

At the same corner as the Egyptian, three tourist-trap museums—the Hollywood Wax Museum, the Guiness World Records Museum and Ripley's Believe It or Not—are wholly forgettable and ludicrously overpriced. All three are commercial rip-offs... believe it or not!

One block west of Mann's Chinese Theater, the **Hollywood Entertainment Museum** ★ *($7.50; Thu to Tue 11am to 6pm; 7021 Hollywood Blvd. at Sycamore St., ☎323-465-7900)* is a light-hearted celebration of movie-making and its history. Opened in 1996, it is located in a space at the Galaxy cinema complex once occupied by an unsuccessful food court. Visitors enter through a rotunda gallery, where they can see sets and other memorabilia from favourite movies and TV shows, as well as exhibits on costumes and makeup. A timeline presents the industry's century-long history, and a7min multiscreen show every 30min presents voices and faces from the past. Then the second part of the visit begins, with a guide leading groups through other rooms where various techniques like sound effects are presented from a historical view point. Another part of the tour demonstrates the various departments found in a typical studio backlot. Original items from popular movies including *Star Trek* are integrated with the other displays.

Across the street lies the **Hollywood Roosevelt Hotel** *(7000 Hollywood Blvd.)*, an integral part of Hollywood lore in the early decades after its 1927 opening. It was briefly home to the Academy Awards, and has been renovated and stripped of the "modernizing" touches that once concealed its impressive Spanish-colonial design, including intricately carved columns and painted ceilings.

On a very different note, **Los Angeles Contemporary Exhibitions (LACE)** *(free admission; Wed to Sat noon to 6pm; 6522 Hollywood Blvd. at Wilcox St., ☎323-957-1777)* is an artist-run gallery with a reputation for conceptual works that move toward new frontiers, using painting and a variety of other media. Some of its exhibitions have won enthusiastic critical acclaim. Next door, **Los Angeles Center for Photographic Studies** *(free admission; Wed to Sat 11am to 6pm; 6518 Hollywood Blvd. at Wilcox St., ☎323-466-6232)* presents a continuing series of exhibitions in a small storefront space.

The **Hollywood Bowl**, located off Highland Avenue 0.75mi (1.2km) north of Hollywood Boulevard, partway to North Hollywood, is a popular venue for summer concerts (see page 323).

West Hollywood, as the name suggests, lies to the west of Hollywood. With its varied and often funky shopping opportunities and its eclectic selection of hotels, restaurants, cafés and night spots, it is regarded as one of L.A.'s hipper areas. The substantial number of elderly residents does not seem to deter from this image. It is also the main centre of the gay and lesbian social scene.

Although it is difficult to pinpoint many specific attractions in West Hollywood, some streets have special character and are thus worth a drive or a stroll. **Sunset Boulevard** follows a sinuous path along the base of the Hollywood Hills between Fairfax Avenue and Doheny Drive to the west. Once referred to as the Sunset Strip, it connects discontinuous rows of shops and restaurants. Further south, **Melrose Avenue** between La Brea Avenue and La Cienega Boulevard was, for a long time, the place to go for avant-garde fashions. Although its popularity has led to the arrival of more mainstream retailers in recent years, the scene still has a certain edge.

One of the most interesting buildings in West Hollywood is the **Pacific Design Center** ★ *(8687 Melrose Ave. near San Vicente Blvd.)*, a giant seven-storey bubble clad in curving cobalt-blue glass. A later bright green addition was equally controversial. Designed by Argentinian architect Cesar Pelli, it has become known locally as the Blue Whale. It houses interior design showrooms for the wholesale trade.

The **Schindler House** ★ *(835 N. Kings Rd., 1½ blocks north of Melrose Ave.)* is regarded as a landmark of Modernist architecture. Named for Rudolph Schindler, the Austrian-born architect who designed this building in the early 1920s as his personal residence, this house has a flat roof and large concrete-walled studio rooms with sliding doors opening to the outdoors. These and other elements were to influence California architecture in the succeeding decades. Heavy alterations after the architect's death were subsequently reversed in a restoration project, and the house is now the site of a small museum established in partnership with Vienna's Museum of Applied Arts (MAK in its German initials). The **MAK Center for Art** *($5; Wed to Sun 11am to 6pm, ☎323-651-1510)* features exhibitions dealing with current issues in art and architecture.

Los Feliz is a neighbourhood to the east of Hollywood that appears to have picked up where Melrose Avenue left off in terms of new horizons in style, particularly along a stretch of Vermont Avenue between Hollywood Boulevard and Franklin Avenue. Occupying a large hilltop estate extending from the southwest corner of Hollywood and Vermont is the **Barnsdall Art Park**, named for oil heiress Aline Barnsdall whose grandiose plans for the site never fully took shape. The site is home to the **Los Angeles Municipal Art Gallery** *(free admission; Wed to Sun 12:30pm to 5pm; 4804 Hollywood Blvd., ☎213-485-4581)*, operating as an extension of Junior Arts Center with its extensive program of studio classes. The gallery presents temporary exhibitions of works by students and professional artists. Next door is the **Hollyhock House** ★ *($2; guided tours every hour Wed to Sun noon to 3pm; ☎323-913-4157)*, an architectural landmark designed by Frank Lloyd

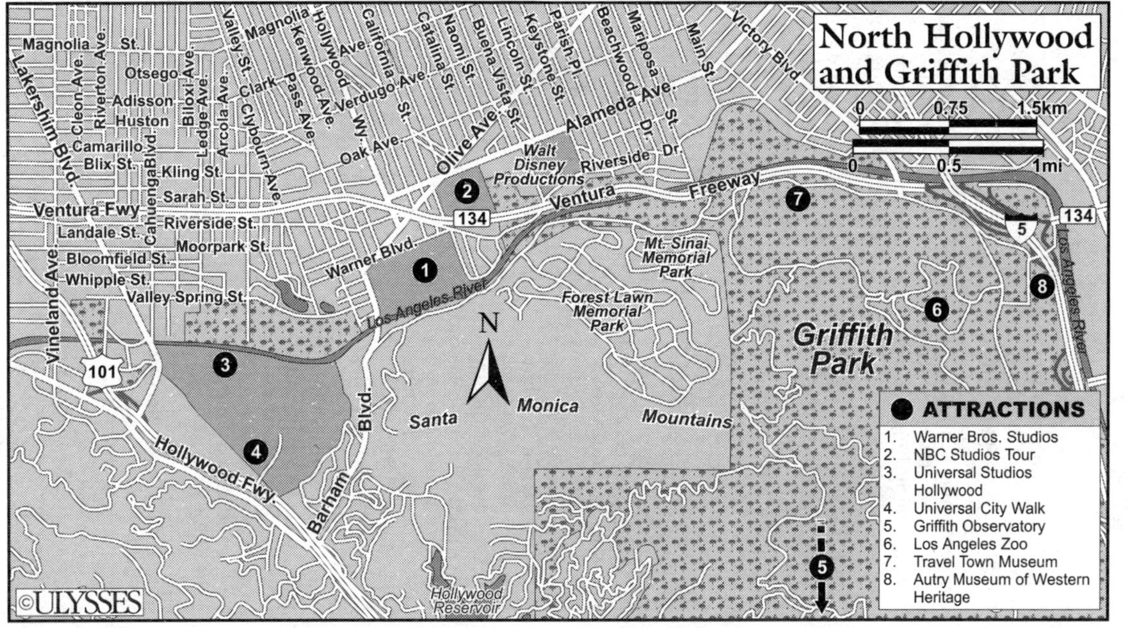
North Hollywood and Griffith Park
0
0.75
1.5km
0
0.5
1mi
ATTRACTIONS
1. Warner Bros. Studios
2. NBC Studios Tour
3. Universal Studios Hollywood
4. Universal City Walk
5. Griffith Observatory
6. Los Angeles Zoo
7. Travel Town Museum
8. Autry Museum of Western Heritage
Griffith Park
Santa Monica Mountains
Mt. Sinai Memorial Park
Forest Lawn Memorial Park
Walt Disney Productions
Hollywood Reservoir
Los Angeles River
Ventura Freeway
Ventura Fwy
Hollywood Fwy
134
101
5
Victory Blvd.
Main St.
Mariposa St.
Beachwood Dr.
Parish Pl.
Keystone St.
Lincoln St.
Buena Vista St.
Naomi St.
Catalina St.
California St.
Hollywood Wy.
Kenwood Ave.
Magnolia Ave.
Valley St.
Pass Ave.
Clark Ave.
Clybourn Ave.
Verdugo Ave.
Oak Ave.
Olive Ave.
Alameda Ave.
Riverside Dr.
Magnolia St.
Lakershim Blvd.
Cleon Ave.
Riverton Ave.
Otsego
Adisson
Huston
Camarillo
Blix St.
Biloxi Ave.
Ledge Ave.
Arcola Ave.
Cahuenga Blvd.
Kling St.
Sarah St.
Riverside St.
Landale St.
Moorpark St.
Bloomfield St.
Whipple St.
Valley Spring St.
Vineland Ave.
Warner Blvd.
Barham Blvd.
N
©ULYSSES

Wright in the late 1910s. Hollyhocks, an abundant flower, form a theme in parts of the design, which incorporates a variety of elements and innovates through the clever use of varied ceiling heights from room to room.

Griffith Park ★★, north of Los Feliz in the Hollywood Hills, provides the most significant area of green space in Los Angeles. Occupying 4,200 acres (1,700ha), this massive and very hilly park (see p 215) encompasses many attractions, including golf courses, hiking trails and numerous picnic grounds, as well as the Forest Lawn Cemetary (immortalized in Evelyn Waugh's novel *The Loved One*), an outdoor theatre, the Griffith Observatory and Planetarium, the Los Angeles Zoo, Travel Town Museum and the Autry Museum of Western Heritage. (By bus: MTA route 96 skirts the eastern side of the park, near the main attractions, running north from downtown L.A. along Olive Street and continuing to North Hollywood.)

The **Griffith Observatory ★★** *(free admission; Tue to Fri 2pm to 10pm, Sat to Sun 12:30pm to 10pm, summer: every day 12:30pm to 10pm; children under five restricted; planetarium shows: $4; 3pm, 7:30pm, also Sat to Sun 4:30pm; laserium shows: $7; Fri to Sat 6pm, 8:45pm, 9:45pm; other days 3pm, 7:30pm; 2800 E. Observatory Rd., Griffith Park, enter via Los Feliz Ave., ☎323-664-1191, www.griffithobs.org)* is housed in a landmark triple-domed building high on a hilltop. Even for those who aren't astronomy buffs, it's worth a visit for the extraordinary view over Los Angeles from the terrace. One dome conceals a triple-beam solar telescope, another a 12in (30cm) Zeiss refracting telescope and, in the middle, the planetarium. The building, which opened in 1935, also houses a science museum that includes displays of meteorites and interactive computer stations where visitors can explore advances in astronomy. On clear evenings visitors can observe the heavens from one of the observatory's telescopes. The 1hr-long planetarium shows narrate aspects of astronomy. Laserium shows, popular with teenagers, feature laser lights set to popular music.

Los Angeles Zoo ★★ *($8.25; every day 10am to 5pm, Jul to Aug until 6pm; 5333 Zoo Drive, Griffith Park, ☎323-666-4090, www.lazoo.org)* features more than 400 species spread over its 80-acre (32ha) grounds linked by winding pathways through abundantly landscaped areas. Not all animals are caged, with moats or space used instead as barriers. The zoo has gradually been reducing its collection to allow the animals more roaming room. Special collections include the Great Ape Forest, the Ahmanson Koala House, Adventure Island (for children) and an aviary.

Almost next door is the **Travel Town Museum ★★** *(free admission; Mon to Fri 10am to 5pm, Sat to Sun 10am to 6pm, Jul to Aug closes 1hr later; 5200 Zoo Dr., Griffith Park, ☎323-662-5874)*, of particular interest to railway buffs. This partly outdoor museum features a miniature railway *(rides $1.75)* and 14 full-sized steam locomotives, the oldest of which dates back to 1864. Among other exhibits are passenger cars (including luxurious sleeping cars and club cars), freight cars, cabooses and an extensive model railway layout. Antique fire engines are also on display.

The **Autry Museum of Western Heritage ★★** *($7.50; Tue to Sun 10am to 5pm; 4700 Western Heritage Way, Griffith Park, ☎323-667-2000)* adopted a cowboy and lasso as its emblem, but the museum's scope is far broader, presenting many aspects of the settlement of the western U.S. by citizens of British heritage and the displacement of earlier inhabitants. The mural-lined galleries do include a section devoted to the Spirit of the Cowboy, but Native American populations and Spanish settlers also receive their due. One gallery presents the bar and other furnishings created in 1880 for a saloon in Montana and portrays some of the wilder aspects of life in the Wild West.

North Hollywood lies at the southern edge of the San Fernando Valley just beyond the Hollywood Hills. It includes Universal City and lies adjacent to Burbank, home to several of the ex-Hollywood studios (see the box on p 128). A new extension to the Metro Red Line speeds access from downtown L.A. and central Hollywood.

Universal Studios Hollywood *($39; every day 9am to 7pm, summer 8am to 10pm; off the Hollywood Freeway, Universal Center Dr. exit, ☎818-622-3801, www.universalstudios.com)* is one of the world's most popular tourist attractions, situated on the grounds of the world's largest movie and television studio and replete with throwbacks to hit-animation features like images of dinosaurs from the film *Jurassic Park.* Obviously, somebody is doing something right. If we haven't given this flashy and heavily hyped theme park a star rating, it's because opinions can vary so wildly. Adolescents will certainly clamour for their parents to fork up the hefty admission price that does, admittedly, include all rides (although the waits can be long, especially in summer). The lavish commercial development of what used to be a simple studio tour has created an interesting phenomenon: movie sets are, by definition, simulations of real scenes. What we see here are simulations of movie sets—in other words, simulations of simulations. The special effects are very special indeed, including simulations of an earthquake in New York and a bridge that collapses practically beneath the wheels of the huge electric carts that ferry visitors around on an introductory 45min tour. Needless to say, food and drink are offered in abundance (although it's not a bad idea to bring along some bottled water). Besides the fake (and a few real) movie sets that visitors can see, there are the rides, some of them suitably stomach-churning, others more tame. Repeat visitors have their favourites. By common consensus, one of the best is the Jurassic Park ride, a sort of slow-moving indoor roller coaster whose riders are confronted at every turn by prehistoric monsters. It may all seem superficial, but it can be fun for those in the right frame of mind and it does present an important element of California culture.

Universal Studios Hollywood

Universal City Walk, adjacent to Universal Studios, is a shopping and entertainment mall designed to look like a traditional shopping street, minus the intrusive automobile traffic and any elements that make real urban streets so creepy. First the suburban malls suck the commercial life from downtown areas, and now they pay the ultimate compliment by simulating city life. Universal City Walk, with its many shops, restaurants, cinemas and even nightclubs, is a security-controlled area where clean-cut suburbanites can walk around outdoors in an environment made to appear less artificial than the typical en-

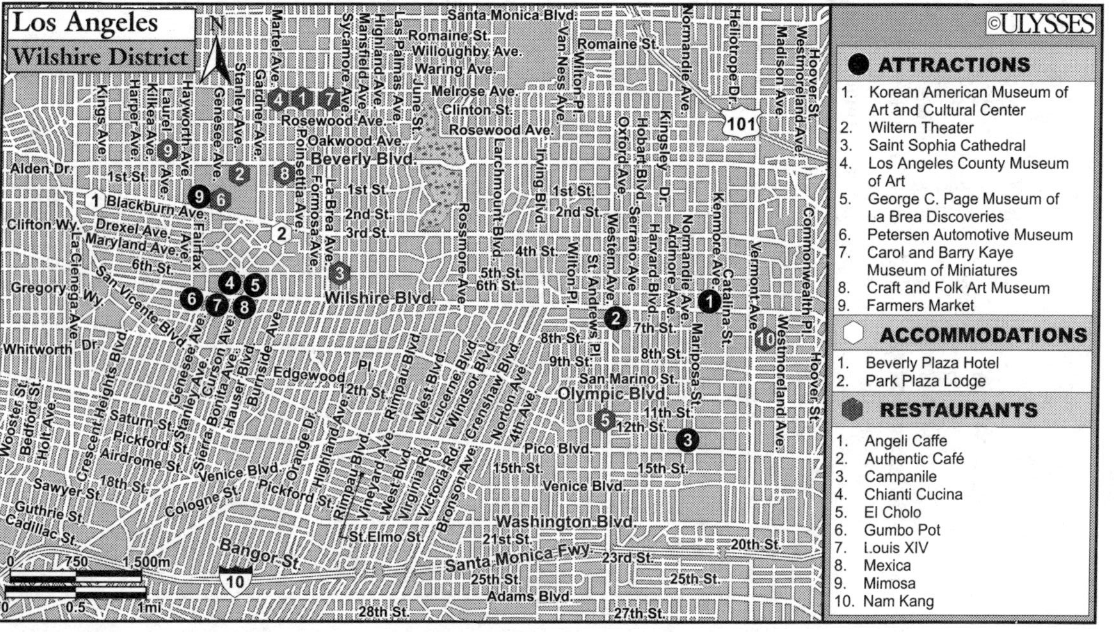

Los Angeles
Wilshire District
©ULYSSES
ATTRACTIONS
1. Korean American Museum of Art and Cultural Center
2. Wiltern Theater
3. Saint Sophia Cathedral
4. Los Angeles County Museum of Art
5. George C. Page Museum of La Brea Discoveries
6. Petersen Automotive Museum
7. Carol and Barry Kaye Museum of Miniatures
8. Craft and Folk Art Museum
9. Farmers Market
ACCOMMODATIONS
1. Beverly Plaza Hotel
2. Park Plaza Lodge
RESTAURANTS
1. Angeli Caffe
2. Authentic Café
3. Campanile
4. Chianti Cucina
5. El Cholo
6. Gumbo Pot
7. Louis XIV
8. Mexica
9. Mimosa
10. Nam Kang
0 750 1,500m
0 0.5 1mi

closed mall. Top marks, though, for design.

Tour D: Mid-Wilshire and Westside

This tour covers the broad area west of downtown Los Angeles, east of Santa Monica, and south of Hollywood. Moving from east to west, it includes the Koreatown district, Wilshire Boulevard's Miracle Mile with its impressive row of museums, the very swank City of Beverly Hills, the Westwood-UCLA area and, finally, Brentwood, crowned by the attention-winning Getty Center, one of the world's most richly endowed art institutions. The Los Angeles County Museum of Art, along the Miracle Mile, is a more than worthy rival.

Wilshire Boulevard, in some respects the most important street in Los Angeles, stretches from downtown L.A. to Santa Monica Beach and is the central artery serving the territory covered here. (It may horrify some wealthy Westsiders to learn that this important thoroughfare, crossing their elegant neighbourhoods, was named for a social reformer and publisher of socialist newspapers. But Gaylord Wilshire, who came from a well-to-do family, also had his capitalist side: he made an astute investment in real estate west of downtown L.A. in the 1880s, in an area that was subsequently developed as a fashionable residential district. More than a century later, the boulevard bisecting this and other districts continues to bear his name.)

Wilshire Boulevard starts at Grand Avenue downtown and runs west past **MacArthur Park**, one of the few significant and appealing patches of greenery in inner-city L.A. A few blocks further west, it crosses through part of **Koreatown ★**, an unofficially designated area that is home to part of the city's large and growing Korean community. It covers an extensive zone reaching from Beverly Boulevard south to Pico Avenue between Vermont Avenue on the east and Western Avenue on the west, and it spills even beyond these limits. While by no means everyone inhabiting this area is of Korean descent, this is a living, working, thriving immigrant neighbourhood (quite unlike the more fossilized Chinatown and Little Tokyo, which have lost most of their residents). Many of the businesses here cater to a mostly Korean clientele, and some have signs in Korean only. The most intensely developed commercial strip lies along Olympic Boulevard between Vermont and Western, with hundreds of shops and restaurants, most located in two-storey mini-malls plagued by a perpetual shortage of parking space. This is where to come for anything Korean, including food and decorative items. The **Korean American Museum of Art and Cultural Center** *(free admission; Tue to Sat 11am to 4pm; 3333 Wilshire Blvd. between Vermont and Normandie Aves., ☎213-388-4229)* presents photos, memorabilia and other items portraying the Korean-American immigrant experience, along with some traditional works of art.

Several interesting buildings, with no relation to Koreatown, are located in this general area. They include the **Wiltern Theater** *(Wilshire Blvd. at Western Ave.)*, a gorgeous turquoise-coloured Art Deco structure erected in 1931; **Saint Sophia Cathedral** *(Fri to Wed 10am to 2pm; 1324 S. Normandie Ave. near Pico Blvd.)*, a Byzantine structure built in 1952 and noted for its fabulously lavish interior with numerous icons, murals and crystal chandeliers, which is the spiritual home of the local Greek Orthodox community; and the former **Bullocks Wilshire Department Store** *(3050 Wilshire Blvd. near Vermont Ave.)*, an elegant 1929 Art Deco landmark, its five storeys topped by a tower, which was closed in 1992 but rescued intact a few years later to serve as the law library of Southwestern University.

The **Miracle Mile**, covering the stretch of Wilshire Boulevard between La Brea and Fairfax avenues, was originally developed as a shopping area in the 1920s to serve the rapidly growing residential areas nearby. Many of the buildings from that period show Art Deco features in various *moderne* styles. Today, the area has lost its importance as a retail zone, and the first few blocks east of Fairfax have been taken over instead by at least a half-dozen museums, dominated by the mammoth Los Angeles County Museum of Art).

Los Angeles County Museum of Art ★★★*($6, seniors and students $4, youth aged 6-17 $1, children under 6 free Mon, Tue, Thu 12 noon to 8pm; Fri 12 noon to 9pm; Sat-Sun 11am to 8pm; Wed closed, 5905 Wilshire Blvd., 3 blocks east of Fairfax Ave.; ☎323-857-6000, www.lacma.org)* The newer and flashier Getty Center has certainly garnered more attention in the art world over the last few years, but the breadth and depth of the collection at Los Angeles County Museum of Art is impressive by any standard. LACMA has set itself the ambitious aim of presenting the art of all major cultures from the ancient world to the present. Generous bequests, along with the recent acquisition of a former department store building to provide added exhibition space, bring it closer to this goal. As with any large museum that takes an encyclopedic approach, a thorough visit can stretch the visitor's time and stamina. Many visitors may choose to focus on the periods or cultures that most interest them. The museum's more than 200,000 works (only a fraction of which are on display) fall under 10 curatorial departments:

• European paintings and sculpture, from the Renaissance to the 19th century, including works by Titian, El Greco, Rembrandt, Millet, Degas and Cézanne;
• American art, with the focus on the 18th and 19th centuries;
• Ancient and Islamic art, with valuable collections from ancient Egpyt, the Near East and the Greek and Roman Empires, as well as ancient Islamic art and objects from the pre-Columbian cultures of the western hemisphere, including sculptures, ceramics and gold masks;
• Far Eastern art (one of the museum's true strengths), with a Chinese collection spanning 3,000 years of bronzes, pottery, porcelain, calligraphy and painting; the Japanese collection (housed in its own pavilion) contains painting, sculpture, lacquerware, ceramics, textiles, painted screens, and small ivory carvings; Korean and Central Asian art are also represented;
• Indian and Southeast Asian art (another strong section), including Indian religious sculpture in stone and bronze, wood carvings, decorative arts, and Buddhist objects from Nepal, Tibet and Cambodia;
• Twentieth-century art, including works by Braque, Picasso, Magritte and several top American artists;
• Prints and drawings, encompassing etchings and woodcuts spanning the centuries from Goya to Picasso;
• Photography, with European and American artists well represented;
• Decorative arts, running the gamut from 14th-century French cathedral windows to early American glass and furniture and including Italian renaissance porcelain, German glassware, French tapestries, and French and English furniture, porcelain and silverware;

• Textiles and costumes, with ancient and modern items spanning many parts of the world.

Even this doesn't tell the whole story. In 1997, for example, the museum received the donation of a sizable collection of Mexican modernist art. The museum has been in its current location since 1965 and has grown with the addition of new buildings. It is laid out in campus style, with five buildings set around a central court.

The largest structure is the Ahmanson Building, with exhibition space on four levels housing the real heart of the permanent collection (visitors should be sure to obtain a floor plan at the entrance to orient themselves more precisely). The Hammer Building is home to prints and photography, as well as to some late 19th- and early 20th-century European art. The Anderson Building is dedicated to 20th-century art, with the more recent objects on the upper level. Finally, the Japanese Pavilion, obviously, houses the Japanese collection.

An additioal building, the former May Company department store a couple of blocks west at the corner of Fairfax Avenue, has been named **LACMA West** and, for the time being, is used mainly for special exhibitions. It also houses a children's gallery and a satellite of the **Southwest Museum** (see page 112), whose main harder-to-reach site is seriously short of space. The LACMA West location presents special exhibitions and rotating shows from the permanent collection. The admission charge varies; sometimes it is free *(☎323-933-4510).*

George C. Page Museum of La Brea Discoveries ★ *($6; Tue to Sun 10am to 5pm; 5801 Wilshire Blvd. at Curson Ave., four blocks east of Fairfax Ave., ☎323-857-6311)* is situated next to a small expanse of bubbling tar-like ooze, known as La Brea tar pits, in which a huge variety of animals, large and small, became trapped over a period of more than 40,000 years. The site has been under excavation by archeologists since 1906 and has yielded a rich treasure trove of bones. Some of these are on display in the form of reconstructed skeletons in a bright, attractive exhibition hall at the museum, named for George C. Page, a local businessman, amateur scientist and philanthropist. The museum (worth an additional star for children) includes a small botanical garden and a 15min film documenting the discoveries. Visitors can sometimes watch archeologists at work in the museum's research wing.

The **Petersen Automotive Museum** ★★ *($7; Tue to Sun 10am to 6pm; 6060 Wilshire Blvd. at Fairfax Ave., ☎323-930-2277, www.petersen.org)* provides a fascinating historical portrayal of L.A.'s love affair with the automobile. The museum, set on three floors in a former department store building, goes beyond a mere collection of automobiles from various decades and presents mock-ups of Los Angeles streetscapes from the pertinent periods to place these vehicles in context. One section documents the role of the automobile in the development of the city. The collection includes large, flashy vehicles once owned by particular Hollywood celebrities.

Carole and Barry Kaye Museum of Miniatures ★ *($7.50; Tue to Sat 10am to 5pm, Sun 11am to 5pm; 5900 Wilshire Blvd., two blocks east of Fairfax Ave., ☎323-937-6464, www.museumofminiatures.com)* is named after the founders whose collection it houses, augmented by many pieces from the personal collection of Walt Disney, the great animator and film producer. It presents a fantasy world of palaces and monuments intricately pieced together by many hundreds of artists. Objects include a replica of the Vatican Palace more than 10ft (3m) high and a model of the Titanic made of 75,000 toothpicks.

Craft and Folk Art Museum ★ *($3.50; Tue to Sun 11am to 5pm; 5814 Wilshire Blvd. four blocks east of Fairfax Ave., ☎323-937-4230)* is set in a charming old house with only limited exhibition space. A series of rotating shows present contemporary and historic displays from different parts of the world.

The **Farmers Market** at the corner of Fairfax Avenue and Third Street, anchored by its distinctive clock

Part of the collection at the Petersen Automotive Museum

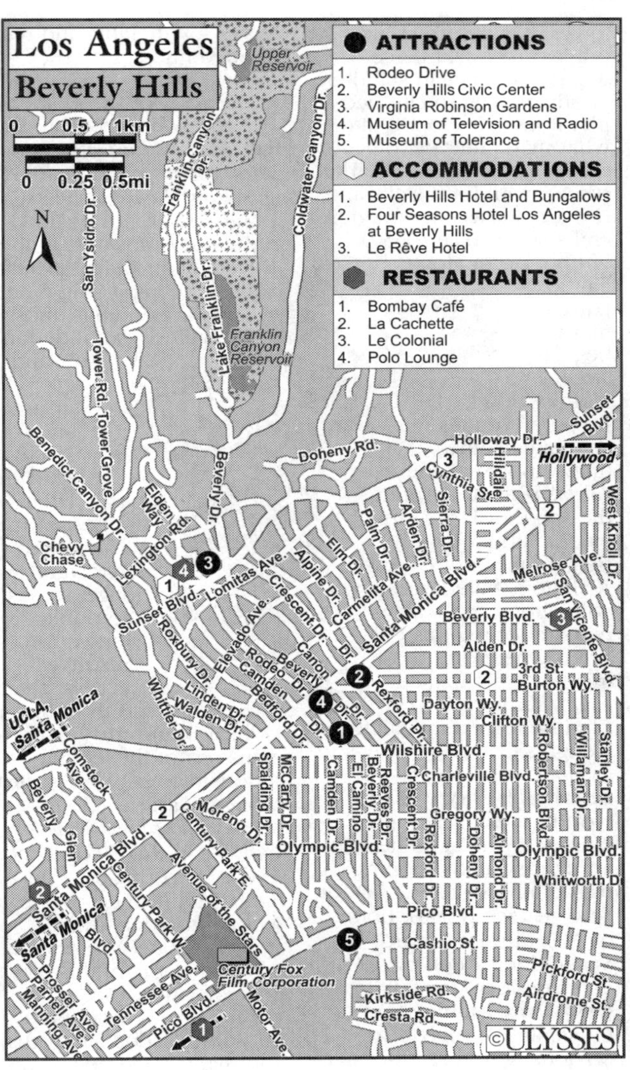

Los Angeles
Beverly Hills
0 0.5 1km
0 0.25 0.5mi
N
ATTRACTIONS
1. Rodeo Drive
2. Beverly Hills Civic Center
3. Virginia Robinson Gardens
4. Museum of Television and Radio
5. Museum of Tolerance
ACCOMMODATIONS
1. Beverly Hills Hotel and Bungalows
2. Four Seasons Hotel Los Angeles at Beverly Hills
3. Le Rêve Hotel
RESTAURANTS
1. Bombay Café
2. La Cachette
3. Le Colonial
4. Polo Lounge
Upper Reservoir
Franklin Canyon Dr.
Coldwater Canyon Dr.
Lake Franklin Dr.
Franklin Canyon Reservoir
San Ysidro Dr.
Tower Rd.
Tower Grove
Benedict Canyon Dr.
Beverly Dr.
Doheny Rd.
Holloway Dr.
Sunset Blvd.
Hollywood
Cynthia St.
Hilldale
West Knoll Dr.
Elden Way
Lexington Rd.
Chevy Chase
Sunset Blvd.
Lomitas Ave.
Crescent Dr.
Alpine Dr.
Elm Dr.
Palm Dr.
Arden Dr.
Sierra Dr.
Carmelita Ave.
Santa Monica Blvd.
Melrose Ave.
San Vicente Blvd.
Beverly Blvd.
Alden Dr.
3rd St.
Burton Wy.
Roxbury Dr.
Elevado Ave.
Rodeo Dr.
Camden Dr.
Bedford Dr.
Canon Dr.
Beverly Dr.
Rexford Dr.
Dayton Wy.
Clifton Wy.
Linden Dr.
Walden Dr.
Whittier Dr.
UCLA, Santa Monica
Comstock Ave.
Wilshire Blvd.
Spalding Dr.
McCarty Dr.
Camden Dr.
El Camino
Beverly Dr.
Reeves Dr.
Crescent Dr.
Charleville Blvd.
Robertson Blvd.
Willaman Dr.
Stanley Dr.
Beverly Glen
Moreno Dr.
Century Park E.
Gregory Wy.
Olympic Blvd.
Olympic Blvd.
Rexford Dr.
Doheny Dr.
Almond Dr.
Whitworth Dr.
Santa Monica Blvd.
Century Park W.
Avenue of the Stars
Santa Monica Blvd.
Pico Blvd.
Cashio St.
Century Fox Film Corporation
Pickford St.
Airdrome St.
Kirkside Rd.
Cresta Rd.
Tennessee Ave.
Prosser Ave.
Parnell Ave.
Manning Ave.
Pico Blvd.
Motor Ave.
©ULYSSES

tower, has outgrown its original role as a place where farmers can sell their goods directly to city people. It has developed into what marketing people refer to as a "festival marketplace," with food stalls and restaurants accompanied by crafts shops (see p 350). Further north along Fairfax, particularly between Melrose and Beverly avenues, is an area sometimes known as the **Fairfax District**. Forming the spine of L.A.'s largest traditional Jewish neighbourhood, Fairfax Avenue is here lined with shops and restaurants reflecting this character. One of the most imaginatively named establishments is a Chinese restaurant called Genghis Cohen!

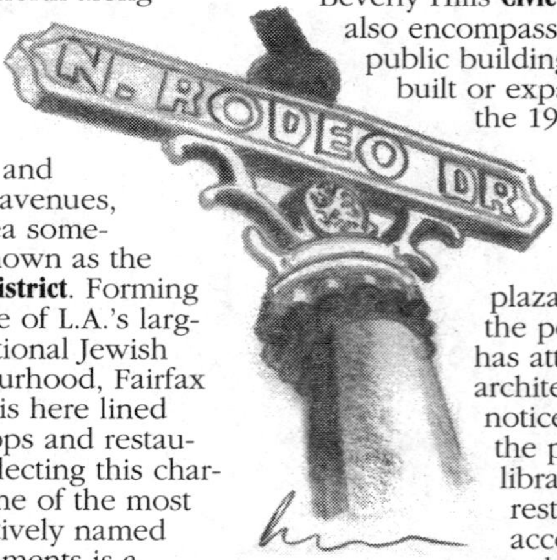

Beverly Hills is one of the world's wealthiest municipalities. Lying at its heart is an ultra-swank shopping district known as the **Golden Triangle** (see p 349), bound by Wilshire Boulevard, Santa Monica Boulevard and Crescent Drive, with **Rodeo Drive** running through the centre. Wealth is so obvious here that it doesn't have to be flaunted in the architecture, which observes low heights and restrained lines.

At the apex of the Golden Triangle is Beverly Hills **City Hall** ★ *(Rexford Dr. at Santa Monica Blvd.)*, built in 1932 in Spanish-revival style with a high tower and a gilded cupola. It forms part of the Beverly Hills **Civic Center** ★, also encompassing other public buildings, most built or expanded in the 1980s and set around an attractive oval plaza. Even the post office has attracted architectural notice, as has the public library. On restricted-access streets north of Santa Monica Boulevard lie the mansions of those with serious money. The **Virginia Robinson Gardens** *($6; by reservation only; 1008 Elden Way, ☎276-5367)* cover most of the almost 6-acre (3ha) estate bequeathed by the widow of a department store magnate. Visitors are taken on tours of the gorgeously landscaped grounds, with their terrace hillsides, shaded footpaths and many hundreds of varieties of plants and flowers.

The **Museum of Television and Radio** *(suggested donation $6; Wed to Sun noon to 5pm, Thu until 9pm; 465 N. Beverly Dr. at Little Santa Monica Blvd., Beverly Hills, ☎786-1000)* is less a museum than a series of private viewing rooms where visitors can view long-ago TV shows contained in extensive archives.

The **Museum of Tolerance** ★★ *($8.50; tour departures: Mon to Thu 10am to 4pm, Fri 10am to 1pm, Apr to Oct until 3pm, Sun 11am to 5pm, closed Sat and on Jewish and civic holidays; 9786 W. Pico Blvd. at Roxbury Dr., south of Beverly Hills and east of Century City; by bus: Santa Monica Route 7, ☎553-8403, www.wiesenthal.com)* is part of the **Simon Wiesenthal Center**, established by the famed investigator of Nazi war crimes. The museum aims to get people thinking about racial or ethnic prejudice and the violent extremes to which it has escalated. Visitors are taken on an hour long tour of exhibits portraying the rise of Nazism in Germany in the 1930s and the calamitous events that followed. Elsewhere in the museum, visitors can wander on their own through a series of interactive displays relating to the Holocaust and to more recent tragedies. Each visitor is given a document bearing the name of a Jewish child born in Europe before the war; later in the visit, the child's fate is revealed (in most cases, it is tragic).

The sprawling campus of the University of California at Los Angeles, known everywhere as **UCLA**, encompasses more than 100 buildings set on 419 acres (170ha) of landscaped grounds west of Beverly Hills. First developed in 1919, it's not especially noteworthy in itself, although it is the site of many special events, and some of its libraries are open to the public. It's also home to the **Fowler Museum of Cultural History** ★ *($5; Thu free; Wed to Sun noon to 5pm, Thu until 8pm; ☎825-4361)*, which presents rotating exhibitions of art from Asia, Africa and Latin America, the **Franklin D. Murphy Sculpture Collection** ★,

Beverly Hills City Hall

Exploring

with more than 50 works including objects by Lachaise and Rodin, and the **Mildred Mathias Botanical Garden**. Locations are clearly marked on large maps at campus entrances. Just south of the campus, **Westwood Village** features a large concentration of cinemas, fast-food restaurants, and shopping. (Many bus routes pass by the UCLA campus, including MTA routes 2, 21, 302, 429, 561 and 576 and Santa Monica Routes 2, 3, 8 and 12.)

The Getty Center

The **Skirball Cultural Centre and Museum** ★ *($8; Tue to Fri 10am to 4pm, Sat noon to 5pm, Sun 10am to 5pm; Sepulveda Blvd. off the 405 Freeway north of Mulholland Dr.; by bus: MTA route 561, ☎440-4500)*, set on lavish grounds in the remote Sepulveda Pass between the Getty Center and the San Fernando Valley, portrays Jewish life through the centuries in many parts of the world, including the arrival of Jewish immigrants to the United States. Exhibits are drawn from an extensive collection of Judaica, with many stressing the theme of religious tradition. Designed by architect Moshe Safdie and opened in 1996, this centre also has an auditorium, conference hall and restaurant.

The Getty Center *(Admission free; parking $5 (reservations required) Tue-Wed 11am to 7pm; Thu-Fri 11am to 9pm; Sat-Sun 10am to 6pm; 1200 Getty Center Drive, ☎310-440-7300, www.getty.edu; By car: 405 Freeway to Getty Center Drive exit; By bus: MTA route 561 or Santa Monica route 14)*

This is the museum the art world has been talking about for years, among the most lavish and richly endowed museums ever built. The museum's billion-dollar campus, designed by architect Richard Meier, opened amid much fanfare in 1997 after 14 years of planning and construction. The collection is impressive,

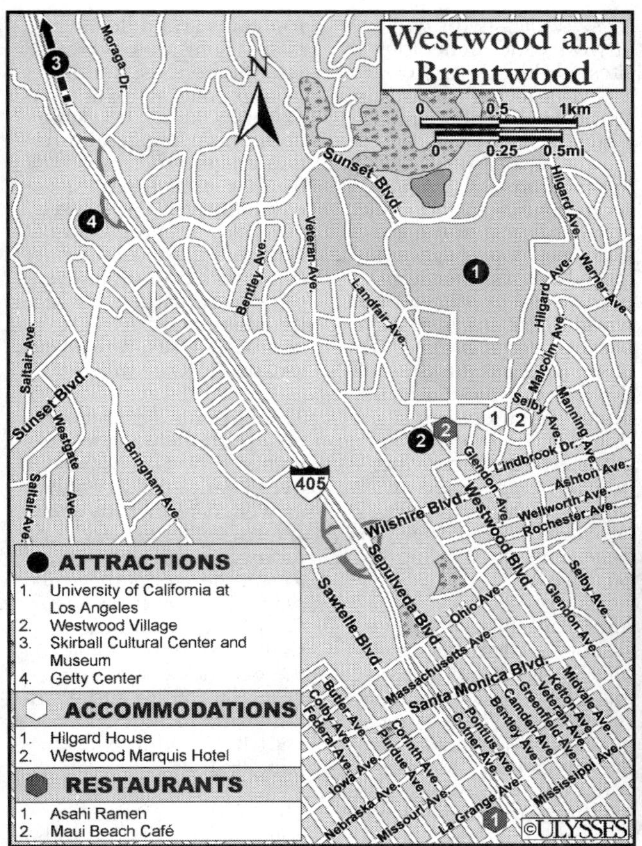

but what most visitors will notice first is the magnificence of the site, perched on a hilltop like a medieval fortress.The Getty Center is endowed by a trust fund established by oil magnate and art collector J. Paul Getty, who died in 1976. Besides the museum, the centre houses various research and educational institutions, including the Getty Research Institute for the History of Art and the Humanities, the Getty Conservation Institute, the Getty Education Institute for the Arts, and the Getty Grant Program. The work done by these bodies helps conserve artworks and archeological sites worldwide and creates arts education programs in schools across the United States.

Preparations for a visit may seem inauspicious. People arriving by car at the museum's remote location in the hills at the northern edge of the exclusive Brentwood district must reserve parking ahead of time. Bus passengers can (and usually do) arrive without advance notice, but there is a slight risk of having to wait in line or, at especially busy periods, of being turned away (reservations are possible). For some, this may be the only experience riding a bus in L.A.

After that, things improve. Visitors are whisked up the hillside by a small railway that offers stunning city and valley views. They emerge on a broad plaza surrounded by gardens, terraces, and a cluster of buildings in white Italian travertine with glass and curved metal forming a harmonious blend of geometric shapes. The entrance pavilion offers a brief orientation film as well as activities for children.

The actual museum consists of a group of five two-story pavilions set around an open courtyard with trees, fountains and reflecting pools. Four are devoted to specific periods; the fifth houses rotating exhibitions. Other buildings house an auditorium, a café and restaurant, and the research institute, which presents exhibitions of rare books and other archival material. Between the museum and the research institute lies the central garden, designed by artist Robert Irwin, that combines trees, flowers and a cascading stream

The museum's permanent collection includes works gathered by Getty himself over nearly half a century as well as numerous acquisitions. Galleries vary enormously in size and lighting to suit the works they display. Many on the upper floor have sophisticated skylight systems. Some of the galleries containing French furniture and decorative arts include rooms with 18th-century wood panelling.

The European Paintings collection covers the 14th to 19th centuries and includes important works by Rembrandt, Titian, Rubens, Veronese, Cézanne, Van Gogh, Monet, Renoir and Manet. The Decorative Arts collection is one of the museum's strengths, with particular emphasis on French items from the mid-17th to early 19th centuries, includ-

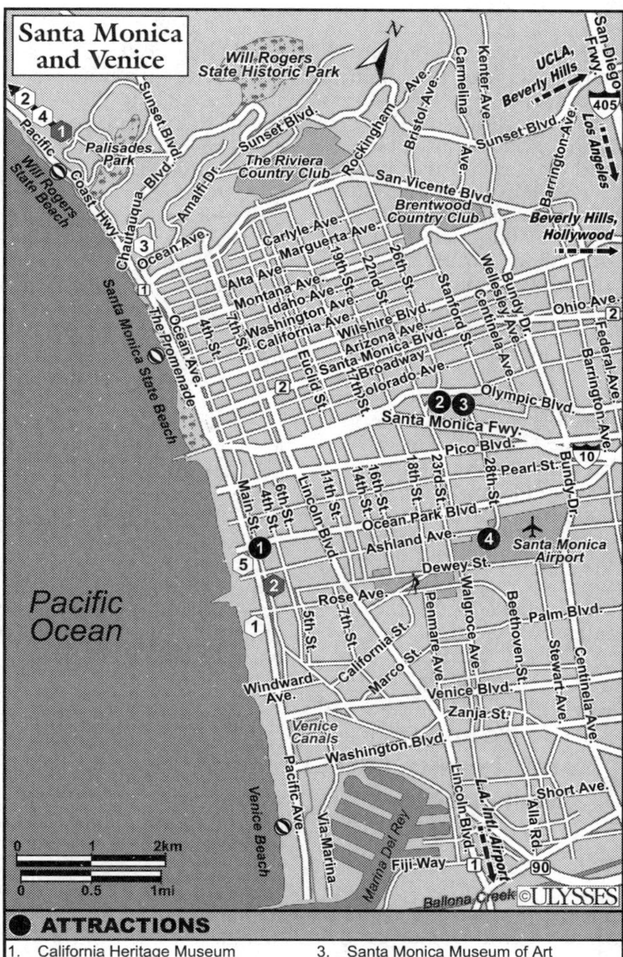

ATTRACTIONS

1. California Heritage Museum
2. Bergamot Station
3. Santa Monica Museum of Art
4. Museum of Flying

ACCOMMODATIONS

1. Cadillac Hotel
2. Casa Malibu Inn
3. Channel Road Inn
4. Malibu Beach Inn
5. Sea Shore Motel

RESTAURANTS

1. Neptune's Net
2. Schatzi on Main

ing furniture, tapestries, carpets, clocks, porcelain and chandeliers. The Drawings collection contains many works by Van Gogh and by earlier artists including Rubens and Leonardo. The Manuscripts collection features illuminated books from Ottoman, Byzantine and Gothic sources. Other collections include Photography and European Sculpture.

Items from the Getty Trust's very extensive collection of classic antiquities were to be exhibited at the Getty Villa in Malibu starting in 2002 once renovations there are complete. Prior to the opening of the Getty Center, the Getty Villa was the main repository for the other collections.

Tour E: Santa Monica and Surroundings

This is the area of Los Angeles that best fits so many Southern California clichés. Here we find broad beaches extending as far as the eye can see, merry crowds, surfers with beautiful bronzed bodies, muscle builders with rugged physical routines, rollerbladers with unimaginable body piercings and barely unimaginable hair colours, more sunglasses than you can shake a stick at, the *dolce vita* of casual café society and, something almost shocking in car-obsessed L.A., two lively but very different streets where cars are banned.

Santa Monica is best known for its beach, its famous pier and its eccentric local politics. Just a couple of blocks from the beach are bookshops and other outward signs of cerebral activity. Few places combine beaches and urban life quite the way Santa Monica does. Besides Santa Monica, this tour covers secluded Malibu to the west and zany Venice to the south. We'll begin in Malibu and follow the curvature of the coastline east and south from there.

Malibu, west of Santa Monica near the western edge of Los Angeles County, projects an image of a hedonistic lifestyle centred around beaches with unmatchable surf, perfect tanned bodies, superb sunsets and a relaxing sense that all is well with the world. It is also a community with large pockets of exclusive wealth and closely guarded enclaves (some of them blocking access to the beach). On a slightly ominous note, Malibu has figured in the head

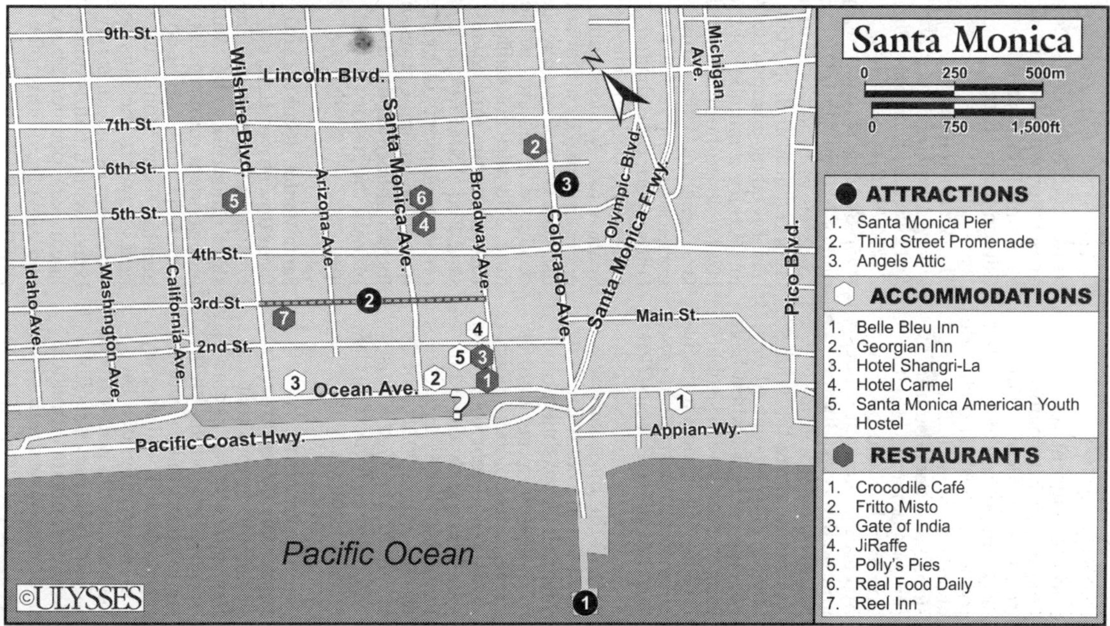

Santa Monica
0
250
500m
0
750
1,500ft
ATTRACTIONS
1. Santa Monica Pier
2. Third Street Promenade
3. Angels Attic
ACCOMMODATIONS
1. Belle Bleu Inn
2. Georgian Inn
3. Hotel Shangri-La
4. Hotel Carmel
5. Santa Monica American Youth Hostel
RESTAURANTS
1. Crocodile Café
2. Fritto Misto
3. Gate of India
4. JiRaffe
5. Polly's Pies
6. Real Food Daily
7. Reel Inn
9th St.
7th St.
6th St.
5th St.
4th St.
3rd St.
2nd St.
Lincoln Blvd.
Wilshire Blvd.
Arizona Ave.
Santa Monica Ave.
Broadway Ave.
Colorado Ave.
Olympic Blvd.
Santa Monica Frwy.
Michigan Ave.
Pico Blvd.
Main St.
Idaho Ave.
Washington Ave.
California Ave.
Ocean Ave.
Pacific Coast Hwy.
Appian Wy.
Pacific Ocean
N
©ULYSSES

lines over recent years in connection with natural disasters, particularly the late-summer brush fires that routinely ravish arid cliffside areas where exclusive mansions have been built in obvious defiance of nature. The area has also been hit by earthquakes, mudslides and tidal waves. But the many miles of natural splendour along the wild Pacific shore that are the very essence of Malibu have long proven an irresistible lure to visitors and residents alike. (For information on beaches, please see p 216).

One of the most famous local landmarks is the **Getty Villa**, which was the home of the Getty Center until its move to its splendid new quarters in Brentwood. The villa is currently closed to the public but is expected to reopen in 2002 as the venue for the Getty Trust's extensive collection of classical antiquities.

Another landmark is **Pepperdine University**, with a gorgeous campus that at first glance looks like an upper-crust country club, set in rolling hills overlooking the sea. The university has been denigrated by people on the political left, in part because of its links with conservative political and religious organizations. In 1998, the Pepperdine law school offered its deanship to Kenneth Starr, the special prosecutor who attempted to hound President Bill Clinton from office.

The **Adamson House** *($2; by guided tour only, Wed to Sat, first tour 11am, last tour 2pm; 23200 Pacific Coast Hwy., ☎456-8432)* is situated along one of Malibu's finest stretches of beach next to a lagoon that is an important bird-breeding ground. Built in 1928 for a member of the last family to hold a Spanish land grant in Malibu, this gorgeous house is set on a landscaped, pine-shaded estate. The building shows Spanish and Moorish influences and makes abundant use of a type of ceramic tile produced in the area at the time. The adjacent **Malibu Lagoon Museum** *(free admission; Wed to Sat 11am to 3pm)* presents elements of local history, including Chumash Indian artifacts and a display on the history of surfing.

Santa Monica, 13mi (21km) from downtown L.A., is what some people imagine all of California to be. An independent municipality with a strong sense of community, Santa Monica is best known to the outside world for its broad, sandy beach with a palm-fringed linear park perched above and a lively, alluring pier protruding into the surf. Sometimes denigrated as the People's Republic of Santa Monica by right-wing critics who are alternately appalled and amused by the municipal council's occasional forays into deep matters of social conscience (for example, homeless people are treated more humanely than in most other suburban areas), this is a place where an above-average number of people take politics seriously and where the candy floss atmosphere of the beach belies the existence of a more substantial side to local life. (Municipal boundaries do extend more than 30 blocks inland.)

Santa Monica has its own downtown area, extending from Ocean Avenue, parallel to the beach, east to Lincoln Boulevard, and from Pico Boulevard north to Wilshire Boulevard. In addition, interesting retail strips line Montana Avenue, a few blocks north, between Seventh and 20th streets, and Main Street from Pico Boulevard all the way south to Venice Beach. Main Street also features a large number of quaint cafés. An electric bus service called the Tide Shuttle *($0.25)* runs at 15min intervals afternoons and evenings between downtown Santa Monica and the Main Street area. The approximately 2mi (3km) between Santa Monica Pier and the heart of Venice Beach make for a wonderful stroll along a beachside footpath. A separate path accommodates cyclists and rollerbladers.

Santa Monica pier ★, at Ocean and Colorado avenues, was built in 1916 and is immediately recognizable by the large Ferris wheel standing guard near the entrance. This Ferris wheel, worth riding for the aerial views of Santa Monica and the Pacific shore, is part of a small amusement area called **Pacific Park** *(rides range from $1 to $4; hours vary by season; ☎260-8744)* that also includes a roller coaster and a beautifully restored carousel dating from 1922. The pier is quite enormous and houses many commercial establishments, including souvenir stalls, pinball arcades, and a variety of snack bars and restaurants with offerings ranging from hot dogs to seafood. It's also possible to rent fishing rods and try your luck right from the edge of the pier. In general, the atmosphere is lively and fun though just a bit tacky. In the summer, free concerts featuring top world musical artists *(☎458-9800)* are presented Thursday evenings starting at 7:30pm (arrive early to be near the stage).

Third Street Promenade ★★★ in downtown Santa Monica is one of North America's liveliest pedestrian-only streets. Covering three long blocks from Broadway to Wilshire Boulevard, the Third Street Promenade succeeds for a variety of reasons. Its mixture of businesses include many restaurants, cafés, cinemas, bookshops, music stores and other establishments that draw large crowds until late in the evening. It is designed with small kiosks, benches and other installations that facilitate pedestrian movement while palliating any sense of physical emptiness. Musicians and other street performers contribute to the vibrant atmosphere. This is justifiably one of the most popular streets in California and well worth a visit.

Angels Attic ★ *($6.50; Thu to Sun 12:30pm to 4:30pm; 516 Colorado Ave. near Fifth St., ☎394-8311)* is a museum of antique dollhouses set in a lovingly restored Victorian house. About 50 dollhouses are on display at any given time, along with toy trains, miniature animals and, of course, dolls.

California Heritage Museum *($3; Wed to Sat 11am to 4pm, Sun 10am to 4pm; 2612 Main St. at Ocean Park Blvd., ☎392-8537)*, set in a house built in 1894, presents late 19th-century decorative arts on the ground floor and rotating exhibitions on particular aspects of California history upstairs.

Bergamot Station ★ *(2525 Michigan Ave. near Olympic Blvd. and 26th St.; by bus: Santa Monica Rte. 5)* is a former transit station from the days when L.A. was served by an extensive tramway network. It was later expanded for industrial use and then abandoned. However, it reopened in 1994 after its ramshackle buildings were resurrected and redeveloped to house numerous art galleries, as well as some architecture and design offices. It has become a major hub in the L.A. art scene, with a number of the top local galleries as well as several smaller galleries specializing in particular types of art. A bright, attractive space in this same complex houses the **Santa Monica Museum of Art ★** *(suggested contribution $3; Wed to Sun 11am to 6pm, Fri until 10pm; ☎586-6488)*,

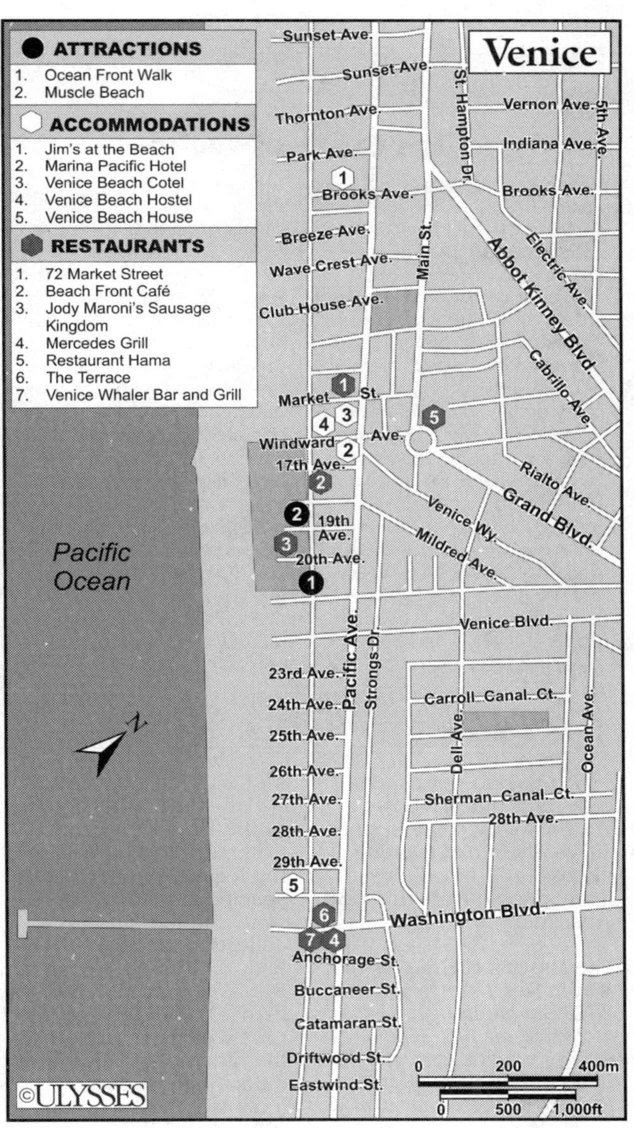
Venice
ATTRACTIONS
1. Ocean Front Walk
2. Muscle Beach
ACCOMMODATIONS
1. Jim's at the Beach
2. Marina Pacific Hotel
3. Venice Beach Cotel
4. Venice Beach Hostel
5. Venice Beach House
RESTAURANTS
1. 72 Market Street
2. Beach Front Café
3. Jody Maroni's Sausage Kingdom
4. Mercedes Grill
5. Restaurant Hama
6. The Terrace
7. Venice Whaler Bar and Grill
Pacific Ocean
Sunset Ave.
Sunset Ave.
Thornton Ave.
Park Ave.
Brooks Ave.
Breeze Ave.
Wave Crest Ave.
Club House Ave.
Market St.
Windward Ave.
17th Ave.
19th Ave.
20th Ave.
23rd Ave.
24th Ave.
25th Ave.
26th Ave.
27th Ave.
28th Ave.
29th Ave.
Anchorage St.
Buccaneer St.
Catamaran St.
Driftwood St.
Eastwind St.
Pacific Ave.
Strongs Dr.
Main St.
St. Hampton Dr.
Vernon Ave.
Indiana Ave.
Brooks Ave.
5th Ave.
Abbot Kinney Blvd.
Electric Ave.
Cabrillo Ave.
Rialto Ave.
Grand Blvd.
Venice Wy.
Mildred Ave.
Venice Blvd.
Carroll Canal Ct.
Dell Ave.
Ocean Ave.
Sherman Canal Ct.
28th Ave.
Washington Blvd.
N
0 200 400m
0 500 1,000ft
©ULYSSES

The Canals of Venice

The Canals of Venice takes its name from the city on Italy's Adriatic coast famed for its numerous canals. The marshland that once covered much of present-day Venice (the one on the Pacific coast) was drained at the turn of the 20th century by tobacco heir Abbot Kinney, who built a network of 16mi (26km) of canals. This was the foundation for what he hoped would become a centre of artistic and cultural inspiration for Americans. He even brought over gondoliers from Italy for the opening ceremonies in 1905, but his project soon floundered. A couple of decades later, with Venice in deep decay, most of the canals were paved over, though about 3mi (5km) of canals survive, still traversed by some of the original narrow bridges. These can be seen in the area east of Pacific Avenue and south of Venice Boulevard. What was until recent times a badly rundown residential area has undergone a quiet gentrification, and real estate values have soared. It would take a huge leap of imagination to see any resemblance to its Adriatic counterpart but, for anyone who cares to wander any distance from the beach, this corner of Venice provides a fascinating century-old reminder of California eccentricity.

which has no permanent collection but presents varied shows by contemporary artists. Its Friday evening discussion series draws many people from the local art scene.

The **Museum of Flying** ★ *($7; Wed to Sun 10am to 5pm; 2772 Donald Douglas Loop N. at 28th St. about 1,312ft or 400m east of Ocean Park Blvd.; by bus: Santa Monica Rte. 8; ☎392-8822, www.mof.org)* is located at Santa Monica municipal airport, which was the headquarters of the Douglas Aircraft Company and birthplace of the legendary DC-3. This specific airplane is represented in the museum's collection along with Spitfires, a Grumman Bearcat, a P-47 Thunderbolt and more than 20 other vintage aircraft which are sure to stir the blood of aviation history buffs. Some of these planes look as if they are ready to roll out and fly. Docents, some of them retired military pilots, are happy to show visitors around. For an extra $2, visitors can spend several minutes in a flight simulator. The museum also has an interactive children's section.

Venice, directly south of Santa Monica, is where individuals of all sorts come to see people who are just slightly weird—or to be a little weird themselves. For decades this has been L.A.'s haven of counterculture. People who were emblematic of the Beat generation of the 1950s, the hippie movement of the 1960s, and various cults and New Age trends since then have felt right at home along Venice's colourful shoreline. It's no different today.

Ocean Front Walk ★★★, also known as the Boardwalk (although there are no boards), is one of the zaniest, most effervescent, most kaleidoscopic, most carnivalesque spots in all of North America. Running alongside **Venice Beach** (and banned to vehicular traffic), this delightfully loopy pedestrian thoroughfare is a scene unto itself. Here you will find a colourful assortment of merchandise at the countless street stalls radiating from the corner of Ocean Front Walk and Windward Avenue—tie-dyed T-shirts, nose rings, amazing assortments of sunglasses, psychedelic posters, tattoos, palms readings, you name it. Nearby in a small area called **Muscle Beach**

In-line skates

between 17th and 18th streets, bodybuilders with gigantic muscles pump iron in a continuous show for all to see, next to the basketball and volleyball courts.

The architecture of the area's residential buildings, mostly two or three storeys high, is varied and distinct, forming an interesting backdrop to the beach from the northern tip of Venice all the way to Santa Monica. This lively thoroughfare is bustling with street performers, some of whom stretch the limits in ways that defy description. But more than anything, what makes this place unique is the passing parade of people who aren't there to perform, but who provide a

ATTRACTIONS	
1. Roundhouse Marine Studies Lab and Aquarium	

ACCOMMODATIONS	
1. Barnabey's	6. Marina International Hotel & Bungalows
2. Beach House at Hermosa	7. Moonlite Inn
3. Continental Plaza Hotel Los Angeles	8. Sea Sprite Motel
4. Crowne Plaza Los Angeles Airport	9. Skyways Airport Hotel
5. Grandview Motor Hotel	10. Travelodge at LAX

RESTAURANTS	
1. Le Beaujolais	5. Kincaid's Bay House
2. Encounter at LAX	6. Reed's
3. Fun Fish Market	7. The Kettle
4. Good Stuff	8. Tony's

constant pageant of wild clothing, improbable hair colours, dazzling bikinis, rippling muscles, peculiar sunglasses, or just about anything else to make themselves stand out.

The scene is especially lively on weekend afternoons, when middle-class visitors and their children come to watch the local fauna strut their stuff, creating almost a spontaneous symbiosis with them. There is also a broad sandy beach, a long cycling trail, and the footpath up to Santa Monica. **Windward Avenue**, perpendicular to Ocean Front Walk in the centre of the action, is interesting for its arcaded sidewalks, its murals, and its assortment of cafés and bars.

Tour F: South Bay and Surroundings

This tour takes us along the Pacific shoreline from Marina del Rey south to Palos Verdes. It includes the area around Los Angeles International Airport as well as the communities of Manhattan Beach, Hermosa Beach and Redondo Beach, which together form an area known as South Bay. Here we find great expanses of beach, some of it excellent for surfing, along with some of those famous Pacific sunsets. In terms of cultural stimulation, however, this area is decidedly tepid.

Marina del Rey, extending from Venice in the north to the community of Playa del

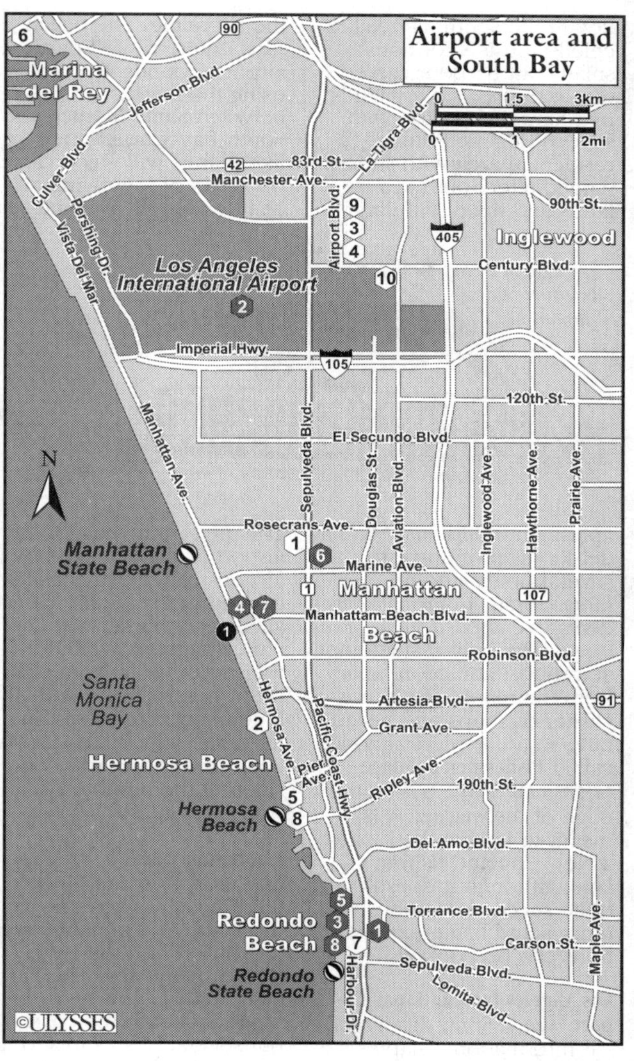

Airport area and South Bay
0 1.5 3km
0 1 2mi
Marina del Rey
Jefferson Blvd.
Culver Blvd.
La Tigra Blvd.
83rd St.
Manchester Ave.
90th St.
Inglewood
Century Blvd.
Airport Blvd.
Pershing Dr.
Vista Del Mar
Los Angeles International Airport
Imperial Hwy.
120th St.
El Secundo Blvd.
Manhattan Ave.
Sepulveda Blvd.
Douglas St.
Aviation Blvd.
Inglewood Ave.
Hawthorne Ave.
Prairie Ave.
N
Rosecrans Ave.
Manhattan State Beach
Marine Ave.
Manhattan Beach
Manhattam Beach Blvd.
Robinson Blvd.
Santa Monica Bay
Hermosa Ave.
Pacific Coast Hwy.
Artesia Blvd.
Grant Ave.
Hermosa Beach
Pier Ave
Ripley Ave.
190th St.
Hermosa Beach
Del Amo Blvd.
Torrance Blvd.
Redondo Beach
Carson St.
Maple Ave.
Sepulveda Blvd.
Redondo State Beach
Harbour Dr.
Lomita Blvd.
©ULYSSES

Rey in the south, is notable chiefly for its enormous small-craft harbour carved out of the coastal lowlands in a hand-like shape with several fingers. Primarily a residential area with streets named after South Sea islands and lined with large

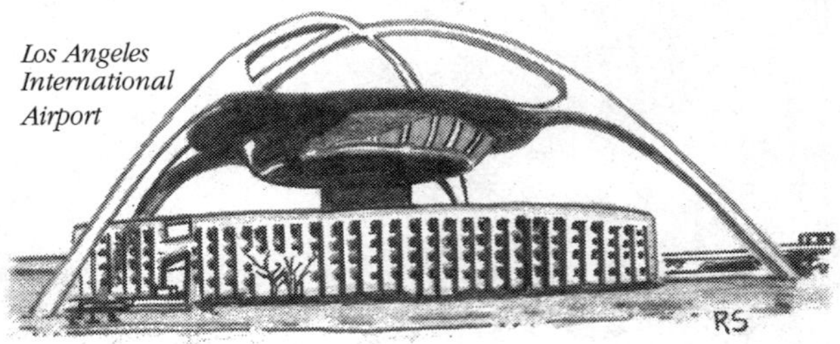

Los Angeles International Airport

apartment buildings, Marina del Rey is also home to several hotels and restaurants. Some additional residents live aboard their boats. The only real attempt at a tourist attraction, apart from the marina itself, is a cluster of shops and restaurants in a commercial zone called **Fishermen's Village** *(13755 Fiji Way)*. Set by the edge of the marina, it is meant to imitate the look of a New England fishing village, although it doesn't quite succeed. Harbour cruises and fishing expeditions can be booked here.

Los Angeles International Airport (see p 58 in the "Practical Information" chapter) covers a vast area extending almost—but not quite—to the shoreline. The beach runs uninterrupted past the airport grounds. Cyclists using the beachside trail between Santa Monica and South Bay who happen to like planes will enjoy close-up views of low-flying aircraft taking off over the sea.

The area to the east of the airport is characterized by airport-related activities. On the southern side are cargo sheds and aircraft maintenance hangars, while further north lies a large cluster of hotels. There is really little of special interest in this area, which has surprisingly few restaurants considering the number of overnight guests.

Manhattan Beach is the first, and most upscale, of the three beach towns that form the South Bay area between the airport and the Palos Verdes Peninsula. The Pacific Coast Highway, running parallel to the coast but several blocks inland, is the principal thoroughfare in the mainly residential

The beaches on the coast of L.A.—Santa Monica, Malibu and Venice—are covered with the tanned, muscle-bound sun-worshippers for which California is famous. - *Michele & Tom Grimm/LACVB*

Since its creation in 1960, the Hollywood Walk of Fame has mmortalized more than 2,000 actors and musicians with small, black-and-gold plaques along Hollywood Boulevard. - *Anne Gardon*

Los Angeles stretches along the Pacific coast from Ventura County, northeast of the city, to Orange County in the southeast, reaching out to the mountains and desert. - *Arnesen Photography/LACVB*

Los Angeles spreads out as far as the eye can see, when viewed from the terrace of the Griffith Observatory, perched on the Hollywood Hills - *Arnesen Photography/LACVB*

South Bay area, distinguished by its long, wide strand of superb sandy beach, replete with the trademark California symbols of surfers and volleyball players, especially on summer weekends, when the beach can be quite crowded (and parking hard to find). By bus, the best bet is MTA route 439 from downtown L.A. via the LAX Transit Center (near the airport) and the Green Line's Aviation station, despite the infrequent service (only once an hour, slightly more often during weekday rush hours). Pedestrian and cycling paths run for many miles along the edge of the beach.

In Manhattan Beach itself, the main perpendicular thoroughfare is Manhattan Beach Boulevard, which is lined with boutiques and restaurants, ending in a long pier. Near the tip of this pier is the **Roundhouse Marine Studies Lab and Aquarium** *(voluntary contribution; Mon to Fri 3pm to sunset, Sat to Sun 10am to sunset; Manhattan Beach Pier, ☎379-8117)*, with several aquarium tanks of interest mainly to children.

Hermosa Beach is a traditional rival to Manhattan Beach. Long considered a more casual and youth-oriented spot, Hermosa Beach has gradually become move upscale, as some of the grand new beachfront villas suggest. It too has its pier, about 1.5mi (2.5km) south of its Manhattan Beach counterpart. The Hermosa Beach pier is an extension of Pier Avenue, whose intersection with the beach has been converted to an attractive pedestrian-only area with numerous snack bars, cafés, restaurants and shops.

Redondo Beach, regarded as a more family-oriented leisure spot, was also a commercial seaport for a brief time, until fierce storms destroyed the main wharf in the early 20th century. A small marina is perched near the north end of this community. Closer to the centre of town, at the end of Torrance Avenue, are Monstad Pier and Fishermen's Wharf, two large and not especially attractive piers that meet at the seaward end. Both house numerous souvenir shops, restaurants and bars, as well as a fishing dock.

Further south lies the **Palos Verdes** Peninsula, where the beach gives way to high bluffs with surf pounding below. Although housing (mostly quite exclusive) has been built in inland zones, this area is surprisingly undeveloped, with only traces of urban influence. A scenic roadway called **Palos Verdes Drive ★** runs near the perimeter, linking Redondo Beach to the north and San Pedro to the east. Along this drive lies the **Point Vicente Interpretative Center** ★ *($2; every day 10am to 5pm, summer until 7pm; 31501 Palos Verdes Dr. W., ☎377-5370).* Marked by a lighthouse, this spot features displays on local history but is most interesting as an observation point for the grey whales that pass here on their annual migration between the Arctic and northwestern Mexico (south from December to February, north from February to April).

The **Wayfarers Chapel** *(free admission; every day 7am to 5pm; 5755 Palos Verdes Dr. W., ☎377-1650)* is something of a curiosity. A high glass structure built in 1949 by the Swedenborgian church to resemble the surrounding redwoods and pines, it forms an enchanting setting and is a popular spot for weddings.

The **South Coast Botanic Garden** ★ *($5; every day 9am to 5pm; 26300 Crenshaw Blvd., ☎544-6815)* is built on a reclaimed garbage dump and is often cited as an imaginative example of land recycling. Its 150,000 plants representing 2,000 species include many from southern Africa, Australia and the Mediterranean. Bisected by a stream, it has several specialized gardens, among them a cactus garden and a fuchsia garden.

Tour G: Long Beach and Surroundings

The southern tip of Los Angeles County, bound by the Palos Verdes Peninsula

● ATTRACTIONS	
1. Warner Grand Theater	6. Fort MacArthur Military Museum
2. Los Angeles Maritime Museum	7. Long Beach Aquarium of the Pacific
3. Cabrillo Marine Aquarium	8. Queen Mary
4. Point Fermin Park	9. Museum of Latin American Art
5. Korean Friendship Bell	10. Long Beach Museum of Art

ACCOMMODATIONS	
1. Hilton – Port of Los Angeles / San Pedro	5. Lord Mayor's Inn
2. Hostelling International – Los Angeles South Bay	6. Pacific Inn
3. Hotel Queen Mary	7. Renaissance Long Beach Hotel
4. Inn of Long Beach	8. The Turret House
	9. Vagabond Inn

RESTAURANTS	
1. Alegria Cocina Latina	4. Shenandoah Café
2. Belmont Brewery Company	5. Sky Room
3. Dragon House Restaurant	6. Taco Company

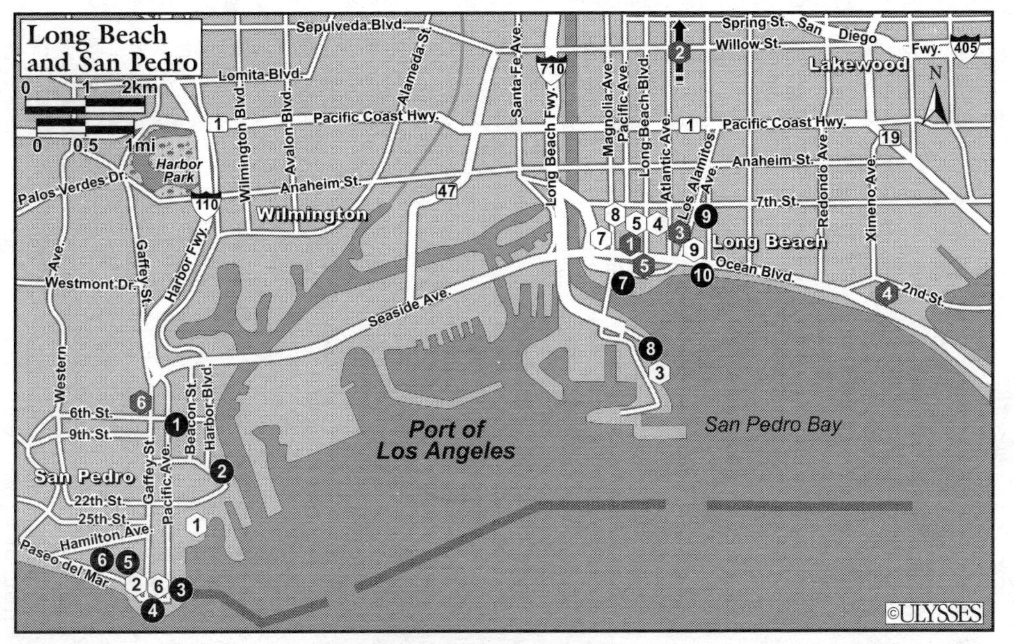

Long Beach and San Pedro
0 1 2km
0 0.5 1mi
Sepulveda Blvd.
Lomita Blvd.
Alameda St.
Santa Fe Ave.
Spring St.
San Diego Fwy.
Willow St.
405
Lakewood
N
710
Pacific Coast Hwy.
Wilmington Blvd.
Avalon Blvd.
Long Beach Fwy.
Magnolia Ave.
Pacific Ave.
Long Beach Blvd.
Atlantic Ave.
Los Alamitos Ave.
Redondo Ave.
Ximeno Ave.
Anaheim St.
7th St.
Harbor Park
Palos Verdes Dr.
110
47
19
Wilmington
Long Beach
Ocean Blvd.
2nd St.
Harbor Fwy.
Western Ave.
Westmont Dr.
Gaffey St.
Seaside Ave.
6th St.
9th St.
Beacon St.
Harbor Blvd.
Pacific Ave.
San Pedro
22th St.
25th St.
Hamilton Ave.
Paseo del Mar
Port of Los Angeles
San Pedro Bay
©ULYSSES

to the west and Orange County to the east and south, is serious commercial-port territory. The twin ports of San Pedro and Long Beach are the busiest in the western United States, and parts of their massive installations can be seen from the high Vincent Thomas Bridge that links the two. Both of these communities, known mainly for their carefully zoned residential and industrial areas, also attempt to draw tourists, though some of the offerings may seem rather bland with the exception of two truly outstanding aquariums, the Cabrillo Aquarium in San Pedro and the Aquarium of the Pacific in Long Beach. The latter also includes a pair of interesting art museums. Santa Catalina Island (often locally referred to simply as Catalina Island) lies 22mi (35km) offshore and provides an interesting getaway.

San Pedro, about 22mi (35km) south of downtown L.A., is a largely working-class area of broad ethnic diversity noted chiefly for the vast marine installations officially designated as the Port of Los Angeles. Pacific Avenue, an unremarkable commercial street, is the main thoroughfare in downtown San Pedro. It does have at least one interesting building, however, the 1,500-seat **Warner Grand Theater** *(478 W. Sixth St. at Pacific Ave.)*, with its huge neon sign, opulent Art Deco lobby, and intricate wood carvings. Rescued by the City of Los Angeles (to which San Pedro was annexed in 1909) and reopened in 1996, this theatre is open only for special performances. Gaffey Street, a couple of blocks west, is another important thoroughfare.

The **Los Angeles Maritime Museum** ★★ *($1; Tue to Sun 10am to 5pm; Berth 84 at the foot of Sixth St., ☎548-7618)* fills seven galleries in the former Municipal Ferry building and portrays contemporary port activity as well as various aspects of the nautical past. Displays include models of more than 700 vessels, including an 18ft (5.5m) replica of the *Titanic*, with a detailed cutaway view of the interior. Among other vessels similarly showcased are the *Golden Hind*, the *Bounty*, the *USS Constitution* ("Old Ironsides") and the *Poseidon*. The museum also has a floating collection of real vessels as well as displays of seafaring artifacts and memorabilia. **Ports O'Call Village**, just south of the Maritime Museum, is a forgettable tourist trap where souvenirs and snacks are sold at numerous stalls in a silly attempt to recreate a

New England fishing village.

One of the biggest draws in San Pedro is the **Cabrillo Marine Aquarium** ★ *(free admission; parking $6.50; Tue to Fri noon to 5pm, Sat to Sun 10am to 5pm; 3720 Stephen White Dr. off Pacific Ave., ☎548-2631)*, located next to Cabrillo Beach near the southeastern tip of San Pedro. Built in 1981, the aquarium doesn't compare in size to the newer Aquarium of the Pacific in Long Beach, but it does contain 38 saltwater tanks displaying a broad variety of marine habitats, with many colourful fish as well as birds and marine mammals. Special children's programs are offered.

A few blocks southwest, **Point Fermin Park** covers a large cliffside area above the shore and the tide pools that form a sanctuary for marine life. The park provides good vantage points for views of the ocean below, with migrating grey whales passing close by, and the port installations to the east. Besides picnic grounds and footpaths, it boasts a picturesque lighthouse built in 1874. Further up the hill is **Angel's Gate Park**, site of the **Korean Friendship Bell** ★. Weighing 16.7 tons (17 tonnes), this U.S. bicentennial gift from the Korean government, installed here in 1976, is sheltered by a colourful and ornate pagoda-style structure. What is perhaps most attractive about this site is its pervasive sense of tranquility, with the ocean stretching out below. Also located in this park is the **Fort MacArthur Military Museum** *(free admission; Tue, Thu, Sat, Sun noon to 5pm; ☎548-2631)*, housed in a military installation built in 1916 to watch for enemy attacks. Exhibits portray the defence of Los Angeles harbour and various civilian and military aspects of the war effort. Visitors can also see an artillery battery.

Long Beach is a prim community with a picture-perfect, pedestrian-friendly downtown area that often looks as if a neutron bomb had hit. Everything is clean and tidy, and big money went into refurbishing the waterfront following the closing of a naval base. Despite this, somehow it all seems peculiarly lifeless, as if it were early Sunday morning all week long. All the same, Long Beach does attract a sizable number of visitors (but why do so many of them seem invisible?), drawn to the numerous meetings held at the gargantuan convention centre, as well as to the Aquarium of the Pacific and Queen Mary Seaport.

Downtown Long Beach lies just east of where the diminutive Los Angeles River flows into the Pacific. Ocean Boulevard runs parallel to the shore across the entire length of Long Beach. Shoreline Drive runs a little closer to the shore in the downtown area, while Pine Avenue is a major perpendicular street, lined with many shops and restaurants over a stretch of several blocks extending up to Sixth Street. Long Beach Boulevard runs parallel, one block further east. The free Passport shuttle bus service operates along four routes, connecting all major attractions with each other and with parking areas. The Long Beach Freeway, bearing route number 710, links Long Beach and downtown L.A. Another way to reach Long Beach from downtown Los Angeles is the Blue Line light rail system, which has its southern terminus in downtown Long Beach. There is no bus or rail service to Long Beach Airport.

Opened in 1998, **Long Beach Aquarium of the Pacific ★★** *($14.95; every day 9:30am to 6pm; 100 Aquarium Way, off Shoreline Dr., ☎562-590-0, www.aquariumofpacific.org)*, is distinguished from the outside by its curved glass walls and undulating roofline. Nearly 1,000,000 gallons (more than 3,000,000L) of sea water fill the 17 major habitat tanks and the 30 smaller "focus tanks" that together house more than 550 species of marine life. Using a familiar U.S. metaphor, the aquarium's exhibition space is supposedly the size of three football fields. Visitors enter by the Great Hall of the Pacific and are wowed by a full-scale model of a blue whale, our planet's largest creature. Three distinct parts of the Pacific are represented in the temperate Southern California and Baja section, the frigid Northern Pacific and Bering Strait section, and the warm Tropical Pacific section. Simulated waves and special sound and atmospheric effects add to the experience. Charming marine mammals such as sea otters can be seen alongside sharks, barracudas and giant spider crabs, who also share quarters with many of the sea's smaller and meeker creatures.

Long Beach's other landmark tourist attraction is the ***Queen Mary*** ★★ *($15; every day 10am to 6pm, until later in summer; Pier J, 1126 Queens Hwy., ☎562-435-3511, www.queenmary.com).* This great relic of the golden era of trans-Atlantic crossings, launched in 1934 and weighing in at more than 71,832 tons (73,000 tonnes), easily qualifies as a shameless tourist trap. Indeed, she has drawn in suckers by the millions since she was moored permanently at Long Beach in 1967, three years after her retirement from service. But this is as close as most of us will ever get to reliving the special ambiance of a bygone period. From lavish hardwood-panelled staterooms to the stunning Art Deco observation lounge, she is a statement in splendour and elegance. With her 12 decks and her 984ft (300m) length, she was the largest passenger vessel of her time. The vessel houses a 385-room hotel and countless gift shops. A former Soviet submarine moored next to the *Queen Mary* can be visited for an extra charge.

The **Museum of Latin American Art** ★ *($5; Tue to Sat 11:30am to 7:30pm, Sun noon to 6pm; 628 Alamitos Ave. at Sixth St., ☎562-437-1689)* has a small permanent collection focussing mostly on contemporary artists and also offers a continuing series of temporary exhibitions. Housed a few blocks northeast of downtown Long Beach in a former roller skating rink dating from 1920, the museum makes an effort to achieve geographic diversity and to move away from the Mexican dominance of the Latin American art scene in the United States. The museum includes a book and crafts shop as well as a small restaurant with a delightful outdoor terrace and a menu reflecting this same geographic diversity. Several private art galleries are located nearby.

Queen Mary

The **Long Beach Museum of Art** ★ *($2; Wed to Sun 10am to 5pm, Fri until 8pm; 2300 E. Ocean Blvd. between Junipero and Temple aves., ☎562-439-2119)* focuses on works by contemporary California artists and has developed a reputation for experimental video works, although the exhibition program is far broader than this may suggest. The museum is housed in a historical mansion on a bluff overlooking the Pacific Ocean a few blocks east of downtown Long Beach.

Tour H: The San Fernando Valley

The cities of Burbank, Glendale, Van Nuys, Encino, Sherman Oaks, Panorama City and San Fernando are an integral part of the San Fernando Valley, which is simply known to Angelinos as "The Valley." Ringed by the Santa Monica Mountains to the south and the San Gabriel Mountains to the east, the Valley covers a surface area of 220 sq mi (570km^2) and is home to 1.5 million people. The temperature here is usually a few degrees higher than in LA, which undoubtedly explains the blanket of smog that shrouds the area throughout most of the year. This was also the epicentre of the earthquake that shook Los Angeles in January of 1994.

But the San Fernando Valley is first and foremost the kingdom of suburbanites. Middle-class families find everything they're looking for here: a place where it's still possible to believe in the "American Dream" of owning a bungalow with a swimming pool, two-car garage and surrounding land. Indeed, the region is largely made up of a series of neighbourhoods with single-family dwellings, shopping malls and highways that link the Valley with the rest of the metropolis. The car, a must in the suburbs, is elevated to cult status. Drive-ins, where the hoi polloi can watch a movie, eat burgers and even receive communion (!) without ever having to leave the seat of their precious cars, have sprung up everywhere around here.

All this may explain why the citizens of downtown L.A. love to deride the lifestyle of Valley residents. But these same people would be well advised to remember that most Hollywood television and movie studios have set up shop here and that the Valley is home to an ever-growing number of gourmet restaurants and one of the most important historic sites in all L.A., the

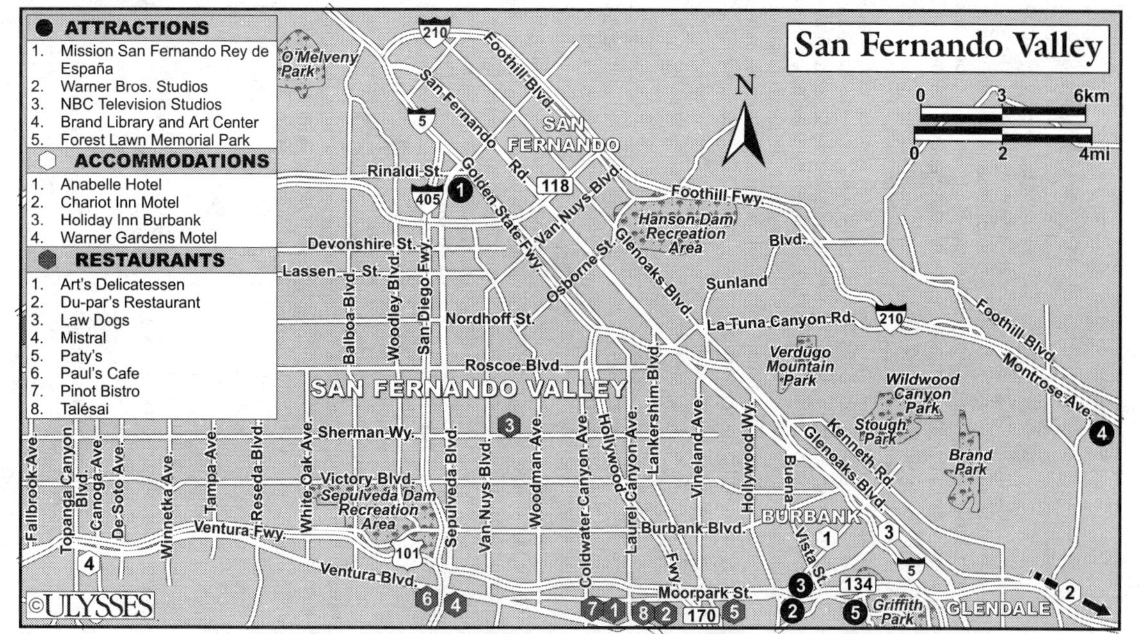
San Fernando Valley
ATTRACTIONS
1. Mission San Fernando Rey de España
2. Warner Bros. Studios
3. NBC Television Studios
4. Brand Library and Art Center
5. Forest Lawn Memorial Park
ACCOMMODATIONS
1. Anabelle Hotel
2. Chariot Inn Motel
3. Holiday Inn Burbank
4. Warner Gardens Motel
RESTAURANTS
1. Art's Delicatessen
2. Du-par's Restaurant
3. Law Dogs
4. Mistral
5. Paty's
6. Paul's Cafe
7. Pinot Bistro
8. Talésai
N
0 3 6km
0 2 4mi
SAN FERNANDO
SAN FERNANDO VALLEY
BURBANK
GLENDALE
O'Melveny Park
Hanson Dam Recreation Area
Verdugo Mountain Park
Wildwood Canyon Park
Stough Park
Brand Park
Sepulveda Dam Recreation Area
Griffith Park
Foothill Blvd.
San Fernando Rd.
Golden State Fwy.
Van Nuys Blvd.
Rinaldi St.
Foothill Fwy.
Glenoaks Blvd.
Osborne St.
Devonshire St.
Lassen St.
Sunland Blvd.
La Tuna Canyon Rd.
Nordhoff St.
Roscoe Blvd.
Montrose Ave.
Kenneth Rd.
Sherman Wy.
Victory Blvd.
Ventura Fwy.
Ventura Blvd.
Burbank Blvd.
Hollywood Fwy.
Moorpark St.
Vista St.
Buena
Fallbrook Ave.
Topanga Canyon Blvd.
Canoga Ave.
De Soto Ave.
Winnetka Ave.
Tampa Ave.
Reseda Blvd.
White Oak Ave.
Balboa Blvd.
Woodley Blvd.
San Diego Fwy.
Sepulveda Blvd.
Van Nuys Blvd.
Woodman Ave.
Coldwater Canyon Ave.
Laurel Canyon Ave.
Lankershim Blvd.
Vineland Ave.
Hollywood Wy.
210
5
405
118
101
170
134
©ULYSSES

Mission San Fernando Rey de España.

The foundation of the mission by Spanish friars in 1797 marked the beginning of local history. But it wasn't until 1870 that the region benefited from a first wave of expansion with the subdivision of Spanish concessions and the arrival of the railway. In 1905, major housing projects were developed on land that had hitherto merely consisted of simple orange groves. And that was all it took to bring on a real-estate boom unprecedented in the history of Los Angeles, which in turn gave rise to a major population boom.

In 1924, a host of world-renowned movie studios radically transformed the local economy. Universal, Warner Bros., Columbia and other studios gradually left Hollywood to settle in the San Fernando Valley. After World War II, the aeronautical industry diversified the local economy, consequently attracting many middle-class families. Bolstered by their numbers, these families created a region that met all their needs, namely the present-day San Fernando Valley.

This tour has been mapped out for visitors with cars. To reach the Mission, where the tour begins, take the Hollywood Freeway (US 101, then CA 170) or the Golden State Freeway (I-5) east of downtown, which links up with the Glendale Freeway, then the Colorado and Hollywood freeways.

Established in 1797 and named after King Ferdinand III of Spain, the **Mission San Fernando Rey de España ★★** *($4; every day 9am to 4:30pm; 15151 San Fernando Mission Blvd.; in San Fernando, take the Brand Blvd. Exit, which runs west to Mission Blvd., ☎818-361-0186)* is the 17th of California's 21 missions. Inspired by Spanish monasteries, but more specifically modelled after those of Mexico, the mission's complex is set around a large quadrangle and includes a long, narrow church. The courtyard's arcaded structures once housed the friars' living quarters (*convento*), barracks, workshops, an infirmary and buildings set aside for single Native American women and children. The resident Franciscans manufactured adobes, bricks of very abundant black clay, their main building material. The adobe bricks were made by mixing straw in with the clay and filling moulds that were then sun-dried.

Long neglected after the friars' departure in 1846, and twice destroyed by earthquakes (in 1818 and

1971), the mission's passage through time is nothing short of miraculous. The gardens and buildings alike have been magnificently restored, notably the workrooms and the monastery, with its Roman-style arches and hand-painted Native American motifs. The church features 16th-century reredos (ornamental screens) covered in gold-leaf, located behind the alter.

Six Flags Magic Mountain ★ *(a pass offers unlimited access to all attractions; 2610 Magic Mountain Pkwy., ☎805-255-4111)*, an amusement park located 9mi (14km) north of the mission via the I-5, at the Valencia Exit, is just the place for thrill-seekers and family outings. Indeed, 200 acres (80ha) of attractions, shows and rides await young and old alike here. Its famous roller-coasters are among the highest and fastest in the world (Riddle's Revenge, Colossus), including one (Superman: The Escape) that takes you from 0 to 100mph (160km/h) in seven seconds. Other attractions accessible to all include a wild "white-water" ride in hollowed-out logs, a bobsled run and a mini-car racetrack.

Burbank is reached via the Golden State Freeway (I-5), Warner Boulevard Exit.

Burbank, the largest city in the eastern part of the San Fernando Valley, has a population of over 100,000. Shored up by the presence of many movie studios, it describes itself as the nation's entertainment centre, indeed the new Hollywood. The local economy, however, has relied on the aerospace industry since the 1930s, when the Lockheed Aircraft Corporation set up shop near the Burbank Airport.

Warner Bros. Studios ★★ *($30, 2hr guided tours, Mon to Fri 9am to 3:30pm, children under eight years of age are not admitted; 4000 Warner Blvd., reservations required, ☎818-972-8687)*, founded in 1925, have produced and continue to produce hit TV series (*ER*, *Friends*) and movies (*Jurassic Park*, *Came-*

lot). A sign of the times, the studios are now occupied by independent producers. Warner Bros. features 34 sound stages employing close to 3,000 people. On the guided tour, don't expect demonstrations of special effects peppered with pyrotechnics, but rather a unique opportunity to get a behind-the-scenes look at a genuine studio. Among other things, you'll get the chance to explore exterior sets used in various film shoots, including a small southern town, a New York street used in some 200 shows and movies, a jungle and an Old West outpost with saloon.

NBC Television Studios ★ *($7, 70min guided tours; Mon to Fri 9am to 3pm; 3000 W. Alameda Ave., reservations required, ☎818-840-3538)*, home to one of the leading American TV stations, are reached via Olive Avenue, past the Ventura Freeway. These studios are now strictly reserved for television, but nevertheless contain recording studios and technical services akin to those of movie studios. Visitors can attend a taping of *The Tonight Show*, one of the most popular TV talk shows in the country.

To reach Glendale, take San Fernando Road at the junction of the Golden State and Ventura freeways and head downtown to Glendale Avenue.

Though only founded in 1883, **Glendale** is now the third largest city in L.A. County. Glendale's development only started with the extension of the Pacific Electric Railway in 1904, which drew hundreds of newcomers to the city. Today, the city is a true melting pot, with the largest Armenian community in California.

Forest Lawn Memorial Park ★★ *(free admission; every day 9am to 5pm; 1712 S. Glendale Ave., ☎818-241-4151)* is probably one of the most impressive cemeteries in the entire country. Spread out over four different locations in the city of Los Angeles—the one in Glendale being by far the grandest—this public-park-like haven of peace was created by Dr. Hubert Eaton. It is the final resting place of a host of celebrities, including Clark Gable, Jean Harlow and Nat King Cole. These the grave sites cannot be visited, however, as they are located in extravagant mausoleums strictly off-limits to the general public, some of which feature reproductions of art masterpieces.

During your visit, be sure to check out the **Great Mausoleum**, where scores of

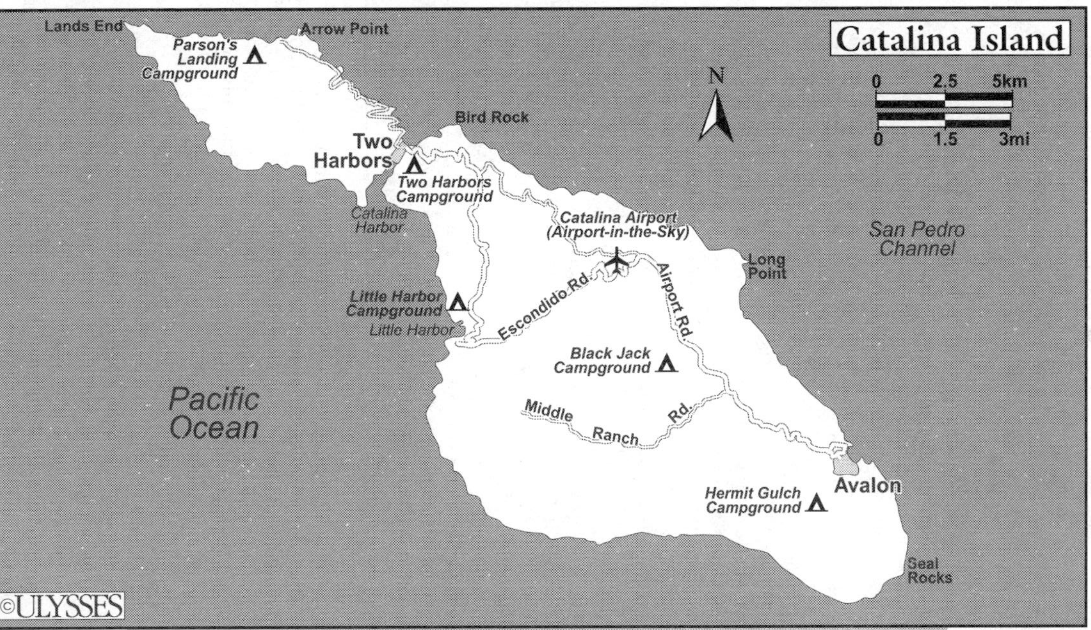

Catalina Island
0
2.5
5km
0
1.5
3mi
N
Lands End
Arrow Point
Parson's Landing Campground
Bird Rock
Two Harbors
Two Harbors Campground
Catalina Harbor
Catalina Airport (Airport-in-the-Sky)
San Pedro Channel
Long Point
Little Harbor Campground
Little Harbor
Escondido Rd.
Airport Rd.
Black Jack Campground
Pacific Ocean
Middle Ranch Rd.
Avalon
Hermit Gulch Campground
Seal Rocks
©ULYSSES

American artists and writers rest in peace. To get there, take Cathedral Drive, located behind the administrative buildings. Inside the chapel are various reproductions of Renaissance masterpieces. First and foremost among these is Rosa Caselli Moretti's stained-glass recreation of Leonardo Da Vinci's ***Last Supper*** (Milan), as well as replicas of Michelangelo's ***Moses***, ***Pieta*** and statues from the Medici chapel (Florence). Farther along, a statue of George Washington stands in front of the **Freedom Mausoleum**, while the Court of David features a reproduction of Michelangelo's ***David***. Finally, Jan Styka's ***Crucifixion***, on display every hour in the Hall of the Crucifixion-Resurrection, is nothing less than the world's largest religious painting.

Take the Glendale Freeway and get off at Verdugo Boulevard, west of Pasadena, or follow the Pasadena-bound Ventura Freeway.

Brand Park, located northeast of Glendale, is home to the **Brand Library and Art Center** *(Tue to Thu 1pm to 6pm, Fri and Sat 1pm to 5pm; 1601 W. Mountain St., ☎818-548-2051)*, which houses over 50,000 books devoted to art and music. Reminiscent of the Taj Mahal, the building is inspired by the East Indian pavilion at the 1893 World Exposition in Chicago. Brand Park also features a fine example of Queen Anne-style architecture: the **Doctor's House** *(☎818-548-2147)*, dating from 1880. Surrounding these unique buildings are the magnificent **Descanso Gardens** *(every day 9am to 4:30pm; 1418 Descanso Dr., La Cañada)*, which feature more than 100,000 slips of 600 different kinds of camellias (in flower from October to May) as well as azaleas and over 1,700 varieties of roses. While here, be sure to visit the teahouse, nestled in a very Zen Japanese garden awash in ponds and waterfalls *(Feb to Nov on weekends)*.

Tour I: Catalina Island

Santa Catalina, more commonly known as Catalina Island, is one of the largest of the Channel Islands archipelago, a partially submerged chain of mountains that extends from Santa Barbara to San Diego. Catalina is also a favourite getaway destination for Angelinos and other day-trippers seeking a relaxing respite from smog-ridden LA. Located just an hour's ferry ride from Long Beach, the island has much to offer travellers in search of exoticism.

Catalina Island lies 22mi (35km) off Long Beach and is easily reached by ferry. **Catalina Express** *($38 return; reservations required in summer and on weekends; take Hwy. 710 toward the* Queen Mary *and follow the signs,*

Catalina Island Casino

☎519-1212 or 800-995-4386) offers ferry service from Long Beach or San Pedro *(take Hwy. 110, Harbour Blvd. Exit toward the Catalina Terminal)* to Avalon in 60min. **Catalina Cruises** *($25 return; ☎800-228-2546)* offers more affordable passenger service to the island from Long Beach, San Pedro or Redondo Beach. Those with deep pockets can also get here by helicopter with **Island Express** *($121 return; ☎510-2535).*

First-time visitors will undoubtedly fall under the spell of this charming place. Coasts studded with sheer cliffs, verdant mountains, canyons, bays and beaches are just a few of the beautiful assets with which the island beguiles visitors. Thousands of nature lovers discover or rediscover Santa Catalina every year. Some come for the hiking, to get a glimpse of what California might look like in a primal state, while others prefer to practise scuba diving in the exceptionally crystalline waters. Indeed, this island offers some of the most gorgeous diving spots in the world. Lastly, scores of vacationers end up here to revel in the Mediterranean-like beauty of **Avalon ★★**, the island's port of entry.

While exploring California in 1542, Don Juan Rodríguez Cabrillo became the first European to discern the aesthetic harmony of the island, where he met Native Americans who had lived

ATTRACTIONS	
1. Green Pleasure Pier	5. The Wolfe House
2. Catalina Island Visitor's Bureau	6. Zane Grey Pueblo
3. Casino	7. Inn on Mt. Ada
4. Wrigley Memorial and Botanical Gardens	

ACCOMMODATIONS	
1. Hermit Gulch Campground	4. The Inn on Mt. Ada
2. Hermosa Hotel & Cottages	5. Seaport Village Inn
3. Hotel Metropole	6. Zane Grey Pueblo Hotel

RESTAURANTS	
1. Busy Bee Cafe	5. The Clubhouse
2. Cafe Prego	6. Mi Casita
3. Casino Dock Cafe	7. Pancake Cottage
4. Channel House	8. Ristorante Villa Portofino

here for more than 7,000 years in the manner of their continental brothers and sisters. Sixteen years later, Spaniard Don Sebastián Viscaíno set foot on the island and named it "Santa Catalina" in honour of Saint Catherine of Alexandria.

Then, in the late 18th century, American and Russian-born hunters, attracted by the abundance of sea otters and their valuable pelts, disrupted the harmony that had been established between the island wilderness and the Native Americans, ultimately causing the annihilation of the latter. Shepherds then grazed herds of sheep and cattle on the island's pastureland, while the well-hidden coves provided refuge to pirates and filibusters lying in wait for their next victims.

In the 1880s, the island began to attract interest as a holiday destination. Every summer, dozens of pleasure crafts dropped anchor in Catalina's many bays. A series of land speculators then saw the island as a golden opportunity to make a fortune by developing it as a unique holiday resort. And yet, no consistent enterprise managed to achieve this end. It wasn't until the island was sold in 1919 to William Wrigley Jr., of Wrigley's chewing-gum fame, that Santa Catalina began to adopt its current appearance. Wrigley developed Avalon and had a mansion and casino built, but left most of the island in its natural state. He also brought his baseball team, the Chicago Cubs, to the island for spring training.

From 1930 on, Avalon became increasingly popular

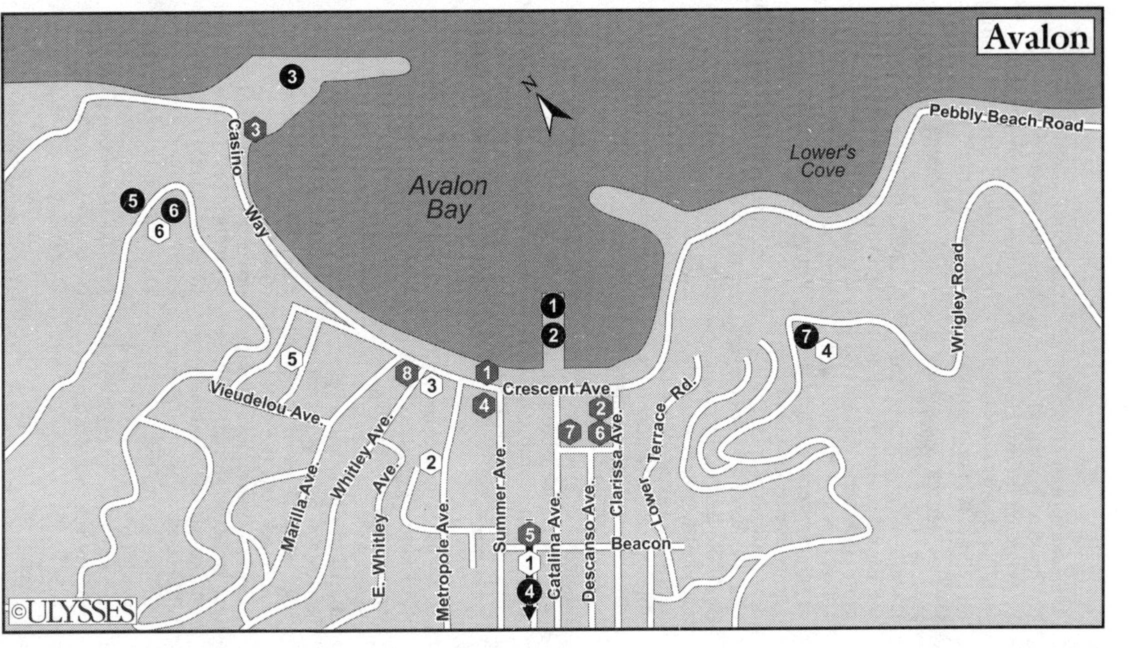
Avalon
Avalon Bay
Lower's Cove
Pebbly Beach Road
Wrigley Road
Casino Way
Crescent Ave.
Vieudelou Ave.
Marilla Ave.
Whitley Ave.
E. Whitley Ave.
Metropole Ave.
Summer Ave.
Catalina Ave.
Descanso Ave.
Clarissa Ave.
Lower Terrace Rd.
Beacon
N
©ULYSSES

with vacationers, especially Hollywood stars and other bigwigs, including Cecil B. DeMille, John Wayne, Zane Grey and Winston Churchill.

It soon became clear that the island had a one-of-a-kind ecosystem with over 400 species of plants, eight of which were endangered. The well-preserved wilderness harbours amazing wildlife: over 100 species of birds have been listed, in addition to many animals, including foxes, black buck antelopes and wild boars. Moreover, Santa Catalina is home to a herd of 400 buffalo whose ancestors were brought to the island in 1925 for the filming of Zane Grey novel's *The Vanishing American*.

It thus became apparent to the island's guardians that it was imperative to take measures to keep the natural charm of the island's interior intact. So it was that in 1975, some 86% of the land was deeded to the Catalina Island Conservancy. Driving was henceforth banned and remains so to this day. While golf carts and a few cars are permitted in Avalon, the rest of the island must be covered on foot, by bike or shuttle.

Although Catalina Island can be seen in one day, scores of charming hotels give visitors the opportunity to extend their stay for one or several nights. A short itinerary must, however, include breakfast along the seafront promenade, touring the island's rugged interior, scuba diving at Casino Point and dinner in Avalon.

From the ferry landing dock at the west end of Avalon Bay, head to Crescent Avenue, a lovely harbour-front promenade dotted with fountains where the tour of the town begins. The charming **Green Pleasure Pier**, at the corner of Crescent Avenue and Catalina Street, splits the bay in two and offers a magnificent view of the town and the mountains in the distance. Along the pier are snack bars, the Harbor Patrol offices and a few jetties for tour vessels, including a glass-bottom boat and a semi-submersible "submarine." These crafts take visitors to one of the island's coves to get acquainted with the spectacular marine life that dwells beneath the calm surface of the ocean. Day and night excursions are organized by the **Catalina Island Company** *(Green Pleasure Pier, ☎510-2000)*.

The same company also offers the **Inland Motor Tour**

($30; 4hr tour), a half-day excursion through the island's interior that includes a horse show and refreshments at Rancho Escondido. As for **Catalina Adventure Tours** *(☎510-2888, www. catalinaadventuretours. com)*, it offers seven different guided tours on both land and sea.

The **Catalina Island Visitor's Bureau** *(1 Green Pleasure Pier, ☎510-1520, www.catalina. com)* offers a warm welcome and precise information to help you plan your stay on the island.

A circular, white-painted structure dominating Casino Point, at the northwest end of Avalon Bay, the majestic **Casino** ★★ *(Casino Way, at the end of Crescent Ave.)* is still considered one of the most faithful examples of the Art Deco architectural style. Built by William Wrigley in 1929, it has since become a famous island landmark. But don't be fooled by its name—the Casino is not a gambling house but actually a reception centre, casino being the Italian word for "gathering place." For the two decades following its construction, the Casino drew scores of people who sailed in from San Pedro to dance all night to live Big Band music. The large ballroom, graced with a huge, round dance floor, was the scene of these lively years. A 55min guided tour *($8.50; ☎510-8687)* will allow you to appreciate the building's Art Deco features.

On the Casino's main floor, the **Catalina Island Museum** ★ *($2; Apr to Dec every day 10am to 4pm, Jan to Apr Fri to Wed 10am to 4pm; Casino Way, ☎510-2414)* houses a small collection of objects that chronicle the island's 7,000 years of history. Also on site is the **Casino Art Gallery** *(free admission; Jun to Sep every day 10:30am to 4pm, Oct to May Fri to Sun 10:30am to 4pm; ☎510-0808)*, which showcases the works of local artists.

A couple of miles south of the bay, via Avalon Canyon Road, lie the **Wrigley Memorial and Botanical Gardens** ★★ *($3; every day 8am to 5pm; Avalon Canyon Rd., ☎510-2288; shuttle service available between Avalon and the memorial)*, which will introduce you to the flora of Southern California and plants unique to the island. The 130ft-high (40m) monument is a Spanish mausoleum erected in memory of William Wrigley Jr. It is graced with glazed tiles and a spiral staircase, whose summit offers an interesting view.

Walking through the island's residential hills provides an opportunity to discover some unique architecture. The **Wolfe House ★**, a fine example of modernism, was built in 1928 by renowned architect Rudolf Schindler. The house is a private property, but a good view can be had from the street or the trail down below. Across the street, the **Zane Grey Pueblo** *(199 Chimes Tower Rd., ☎510-0966)* is a 1926 adobe structure that was home to Zane Grey, a famous writer of western novels. The house is now a rustic hotel.

But the most impressive excursion is unquestionably that which leads into the hills around Avalon. Follow Claressa Street, turn left on Thomas Street, then right on Wrigley Terrace Road, which brings you to a road that overlooks Avalon. At the very top, on the right, stands the **Inn on Mt. Ada** (see p 255), an elegant hotel that was once the Wrigleys' mansion and from which you'll be treated to a magnificent panorama of the ocean and the town.

Although driving is not permitted on the island, it's fairly easy to get around as most places are accessible on foot or by bike. For bicycle or mountain-bike rentals, you can turn to **Brown's Bikes** *(107 Pebbly Beach Rd., ☎510-0986)*. Small electric cars can also be leased at **Cartopia Auto Rental** *(15 Crescent Ave., ☎510-2493)* or **Catalina Auto & Bike Rental** *(301 Crescent Ave., ☎510-0111)*.

Two Harbors ★ is located on a 2,625ft-wide (800m) isthmus that links the two halves of the island. The only developed area, apart from Avalon, it features a small jetty, a marina, campground, picnic area and other services for excursionists.

Safari Shuttle Bus *(☎510-2800)* offers shuttle service to Two Harbors with the option of returning to Avalon by boat in the course of the afternoon. The **Catalina Island Conservancy** *(125 Claressa Ave., ☎510-0143)* organizes ecotours of the island in all-terrain vehicles.

Tour J: Inland Orange County

Anaheim

Long before Disneyland ever existed, the city of Anaheim was established by German immigrants as an important wine-producing colony for the budding metropolis of Los Angeles.

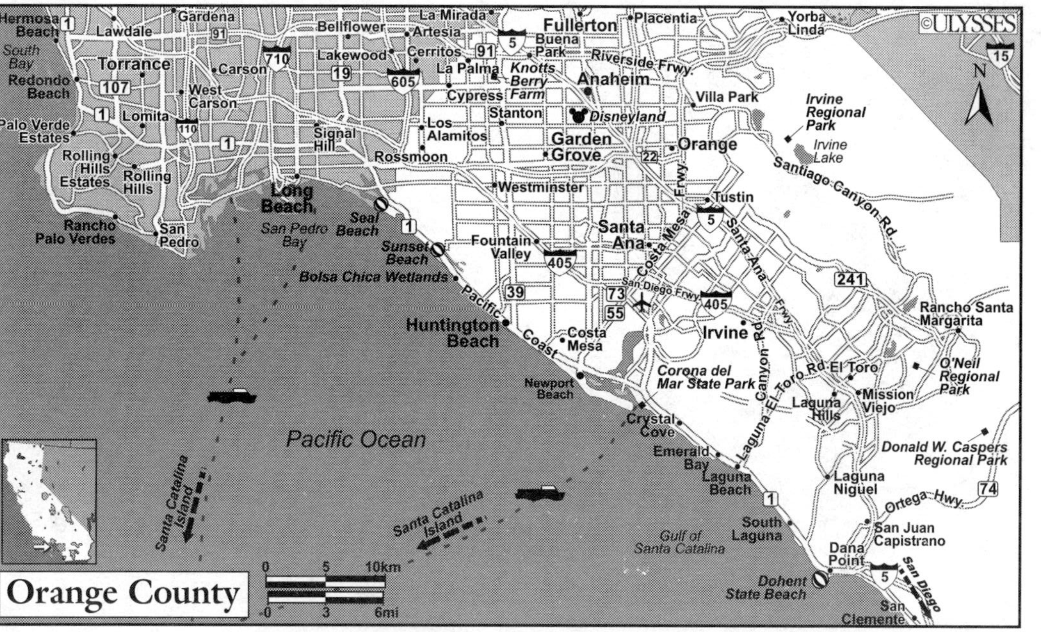
Orange County
©ULYSSES
N
Hermosa Beach
South Bay
Redondo Beach
Palo Verde Estates
Rolling Hills Estates
Rolling Hills
Rancho Palo Verdes
San Pedro
Lawdale
Torrance
Lomita
Gardena
West Carson
Carson
Long Beach
San Pedro Bay
Signal Hill
Bellflower
Lakewood
La Mirada
Artesia
Cerritos
La Palma
Cypress
Los Alamitos
Rossmoon
Seal Beach
Sunset Beach
Bolsa Chica Wetlands
Huntington Beach
Pacific Coast
Fountain Valley
Westminster
Stanton
Garden Grove
Knotts Berry Farm
Buena Park
Fullerton
Placentia
Anaheim
Disneyland
Riverside Frwy.
Villa Park
Orange
Yorba Linda
Irvine Regional Park
Irvine Lake
Santiago Canyon Rd.
Tustin
Santa Ana
Costa Mesa Frwy.
Santa Ana Frwy.
San Diego Frwy.
Costa Mesa
Newport Beach
Irvine
Corona del Mar State Park
Crystal Cove
Emerald Bay
Laguna Beach
Laguna Canyon Rd
El Toro Rd
El Toro
Laguna Hills
Mission Viejo
Rancho Santa Margarita
O'Neil Regional Park
Donald W. Caspers Regional Park
Laguna Niguel
Ortega Hwy.
San Juan Capistrano
South Laguna
Dana Point
Dohent State Beach
San Clemente
San Diego
Gulf of Santa Catalina
Pacific Ocean
Santa Catalina Island
Santa Catalina Island
0 5 10km
0 3 6mi
1
91
107
110
710
19
605
5
22
405
39
73
55
241
74
15

Disneyland

Anaheim, though best known for Disneyland, features a multitude of other attractions nearby as well as fantastic shopping, dining and entertainment possibilities. Most visitors choose to stay in Anaheim when visiting inland Orange County due to its wide spectrum of accommodations and its central location. Most area attractions are within a short drive on Interstate 5, which runs through the city. Alternatively, the hotels listed in this guide also provide a free or low-cost shuttle to all the region's attractions. The city of Orange is only a few minutes east of Anaheim and features both charming antique shopping and the newest outdoor mall in the county.

Disneyland ★★★ *(adults $41, children $31; 1313 Harbor Blvd.; ☎781-4565; www.disneyland.com)* was Walt Disney's vision of the "happiest place on earth" and has been the main attraction in California for the past 45 years. What started as a mere 18 rides has grown to over 60, with plans for many more. The Magic Kingdom, however, is more suited to young children than teenagers. Teenagers will probably enjoy Knott's Berry Farm better, with its intense rides and slightly more mature attractions. For young children though, Disneyland is a dream come true.

Passes are available for one, two or three days and allow unlimited re-entry into the park. During the low season, it is possible to ride everything in one day. If you are visiting in the summer, however, two days may be more realistic as lineups are common. A new feature of the park is Fastpass, allowing guests to use their entry pass to "reserve" a time to come back to the ride. This is an invaluable service as it helps you avoid the majority of lineups. The Fastpass is currently available at Space Mountain, Splash Mountain and Roger Rabbit's Car Toon Spin.

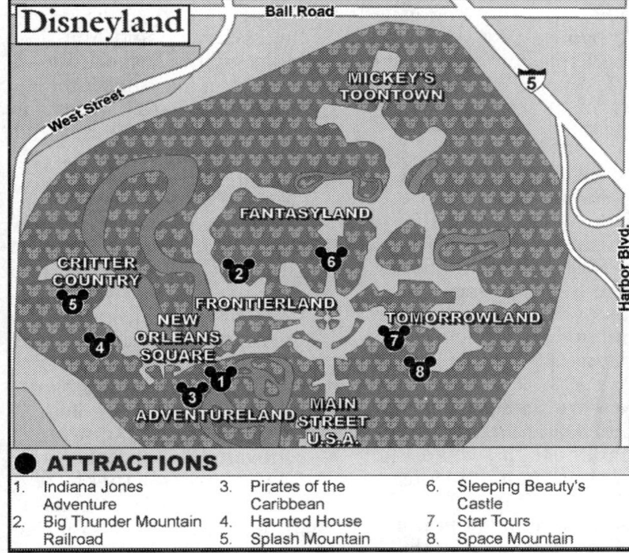

Disneyland consists of eight different "lands," each with their own distinctive theme.

Main Street, U.S.A. features a variety of shops in an early 20th century atmosphere. Make sure to check out the main street cinema to see Mickey's first cartoon, *Steamboat Willy*.

Tommorrowland ★★★ is the highlight of the park, including attractions like Star Tours, Space Mountain, and Autotopia. Lineups can last up to 1hr or more at the rides, but Innoventions is both fun and educational without the wait.

Mickey's Toontown ★★ is a especially popular attraction with the very young. Rides such as Gadget's Go Coaster and Goofy's Bounce House cater to children as young as three.

Fantasyland ★★ has a theatre offering live entertainment and several fun rides with very little waiting involved. Popular spots include the Sleeping Beauty Castle and King Arthur's Carousel.

Frontierland ★★ transports you back to the Wild West with attractions like a full-sized riverboat, the Big Thunder Mountain Railroad ride and a shooting gallery, to name a few. After dark, the Fantasmic show pits Mickey and his friends against the usual Disney villains.

Adventureland ★★★ is home to Tarzan's 70 ft (23m) treehouse and a great jungle cruise, complete with hippos and headhunters. The Indiana Jones ride is also worthwhile, but the lineups are sometimes daunting.

New Orleans Square ★★ has the classic Pirates of the Caribbean, as well as the famous Haunted House. The Blue Bayou Restaurant here is the most popular (and expensive) in the park. It is also the only restaurant with table service. Same-day reservations should be made by calling ☎956-6755. **Critter Corner** ★★ is enchanting as characters from the world of Winnie the Pooh come to life. Hit the water on the Davey Crocket Canoes or get wet at Splash Mountain.

Edison Field

If you want to get to know the history behind Anaheim, try the **Anaheim Museum** ★ *(241 S. Anaheim Blvd.; ☎778-3301)*, located in the beautifully restored 1908 Carnegie Library Building. In addition to a series of changing exhibits, the museum also chronicles the changes that have occurred in the Anaheim area over the past 150 years, from vineyards to orange groves to Disneyland.

If sports are your passion, Anaheim has two professional teams. The newly-renovated **Edison Field** *(200 Gene Autry Way; ☎940-2240)* is home to baseball's **Anaheim Angels**, who slug it out April through October. The trademark Outfield Extravaganza features six water geysers, dramatic lighting and pyrotechnics. Across Highway 57 is the **Arrowhead Pond of Anaheim** *(2695 E. Katella Ave.; ☎704-2500)*, home to NHL's **Anaheim Mighty Ducks**, who take to the ice October through April.

Adventure City ★ *($5, unlimited rides $11; daily 10am to 5pm; 1238 S. Beach Blvd.; ☎236-9300)* is an affordable little theme park aimed at two to 12 year olds.

Seventeen rides from rollercoasters to merry-go-rounds are complimented by face painting, puppet shows, a petting farm and a children's theatre. You should definitely spring for the unlimited pass. Next door, at the **Hobby City Doll & Toy Museum** *(free; 1238 S. Beach Blvd.; ☎527-2323)* visitors can browse through a variety of craft, art, and collectibles shops and explore a half-scale model of the White House and over 4000 antique and foreign dolls and toy soldiers.

Just south of Anaheim in nearby Garden Grove, the 3,000-seat **Crystal Cathedral** ★★★ *(13280 Chapman Ave., Garden Grove; ☎971-4069)* is an incredible sight to behold. Designed by architect Philip Johnson, this fascinating structure is comprised of over 10,000 panes of mirrored glass that shine brilliantly in the California sun. The 236 ft (79m) steeple houses a 52-bell carillon and a 24hr prayer chapel. Throughout the expansive grounds of the church is a collection of biblically-inspired statues that are set amid reflecting pools, fountains and myriad flowers. The "Glory of Christmas" and "Glory of Easter" shows are famous for their high production value, complete with flying angels, special effects and orchestral sound.

Buena Park

The highlight of Buena Park is Beach Boulevard, known as the "entertainment corridor." Most of the main attractions are located on this street, interspersed with various dining and shopping opportunities.

For the ultimate in high-speed, adrenaline-pumping rides, head to **Knott's Berry Farm** *(Adults $38, children $28; 8039 Beach Blvd.; ☎220-5200; www.knotts.com)*, just 10min northwest of Disneyland. From its humble beginnings as a chicken restaurant and roadside produce stand, Knott's is now the second most visited tourist site in California. The

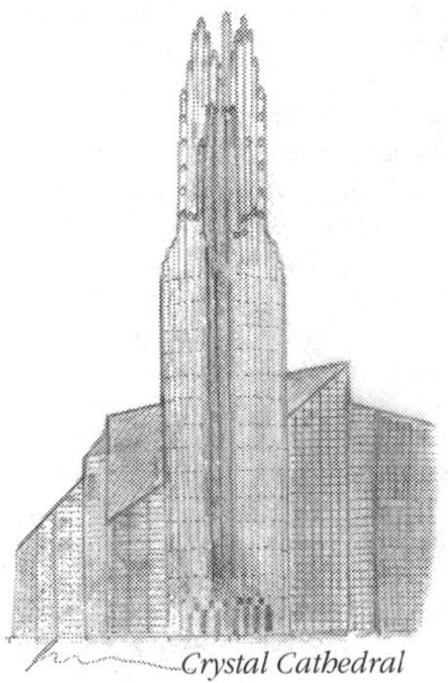
Crystal Cathedral

two newest attractions are the Supreme Scream, which drops its riders 30 storeys in three seconds, and the Ghost Rider, a colossal wooden roller coaster. There are 165 rides, shows and attractions in all, covering 150 acres (61ha). The park is divided into six themed areas: the Wild West Ghost Town, Indian Trails, Fiesta Village, The Boardwalk, Wild Water Wilderness and Camp Snoopy. At Camp Snoopy, children can experience smaller versions of the adult rides.

Right next to Knott's is **Soak City U.S.A.** ★★ *($20; 8039 Beach Blvd.; ☎220-5200)*, harbouring 15 acres (7ha) of water rides with a California surf theme. With its huge wave pool, tube slides and children's water lagoon, this is a great place to enjoy the California sun.

The **Mott's Miniature Museum** ★★ *(7900 La Palma Ave.; ☎527-1843)* is adjacent to the park. Several great exhibits are showcased here, including the History of American Living, which features six scale homes, ranging from the 18th century to modern day, complete with a miniature working television. The highlight here is the Microscopic Miniature display, where visitors must use magnifying glasses to see fully dressed fleas or "The Last Supper" painted on a pinhead.

The **Movieland Wax Museum** ★ *($13; 7711 Beach Blvd.; ☎522-1155)* is home to almost 300 celebrity wax figures on display in 115 realistic sets. Everyone featured in here, from Michael Jackson to John Wayne, is life-size and incredibly lifelike. While the static displays are interesting and of amazing quality, Ripley's Believe It Or Not Museum is less expensive and far more intriguing.

Though not for the faint-of-heart, the **Ripley's Believe It Or Not Museum** ★★ *($9; 7850 Beach Blvd.; ☎522-1152)* is an interesting and, at times, shocking adventure into the strange, the amazing and the wonderful. Through a 10,000 sq ft (930m^2) collection of artifacts, wax sculptures and displays, visitors can observe some of the strangest things the world has to offer. Robert L. Ripley, born in nearby Santa Rosa on Christmas Day 1893, visited 198 countries during his lifetime, searching for just the things you now see in his museum. The work still continues in his memory, with more unbelievable exhibits added every year.

Santa Ana to Costa Mesa

Santa Ana and Costa Mesa are situated just south of Anaheim on Harbor Boulevard. This area is considered by many to be the artistic and cultural centre of Orange County, since it is home to the Bowers Museum, Orange County Theatre District and the Artist's Village. Costa Mesa has the added advantage of being conveniently located a quick 20min drive from the sands of Newport Beach.

The **Artist's Village** in downtown Santa Ana *(Broadway to Sycamore St. on Second St.)* is home to more than 55 studios and galleries that showcase their works at 7pm on the first Saturday of the month. Stroll through the village and take in the local artwork hanging in windows and displayed in the various galleries.

The **Bowers Museum of Cultural Art and Kidseum** ★★ *($8; 2002 N. Main St., Santa Ana; ☎567-3600)* is dedicated to the preservation, study and exhibition of the cultural arts of the Americas, Africa and the Pacific Rim. Inside the museum walls and warm, open-air space, 85,000 objects are showcased including many one-of-a-kind and historical artifacts. Next door, the Kidseum offers interactive displays and activities for children to learn about local history and world cultures.

Learning is actually quite entertaining at the **Discovery Science Centre** ★★★ *($9.50; 2500 N. Main St., Santa Ana; ☎542-CUBE; www.discoverycube.org)*. Eight different areas feature interactive exhibits highlighting everything from the principles of flight and space exploration to human performance and perception. A 3-D laser theatre show is also included with admission. Kids will especially love the musical floor, bed of nails and mini-tornadoes.

Costa Mesa

Modern and contemporary U.S. art is featured at the **Orange County Museum of Art** ★ *(3333 Bristol St., Suite 1000; ☎662-3366)*. A lecture series takes place on Tuesday and Friday nights and features screenings of classic films. Sculptures, a meditative garden and a beautiful stained-glass enclosure are hidden here amid the shops and restaurants of South Coast Plaza.

The **Orange County Theatre District** offers over 3,000 seats overall at its various venues. The **Orange County Performing Arts Centre** *(600 Town Center Dr.; ☎556-2787)* features national and international selections of ballet, opera ballet, opera, musical theatre, classical music, and jazz throughout the year. The bold-looking building is a local landmark with its gigantic window providing a view of the elegant, modern interior.

The Tony Award-winning **South Coast Repertory** *(655 Town Center Dr.; ☎708-5500)* stages creative new and classic drama and has drawn national attention for productions such as David Henry Hwang's *Golden Child*, which was first produced at South Coast Repertory and is now on Broadway.

The **Santa Ana Zoo in Prentice Park** ★★★ *($3.50; 1801 Chestnut Ave., Santa Ana; ☎647-6575; www.santaanazoo.org)* is home to more than 250 exotic animals from various habitats around the world. The highlight here is definitely the monkeys who never fail to entertain. An extensive rainforest exhibit, walk-through aviary and children's petting zoo add to the list of attractions.

The annual Orange County Fair takes place in the last two weeks of July at the **Orange County Fair & Exposition Center** *(88 Fair Dr.; ☎708-1567)* in Costa Mesa. During the rest of the year, the grounds host a **Farmer's Market** *(Thurs. 8:30am to 1pm; ☎723-6616)* and **International Speedway Racing** *($9; Sat. 7:30pm to 10pm; ☎492-9933)*.

Tour K: The Beaches of Orange County

Seal Beach

Seal Beach is a small, attractive town that seems to have been forgotten in the rush to develop the Californian coast. The pace of life here is slower, the locals friendlier, and visitors return year after year hoping that their secret will still be safe. The small town atmosphere is best experienced in a short walk down charming Main Street, past the unique shops and casual restaurants. There are less than 100 beds available in Seal Beach, so visitors should make their reservations well in advance.

The **beach ★★★** is the main attraction in town. A handful of shops along main street rent surf boards, boogie boards and sailboards for the water. Landlubbers will find kites and bicycles available. Over 30mi (48km) of bike paths wind throughout the area.

Seal Beach Pier is one of the longest wooden piers in the United States. Originally constructed in 1938, it was destroyed by a violent Pacific storm in 1983. The pier was rebuilt in 1984 through the concentrated efforts of the entire community. Fishing is possible along the pier. Ruby's Diner (see p 303) is at the end of it, looking out onto the ocean.

The **Seal Beach Historical and Cultural Society** *(second and fourth Sat of each month 1pm to 4pm; ☎683-1874)* is located in a red, 1925 railway car on Electric Avenue, just west of Main Street. This small museum features photographs of early Seal Beach, sea shells, Native American artifacts and a small reference library.

The **Anaheim Bay National Wildlife Refuge** is accessible to visitors on the last Saturday of the month *(☎598-1024)*, when a shuttle runs through the 1000-acre (404ha) reserve. The refuge is a salt marsh habitat that is a breeding ground for various fish and migratory birds. The tour is free and departs from the main gate of the naval base at 9am. There is only limited access to the refuge because it is located within the **U.S. Naval Weapons Support Facility** *(www.sbeach.navy.mil)*. Giant naval vessels can be seen coming in and out of Anaheim Bay.

The main event in Seal Beach is the **Seal Beach Car Show** *(info ☎799-0179)* at the end of April. Thousands of people from all over California come to this sleepy beach town to watch the hotrods and vintage cars compete for prizes.

Huntington Beach

In the 1920s, oil was discovered in Huntington Beach. This led to a population boom as speculators and residents drilled in their backyards looking for the coveted "black gold." By the 1950s, however, the oil had run dry, and Huntington began to develop its present claim to fame as "Surf City USA." In the downtown core, surf shops dominate the commercial area. Scores of bronzed surfers can be found lounging on the beaches and in the sidewalk cafés or, more likely, catching one of Huntington's famous waves by the pier. Huntington is home to the US Open Surfing Championship and the Bud Surf Tour. It was recently rated the "most heavily surfed beach on the West Coast" by *Surfer's Almanac.*

There are fabulous shopping, dining and nightlife opportunities to be had here. Huntington Beach is a laid-back, vibrant town, where "no shirt, no shoes, no service" doesn't necessarily apply.

The **beaches** of Huntington are the city's main attraction, stretching for 8mi (13km) east and west of downtown. Just west of the city, **Bolsa Chica Beach ★★★** tends to be less crowded than its counterparts, and fronts the ecological reserve of the same name (see p 192). The **Huntington City Beach ★★** surrounds the pier, and is a popular place to watch local surfers. **Huntington State Beach ★★** is a 2mi-long (3.2km) sandy beach with six wheelchair ramps that reach almost to the water. All beaches include picnic facilities, outdoor showers and free parking nearby. Rangers and lifeguards are on duty year-round at both the state and city beaches.

The **Huntington Beach Pier ★★** is the longest concrete municipal pier in California, extending 1,850ft (616m) into the Pacific. Originally built as a wooden pier in 1903, it has been rebuilt twice after storm damage. The current pier was opened in July 1990. This is a Mecca of activity during the day, the perfect place to see and be seen, lounge in the sun, or watch the surfers tackle the waves. Fishing is allowed from the pier and doesn't require a licence. Ruby's Diner (see p 303) sits at the end of the pier, a busy but friendly spot for a meal at sundown.

Some of the most revered artifacts in the history of surfing can be found at the **International Surfing Museum ★★** *($2; Wed to Sun noon to 5pm; 411 Olive Ave.; ☎960-3483; www.surfingmuseum.org).*

The music of the Beach Boys pervades the museum and surf videos help set the mood. A permanent display chronicles the evolution of the surfboard, and an original Duke Kahanamoku hardwood board hangs among other treasures of its kind. The north wall of the museum is covered with a beautiful mural depicting surfers in action—a favourite photo opportunity for visitors.

The **Huntington Beach Surfing Walk of Fame** ★ pays homage to the heroes of Surf City. Granite stone is inlaid in the sidewalk that extends outward from the corner of Main Street and the Pacific Coast Highway.

Huntington Central Park *(☎960-8895)* consists of over 350 acres (142ha) of majestic trees, grassy lawns, ponds and fountains. Throughout the park there are several great playgrounds, barbeques, sports facilities and 6mi (9km) of trails. The park is located on both sides of Golden West Street, near Talbert. The **Shipley Nature Centre** and **Central Library and Cultural Centre** are also located in the park.

In the north end of the park, near Slater Avenue and Golden West Street is the **Shipley Nature Centre** ★★ *(free; 9am to 5pm; ☎960-8847)*. The centre consists of an 18-acre (7.2ha) forest with a variety of wildlife habitats that are home to a community of raccoons, snakes, turtles, opossums and coyotes. Guests can explore the half-mile interpretive trail that will take them through the forests, grasslands and freshwater marsh of the park's centre.

The **Huntington Beach Cultural Centre and Central Library** ★ *(7111 Talbert Ave.; ☎960-8839)* serves as the city's main library, but also houses the Huntington Beach Playhouse Community Theatre group and the Children's Storytime Theatre. The impressive lobby is adorned with fabulous fountains, pools and cascading waterfalls.

At Center Avenue, just off the San Diego freeway, is the **Old World Village** ★ *(7561 Center Ave.)*. This shopping, dining and entertainment centre is an attempt to recreate a German alpine town. Wander down the cobbled streets and check out the European-inspired shops, have a little wiener schnitzel and sauerkraut and, when night falls, there are drinks and dancing. In late September and early October, this is the epicenter of the Oktoberfest celebrations.

ATTRACTIONS	
1. Mariners Mile	10. Newport Harbor Nautical Museum
2. Lido Marina Village	11. Environmental Nature Center
3. Cannery Village	12. Orange County Museum of Art
4. Cannery Wharf Park	13. Newport Sports Collection Foundation
5. Newport Pier	14. Sherman Library and Gardens
6. Balboa Pier	15. Big Corona and Little Corona Beaches
7. Balboa Pavilion/Balboa Fun Zone	
8. Balboa Island Car Ferry	
9. Balboa Island	

ACCOMMODATIONS	
1. Balboa Bay Club	5. Newport Channel Inn
2. Balboa Inn	6. Newport Classic Inn
3. Doryman's Inn	7. Portofino Hotel
4. Four Seasons Hotel	

RESTAURANTS	
1. Alta Coffee	7. Roy's Newport Beach
2. Alysia 101	8. The Spaghetti Bender
3. The Blue Beet Café	9. The Tale of the Whale
4. The Chart House	10. Tutto Mare Ristotrante
5. Hornblower Cruises	11. Veg a Go-Go
6. The Riverboat Restaurant	

The **Newland House Museum** *($2; Wed and Thu 2pm to 4:30pm, Sat and Sun 12-4pm; 19820 Beach Blvd.; ☎962-5557)* is a Queen Anne-style Victorian farm house, located a fair distance from downtown on the corner of Beach Boulevard. and Adams Avenue. The house has a wonderful view of the Santa Ana Gap, a marshy lowland between Huntington Beach and Costa Mesa. Inside, the furnishings and decor have been lovingly preserved for visitors.

The **Bolsa Chica Ecological Reserve** ★★ *(tours 9am and 10:30am, first Sat of the month, Sep to Apr; Warner Ave. at the Pacific Coast Hwy.; ☎800-628-7275 ext.119)* is a protected wetland reserve that serves as a rest area for birds migrating along the Pacific Flyway. Its 530 acres (214ha) are also home to a variety of wildlife that is relatively easy to spot. The reserve has limited access to protect its flora and fauna, but there is a 1.5mi (2.5km) interpretive loop trail, with informative signs posted along it. Note the oil pumps that continue to operate in the reserve.

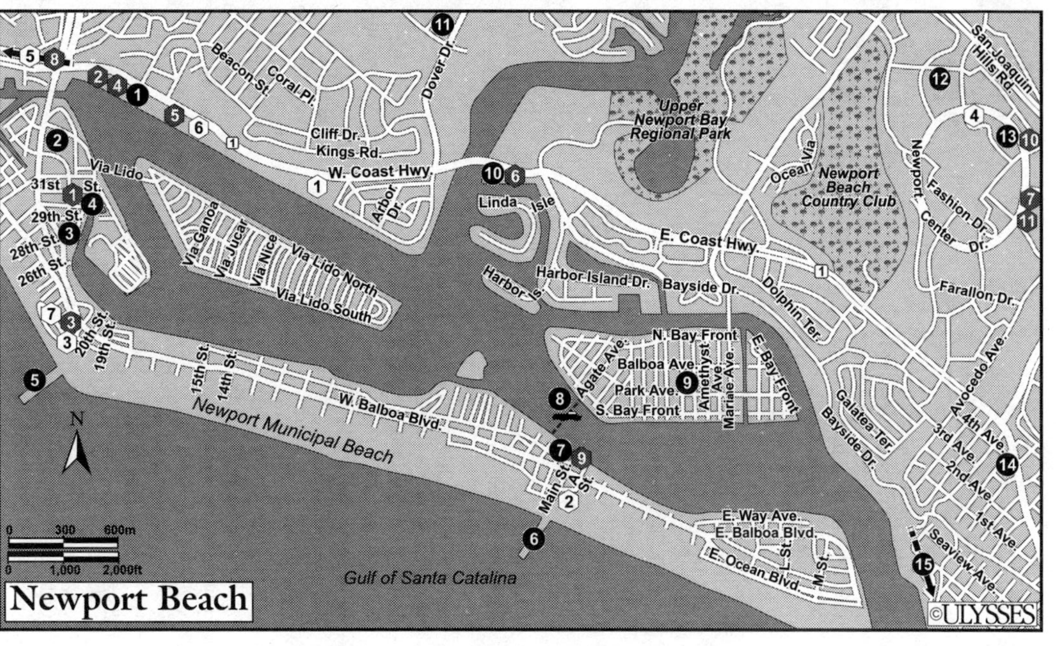
Newport Beach
Beacon St.
Coral Pl.
Cliff Dr.
Kings Rd.
Dover Dr.
W. Coast Hwy.
Arbor Dr.
Via Lido
31st St.
29th St.
28th St.
26th St.
20th St.
19th St.
Via Ganoa
Via Jucar
Via Nice
Via Lido North
Via Lido South
15th St.
14th St.
W. Balboa Blvd.
Newport Municipal Beach
Upper Newport Bay Regional Park
Linda Isle
Harbor Is.
Harbor Island Dr.
Bayside Dr.
E. Coast Hwy.
Ocean Via
Newport Beach Country Club
Dolphin Ter.
N. Bay Front
Agate Ave.
Balboa Ave.
Park Ave.
S. Bay Front
Amethyst Ave
Mariaie Ave.
E. Bay Front
Main St.
A St.
Galatea Ter.
Bayside Dr.
E. Way Ave.
E. Balboa Blvd.
E. Ocean Blvd.
L St.
M St.
San Joaquin Hills Rd.
Newport Center Dr.
Fashion Dr.
Farallon Dr.
Avocedo Ave.
4th Ave.
3rd Ave.
2nd Ave.
1st Ave.
Seaview Ave.
Gulf of Santa Catalina
N
0 300 600m
0 1,000 2,000ft
©ULYSSES

Newport Beach

Every weekend, thousands of Orange County residents flock to Newport Beach for the fine restaurants, festive atmosphere and vibrant nightlife. Much more than just a beach, the Newport area is comprised of several small and distinct villages that compliment what most people refer to as Newport Beach. Stretching for 6mi (9km) along the Californian shoreline, this area has some of the most expensive real estate in Orange County and is a popular spot for Californians to unwind. Newport harbour is also one of the largest small-yacht harbours in the world, home to over 9,000 boats and the famous *Dory Fishing Fleet* (see p 197). Shoppers will delight in the upscale Fashion Island shopping centre (see p 357). The tourism industry is well developed in Newport Beach, but the adjacent community of Corona del Mar *(www.cdmchamber.com)* provides some respite with its quaint, small town atmosphere. Newport is also a convenient gateway to Catalina Island, 26mi (42km) offshore.

The stretch of Pacific Coast Highway between Newport Boulevard and Dover Drive is known as **Mariners Mile ★★**. Along this mile is a great collection of restaurants, shops and galleries that all share a common nautical theme. This is also a good area to charter a cruise and get a terrific view of the harbour.

Just off Newport Boulevard from the Pacific Coast Highway, visitors will discover the **Lido Marina Village**. This charming sector of Newport brings to mind a European open-air marketplace as you stroll down the cobblestone street of **Via Oporto,** browsing through the many galleries, boutiques and antique shops. There are also several quaint cafés and restaurants that look out on the bay.

A few blocks east of the Lido Marina Village is **Cannery Village ★★**, which covers eight square blocks in an area that was once the centre of the Newport commercial fishing industry. In the early 1900s the area was filled with boat repair shops, boat yards and, of course, canneries. Today the village retains its nautical atmosphere, but the old buildings now house an eclectic collection of art galleries, antique shops and restaurants. Aspiring local artists converge on **Cannery Wharf Park** *(where 30th St. meets the bay)* Sunday afternoons to sell their latest works.

The **Newport Municipal Beach** ★ stretches from the Santa Ana River Jetty and along the Balboa Peninsula to the Entrance Channel of Newport Harbor. Sun seekers are best to stay to the west end of the beach to avoid the considerable crowds that invade this beach on the weekends. Beach parking is available at either of the piers, or at one of the numerous beachfront lots *($7 maximum).* **The Wedge**, by the Entrance Channel, is an excellent surfing spot, but once again, it fills up quickly. Inexperienced surfers and swimmers should try to remain within sight of the lifeguard towers. Beach volleyball courts and campfire spots are available. Numerous small beaches run along the inland shore of the Balboa Peninsula. At Bay Avenue, between 18th and 19th Streets is a calm **beach** that is lifeguard-supervised.

Big Corona and Little Corona Beaches ★★ are found just east of the Entrance Channel, in front of Corona del Mar. These smaller, less crowded beaches are great for families, watching yachts come into the harbor, and scuba diving.

The large, imposing structure of the **Orange County Museum of Art** ★ *($5; Tue to Sun 11am to 5pm; 850 San Clemente Dr.; ☎759-1122; www.ocma.net)* hosts temporary exhibits of various contemporary paintings, sculpture and photography, with emphasis on Californian art from the 19th century to the present. The bookstore specializes in contemporary art books. Lunch is served in the lush Sculpture Garden Café from 11:30am to 2:30pm weekdays. Workshops and classes are available.

The **Newport Harbor Nautical Museum** ★ *($4; Tue to Sun, 10am to 5pm; 151 E. Pacific Coast Hwy.; ☎673-7863; www.newportnautical.org)* celebrates all things nautical aboard the riverboat *Pride of Newport* in the Newport Harbor. A collection of historical photographs, videos and maritime paintings by renowned artist Arthur Beaumont serve to educate visitors on Newport Harbor and the surrounding area. Also exhibited is an interesting display of ships in bottles and navigational instruments. The museum shares the ship with the Riverboat Restaurant (see p 308).

Sports fans will be amazed by the **Newport Sports Collection Foundation** *(free; Mon to Fri 10am to 6pm, Sat 10am to*

3pm; 620 Newport Center Dr.; ☎721-9333). Over 10,000 game-worn jerseys, helmets and equipment cover the walls of the 10 rooms in this unique museum. The aim of the museum is to promote sports as a way to keep children away from gangs and drugs. Baseball, football, basketball, golf, hockey and the Olympics are all represented. Professional athletes come here occasionally to speak to the visiting children.

The **Upper Newport Bay Ecological Reserve** *(2400 Irvine Ave.; ☎646-8009)* is a 752-acre (304ha) coastal wetland reserve that supports six ecological habitats. A variety of fish, mammals and over 200 species of birds call this reserve home. Fishing is available year round, with the best spots being near Big Canyon and North Star Beach. Canoe and kayak tours, sunset cruises and family campfire programs are offered throughout the year from the **Newport Aquatic Centre** *(☎714-644-3151)* at North Star Beach. There is also a 10mi (16km) loop trail that winds through the reserve. Free naturalist-guided walking tours are offered the first and third Saturday of the month.

An entire city block in Corona del Mar is devoted to the **Sherman Library and Gardens ★★** *(daily 10:30am to 4pm; 2647 E. Pacific Coast Hwy.; ☎673-2261).* The facility was named for Moses H. Sherman, an educator and California pioneer. The historical research library (weekdays only) is an important repository of information on the Pacific Southwest over the past 100 years. The luxuriant gardens feature over 2,000 plant species from rare desert cacti to exotic tropical bromelia and orchids, highlighted by fountains and sculptures. The **Discovery Garden ★** is designed for those with impaired vision, relying on the sense of touch, and is wheelchair accessible.

Newport Pier *(McFadden Pl. between 20th and 22nd Pl.)* is on the site of historic McFadden Wharf, which was destroyed by a violent storm in 1939. The original wharf was an important stop for coal steamers in the early 1900's. The **Balboa Pier** *(Main St. and E. Balboa Blvd.)* was built in 1909 and is the site of the first water-to-water hydroplane flight, in 1912, to Santa Catalina Island and back. Today, both piers have become a popular hangout for tourists and locals alike. Fishing is allowed from the piers without a licence.

Newport Beach's **pleasure craft harbor** is one of the largest of its kind in the world and provides avid boaters with the opportunity to admire some extravagant yachts. The harbour is also home to the ***Dory Fishing Fleet***, which pulls in promptly at 9am every morning. Started in 1889, this fleet is the last beachside cooperative of its kind in the United States. Upon their return, the local chefs crowd in to get their pick of the freshest seafood. It's hard not to get caught up in the marine atmosphere and you'll want to get out on the water yourself. **Balboa Boat Rentals** *(beside the Balboa Ferry dock; ☎673-7200)* rents by the hour or half day at reasonable prices. Double kayaks and pedal boats cost \$50/half-day, while motor and fishing boats run \$100 and more. Alternatively, bay cruises are available from Newport Harbor Sightseeing *(\$6; every day 10am to 7pm; ☎673-5245)* leaving from the **Balboa Pavilion**.

The **Environmental Nature Center** *(every day 9am to 5pm; 1601 16th St.; ☎645-8489)* is a great way for children aged five and over to experience nature firsthand. Guided walking tours are available of the 2.5 acre (1.2ha) wildlife habitat that also supports 13 Californian plant communities.

In 1905, the Newport Investment Company erected the **Balboa Pavilion** *(400 Main St.)* as an open-air building with a Victorian-era balustrade edging the second floor. In 1906, it became the southern terminus for the Pacific Electric Railway, which connected the beach to downtown Los Angeles. Today it is home to **The Tale of the Whale** restaurant (see p 307), a snack bar and a number of fishing and cruise services. The pavilion also serves as the centre of the **Balboa Fun Zone** *(every day 10am to 10pm; ☎673-0408)*, which has been a tradition in Newport since 1936. Admission is free, but there is a small cost to ride the Ferris wheel, carousel and bumper cars. Kids love the festive atmosphere, and some of the best views of the harbor are to be had from atop the restored Ferris wheel.

Balboa Island

Be sure to catch the **Balboa Island Car Ferry** *($1/car or $0,35/pers.)* to get to the island. Alternatively, you can reach the island by car off the Pacific Coast Highway at Jamboree Road, but parking is in such short supply that it is better to explore the island on foot. The island is primarily residential, with a wonderful architectural mix of Cape Cod and modern Californian homes packed into its tight little streets. Along **Park Avenue** ★★ is a colourful collection of gift shops, galleries and restaurants. The North Bay front walkway is a nice stroll that allows some great views of the harbor.

Laguna Beach

Laguna Beach is a small, eclectic town and the heart of the artistic community on Southern California's coast. An artist's colony was established here amidst the 30 white-sand beaches and bays of Laguna Beach in 1917. The varied topography and numerous ocean lookouts continue to inspire the works of the Californian impressionist school.

Laguna is the centre of the Californian Plein-Air movement, artists influenced by Monet-style French impressionism. During the 1920s, Laguna Beach was a haven for some Hollywood's superstars, from Charlie Chaplin and Douglas Fairbanks to Mary Pickford and Bette Davis. For a town this size, it has a surprising number of quality restaurants, yearly festivals, and quaint boutique shops. Almost everything in town is within a few minutes' walk from the beach.

A fascinating pastime in Laguna Beach is touring the many **art galleries** in the area. During the depression, members of the Laguna Beach artistic community would display their works by the sides of the Pacific Coast Highway or hanging from the eucalyptus trees, hoping to make a sale to one of the passing motorists. Today, a multitude of art galleries line the highway where the artists once stood. In north Laguna, **Gallery Row** ★★★ covers the 300 and 400 blocks of the North Pacific Coast Highway. These two blocks are home to over 20 galleries, that proudly display their original artwork. In South Laguna there is a complete palate of galleries, crafts and artists studios waiting to be explored between the 900 and 1800

Laguna Beach
©ULYSSES
0 250 500m
0 750 1,500ft
N
ATTRACTIONS
1. Edwards South Coast Cinema
2. Main Beach Park
3. Laguna Art Museum
4. Gallery Row (North Laguna)
5. Hortense Miller Garden
6. Friends of the Sea Lion Marine Mammal Centre
7. Gallery Row (South Laguna)
8. Bette Davis House
9. Laguna Beach Visitors Bureau
ACCOMMODATIONS
1. Casa Laguna Inn
2. Crescent Bay Inn
3. Hotel Laguna
4. Inn at Laguna Beach
5. Laguna Brisas Spa Hotel
6. Laguna Riviera
7. Surf and Sand Hotel
8. Tides Motel
RESTAURANTS
1. 230 Forest Ave.
2. Aegean Cafe
3. Bombay Duck Bistro & Grill
4. C'est La Vie
5. Claes Seafood Etc.
6. French 75
7. Gina's Pizza
8. Goko Cafe & Deli
9. Madison Square & Garden Cafe
10. Nature's Oven II
11. Romeo Cucina
12. Ruby's Auto Diner
13. Tivoli Terrace
14. Wahoo's Fish Tacos
15. The White House
Gulf of Santa Catalina
Pacific Ocean
Heisler Park
North Coast Hwy.
South Coast Hwy.
Cliff Dr.
Hillcrest Dr.
Chiquita St.
La Brea St.
Fairview St.
Wawe St.
Hawthorne Dr.
Myrthie St.
Locust St.
Jasmine St.
Holly St.
High Dr.
Aster St.
Poplar St.
Cypress Dr.
Cedar Way
Acadia Dr.
Broadway St.
Ocean Ave.
Forest Ave.
3rd St.
2nd St.
Mystic Vw.
Vista Ln.
Mystic Way
Park Ave.
Legion St.
Catalline St.
Goff St.
Glenneyra St.
Wilson St.
Clee St.
St. Anns Dr.
Thalia Dr.
Seaview St.
Anita St.
Oak St.
Brooks St.
Cress St.
Mountain Rd.
Dunning Dr.
Carmelita St.
Agate Rd.
Flora St.
133

blocks of the South Pacific Coast Highway. The first Thursday of each month is the **Laguna Beach Artwalk**, when the multitude of area art galleries remain open until 9pm.

The Mediterranean-revival style **Edwards South Coast Cinema** *(156 Pacific Coast Hwy.; ☎497-1711)* was built in 1934 and was the first building in Laguna to be constructed of steel and concrete. It currently has two theatres showing recent releases.

Main Beach Park ★★ is located in the middle of downtown Laguna Beach, at the intersection of Laguna Canyon Road and the Pacific Coast Highway. The beach area has two half-court basketball courts, sand volleyball courts, benches, picnic tables, public showers and restrooms. A walk along the wooden boardwalk will take you into the **Heisler Park Area ★★**.

The walking trails of **Heisler Park ★★★** wind along the bluffs of Cliff Drive past public art displays, striking ocean views and through the **Glenn E. Vedder Ecological Reserve**. The reserve is a beautiful diving spot, and the natural tide pools are fascinating. Natural tide pool tours are available from Laguna Outdoors *(☎874-6620)*. This is a perfect way to explore the incredible Californian coastline, but be careful not to remove anything from the protected areas of the beach.

The **Laguna Art Museum ★★** *($5; Tue to Sun 11an to 5pm; 307 Cliff Dr. at Pacific Coast Hwy.; ☎494-8971; www.lagunaartmuseum.org)* focuses on the art of California, but also has exhibitions of historical, modern and contemporary American art.

The **Friends of the Sea Lion Marine Mammal Centre ★** *(donations welcome; daily 10am to 4pm; 20612 Laguna Canyon Rd.; ☎494-3050)* is a volunteer, non-profit organization that has been providing medical care to sick or wounded seals and sea lions since 1971. Visitors can take a guided tour of the facility, watch a slide show, and see the recovering animals. Very little human interaction is allowed, however, as the centre tries to keep these ani-

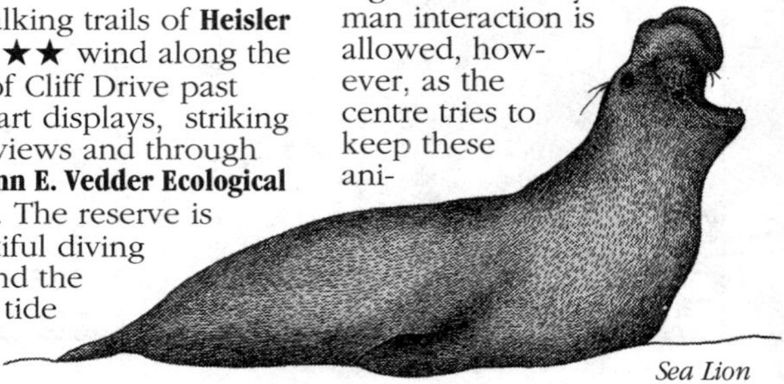

Sea Lion

mals wild, for a more successful re-release to their natural habitat.

The **Hortense Miller Garden** ★★ *(22511 Allview Terrace; ☎497-0716, ext.6; no children under 13)* can be found on the upper slopes of Boat Canyon and features over 1,500 plants from around the world on 2.5 acres (1ha) of superbly landscaped grounds. Hortense, who is 91 years old, still greets guests as they arrive. A feast for the senses, tours last 2hrs and must be booked in advance.

The **Bette Davis House** *(1991 Ocean Way)* is an English Tudor home which overlooks beautiful Wood's Cove. Built in 1929, Bette Davis lived here during the early 1940s.

Dana Point

In the early days, Dana Point was called San Juan Point and served as an anchoring place for mission supply ships. It was also an important site in the hide trade, as hides tanned on the local ranches were thrown over the cliffs to trade ships from New England. Richard Henry Dana, a seaman aboard the *Pilgrim*, one of these trade ships, called the area "the only romantic spot in California" in his book *Two Years Before the Mast*. The town of Dana Point is indeed a romantic place, as the dramatic cliffs and secluded Pacific lookouts attest. The place has somehow managed to retain its small town charm while developing a decent tourism industry with the local harbour.

The focal point of the community, **Dana Point Harbor** *(www.danapointharbor.com)*, houses two marinas which can accommodate 2,500 small craft inside a 1.5mi (2.4km) jetty. In addition to the usual harbour facilities, the area offers windsurfing, jet skiing and certified dive charters. Dana Wharf Sportfishing *(34675 Golden Lantern; ☎496-5784; www.danawharfsportfishing.com)* offers sportfishing charters and whale-watching cruises (Dec to Mar). The harbour is also host to the Festival of Whales (February), the Tallships Festival (September) and the Holiday Boat Parade (December).

The west end of the harbour is home to the **Tallship *Pilgrim*** ★★ *(free; Sundays 10am to 2:30pm; 24200 Dana Point Harbor Dr.; ☎496-2274)*, which is a full-sized replica of the square-rigged vessel that Richard Henry

Dana first sailed into this cove in 1835. Tours of the ship are led by docents in period costume, who explain what life was like aboard one of these seafaring vessels. During the summer months, there are children's programs as well as a "musical marine theatre" series.

The *Pilgrim* also marks the site of the **Orange County Marine Institute ★★★** *(24200 Dana Point Harbor Dr.; ☎496-2274; www.ocean-institute.org)* which operates the 70 ft (23m) *R/V Sea Explorer*, a marine educational vessel with a fully equipped floating laboratory dedicated to environmental education. A variety of programs are offered to allow visitors to get hands-on experience of the challenges faced by marine biologists. Programs are a very reasonable $20 and include a blue whale safari, bioluminescence night cruise (during the new moon only), and a marine wildlife cruise.

Doheny State Park ★★ *($5/car; 25300 Dana Point Harbor Dr.; ☎496-6172; camping $17-$22 - no hook-ups)* is 62 acres (25ha) of green grass and white sand under grand palm trees. The interpretive centre at the park entrance has a small group of aquariums that display the fish found in this area. There are also exhibits about local animals, fossils and skeletons. The **beach ★★** at Doheny Park is a beautiful stretch of well-tended white sand with volleyball courts and fire pits scattered throughout its 1mi (1.6km) length. Towards the west end of the beach is a rocky area that attracts divers and anglers. The nearby estuary is a great place for spotting flocks of migrating birds.

For one of the most picturesque views on the California Coast try **Heritage Park** *(corner of El Camino and Old Green Lantern)*, a lovely terraced park overlooking the marina and the Pacific. Only a block to the west on El Camino, the **Lantern Lookout Park** provides another panoramic vista.

For more information on the surrounding area, check out the small museum of the **Dana Point Historical Society** *(free; 34085 Pacific Coast Hwy.; ☎248-8121)*. The society has a small collection of old photos and artifacts from early Dana Point.

San Clemente

Visitors to San Clemente will notice that this town, just south of Dana Point on the Pacific Coast Highway, is subtly different from its neighbours. The town's founder, Ole Hanson, envisioned a Spanish city by the sea, with white stucco walls under red tiled roofs. The city has continued to follow this architectural style, turning San Clemente into a charming and popular beach town. The city offers almost 10mi (16km) of beach and a 1,200-ft (400m) long fishing pier reaching out into the Pacific.

The **beach** ★★ is the real draw here, since the town has few other interesting attractions. It is a good place, however, to relax and enjoy the surf and sand. Going north or south from the pier, the land rises and paths wind down from the bluffs to the sand.

Step back in time at the **San Clemente Heritage Centre** ★ *($2.75; Mon to Sat 10am to 5pm; 415 North El Camino Real; ☎369-1299)*, which has several rooms highlighting different aspects of the town's history. Exhibits include a tribute to the legends of surfing, the Nixon years, and an art gallery showcasing local artists.

The most popular festival in San Clemente is the **Ocean Festival**, held at the base of the pier on the third weekend of July. The festival features a fishing derby, lifeguard competitions, an art show and sand castle competition, as well as live entertainment.

San Juan Capistrano

The historic city of San Juan Capistrano is the oldest settlement in Orange County, with three adobe houses in the Los Rios district that date back to 1794. The community here treasures its connections to the past, working to promote and protect the many historically significant structures in the area. Walking the streets of town will give visitors a sense of what early Southern California was like, where the great Mission was the centre of the community,

Mission San Juan Capistrano

Exploring

just as it is today in San Juan Capistrano.

The **Mission San Juan Capistrano** ★★★ *($6; every day 8:30 to 5pm; corner of Camino Capistrano and the Ortega Hwy.; ☎248-2048; www. missionsjc.com)* is the third most visited attraction in Orange County—after Disneyland and Knott's Berry Farm—drawing over 500,000 visitors per year and dubbed the "Jewel of the Missions." Stepping onto the grounds evokes a sense of awe as centuries-old bells toll off the slow passage of time. The mission is at once beautiful and romantic, spiritual and spellbinding. Preservation and restoration efforts have left just enough undone to convey a sense of nostalgia within the adobe walls. Inside, Moorish fountains sit among lush gardens. Visitors can wander through the early soldier's barracks, friar's quarters and cemetery to get a look at the small Serra Chapel, the oldest building in California. Inside the chapel is a magnificent gold baroque altar, which is 350 years old. Guides are available to tour the mission, but should be reserved in advance.

Just west of the mission, a beautiful white dome sits four storeys above San Juan and marks the site of the **Train Depot** *(26701 Verdugo St.)*, completed October 8, 1894. This historic landmark is served by Amtrak and the Metrolink and is home to Sarducci's restaurant (see p 314) and the Freight House Saloon (see p 337). A lovely mural depicting life in San Juan has been restored in the bar area of the saloon.

Across the tracks from the depot is the **Los Rios Historical District** ★★, with houses ranging from five decades to two-centuries old. The Montanez, Rios, and Silvas adobes are all that remain of the 40 adobes that once lined this street. The **O'Neill Museum** *(31831 Los Rios St.)* dates back to the late 1800s and is now home to the offices of the San Juan Capistrano Historical Society. For those who wish to explore this area fully, self-guided walking tour maps are available from the society and at many establishments downtown.

Children will love the **Jones Family Mini-Farm**, behind the Olivares House at Los Rios and River Streets. This 3-acre (1.2ha) farm is home to the largest horse in Orange County, as well as other farm animals. Children can take a pony ride *($2)* or feed and interact with the barnyard animals at the petting zoo *($0.50)*. The farm strives to recreate life in San Juan in the early 1900s.

Photography buffs will really enjoy the **House of Photographic Arts** *(27182 Ortega Hwy.; ☎494-1257)* which showcases historical and modern photography by established as well as up-and-coming photographers.

Oceanside

Over the past two centuries, local missionaries and ranch workers have been saying "let's go to the ocean side" on warm days, and thus this quaint resort was born. Oceanside is situated halfway between Los Angeles and San Diego. The small town serves as the area's transportation hub, with trains and buses heading for destinations to the north, south and east. This makes it a good home base to explore the region. The 3.6mi (5km) of wide, white beaches provide an excellent location for all types of water sports, whether it be surfing, sailing, fishing or just plain lounging on the beach. The San Luis Rey Mission acts as the cultural centre of Oceanside, and offers a chance to explore the rich history and culture of the region.

The clean, white-sand **beaches** ★★ of Oceanside fortunately don't draw the same crowds as its counterparts. There is, however, plenty to do here. **The Strand** ★ is a paved path running parallel to the water that is perfect for jogging or in-line skating. The beachfront is divided into eight beaches even though it is one continuous stretch of sand. The beaches north of the pier have much more sand and more room to play. Most of the beaches have firepits, volleyball courts, public restrooms and showers. There is paid parking on both sides of the pier and metered parking on the street.

At 1,942 ft (647m), the **Oceanside Pier** ★★ *(Pier View Way and Pacific St.)* is the longest wooden pier in

Oceanside Pier

Southern California. As with most of the piers along the coast, it is alive with activity from sunrise to sunset. No license is required for pier fishing and there are snack shops along the way if you don't make a catch. An electric tram service is available for those with limited mobility, who can't make the considerable walk to the end.

Over 1,000 boats make their home at the **Oceanside Harbor** ★★ *(1540 Harbor Dr. N; ☎966-4580)*. A variety of services are available here, including whale-watching tours, deep-sea fishing trips and boat rentals. Around the harbour lighthouse is a quaint, Cape-cod style village with a fine selection of shops and restaurants.

Fifty-two trains pass through the **Oceanside Transit Centre** *(235 Tremont St.)*, making Oceanside one of the easiest beaches to reach by public transit. This also makes Oceanside a great home base for those who don't want to battle with traffic. The **Metrolink** *(☎203-808-LINK)* service is intended for commuters but is useful for tourists as well. Commuter trains head north as far as Los Angeles Union Station in the early morning, Monday through Friday. The same trains run south in the evening, but there is no service during the day, so contact Metrolink to plan your travels ahead of time. The **Coaster Beach Train** *($3.00 - $3.75 one way; ☎800-262-7837)* operates throughout the day in both directions as far as San Diego *(1hr)*, making stops along the coast. The last train back from San Diego runs at 6:42pm. **Amtrak** *(☎800-872-7245)* and **Greyhound** *(☎722-1587)* also serve Oceanside from this terminal.

The **Oceanside Historical Society** *(Thu to Sat 10am to 2pm; 305 N. Nevada St.; ☎722-4786)* is located in the historic Gill Fire Station building. The museum has a collection of images from early Oceanside and the staff is very knowledgeable. The society sponsors a monthly historical walking tour of the downtown area on the third Saturday of the month, April through September. Alternatively, a self-guided tour and map are available.

The **Star Theater** ★ *(402 N. Pacific Coast Hwy.; ☎721-5700)* has been lovingly restored to its 1956 grandeur, with its classic neon facade that is visible for blocks. Inside is the largest screen in the county and a seating capacity of 920.

The Spanish-revival style **Oceanside Museum of Art** ★

($3; Tue to Sat 10am to 4pm, Sun 1pm to 4pm; 704 Pier View Way; ☎721-2787) is across from **City Hall** in the **Civic Centre Plaza** ★ *(300 N. Pacific Coast Hwy)*. The museum features exhibitions on loan from major art museums around the world and showcases their own collection of regional, ethnic and local artists. The prime emphasis is on art education for children, and every effort is made to ensure they enjoy the visit. If you are in the area on a Thursday, check out the **Oceanside Farmers' Market** *(Thurs 9am to 12:30pm; Corner of N. Pacific Coast Hwy and Pier View Way)* in the plaza, a chance to taste legendary Californian produce straight from the farm.

For an enlightening perspective on surfing culture and history, check out the **California Surfing Museum** ★ *(free; closed Tue; 10am to 4pm; 223 N. Coast Hwy.; ☎721-6876)*. In addition to the many photos, surfboards and memorabilia, the museum features a new exhibit every six months that pays homage to one of surfing's legends.

Along the north side of Oceanside is **Camp Pendleton** *(Oceanside Harbor/Camp Pendleton ramp off Interstate 5; ☎725-5569)*, the world's largest U.S. Marine Corps Amphibious Training Base. The base is home to 37,000 people, over 75 head of buffalo, and a few attractions. An 1827 adobe ranch house serves as the home of the commanding general. The adobe Chapel and Bunkhouse Museum have period rooms that depict early life on the ranch. Visitors can take a self-guided walking or driving tour of the base, but check with the guard shack for a map to find out the "rules."

Nicknamed the "King of the Missions," the **San Luis del Rey Mission and Museum** ★★★ *($4; every day 10 am to 4:30pm; 4050 Mission Ave.; ☎757-3651; www.sanluisrey.org)* was founded on June 13, 1798 by Father Fermin Francisco de Lausen and is located about 3mi (5km) east of town. Named after St. Louis IX, King of France and patron of the Secular Franciscan order, it was the 18th Spanish mission in California and also the largest. The present structure was built between 1811 and 1815 with timbers from Mt. Palomar and adobe made on site. Since the 1890s the building has been under constant restoration and the brilliant white walls and perfect arches look better today than ever. The mission provides guided and self-guided tours through the sunken gardens and along the arched colonnade after a visit to the museum.

Visitors are also welcome to take part in weekend mass.

Behind the mission, the **Heritage Park Village and Museum** ★★ *(free; grounds open every day 9am to 4m; ☎966-4545)* awaits visitors. The park is a collection of buildings from the late 19th and early 20th century that have been carefully brought in and assembled as a recreation of an old Californian town. Take a stroll back through time as you pass the town's first General Store, the Portola Inn, the Blacksmith Shop and even the old City Jail. Each building is period-furnished and faces onto a lovely park and gazebo. Unfortunately, the buildings are only open on Sundays from 1pm to 4pm. Guided tours are also available during the summer.

Windmills

Tour L: Palm Springs

The Agua Caliente Cahuilla Indians were the first people to settle in the Palm Springs area. They were attracted by the ample flora and fauna of today's Indian Canyons and the bubbling hot springs in the area were said to have magical healing powers. By the mid-1800s the Mormons of San Bernardino had made their way to this area, bringing with them smallpox which decimated the Cahuilla population. Even today the tribe numbers under 300. In 1884 John McCallum became the first white settler to the area, building the now-famous McCallum Adobe that still stands today. By 1940, the population numbered just over 5,000, and swelled seasonally to almost 9,000 as tourists and the Hollywood film community began to discover this oasis in the desert. After the Second

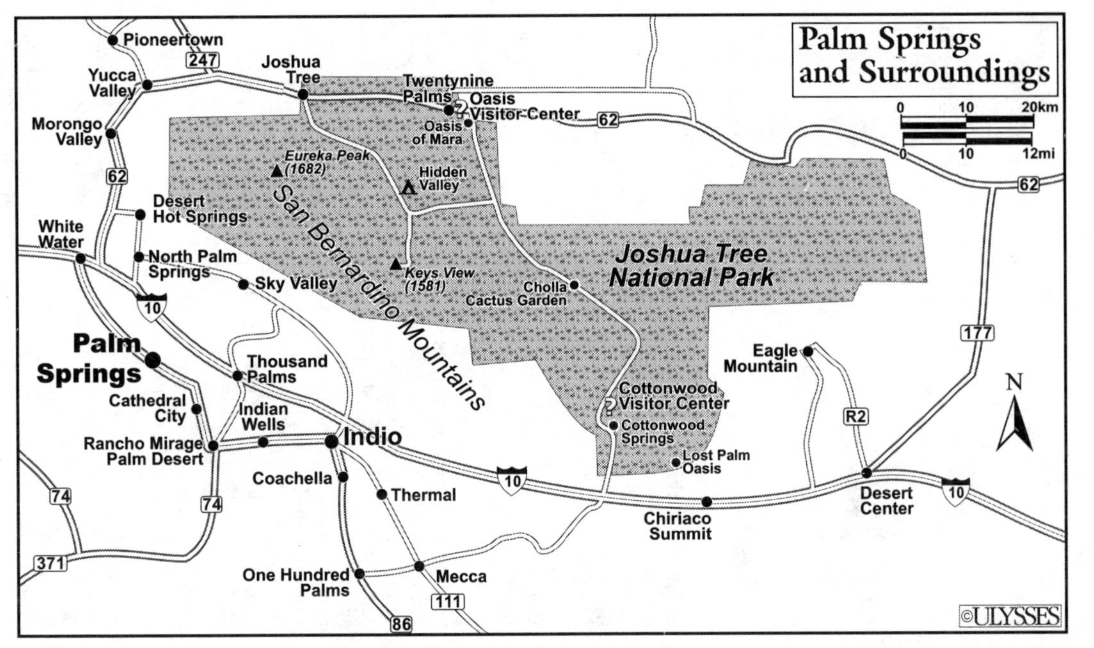

Palm Springs and Surroundings
0
10
20km
0
10
12mi
Pioneertown
247
Joshua Tree
Yucca Valley
Twentynine Palms
Oasis Visitor Center
Oasis of Mara
62
Morongo Valley
Eureka Peak (1682)
Hidden Valley
Desert Hot Springs
San Bernardino Mountains
White Water
North Palm Springs
Sky Valley
Keys View (1581)
Cholla Cactus Garden
Joshua Tree National Park
10
Palm Springs
Thousand Palms
Eagle Mountain
177
Cathedral City
Indian Wells
Cottonwood Visitor Center
Cottonwood Springs
R2
N
Rancho Mirage
Palm Desert
Indio
Lost Palm Oasis
Coachella
Thermal
Desert Center
74
Chiriaco Summit
371
One Hundred Palms
Mecca
111
86
©ULYSSES

Ocotillo

World War, the secret was out and Palm Springs became the "playground of the stars," with regular visits from the Brat Pack and other Hollywood celebrities. Bob Hope was appointed honorary mayor.

Until the early 1990s, Palm Springs had a reputation as a party resort town, and thousands of students descended on the town during spring break. After a small riot one year, Mayor Sonny Bono created new laws to discourage this influx of students, much to the dismay of local bar and hotel owners. Today Palm Springs has adopted a more subdued atmosphere, but continues to attract visitors in record numbers. The warm, dry climate and cosmopolitan restaurants, shopping and hotels keep visitors coming back year after year.

The tour starts at the world-famous Desert Museum.

A must-see on your visit is the **Palm Springs Desert Museum** ★★★ *($7.50; Tue to Sat 10am to 5pm, Sun noon to 5pm; 1101 Museum Dr.; ☎325-0189)*. Art exhibits include a large permanent collection of contemporary and Western American art, with special emphasis on California. The natural science galleries are the most interesting, however, focusing on the history and culture of the local indigenous peoples, the flora and fauna of the desert and containing a special wing devoted to Death Valley. Here you can learn about the Cahuilla Indians as well as the rattlesnakes, desert tortoises and lizards that inhabit the desert around you, while a seismograph records earthquake activity all over Southern California. A wonderfully landscaped **sculpture garden** awaits after the galleries. Also located in the museum is the **Annenberg Theater**, *(☎325-4490)*, a 450-seat, state-of-the-art theatre facility that presents ballet, opera and classical music.

Walk north to Amado Road and turn right (east).

Stop in to the **Palm Springs Chamber of Commerce** ★ *(190 W. Amado Rd.;☎325-1577)* for more information, a free map, and coupons to the area's attractions. The friendly staff would be happy to recommend some attractions to you.

Continue east to Palm Canyon Drive and turn right (south).

Palm Canyon Drive ★★★ is the main street and the heart of Palm Springs. Walking down this street you will find all sorts of small boutiques, opulent hotels and art galleries. Also of interest is the Palm Springs walk of stars, with gold stars inlaid in the sidewalk to honour such Palm Springs regulars as Frank Sinatra and Marilyn Monroe.

Across from the Mercado Plaza shopping centre, is the **Plaza Theater ★** *(128 S. Palm Canyon Dr.; ☎327-0225)*, which is home to the critically acclaimed Palm Springs International Film Festival. The **Fabulous Palm Springs Follies** *(☎864-6514)* also perform here, a group of actors 50 years of age and over that present a music, dance and humour of the 1930s and 40s.

Some of the greatest works of Southwest and Latino art are showcased at **Adagio Galleries ★★** *(193 S. Palm Canyon Dr.; ☎320-2230)*. The gallery has recently been expanded and hosts major showings throughout the year of such artists as Frank Howell, Nivia Gonzalez and John Nieto.

Learn about the original people of Palm Springs at the **Agua Caliente Cultural Museum Information Center ★** *(free; Mon to Sat 10am to 4pm, Sun noon to 3pm; 213 S. Palm Canyon Dr. ☎323-0151)*. Displays highlighting the history and accomplishments of the Agua Caliente Cahuilla Indians feature artifacts, music and photographs. The Flora Patencio Basketry exhibit highlights her famous work and a desert landscape diorama that shows how the Cahuilla Indians lived and worked with their environment.

The **Village Green Heritage Center ★★** *(221-223 S. Palm Canyon Dr.)* is dedicated to the pioneers that helped build Palm Springs out of rough desert country. The centre is a collection of heritage buildings that strives to educate visitors on the rich history of the area.

The **McCallum Adobe** was the first pioneer home in Palm Springs, built in 1885. It is now home to the **Palm Springs Historical Society ★** *($0.50; Oct to May; 221 South Palm Canyon Dr.; ☎323-8297)*.

Next to the adobe is **Miss Cornelia White's house ★**, built nine years later out of

● ATTRACTIONS	
1. Palm Springs Desert Museum / Annenberg Theater	6. Village Green Heritage Center
2. Palm Springs Chamber of Commerce	7. Reflections of ...
3. Plaza Theater	8. Spa Hotel and Casino
4. Adagio Galleries	9. J. Behman Gallery & Desert Fine Arts Academy
5. Agua Caliente Cultural Museum Information Center	10. Palm Springs International Airport

ACCOMMODATIONS	
1. Ballantine's Hotel	5. Octillo Lodge
2. Hyatt Regency Suites	6. Ramada Resort and Conference Center
3. L'Horizon Garden	7. The Royal Sun
4. Motel 6	

RESTAURANTS	
1. Capra's	8. Muriel's Supper Club
2. Delhi Palace	9. Peabody's Coffee Bar and Music Studio
3. Jamba Juice	10. The Rock Garden Café
4. Kaiser Grill	11. Sherman's Deli and Bakery
5. Kiyosaku	12. Sorrentino's Seafood House
6. LalaJava	13. Village Pub
7. Las Casuelas Terraza	

railway ties and home to Palm Springs' first telephone. Both contain personal memorabilia of the original owners and are worth a quick visit.

Ruddy's General Store Museum ★★ *($.050; Oct to Jun, Thu to Sun 10am to 4pm Jul to Sep Sat and Sun 10am to 4pm; ☎327-2156)* is probably the most fun of the three museums. Inside, over 6,000 *unused* items line the shelves. Take a minute to wander through and marvel at the collection of everyday goods from the late 1930s.

Reflections of... *(285 S. Palm Canyon Dr.; ☎800-921-7787)* has one of the largest collections of Art Glass in the United States. Over 300 artists are featured, who were chosen for their skill in creating vases, sculptures, paperweights and oil lamps. You might want to leave the kids outside.

Turn left (east) on Baristo Road to South Indian Canyon Drive. Turn left (north on Indian Canyon.

Three blocks north of Baristo Road is the **Spa Hotel and Casino** *(24hrs; 100 N. Indian Canyon Dr.; ☎325-1461)*. Here you can try

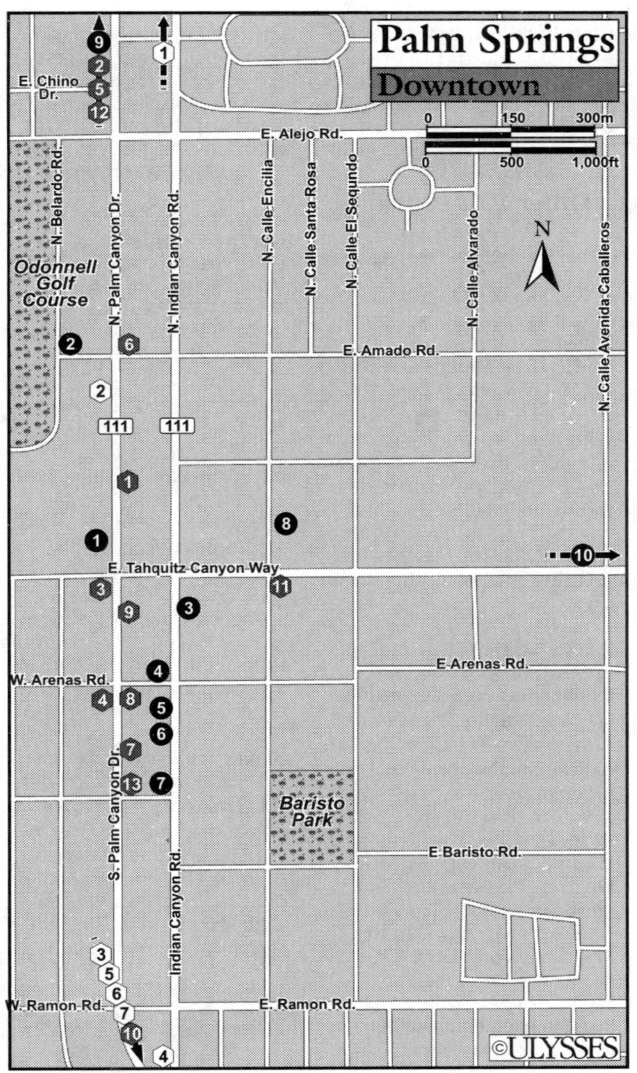

Palm Springs
Downtown
0
150
300m
0
500
1,000ft
N
E. Chino Dr.
E. Alejo Rd.
N. Belardo Rd.
N. Palm Canyon Dr.
N. Indian Canyon Rd.
N. Calle Encilia
N. Calle Santa Rosa
N. Calle El Sequndo
N. Calle Alvarado
N. Calle Avenida Caballeros
Odonnell Golf Course
E. Amado Rd.
111
111
E. Tahquitz Canyon Way
E Arenas Rd.
W. Arenas Rd.
S. Palm Canyon Dr.
Indian Canyon Rd.
Baristo Park
E Baristo Rd.
W. Ramon Rd.
E. Ramon Rd.
©ULYSSES

your luck at the slots or sit in on a hand of poker or blackjack. The interior doesn't meet Vegas standards, but it's a great place to spend a rare wet afternoon.

Other Palm Springs Attractions

If you need to beat the desert heat, grab your bathing suit and head over to the **Oasis Water Park** ★★ *(1500 Gene Autry Trail; ☎327-0499)*. Thirteen water slides with such intimidating names as the Black Widow and the Scorpion provide the thrills while the giant wave pool and lazy Whitewater River are perfect for relaxing and catching some rays.

For cutting-edge contemporary art, stop by the **J. Behman Gallery & Desert Fine Arts Academy** *(1103 N. Palm Canyon Dr.; ☎320-6806)*. The gallery showroom displays pieces created by the students of this full-time art school and is a refreshing change from the classics. Drop in on Saturdays for a children's craft class or on Friday for an adult figure drawing workshop.

Over 50 years in the making, **Moorten Botanical Gardens** ★★ *(everyday; 1701 S. Palm Canyon Dr.; ☎327-6555)* features over 3,000 varieties of desert plants. Several different habitats have been constructed to provide for the differing needs of the plants. Stroll through and marvel at the incredible diversity of desert fauna.

On the north side of the Palm Springs airport is the **Palm Springs Air Museum** ★★ *($7.50; everyday 10am to 5pm; 745 N. Gene Autry Trail; ☎778-6262)*. This gigantic museum is dedicated to preserving the fighters, bombers and trainers from the U.S. armed forces. Two main display hangars house everything from the B-17 *Flying Fortress* to the P-38 *Lightning*. Climb up the many ladders and take a look in the cockpit. Get some hands-on experience in one of their flight simulators. Flight demonstrations are held occasionally and there is a unique gift shop

Hadley Fruit Orchards ★★ *(free; everyday 9am to 5pm 122 La Plaza; ☎325-2160)* is a working farm that grows a variety of fruits, dates and nuts. Walk through the orchards then sample some of their goods including their signature date shakes.

Outdoors

With its heavenly climate, 70mi (115km) of beaches, mountain chains and health-conscious lifestyle, Los Angeles offers a wide range of parks, beaches and outdoor activities to keep you busy 365 days per year.

Parks

Angeles National Forest

Wilson Mountain stands proudly in Angeles National Forest, a park that stretches north of Pasadena. You can drive up towards its peak and enjoy a spectacular view of all of Los Angeles. The **Chilao Visitor's Center** is located a dozen miles north of Wilson Mountain and features a lovely forest exhibit. The center also serves as the starting point of several hiking trails.

Griffith Park

With its 9,885 acres (4,000ha), Griffith Park is Los Angeles's biggest recreation area. The park's trees, hills and tangled, winding trails are laid out in the English style that was used at the turn of the century in urban park landscaping.

Adorned with a few monuments, and featuring playgrounds, bicycle paths, a golf course and horseback riding trails (see p 229), Griffith Park is a tourist attraction in itself (see p 134).

Hancock Park

After visiting the L.A. County Museum of Art, stop and have a well deserved rest on the cool grass in Hancock Park *(Wilshire Blvd., Museum Row)*. The **La Brea Tar Pits**, featuring replicas of prehistoric animals that stand where a great number of fossils were uncovered (and which are today on display at the site's Page Museum) are also worth a visit.

Placerita Canyon State & County Park

If you sometimes get the impression that Los Angeles County is nothing but a succession of suburban concrete houses, you should know that the Placerita Canyon State & County Park *(19152 Placerita Canyon Rd. Newhall, ☎815-259-7721)* has 700 acres (284ha) of oak forest and an indigenous chaparral. Many trails cut through the park, which also features a nature interpretation centre.

Beaches

L.A.'s beaches are an integral part of the Southern California lifestyle. No other public attraction is as popular as the vast, white-sand beaches that are bathed by the Pacific Ocean.

Below is a list of such beaches, namely those that are the most accessible. They are, for the most part, safe and well-maintained, and swimming is almost always enjoyable (make sure to respect the "no swimming" signs in certain areas), even if the water is rather cold in winter. Beaches are officially open (i.e. supervised by lifeguards) every day of the year between 9am and 9:30pm.

For any information on Los Angeles's beaches, call ***☎457-9701*** for Malibu, ***☎578-0478*** for Santa Monica or ***☎379-8471*** for Manhattan and Redondo.

Will Rogers State Beach

Located less than 2mi (3km) north of the Santa Monica Pier, Will Rogers State Beach *(15100 Pacific Coast Hwy., Pacific Palisades, ☎310-394-3266)* is popular with families, young single people and the gay community. Sports enthusiasts are drawn here by the facilities such as a dozen volleyball nets, gym equipment and a playground for the little ones. Be careful, as the water may sometimes be affected by pollution, especially after a storm.

Installations and services: bathrooms, lifeguards, snack bar, volleyball nets, gym, parking lot.

Santa Monica State Beach

Santa Monica State Beach, which is located at the end of the Santa Monica Freeway (I-10), is no doubt worthy of the title of Los Angeles's most famous beach. It is also the most easily accessible beach from downtown and is the ideal spot for sunbathing or meeting interesting people. Music concerts are also held here in summer.

Installations and services: bathrooms, lifeguards, parking lot (rather pricy), bicycle path, volleyball nets, fun fair, showers, snack bar.

Venice City Beach

Venice's beautiful white-sand beach is bathed by a blue and inviting sea. This is a paradise for in-line skaters, walkers and cyclists, not to mention volleyball enthusiasts and sun worshippers. But what really grabs your attention here is the succession of T-shirt merchants, jewellers and pizza shops that stretches for over a mile. Added to these attractions is a blend of musicians, magicians, fortune-tellers and dancers who try to outdo each other to elicit some change from the procession of passersby, who stroll along the beach all summer. Outdoor aerobic classes are also given at **Muscle Beach** *(corner 18th Ave.)*, an actual fitness club equipped with weights and exercise equipment, located right on the beach.

Installations and services: bathrooms, bicycle and in-line skate rentals, parking lot, showers, snack bar.

Manhattan Beach

The extremely lively Manhattan Beach attracts a great number of beach volleyball enthusiasts. Several nets are set up for anyone who wishes to practise this sport, which is becoming increasingly popular in the United States. This beach also serves as a meeting place for young, tanned and muscled professionals who come to see and be seen.

Hermosa Beach

Hermosa Beach is located just south of its sister beach, Manhattan Beach. The only obvious difference seems to be its patrons, who consist mainly of rebellious teenagers.

Installations and services: bathrooms, lifeguards, volleyball nets, snack bar, showers.

Redondo Beach

Redondo Beach marks the starting point of a long and lively sandy beach that stretches more than a mile southward. A whole slew of activities awaits travellers who venture here, including restaurants, stores, boat excursions, snorkelling around a shipwreck and fishing. Rock and jazz concerts are also held in summer.

Installations and services: parking lot, lifeguards, snack bar, bathrooms, showers, volleyball nets.

Crescent Beach

Located across from the port, this beach is the heart of Avalon, and is bordered by the city's main artery, which makes it rather hectic. A jetty divides the beach in two, with the ferry's quay on one side and Avalon's famous casino on the other. You can get here by taking Crescent Avenue.

Installations and services: bathrooms, showers, beach equipment rental on the street bordering the beach.

Huntington Beach

The **beaches** of Huntington are the city's main attraction, stretching for 8mi (13km) east and west of downtown. Just west of the city, **Bolsa Chica Beach** tends to be less crowded than its counterparts, and fronts the ecological reserve of the same name (see p 192). The **Huntington City Beach** surrounds the pier, and is a popular place to watch local surfers. **Huntington State Beach** is a 2mi-long

(3.2km) sandy beach with six wheelchair ramps that reach almost to the water. All beaches include picnic facilities, outdoor showers and free parking nearby. Rangers and lifeguards are on duty year-round at both the state and city beaches.

Big Corona and Little Corona Beaches are found just east of the Entrance Channel, in front of Corona del Mar. These smaller, less crowded beaches are great for families, watching yachts come into the harbor, and scuba diving.

Newport

The **Newport Municipal Beach ★** stretches from the Santa Ana River Jetty and along the Balboa Peninsula to the Entrance Channel of Newport Harbor. Sun seekers are best to stay to the west end of the beach to avoid the considerable crowds that invade this beach on the weekends. Beach parking is available at either of the piers, or at one of the numerous beachfront lots *($7 maximum)*. **The Wedge**, by the Entrance Channel, is an excellent surfing spot, but once again, it fills up quickly. Inexperienced surfers and swimmers should try to remain within sight of the lifeguard towers. Beach volleyball courts and campfire spots are available. Numerous small beaches run along the inland shore of the Balboa Peninsula. At Bay Avenue, between 18th and 19th Streets is a calm **beach** that is lifeguard-supervised.

Oceanside

The clean, white-sand **beaches ★★** of Oceanside fortunately don't draw the same crowds as its counterparts. There is, however, plenty to do here. **The Strand** is a paved path running parallel to the water that is perfect for jogging or in-line skating. The beachfront is divided into eight beaches even though it is one continuous stretch of sand. The beaches north of the pier have much more sand and more room to play. Most of the beaches have firepits, volleyball courts, public restrooms and showers. There is paid parking on both sides of the pier and metered parking on the street.

Outdoor Activities

Cycling

We don't recommend the bicycle as your mode of transportation on the streets of Los Angeles. The heavy traffic and aggressive behaviour of some motorists often turns the city's streets into a real jungle that is openly hostile toward cyclists, in-line skaters and sometimes even regular pedestrians.

Los Angeles has nearly as many bicycle paths as highways, and they are rarely congested. Many of the paths run along parks, rivers, aqueducts and lakes, thus offering a variety of beautiful panoramas of the region. A good example is the flat 9mi (14.5km) path that surrounds the **Sepulveda Dam Recreation Area**, right in the heart of the San Fernando Valley.

An exceptional bicycle path runs along the Pacific Ocean coastline. This long, protected route stretches around 20mi (30km) between Temescal Canyon and Redondo Beach. To rent a bicycle, head to **Rental on the Beach** *(2100 Ocean Front Walk, Venice, ☎821-9338)* or **Perry's Beach Rental** *(2400 Ocean Front Walk, Venice, ☎452-7609).*

Griffith Park also has 14mi (23km) of bicycle paths, ranging from beginner to expert levels. The **Crystal Springs Loop**, which follows Crystal Springs Road and Zoo Drive to the park's eastern limit, will take you to the carousel as well as Travel Town; the **Mineral Wells Loop**, a rather steep climb, runs past the Harding Golf Course before leading back down to Zoo Drive to reach Travel Town and the zoo garden. For bicycle rentals, head to **The Annex** *($7.50/half-day, $15/day, $25/two days; 3157 Los Feliz Blvd., ☎323-661-6665).*

The **West Fork Trail** in the San Gabriel Mountains no doubt remains the most panoramic path in the entire Los Angeles area. This easy, paved 6.7mi (11km) trail runs parallel to the western branch of the San Gabriel River. Take Route 210 until Azusa, then go north on Route 39 for 0.6mi (1km) until you reach a parking lot located not far past the Rincon Ranger Station.

T.Z. Bike Tours also organizes guided bicycle tours in the Santa Monica Mountains and the Angeles Crest (San Gabriel Mountains), for amateurs and professionals alike. For information, call **Super-Go** *(☎451-9977)* or **I. Martin** *(☎323-653-6900)*.

For additional information on the region's bicycle paths, ask for the brochure published and distributed by the Transportation Commission *(☎213-623-1194)*.

In-line Skating

In-line skaters wishing to roll down Los Angeles's streets should also heed the warnings given to cyclists. You are better off practising this activity on the above-mentioned bicycle paths, even though cyclists enjoy the right of way. **Venice** is L.A.'s, and perhaps even the world's, in-line skating capital. The **Ballona Creek Trail** in Marina del Rey *(starting at Fisherman's Village)* is another great option.

Boardwalk Skates *($4/hr, $12/day; 201½ Ocean Front Walk, Venice, ☎450-6634)* rents in-line skates, as does **Skatey's** *($5/hr, $10/day; 102 Washington St., Venice, ☎310-823-7971)*.

To practise this activity indoors, go to **Moonlight Rollerway** *(5110 San Fernando Rd., Glendale, ☎818-241-3630)* or **Skateland** *(18140 Parthenia St., Northridge, ☎818-885-1491)*.

Palm Springs

Bighorn Cycles *(302 N. Palm Canyon Dr.; ☎325-3367)* offers mountain bikes for as low as $29/day, with kids' bikes and city cruisers also available. Bighorn also leads tours through Indian Canyons *($49)* and the estates of Palm Springs *($35)*.

Jogging

Exposition Park is popular with joggers, where they can practise their favourite sport in the company of students and downtown professionals. Other locations offer specially designed, beautiful trails, including **San Vicente Boulevard** in Santa Monica, the **Lake Hollywood Reservoir**, east of **Cahuenga Boulevard** in the Hollywood Hills, as well as the 22mi (35km) bicycle path adjacent to the beach, particularly near Venice and Santa Monica.

Golf

The Los Angeles region abounds in magnificent golf courses.

The **Rancho Park Golf Course** *(1040 W. Pico Blvd., West Hollywood, ☎310-838-7373)*, an 18-hole course with a practice green, is no doubt one of the most challenging. Several quality golf courses are located in the San Fernando Valley. The **Balboa and Encino Golf Course** *(1821 Burbank Blvd., Encino, ☎818-995-1170)* is a good choice, as is the **Woodley Lakes Golf Course** *(331 Woodley Ave., Van Nuys, ☎818-780-6886)*, which is dotted with trees.

For its part, Griffith Park offers two magnificent 18-hole golf courses: the **Harding Municipal Golf Course** and the **Wilson Municipal Golf Course** *(accessed by the entrance on Riverside Dr. and Los Feliz Blvd. 4730 Crystal Springs Dr., ☎323-663-2555)*. The **Roosevelt Municipal Golf Course** *(entrance on Vermont Ave., 2650 N. Vermont Ave., ☎323-665-2011)* offers a nine-hole course.

Other lovely nine-hole golf courses are also open to the public, such as the **Los Feliz Municipal Golf Course** *(3207 Los Feliz Blvd., ☎323-663-7758)*, **Hulmby Park** *(601 Club View Dr., Beverly Hills, ☎310-276-1604)* and finally the **Penmar** *(1233 Rose Ave., Venice, ☎310-396-6228)*.

The **Catalina Island Visitors Golf Course** *(☎310-510-0530)* on Catalina Island, is a nine-hole course located in an enchanting setting.

Palm Springs

Palm Springs has dozens of fantastic golf courses to choose from in both a desert and classical layout. Here are a few resources for last minute tee times.

Next Day Golf (☎345-8463) and **Stand-by Golf** (☎321-2665) offer a good selection of guaranteed tee times at public, semi-public and private golf courses in Palm Springs. Call a day in advance.

Hiking

Hikers have a wide variety of excursions to choose from, with a great selection available throughout the entire region.

Griffith Park *(4730 Crystal Springs Dr.)*, located in the Hollywood Hills, is a good choice for walkers. With close to 56mi (90km) of trails, this park borders the Hollywood Hills, at the edge of the Santa Monica Mountains. For additional information and to obtain maps of the region, get in touch with the local ranger station *(☎213-665-5188)*. **Mount Hollywood Loop Trail** (6mi or 9.7km) is among the area's best. Starting on the outskirts of the carousel, it runs along a stream, crosses lands inhabited by deer and coyotes, and finally exits the canyon to climb the chaparral-covered slopes of Hollywood Mountain. Trails also skirt around the **Lake Hollywood Reservoir** *(Hollywood Fwy., Barham Boulevard exit, turn onto Lake Hollywood Dr. to reach the reservoir)*.

The San Gabriel Mountains are crisscrossed from every angle by trails created to be explored. At the very end of Chaney Trail Road, in Altadena, you will discover a charming area for a recreational hike through a canyon dotted with trees. The **Lower Millard Canyon Falls Trail** (0.5mi or 0.8km) leads to a 4.6ft (15m) waterfall surrounded by enormous rocks. If your thirst for adventure has not been quenched thus far, follow the **Upper Millard Canyon Trail** (2.5mi or 4km). For a more ambitious hike starting at the same point, follow the **Mount Lowe Railway Trail** (3.5mi or 5.6km), at the end of which you will see the abandoned tracks of the Mount Lowe Railway (a.k.a. the Alpine Division Trolley), as well as the ruins of the Alpine Tavern lodge. This trail is of medium difficulty, and the view of Los Angeles it affords is spectacular.

Mountainous wilderness areas perfect for hiking, such as the Santa Monica Mountains, still exist near Los Angeles. The Santa Monica Mountains' bushy, grassy-hill setting is marked by gurgling brooks and breathtaking canyons. Several hiking trails wind through the **Santa Monica Mountains National Recreation Area** *(information ☎805-370-2301)*. The **Inspiration Point Trail** (2mi or 3.2km) will let you discover a view of Westside during a visit to the Will Rogers State Historic Park. The Topanga Canyon State Park also offers more than 30mi (50km) of trails, including the Musch Ranch Loop Trail (2.5mi or 4km), which cuts through five vegetation ecosystems. With its plunging views of the sea and the Santa Ynez Canyon, you can admire the heights of the Palisades Highlands from the Santa Ynez Canyon Trail (6.2mi or 10km).

If possible, go in springtime when the wildflowers display their vivid colours.

Fans of U.S. TV and movies will want to trek down the **Century Ranch Trail** (2.3mi or 3.7km), in Malibu Creek State Park, to see the shooting location of the *M*A*S*H** TV series and the movie *Love Is A Many Splendoured Thing*. The trail runs along Malibu Creek and leads to Rock Pool, The Gorge and Century Lake.

The **Palos Verdes Peninsula Trail** (5mi or 8km) follows a stretch of rocky headland sculpted by the waves, and runs along a pebbly beach that skirts around quiet coves from which you can observe marine life in numerous pools. The trail begins at Malaga Cove and ends at the Point Vicente lighthouse.

Near Malaga Cove, in the Plaos Verdes Estate Shoreline Preserve, the **Seashore-Shipwreck Trail** (1.9mi or 3km) lets you discover the shipwreck of the *Dominator*, an old Greek vessel that is slowly disintegrating on the beach. The trail, which skims the shoreline by threading through pools and coves, is marked by numerous large rocks you have to climb over.

In the San Fernando Valley, the **Mount Lukens Stone Canyon Trail** (3.3mi or 5.3km) which climbs a 5,075ft (1,547m) peak (the highest in the Los Angeles area), is a rather arduous climb. On a clear day you can see the Pacific in the distance, beyond a blanket of residential areas and rolling hills. The trail begins at Sunland, bordering Doske Road. Don't forget to bring along a supply of water.

Hikers who want to trek through Catalina Island must obtain a permit beforehand from the **Santa Catalina Island Conservancy** *(free; every day 9am to 5pm; Third St., corner Claressa St., ☎510-2595)* in Avalon or Two Harbours *(free; Box 5086, Two Harbours, ☎510-0303)*. The interior is dry and desert-like, so bring a lot of water. Airport Road, which is paved, climbs through the surrounding hills, and is the only way to get there. The entire coast will unravel itself before your eyes, as will the oak, pine and eucalyptus forests that adorn the edges of the road. From the airport, you can follow a figure-eight-shaped path that features most of the island's scenery. Catalina Island protects around 400 species of vegetation, some of which are found nowhere else in the world. Animal wildlife (quails, turkeys, mountain goats, foxes, deer, boars) is just as abundant, as are the bisons that a movie studio introduced in the 1920s for the filming of a western. The **Catalina Island Visitor's Bureau** *(☎310-510-1520)* will provide you with a list of establishments and all the necessary information. You'll have the opportunity of visiting interesting attractions on the island, such as **Black Jack Mine**, **Ripper's Cove**, **Emerald Bay**, **Parson's Landing**, **Little Harbour**, **Rancho Escondido**, **Middle Ranch** and **Eagle's Nest Lodge**.

The Beaches of Orange County

Newport Beach

The **Upper Newport Bay Ecological Reserve** *(2400 Irvine Ave.; ☎646-8009)* has a 10mi (16km) loop trail that winds through the reserve. Free naturalist-guided walking tours are offered the first and third Saturday of the month.

Huntington Beach

The **Bolsa Chica Ecological Reserve** *(tours 9am and 10:30am, first Sat of the month, Sep to Apr; Warner Ave. at the Pacific Coast Hwy.; ☎800-628-7275 ext.119)* has a 1.5mi (2.5km) interpretive loop trail, with informative signs along it. Keep an eye open for the many birds that make this reserve their temporary home.

Palm Springs

Exploring **Indian Canyons** is a popular route for hikers, as are the trails that lead from **Mountain Station** into San Jacinto State Park. Maps are available at the Indian Canyons Ranger Station and in the Mountain Station gift shop.

Tennis

The city's various parks feature several outdoor tennis courts. For a complete list, contact the **L.A. Department of Recreation and Parks** *(200 N. Main St., Los Angeles, ☎213-473-7070)*.

Lincoln Park *(corner Lincoln St. and Wilshire Blvd., Santa Monica)*, **Westwood Park** *(1375 Veteran Ave., West L.A.)*, **Barrington Recreationnal Center** *(Barrington Ave., south of Sunset Blvd., East L.A.)* and **Griffith Park** *(Riverside Dr., south of Los Feliz Blvd. and north of the entrance on Vermont Ave.)* all have lit courts.

Merchant of Tennis *(118 S. La Cienaga Blvd., West Hollywood, ☎310-855-1946)* offers lit courts until 3am.

Fishing

The waters surrounding Los Angeles abound in sport fishing favourites: barracudas, sea bass, halibuts and even sharks.

Marina del Rey Fishing *(Dock 52, Fiji Way, ☎822-3625)* for half-day excursions *($22)*.

Redondo Sport Fishing Company *(233 N. Harbour Dr., ☎372-2111)* also offers half-day excursions, for $23 per person.

L.A. Harbour Sport Fishing *(☎547-9916)*.

Scuba Diving

Scuba diving and snorkelling enthusiasts will get their fill along the entire Los Angeles coast. Leo Carrillo State Beach, Catalina Island and the Channel Islands are some of the West Coast's best diving locations. **New England Divers** *(2936 Clark Ave., Long Beach, ☎562-421-8939)* and **Dive'n Surf** *(504 N. Broadway, Redondo Beach, ☎372-8423)* will provide you with all the equipment you need for this adventure.

Catalina Island is well known by divers throughout the world. With its suburb location at the junction of the northern and southern halves of the Pacific Ocean, it attracts a surprising variety of marine life, including large fish that suddenly appear from the depths and small colourful species that inhabit the thick clumps of kelp along the coast. The island also features a good number of caves and rusted shipwrecks scattered on the floor of coastal waters. Several establishments organize excursions and rent diving suits.

Catalina Diver's Supply
Box 12, Avalon
☎800-353-0330
☎ 510-0330
⇌ 510-0695
www.catalina.com/cds

Catalina Scuba Lux
12 Catalina Ave., Avalon
☎ 510-2350
www.scubalux.com

Catalina Snorkeling Adventures
Box 1534, Avalon
☎ 510-8558
www.catalinasnorkeling.com

The **Casino Point Marine Park**, located at the tip of the Casino, is a great place to go scuba diving. It was designated a marine park in 1965 and is a diver's paradise. Equipment rental on the spot.

The Beaches of Orange County

Visitors can fish from the piers in most beach towns without a licence.

Newport Beach

Davey's Locker Sportfishing *(400 Main St., Balboa; ☎673-1434)* offers individual ticket sales for half-day, 3/4 day, full-day and shark fishing trips year round. Whale-watching excursions are also available January to March.

Dana Point

Dana Wharf Sportfishing *(34675 Golden Lantern; ☎496-5794)* offers half-day, full-day and week-long sportfishing trips.

Bird-Watching

The Beaches of Orange County

Many of the parks and wildlife reserves on the coast are in the path of the Pacific Flyway, serving as welcome stops for the numerous species of birds migrating along this route. There are also several species that make these wildlife refuges their home year round.

Seal Beach

The **Anaheim Bay National Wildlife Refuge** is accessible to visitors on the last Saturday of the month *(info ☎598-1024)*, when a shuttle runs through the 1000-acre (404ha) reserve. The refuge is a salt marsh area that is a breeding ground for various fish and migratory birds. The tour is free and leaves from the main gate of the base at 9am. There is only limited access to the refuge because it is located within the **U.S. Naval Weapons Support Facility** *(www.sbeach.navy.mil)*. Giant naval vessels can be seen coming in and out of Anaheim Bay.

Huntington Beach

The **Bolsa Chica Ecological Reserve** *(Warner Ave. at the Pacific Coast Hwy.; ☎800-628-7275 ext. 119)* is a protected wetland reserve that serves as a rest area for birds migrating along the Pacific Flyway. The 530 acres (214ha) are also home to a variety of wildlife that is relatively easy to spot. (See "Exploring," p 192).

Newport Beach

The **Upper Newport Bay Ecological Reserve** *(2400 Irvine Ave.; ☎646-8009)* is a 752-acre (304 ha) coastal wetland reserve that supports six ecological habitats. A variety of fish, mammals and over 200 species of birds call this reserve home.

San Juan Capistrano

Every year the swallows of Goya, Argentina, return to their nests at Mission San Juan Capistrano, drawing the largest crowd of bird-watchers in California.

Kayaking

You can go sea kayaking on Catalina Island, where both short and long excursions along the island's small bays are organized.

Descanso Beach Ocean Sports
Box 38, Avalon
☎ ***510-1226***
www.kayakcatalinaisland.com

Wet Sport Rental & Catalina Kayaks
Box 231, Avalon
☎ ***510-2229***
www.catalinakayaks.com

Cruises

The Beaches of Orange County

Newport Beach

Balboa Boat Rentals *(beside the Balboa Ferry dock; ☎673-7200)* rents by the hour or half day at reasonable prices. Double kayaks and pedal boats cost $50/half-day, while motor and fishing boats run at $100 and more.

Adventures at Sea *(3101 W. Pacific Coast Hwy., Suite 209; ☎650-2412; www.boatcharter.com)* offers dinner cruises, sailing and sportfishing and Catalina Island excursions from the Newport Harbor.

Surfing

Why not take advantage of your stay in L.A. by trying this sport which is practically synonymous with the Southern California lifestyle? The surfing craze can only be appreciated after having ridden a wave or two. The establishments that follow will be happy to rent you a surfboard.

Malibu Ocean Sports
22935 Pacific Coast Hwy., Malibu
☎*456-6302*
For surfing lessons.

Fun Bunns
111 Manhattan Ave.

Jeffer's
39 14th St.

Zuma Jay Surf Boards
22775 Pacific Coast Hwy.

The Beaches of Orange County

Any area with access to the beach has a surf shop or two nearby that will rent surf boards and wetsuits, as well as give you some pointers as to where the surf is good that day. **Huntington Beach** calls itself "Surf City U.S.A." and has a plethora of surf shops where you can rent a board at a reasonable price. Most of the surfing takes place near the pier, which is excellent for beginners, as there are generally lifeguards on duty in case you run into trouble. Great spots include the **Huntington Pier**, **The Wedge** at Newport Beach and **The Strand** at Oceanside.

Whale-watching

The fall and winter months are favourable for spotting cetaceans swimming along the coast during their annual migration. Aboard specially chartered boats, you can witness these large marine mammals shooting water from their blowholes and waving their tail before diving to the ocean's depths.

Spirit Cruises
☎*831-1073*

Long Beach Sport Fishing
☎*(562) 432-8993*

Catalina Cruises
☎*(562) 491-5559*

Star Party Cruises
☎*(562) 799-7000*

Horseback Riding

Griffith Park Horse Rentals
480 Riverside Dr., Burbank
☎*(818) 840-8401*
For pleasant horseback rides along Griffith Park trails.

Bar S. Stalles
1850 Riverside Dr., Glendale
☎*(818) 242-8443*

Palm Springs

Smoke Tree Stables *(2500 Toledo Ave.; ☎327-1372)* specializes in equestrian tours of Indian Canyons. Rides are available by the hour or by the day.

Fitness Centres

Bodies in Motion
$20/day
1950 Century Park E., Century City
☎ 836-8000

24 Hour Fitness
$15/day
☎800-204-2400

Crunch Fitness
$22/day
8000 Sunset Blvd., West Hollywood
☎(323) 654-4550

Gold's Gym
30 Hampton Dr., Venice
☎392-6004
101 N. Cole Ave., Hollywood
☎(323) 462-7012

Hot-Air Ballooning

Palm Springs

Balloon Above the Desert *($155; ☎800-342-8506, ☎776-5785)* offers customized balloon flights not only in Palm Springs, but all over California. The flight lasts 60-75min and departs at 6am or 3pm. Hotel pickup and drop-off is available.

Ice Skating

Though not a sport traditionally associated with L.A., should you get the urge to ice skate, the following addresses can accommodate you.

Ice Skating Center
310 E. Green St.
☎(626) 578-0800

Ice Arena
4545 Sepulveda Blvd.
☎398-5718

Cross-Country Skiing

Southern California's cross-country ski season usually runs from mid-November to mid-March. Idyllwild, near Palm Springs, has several cross-country ski trails. For information, call the **Idyllwild Chamber of Commerce Information Line** *(☎909-659-3259)*.

Downhill Skiing and Snowboarding

Yes, you can ski not far from Los Angeles. **Waterman Mount** *(☎326-440-1041)*, located north of Pasadena in the San Gabriel Mountains, has a few chair-lifts and runs for all levels of skiers and snowboarders. **Baldy Mount** *(exit on I-10, above Mountain Ave., ☎909-981-3344)* is another ski location farther east.

Big Bear is a major ski resort offering several services (including accommodations) only 90min from L.A. It's one of the West Coast's most popular resorts with night skiing, several chair-lifts and a good number of snow-making machines. For information, call the **Chamber of Commerce** *(☎909-866-4607)*.

Ullysses's Favourite Hotels

For business people:

Hotel Inter-Continental (see p 237)

Los Angeles for tighter budgets:

Figueroa Hotel (see p 235)
Westwood Marquis Hotel (see p 242)
Pasadena Hilton (see p 238)
Renaissance Long Beach Hotel (see p 252)

For panoramic rooftop views:

Le Rêve Hotel (see p 242)

For the attention to design and decor:

Mondrian (see p 241),
The Argyle Hotel (see p 241)
Hotel Queen Mary (see p 251)

Cozy B&Bs:

The Venice Beach House (see p 246)
Lord Mayor's Inn (see p 251)

For luxury:

Beverly Hills Hotel and Bungalows (see p 243)
Ritz-Carlton Huntington Hotel and Spa (see p 238)

For the best bargains:

Saga Motor Hotel (see p 237)
Hostelling International (see p 249)

For the ambiance:

Barnabey's Hotel (see p 250)

For the most beautiful views:

Zane Grey Pueblo Hotel (see p 254)
The Inn on Mt. Ada (see p 255)

For romatics:

Beach House at Hermosa (see p 249)

Accommodations

Choosing accommodations in a big city is often a daunting task.

In a sprawling, decentralized city like Los Angeles, distance poses an added consideration.

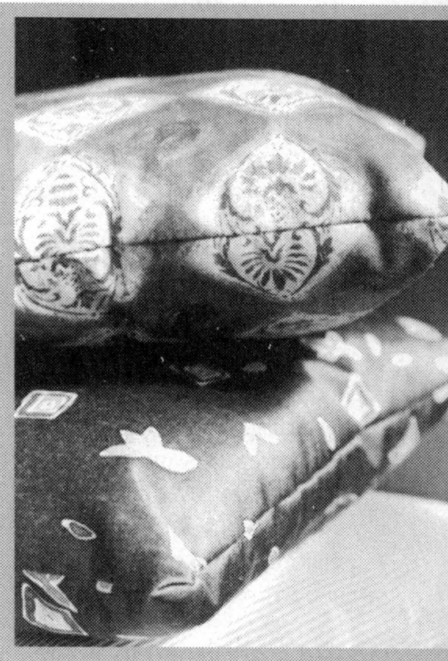

In most cities, staying downtown would be an obvious choice for many travellers, but this is less true in Los Angeles. After dark, downtown L.A. offers few attractions, and some areas can be a bit scary. Furthermore, many downtown hotels are skewed toward either extreme of the price scale, with a selection of high-end establishments catering mainly to business travellers and, at the opposite end, faded skid-row hostelries where most guests pay by the week or month—or even by the hour. For travellers seeking a modicum of comfort and security, but lacking the benefits of a generous expense account, the choice is narrower, although we do offer several suggestions within this chapter.

Several other parts of the city offer a viable alternative to the downtown area. Venice Beach will be a natural choice for many young budget travellers both because of its attractive ambiance and the ready availability of low-priced accommodations. There are also some possibilities in Hollywood. The overall choice is broader for mid-range and higher-end travellers. With the great strength of the U.S. dollar in recent years, prices across the whole spectrum may seem high to some visitors from abroad.

Even for the most impecunious of travellers, time is money. It doesn't make sense to waste it unnecessarily on L.A.'s clogged freeways or tortoise-like public transit. Before deciding on accommodations, readers may wish to consider which parts of the city they are most likely to visit and make their choice accordingly.

The prices in this guide are for one standard room, double occupancy in high season.

$	$40 or less
$$	$40 to $80
$$$	$80 to $130
$$$$	$130 to $200
$$$$$	$200 or more

Downtown Los Angeles

See map on p 103.

Stillwell Hotel
$$
≡, ℜ, *bar*
838 S. Grand Ave. between Eighth and Ninth sts.
☎(213) 627-1151
☎800-553-4774
≠(213) 622-8940
H.STILLWELL@aol.com
This is an older but refurbished 250-room hotel located about midway between the convention centre and the heart of the downtown area. Although far from luxurious, it is a friendly spot offering a decent level of comfort for the price and interesting decorative touches.

Metro Plaza Hotel
$$
≡
711 N. Main St. at Cesar Chavez Ave.
☎(213) 680-0200
☎800-223-2223
res@metroplazahotel.com
Conveniently located near Union Station, Olvera Street and Chinatown, this hotel has 80 plain but functional rooms.

Best Western Dragon Gate Inn
$$$
≡, ℜ
818 N. Hill St. between Alpine St. and College St.
☎(213) 617-3077
☎800-282-9999
⇌(213) 680-3753
www.bestwestern.com
This hotel, located in the heart of Chinatown, includes a shopping gallery set around a central atrium and was renovated in 1999. The 57 rooms are simply furnished, most with refrigerators and coffee-makers. A light breakfast is included in room rates.

Figueroa Hotel
$$$
≡, ≈, ℜ, *bar*
939 S. Figueroa between Ninth and 10th sts.
☎(213) 627-8971
☎800-421-9092
⇌(213) 689-0305
This is a high-rise version of classic L.A.-style Spanish revival architecture. Built in 1927, it features ceramic tiles, wrought-iron chandeliers and wood-beamed ceilings in the common areas. The 285 rooms are spacious and comfortable, although decorators have chosen a curious blend of styles. The main restaurant is next to the garden-lined pool area; upstairs is a coffee shop for lighter fare. Located near the convention centre, the hotel tends to be fully booked during major events.

Kawada Hotel
$$$
≡, ℜ, *K*
200 S. Hill St. at Second St.
☎(213) 621-4455
☎800-752-9232
reservations@kawadahotel.com
Located in the northern part of the downtown area near city hall, this hotel looks from the outside like an old low-rise office building. Inside, however, the 115 mainly small rooms are bright, pleasant and highly functional, most with kitchenettes.

Miyako Inn
$$$-$$$$
≡, ⊙, ℜ, *bar*
328 E. First St. between San Pedro and Central Aves.
☎(213) 617-2000
☎800-228-6596
⇌(213) 617-2700
miyakola@earthlink.net
Located in the Little Tokyo district, this establishment includes a fitness club and karaoke lounge. Many of the 174 rooms have mats, screens and low beds in the Japanese style.

Hyatt Regency Los Angeles
$$$-$$$$$
≡, ℑ, *bar*
711 S. Hope St. at Seventh St.
☎(213) 683-1234
☎800-233-1234
⇌(213) 612-3179
hregencyl@aol.com
Located near the heart of the financial district, adjacent to Macy's Plaza, this 24-storey, 482-room hotel

offers the standard comforts of a business-style establishment and panoramic views from many rooms.

New Otani Hotel
$$$$-$$$$$
≡, ⏲, ℜ, *bar*
120 S. Los Angeles St. between First and Second sts.
☎*(213) 629-1200*
☎*800-421-8795*
⇄*(213) 253-9269*
www.newotani.com
Housed in a 21-storey building located in the heart of Little Tokyo, this hotel offers a blend of American and Asian styles in its common areas and its 414 rooms. Features include a large Japanese garden and a two-storey shopping arcade. Special Japanese cultural packages are available.

Westin Bonaventure Hotel
$$$$-$$$$$
≡, ≈, ⏲, ℑ, *bar*
404 S. Figueroa St. at Fourth St.
☎*(213) 624-1000*
☎*800-228-3000*
⇄*(213) 612-4800*
A 35-storey landmark with 1,356 rooms in five gleaming cylindrical towers perched like a spaceship on the western side of the downtown area, this vast convention hotel is almost a city within a city. On the premises are more than 40 shops, restaurants and bars. The rooms are large and comfortable, many with wonderful views.

Wyndham Checkers Hotel
$$$$-$$$$$
≡, ⏲, ℑ, *bar*
535 S. Grand Ave. between Fifth and Sixth sts.
☎*(213) 624-0000*
☎*800-996-3426*
⇄*(213) 626-9906*
checkersla@aol.com
This hotel offers 188 very comfortable rooms and suites. Elegant touches include a rooftop spa, woodpanelled library, and marble bathrooms. Built in 1927 and classed as a historical monument, the hotel has an intricate stone facade.

Regal Biltmore Hotel
$$$$$
≡, ≈, ⏲, ℑ, *bar*
506 S. Grand Ave. at Fifth St.
☎*(213) 624-1011*
☎*800-245-8673*
⇄*(213) 612-1545*
www.thebiltmore.com
A landmark hotel in the heart of the downtown area, this 11-storey building, built in 1923, has an elegant marble-lined lobby with a truly palatial atmosphere. The hotel's Crystal Ballroom was the setting of the Academy Awards in the 1930s and 1940s. The 683 rooms and suites are grandly furnished and very comfortable.

Hotel Inter-Continental Los Angeles
$$$$$
≡, ≈, ⊙, ℑ, *bar*
251 S. Olive St. between Second and Third sts.
☎***(213) 617-3300***
☎***800-327-0200***
⇄***(213) 617-3399***
Located on Bunker Hill near the Museum of Contemporary Art, this 17-storey, 434-room establishment is the newest of the big downtown hotels, conservative but chic in style, with attention to service. Features designed for business travellers include two phone lines in each room and a business centre. Weekend specials are sometimes offered.

Pasadena and Surroundings

See map on p 117.

Saga Motor Hotel
$$ bkfst incl.
≡, ≈, ℜ
133 E. Colorado Blvd. (between Allen and Sierra Bonita)
Pasadena, CA 91106
☎***(626) 795-0431***
☎***(800) 793-7242***
⇄***(626) 792-0559***
The Saga Motor Hotel is the best thing there is in the heart of Pasadena. Recent renovations have not done away with all the charm of this 1950s hotel, whose rooms are clean, though small and somewhat Spartan. It's best to opt for those around the outdoor swimming pool to avoid street noise. A good choice for this category of hotel.

Westway Inn
$$
≡, ≈
1599 E. Colorado Ave. across from Pasadena City College
⇄***(626) 304-9678***
⇄***(626) 449-3493***
This 61-room motel is one of the more attractive places to stay along Pasadena's motel row. Its rooms are modern, with refrigerators, and service is friendly.

Pasadena Hotel Bed & Breakfast
$$$-$$$$ bkfst incl.
sb/pb, ≡
76 N. Fair Oaks Ave., between Union and Holly sts.
☎***(626) 568-8172***
☎***800-653-8886***
⇄***(626) 793-6409***
This establishment offers 12 guest rooms in a historic house located in Old Pasadena. Rooms are small but comfortable (in most cases, the bathroom is down the hall). They are complemented by an elegant sitting room downstairs. Breakfast and afternoon tea, served in a courtyard, are included in room rates.

Bissell House
$$$-$$$$
≡, ≈
201 Orange Grove Ave. at Columbia St.
☎(626) 441-3535
☎800-441-3530
≡(626) 441-3671
www.virtualcities.com
This historical gingerbread house, built in 1887, is located along Pasadena's traditional millionaire's row. Tall hedges provide shelter from the busy street outside. The five rooms have antique furnishings, including old-fashioned bathtubs. A large breakfast and afternoon snacks are included in room rates.

Pasadena Hilton
$$$$
≡, ⏲, ≈, ℜ, ℝ
168 S. Los Robles Ave.
Pasadena, CA 91101
☎(818) 577-1000
☎800-HILTONS
⇆(818) 584-3148
www.hilton.com
Located a stone's throw from the Pasadena Convention Center and the old town, the Pasadena Hilton is a good choice for business people. Indeed, the warmly furnished rooms feature a computer, VCR, audiovisual equipment and a comfortable ergonomic "smart desk." The vast lobby is noteworthy for its attractive decor.

Doubletree Hotel
$$$$-$$$$$
≡, ≈, ⏲, ℑ, *bar*
191 N. Los Robles Ave. near Walnut St.
☎(626) 792-2727
☎800-222-8733
⇆(626) 795-7669
This modern hotel is adjacent to the very picturesque city hall near the Old Pasadena district. Set on wide landscaped grounds with a Mediterranean theme, this 12-storey, 360-room hotel offers large, comfortable rooms with a range of amenities. Special rates apply most weekends.

Ritz-Carlton Huntington Hotel & Spa
$$$$$
≡, ⏲, ⊛, ≈, ℜ, ✪, ⌂
1401 S. Oak Knoll Ave.
Pasadena, CA 91106
☎(626) 568-3900
☎800-241-3333
⇆(626) 568-3700
www.ritzcarlton.com
The Los Angeles branch of the Ritz-Carlton, an international chain of prestigious hotels, is located in the foothills of the San Gabriel Mountains, in the highly residential city of Pasadena. This luxury hotel, one of the poshest in town, offers 392 rooms with delightful Georgian decor and a view of the 125 acres (50ha) of refined and tasteful Japanese gardens. The landmark hotel occupies an imposing Mediterranean-style building (1906), as evidenced by the terracotta ridge-tiled

roof. Among the dizzying array of services offered, those of the spa prove to be particularly praiseworthy, including several whirlpools, 17 treatment rooms, a sauna and a eucalyptus-steam room.

Hollywood and Surroundings

See map on p 123.

Hollywood International Hostel
$.
sb
6820 Hollywood Blvd. near Highland Ave.
☎(323) 463-0797
☎800-750-6561
⇄(323) 463-1705
Multi-bunk rooms are available here, each with three or four beds, as well as a handful of- private rooms at $40 per room. Facilities for guests include a kitchen, a TV lounge, a laundry room and a game room with pool tables. Check-in is available 24hrs a day, and the general atmosphere is lively. The majority of guests are from abroad.

Saharan Motor Hotel
$-$$
≡, ≈
7212 Sunset Blvd. at Poinsetta Place, four blocks west of La Brea Ave.
☎(323) 874-6700
⇄(323) 874-5163
sahara-jaco@worldnet.att.net
This is a garish, 1960s-style motel whose 63 rooms are better than they look from the outside. The immediate area can be noisy at night.

Liberty Hotel
$$
≡,
1770 Orchid Ave. near Franklin Ave.
☎(323) 962-1788
This spot is located in downtown Hollywood near Mann's Chinese Theater. Recently renovated, it offers 21 bright, spacious rooms as well as a communal kitchen and laundry facilities.

Highland Gardens Hotel
$$
7047 Franklin Ave. near Sycamore Ave.
☎(323) 850-0536
☎800-404-5472
⇄(323) 850-1712
This spot provides 70 pleasant rooms and suites set around a lush courtyard. Multi-bedroom suites with private kitchen are available at higher rates. The hotel is located near downtown Hollywood toward the Hollywood Hills.

Hollywood Hills Magic Hotel
$$-$$$
≡, *K*, ≈
7025 Franklin Ave. near Sycamore Ave.
☎***(323) 851-0800***
☎***800-741-4915***
⇄***(323) 851-4926***
www.magichotel.com
Offering 49 spacious rooms and suites with modern decor set around a courtyard and large heated pool, this spot is considered family-friendly and provides great value for the money. Located near downtown Hollywood at the base of the Hollywood Hills, it takes its name from the Magic Castle, a private club just up the hill where top-rated magicians perform. (The hotel can arrange reservations.)

Universal City Inn
$$-$$$
≡, ≈
10730 Ventura Blvd. between Lankershim Blvd. and Vineland Ave. in Studio City
☎***(818) 760-8737***
⇄***(818) 762-5159***
This 37-room motel is located just off the Ventura Freeway in North Hollywood within walking distance of Universal Studios. Rates here provide substantially better value than at hotels directly adjacent to the park. The rooms are modern and spacious.

Hollywood Orchid Suites
$$-$$$
≡, *K*, ≈
1753 N. Orchid Ave. between Hollywood Blvd. and Franklin Ave.
☎***(323) 874-9678***
☎***800-537-3052***
⇄***(323) 467-7649***
www.orchidsuites.com
Set in a former apartment building on a quiet side street in downtown Hollywood, this hotel offers 36 pleasant rooms of various sizes. Each has kitchen facilities, and a few have balconies. The lobby is not very appealing.

Park Sunset Hotel
$$$
≡, *K*, ≈
8462 Sunset Blvd. just east of La Cienega Blvd.
☎***(323) 654-6470***
☎***800-821-3660***
⇄***(323) 654-5918***
Located along a busy part of the famous Sunset Strip, this three-storey, 82-room hotel is set well back from the street and the noise. Rooms are pleasantly decorated, and a few have kitchens or balconies.

Best Western Sunset Plaza Hotel
$$$
≡
8400 Sunset Blvd. Two blocks east of La Cienega Blvd.
☎***(323) 3654-0750***
☎***800-421-3652***
⇄***(323) 650-6146***
This hotel offers 88 spacious and pleasantly deco-

rated rooms, some with full kitchen. A light breakfast is included in room rates. This Sunset Strip spot is friendly for families.

Hollywood Roosevelt Hotel
$$$-$$$$
≡, ≈, ⊙, ℑ, *bar*
7000 Hollywood Blvd. at Orange Dr.
☎(323) 466-7000
☎800-950-7667
⇄(323) 462-8056
sales@hollywoodroosevelt.com
This landmark establishment is a step back in time to a more romantic Hollywood era. Located in downtown Hollywood across from Mann's Chinese Theater and built in 1927, the 12-storey Roosevelt is a restored Art Deco monument displaying a Spanish revival influence. It is surrounded by lush gardens. The original home of the Academy Awards, it is replete with Hollywood lore and was once a hangout for literary figures. Its 328 rooms and suites are rather ordinary, however, in contrast to the magnificent lobby.

The Argyle Hotel
$$$$-$$$$$
≡, ≈, ⊙, ℑ, *bar*
8358 Sunset Blvd. three blocks east of La Cienega Blvd.
☎(323) 654-7100
☎800-225-2637
⇄(323) 654-9287
www.argylehotel.com
Dating from 1929, this 15-storey Art Deco gem has 64 exquisitely decorated rooms, each with Art Deco reproductions and distinctive furniture, as well as modern conveniences like VCRs and CD players. Rooms are a little on the small side, but many offer superb city views.

Mondrian
$$$$$
≡, *K*, ≈, ⊙, ℑ, *bar*
8440 Sunset Blvd. two blocks east of La Cienega Blvd.
☎(323) 650-8999
☎800-525-8029
⇄(323) 650-5215
This masterpiece of design was created from what was once an ordinary apartment building in West Hollywood. Guests in the 53 rooms and 185 suites enjoy superb city views (the designer set out to create a "hotel in the clouds") along with elegant minimalist decor and a sophisticated, if somewhat overbearing, level of service. Suites include kitchenettes.

Mid-Wilshire and Westside

See map on p 137.

Park Plaza Lodge
$$
≡,
6001 W. Third St. near Martell Ave. between La Brea and Fairfax
☎(323) 931-1501
⇄(323) 931-5863
This hotel is located near the Farmers Market in the Fairfax district and lies within walking distance of the Los Angeles County Museum of Art. Rooms are spacious and decently furnished. Good value.

Hilgard House
$$$
≡
927 Hilgard Ave. between Weyburn Ave. and Le Conte Ave.
☎ 208-3945
☎800-826-3934
⇄208-1972
reservations@hilgardhouse.com
This 53-room hotel is located near UCLA and Westwood Village.

Beverly Plaza Hotel
$$$-$$$$
≡, ≈, ⏲, ℑ, *bar*
8384 W. Third St. at La Cienega Ave.
☎(323) 658-6600
☎800-624-6835
⇄(323) 653-3464
info@BeverlyPlazaHotel.com
This spot offers 98 rooms in a six-storey building near the Beverly Center. Rooms are spacious and very pleasantly decorated.

Le Rêve Hotel
$$$$-$$$$$
≡, *K*, ≈, ℑ, *bar*
8822 Cynthia St. one block north of Santa Monica Blvd.
☎854-1114
☎800-835-7997
⇄657-2623
Located between West Hollywood and Beverly Hills, this spot offers 80 suites with a floral motif and French influence. Most have balconies and kitchenettes. The rooftop garden and pool area provide panoramic views.

Westwood Marquis Hotel
$$$$$
≡, ℑ, *bar*
930 Hilgard Ave. between Weyburn Ave. and Le Conte Ave.
☎208-8765
☎800-421-2317
⇄824-0355
www.whotels.com
This elegant 257-room all-suite establishment is located near UCLA and Westwood Village. The hotel is set on beautifully landscaped grounds and offers a sophisticated level of service.

Beverly Hills Hotel and Bungalows
$$$$$
≡, ⏲, ≈, ⊛ ✪, ⇆, ℜ
9641 Sunset Blvd.
Beverly Hills, CA 90210
☎ ***276-2251***
☎ ***(800) 283-8885***
www.thebeverlyhillshotel.com

The legendary Beverly Hills Hotel reopened its doors in 1995 after getting a major facelift that set its current owner, the sultan of Brunei, back some $100 million. A brilliant success! The Pink Palace once again offers luxury and comfort to its rich and famous clientele. Each of the deliberately ostentatious rooms and suites boasts original artwork and the latest in technology, including a personal fax machine, three telephones and a sound system that can be appreciated at its true worth thanks to the soundproof rooms. Moreover, every unit features an oversized marble bathroom, a walk-in closet and a small living room. All this and an outdoor swimming pool, two tennis courts and five-star service, too.

Impressive as this may be, the hotel is primarily known for its 21 bungalows scattered throughout a 62-acre (25ha) garden, where the word "luxury" takes on its full meaning. Since its opening in 1912, generations of Hollywood legends have been drawn here by the prestige and luxury of complete privacy afforded by these bungalows, including Charlie Chaplin, Gloria Swanson, Marlene Dietrich, Yves Montand and Frank Sinatra. It's even said that Elizabeth Taylor slept here with six of her nine husbands. Marilyn Monroe particularly appreciated this hideaway, making the most of it to enjoy trysts with John F. Kennedy and Robert F. Kennedy, among others. More recently, Matt Damon and Uma Thurman have been spotted here. Those interested in joining this prestigious coterie of celebrities will have to lay out the modest sum of $775 per night to stay in one of these famed bungalows.

Lastly, to fill your nights, the hotel offers four restaurants, including the famous Polo Lounge (see p 288), with its unique atmosphere.

Four Seasons Hotel Los Angeles at Beverly Hills
$$$$$
≡, ⊛, ⏲, ≈, ℜ
300 S. Doheny Dr.
Beverly Hills, CA 90048
☎ ***(310) 273-2222***
☎ ***(800) 332-3442***
⇆ ***(310) 859-3824***
www.fourseasons.com

Those in Los Angeles to stargaze (we're talking celebrities—not celestial bodies, of course) must book a room at the Four

Seasons Hotel Los Angeles at Beverly Hills. Indeed, it's said that more movie stars parade through the hotel's splendid lobby every day than any other place in the city. The 285 spacious rooms are surprisingly bright, with light streaming in from the balcony, and decorated with eclectic furnishings. Each room also features a VCR and sound system, as well as high-speed Internet access. Moreover, guests have access to a fitness centre, an outdoor swimming pool and limousine service to the upscale boutiques of Rodeo Drive. What's more, with the staff outnumbering clients, guests enjoy the highest level of personal service.

Santa Monica and Surroundings

See map on p 149.

Venice Beach Cotel
$
sb
25 Windward Ave. one block from the beach
☎399-7649
⇄399-1930
This hostel offers a total of 98 beds, most of them in dorms with three to six beds each, the remainder in 16 private rooms *($36 sb, $48 pb)*. Accommodations are simple but satisfactory. The entrance is upstairs.

Jim's at the Beach
$
sb
17 Brooks Ave. half a block from the beach
☎399-4018
hostel_info@yahoo.com
This is the author's choice as the best hostel at Venice Beach. The atmosphere is just a little friendlier, the rooms more appealing, and the common areas more comfortable. Beds are mainly six to eight per dorm, and breakfast is included in the price. On Sundays a special barbecue is offered. Guests have the use of a spacious kitchen, laundry facilities and computers. There is no curfew.

Venice Beach Hostel
$
sb
1515 Pacific Ave. at Windward Ave. one block from the beach
☎452-3052
⇄821-3469
vbh@caprica.com
Venice Beach Hostel offers dorms with four to six beds as well as smaller dorms and a few private rooms *($45-$55 pb, tv)*. Some dorms are set aside for women only. Amenities include laundry facilities and refrigerators with private locked compartments. The hallways are lined with murals and posters. Facilities are plain and a bit tattered, although the atmosphere is friendly. There is no curfew.

Santa Monica American Youth Hostel
$
sb
1436 Second St. south of Santa Monica Blvd.
☎393-9913
This spot offers about 200 beds mostly in dorms as well as some private rooms *($28/pers. for two or more).* Housed in a large brick building that was once a town hall, this well managed spot includes a pleasant courtyard, big kitchen, laundry room, library and travel store. It is located near the Third Street Promenade and the beach.

Sea Shore Motel
$$
≡
2637 Main St. at Hill St. facing the beach
☎392-2787
⇄392-5167
This German-run spot is popular with European visitors. The hotel is located by the sea, although it is some distance from downtown Santa Monica. Rooms are comfortable if somewhat ordinary. Good value.

Cadillac Hotel
$$$
⊙
8 Dudley Ave. facing Venice Beach
☎399-8876
⇄399-4536
www.thecadillachotel.com
This is a restored hotel dating back to 1905. Many of its 34 rooms have sea views. The lobby shows Art Deco influences, while the rooms, redecorated several times over the decades, manage to be both funky and a little tired-looking.

Hotel Carmel
$$$-$$$$
≡
201 Broadway Ave. at Second St. Santa Monica
☎451-2469
⇄393-4180
This establishment is ideally located around the corner from Santa Monica's lively Third Street Promenade and near Santa Monica beach. However, despite the recent renovation of some rooms this aging hotel does not live up to its potential. The 104 rooms vary in size and decor, some of them located down long hallways. Most offer a reasonable level of comfort, although the decor tends to be quite plain. Rooms on the street side can be noisy. The lobby is spacious but mostly empty, and there is just one creaking elevator to serve this four-storey building.

Marina Pacific Hotel
$$$-$$$$
≡,
1697 Pacific Ave. one block from the beach
☎452-1111 ou 800-421-8151
⇄452-5479
www.mphotel.com
This imposing spot offers 96 spacious but rather nonde-

script rooms near the heart of the action at Venice Beach. Double windows cut down on noise. Service is friendly.

The Venice Beach House
$$$-$$$$
sb/pb
15 30th Ave. near the beach
☎823-1966
This delightful spot is located on a quiet pedestrian-only street about 200ft (60m) from the beach and a few blocks south of the central scene in Venice Beach, although there are several restaurants nearby. This lovingly maintained property is listed on the National Register of Historic Places. Its nine guest rooms vary in size; all provide a warm, cozy atmosphere and are adorned with antique furniture. The large veranda, facing a garden, is a wonderful place to relax. A light breakfast is included in room rates.

Casa Malibu Inn
$$$-$$$$
22752 Pacific Coast Hwy., one-quarter mile (400m) from the Malibu pier
☎456-2219
☎800-831-0858
⇄456-5418
casamalibu@earthlink.net
Offering 21 tastefully decorated rooms in a two-storey motel-style structure set around a garden, this hotel has a sparkling private beach. Some of the rooms have kitchenettes or private balconies.

Belle Bleu Inn
$$$-$$$$$
≡, K
1670 Ocean Ave. near the Santa Monica pier
☎393-2363
⇄393-1063
This spot offers 26 suites in a central location close to the beach. Rooms feature hardwood floors, kitchen or kitchenette, and, in most cases, patios facing the beach.

Hotel Shangri-La
$$$$
≡
1301 Ocean Ave., Santa Monica, near Wilshire Blvd.
☎394-2791
☎800-345-7829
⇄451-3351
www.shangrila-hotel.com
This hotel is ideally located overlooking the Pacific at the edge of downtown Santa Monica. Most of the 55 rooms are set around a verdant courtyard, and many have ocean views. Much of the decor reflects an Art Deco influence, although some of the furniture is more mid-20th-century suburban.

Channel Road Inn
$$$$-$$$$$
ℑ, ⊛
219 W. Channel Rd. one block from the beach
☎459-1920
⇄454-9920
www.channelroadinn.com
This charming spot offers 14 rooms in a carefully restored house. Full breakfast, afternoon tea and hors d'œuvres are included in room rates. Rooms, some with sea views and several with fireplaces or whirlpool baths, are furnished mostly in wood with decorative touches like Amish quilts. Guests are generally pampered.

Malibu Beach Inn
$$$$-$$$$$
⊙
22878 Pacific Coast Hwy. near Malibu pier
☎456-6444
☎800-462-5428
⇄456-1499
reservations@malibubeachinn.com
This hotel offers 46 rooms facing a quiet beach that is ideal for bathing. The building and grounds are laid out in early Mexican style. Rooms are pleasingly decorated in deep colours, and each has a balcony or porch facing the sea.

The Georgian Inn
$$$$-$$$$$
≡, ≈, ⊙, ℑ, *bar*
1415 Ocean Ave. between Santa Monica Blvd. and Broadway Ave.
☎395-9945
☎800-538-8147
⇄451-3374
www.georgianhotel.com
Superbly located overlooking the Pacific Ocean at the edge of downtown Santa Monica, this eight-storey Art Deco treasure, built in 1933, has a bright pastel exterior, done in a style reminiscent of Miami Beach. The breakfast room was once a speakeasy, popular with some Hollywood stars of the era. Most of the 84 rooms offer ocean views, and guests are pampered with a wide range of services.

South Bay and Surroundings

See map on p 159.

Moonlite Inn
$
⊗
635 S. Pacific Coast Hwy.
☎540-4058
The Pacific Coast Highway, the large thoroughfare that runs through South Bay, offers budget travellers several motels with rooms for less than $40 a night. Though not all are recommended, the Moonlite Inn is a good choice, and has the

Accommodations

advantage of being located relatively close to the beach and some decent restaurants. Suitably clean and comfortable, but utterly lacking in charm.

Skyways Airport Hotel
$$
≡, *K*
9250 Airport Blvd. several blocks north of Century Blvd.
☎***670-2900***
☎***800-336-0025***
This is one of the more economical hotels among the cluster of establishments immediately to the east of LAX airport. Some of the 69 rather nondescript rooms have kitchenettes.

Travelodge at LAX
$$-$$$
≡, ℜ, ≈
5547 W. Century Blvd.
Los Angeles, CA 90045
☎***649-4000***
☎***(800) 421-3939***
⇋***649-0311***
Located near the airport, as its name indicates, Travelodge at LAX offers good value for the money. Noteworthy assets include a refreshing tropical garden around the swimming pool and balconies off some of the rooms. Free airport shuttle service and a car-rental desk are among the services offered, as is day-and-night room service (a rare commodity in a hotel of this category).

Sea Sprite Motel
$$-$$$$
≡, *R*, ≈
1016 The Strand at 10th St., Hermosa Beach
☎***376-6933***
⇋***376-4107***
Well suited to beach-goers, this family-oriented spot is located just a few steps from the golden sands. It offers a playground and volleyball court as well as refrigerators and microwave ovens in the rooms.

Grandview Motor Hotel
$$$
≡,
55 14th St., off Hermosa Ave., Hermosa Beach
☎***374-8981***
⇋***374-8983***
Located just a few steps from the beach, this three-storey hotel is grand in name only: it totals just 17 rooms, but they are spacious and reasonably comfortable, with refrigerators and balconies. The atmosphere is friendly.

Continental Plaza Hotel Los Angeles
$$$-$$$$
≡, ≈, ⊙, ℑ, *bar*
9750 Airport Blvd. 600ft (200m) north of Century Blvd.
☎***645-4600***
☎***800-529-4683***
⇋***645-7489***
This hotel offers 570 large, nondescript rooms near the airport. The fitness centre is open 24 hours a day.

Crowne Plaza Los Angeles Airport
$$$$
≡, ≈, ⊙, ℑ, *bar*
5985 W. Century Blvd. near Airport Blvd.
☎642-7500
☎888-315-3700
⇌417-3608
www.crowneplaza.com/hotels/laxap
Offering 615 corporate-style rooms near the airport, this spot has the usual business-oriented amenities.

Marina International Hotel & Bungalows
$$$$-$$$$$
≡, ≈, ⊙, ℑ, *bar*
4200 Admiralty Wy. at Palawan Wy., Marina del Rey
☎301-2000
☎800-882-4000
⇌301-8867
This establishment provides views of a vast marina from the 110 large, pleasant rooms in the main tower and the 25 bungalows with private patios or balconies.

Beach House at Hermosa
$$$$$ bkfst incl.
≡, *K*, ≈, ⊛
1300 The Strand
Hermosa Beach, CA 90254
☎374-3001 ou (888) 895-4559
⇌372-211
www.beach-house.com
In our opinion, the Beach House, located right on Hermosa Beach, wins the prize for the best hotel in South Bay. Everything here exudes comfort and casual luxury in a romantic seaside-resort setting. The rooms, adorned with elegant white-wood furnishings and blond woodwork, are not only pleasant, but also offer a beautiful view of the ocean. What's more, each of them features an oversized chrome-plated bathroom with Aveda beauty products, a coffee maker, hair dryer and a large bath for relaxing soaks. Noteworthy among the other standard amenities are the full kitchen, sofa bed, bathrobes, minibar and stereo system with CD player. In the morning, a hearty continental breakfast can be enjoyed in the appealing main-floor lobby, on your room's balcony or—why not!—right on the beach. Those concerned that the bustling Strand will disturb such an idyllic setting can rest easy: the double-glazed windows and soundproof walls keep the noise at bay.

Long Beach and Surroundings

See map on p 163.

Hostelling International – Los Angeles South Bay
$
sb, K
3601 S. Gaffey St., Building 613
San Pedro, CA .
☎(562) 831-2836
Fort MacArthur's former barracks house this local

youth hostel. This very affordable "crash pad" is located in the heart of San Pedro, close to the beaches, within Angel's Gate Park. The place features a large communal kitchen, a veritable microcosm of the United Nations. Women and men sleep in separate dorms, except for those travelling as a couple.

Vagabond Inn
$$
≡, ≈
150 Alamitos Ave. near First St., Long Beach
☎(562) 435-7621
Located between downtown Long Beach and Sunset Beach, this friendly spot offers 62 nondescript motel-style rooms, some with refrigerator and microwave. Room rates go higher on summer weekends.

Inn of Long Beach
$$
≡, ≈
185 Atlantic Ave. at Broadway, Long Beach
☎(562) 435-3791
☎800-230-7500
⇄(562) 436-7510
This friendly place offers renovated rooms set around a central courtyard and pool.

Pacific Inn
$$-$$$
≡,
516 W. 38th St. at Pacific Ave., San Pedro, CA.
☎514-1247
⇄831-5538
This spot offers 24 pleasantly furnished rooms in a motel-type setting. Some have kitchenettes. Several attractions are within easy walking distance.

Barnabey's Hotel
$$$ bkfst incl.
≡, ⊛, ≈, ℜ
3501 Sepulveda Blvd. (corner Rosecrans Ave.)
Long Beach, CA 90266
☎545-8466
☎(800) 552-5285
⇄545-8621
Located barely 2mi (3km) from the beach but miles away from the atmosphere of South Bay, Barnabey's Hotel takes you back to the early-20th-century Edwardian era. This large hotel has a delightfully British cachet, with its 120 comfortably furnished rooms, all of which feature an old-style decor of antiques and old-fashioned wallpaper. The lobby is adorned with dark-oak wood panelling, honey-coloured clocks and crystal chandeliers. An authentic English pub and a restaurant, the award-winning Auberge, which serves an English breakfast among other things, are at guests' disposal.

Hotel Queen Mary
$$$
≡, ⊛, ⊘, ℜ
1126 Queens Hwy.
Long Beach, CA 90802
☎(562) 432-6964
☎(800) 437-2934
⇆(562) 432-7674
Long Beach offers visitors the rare opportunity to stay aboard a legendary luxury ocean liner without having to pay the price of a cruise. The Hotel Queen Mary allows you to sample the good life of the British aristocracy of the interwar years and to enjoy great creature comforts on board, such as the upper deck where "passengers" can bask in the sun. Also to be admired are the famous Art Deco-style trimmings. However, because this is a ship, some rooms are small and the portholes let in little light. But it's amazing what you can put up with to stay in such surroundings. Guests can have something to eat, run errands and relax in one of the many lounges without ever having to bail out.

Lord Mayor's Inn
$$$-$$$$
435 Cedar Ave. between Fourth and Fifth sts., Long Beach
☎(562) 436-0324
www.lordmayors.com
This bed and breakfast is set in a carefully restored Edwardian house built in 1904 in a residential neighbourhood a couple of minutes' walk north of downtown Long Beach. A baby grand piano stands guard at the entrance. Each of the five rooms is furnished with period antiques and fine linens. Seven additional rooms, most with private bath, are set in adjacent cottages. Breakfasts (included in room rates) are a special treat.

The Turret House
$$$-$$$$
556 Chestnut Ave. between Fifth and Sixth sts.,Long Beach
☎(562) 983-9812
☎888-488-7738
www.turrethouse.com
Set is set in a beautifully restored 1906 mansion located on a quiet residential street just north of downtown Long Beach, this spot offers five guest rooms, each with its own name, fastidiously decorated with antique furnishings. A player piano shares duties with a VCR. A sumptuous breakfast and evening refreshments are included in room rates.

Hilton – Port of Los Angeles/San Pedro
$$$$
≡, ⊛, △, ≈, ⊘, ℜ
2800 Via Cabrillo Marina
San Pedro, CA 90731
☎514-3344 ou (800) HILTONS
⇆514-8945
www.hilton.com
Another hotel in the chain that is renowned as a

worldwide accommodation classic, this time located at the Cabrillo Marina, in the port of San Pedro. The building's architecture and design will transport you to the Mediterranean coast, but the never-ending list of services for business travellers will remind you that you're well and truly in North America. Not to be missed is Madeo Ristorante, the hotel's refined restaurant, which offers your palate a culinary trip through Italy in an inspired setting.

Renaissance Long Beach Hotel
$$$$ bkfst incl.
≈, ⊛, ⌚, ≡, ℜ
111 E. Ocean Blvd.
Long Beach, CA 90802
☎(562) 437-5900
⇆(562) 499-2512
The Renaissance Long Beach Hotel is just the place for business people and conventioneers passing through Long Beach. In fact, the establishment is located right near the Long Beach Convention & Entertainment Center and has 16,000 sq ft (1,500m^2) of meeting space. Some 370 spacious, elegant rooms with modern decor make up the upper floors. The Renaissance Club rooms, housed on the two top floors and to which only their occupants have access, are even larger and more private. They also include access to a private lounge where a complementary morning breakfast and early-evening hors d'oeuvres are served. Moreover, the hotel offers a top-notch, well-equipped exercise room with a whirlpool and swimming pool, as well as three restaurants and a business centre.

The San Fernando Valley

See map on p 169.

Chariot Inn Motel
$$ bkfst incl.
≡, ℝ
1118 E. Colorado St.
Glendale, CA.
☎/⇆(818) 507-9774
The Chariot Inn Motel offers travellers passing through Glendale 31 spacious rooms. A TV and refrigerator complement the furnishings, which though old-fashioned are still in good condition. Although there's no restaurant on the premises, continental breakfast is served every morning in the lobby.

Warner Gardens Motel
$$ bkfst incl.
≡, ℝ, ≈
21706 Ventura Blvd.
Woodland Hills, CA 91364
☎(818) 992-4426
☎(800) 824-9292
⇆(818) 704-1062
For those looking to stay near the shops and restaurants of popular Ventura

Boulevard, the Warner Gardens Motel is a good bargain. While not the height of luxury, the motel offers clean, fair-sized, inexpensive rooms. Among the perks that enhance a stay here are a refrigerator and microwave oven in each of the rooms, as well as an outdoor whirlpool and swimming pool.

Anabelle Hotel
$$$-$$$$
⊙, ≈, ℝ, ℜ
2011 W. Olive St.
Burbank, CA 91506
☎(818) 845-7800
☎800-782-4373
⇆(818) 845-0054

The Anabelle Hotel defines itself as "a small luxury hotel," which admittedly seems to fit its character. "Classicism" and "old-world charm" are epithets that apply to the 47 rooms, tastefully decorated with beautiful antiques. What's more, the staff is congenial, downright friendly even, to a clientele that doesn't always ask for much. A final noteworthy asset is its convenient location, a few minutes' walking distance from the NBC Television Studios and Warner Bros. Studios.

Holiday Inn Burbank
$$$$
⌂, ≈, ℜ
150 E. Angeleno Ave.
Burbank, CA 91502
☎(818) 841-4770
☎800-HOLIDAY
⇆(818) 566-7886

Like most of this international hotel chain's other establishments, Holiday Inn Burbank offers spacious, comfortable rooms. At the foot of the many towers that make up its imposing structure, the no-less-impressive lobby greets travellers who have opted for this sure bet of urban accommodation, which houses 382 rooms and 108 suites.

Catalina Island

See map on p 173.

If you plan on spending the night on Catalina Island anytime during the summer, especially on weekends, be sure to make reservations so as to avoid any nasty surprises. **Catalina Island Accommodations** *(☎510-3000)* can help you to this end. Note that hotel rates during the low season (Oct to Apr) are generally reduced by 50%.

Hermit Gulch Campground
$
sb
Avalon Canyon Rd.
☎*510-8368*

This campground set in the magnificent Avalon Canyon is ideal for both equipped and non-equipped outdoor enthusiasts, as camping gear is rented on site. Located 1.25mi (2km) from Avalon, on the way to Two Harbors, campers can get to this site either by taking the Catalina Safari bus or by walking. Free permit required *(☎888-510-7979)*.

Hermosa Hotel & Cottages
$$
pb/sb, K
131 Metropole St. (P.O. Box 646)
Avalon, CA 90704
☎(877) 241-1313
www.catalina.com/hermosa

The Hermosa Hotel will suit budget travellers for whom comfort is not a priority. This is, in fact, one of the few bargains on the island, especially during the high season. The rooms are clean and suitable for those who are not too demanding with regard to the decor.

Zane Grey Pueblo Hotel
$$-$$$ bkfst incl.
⊗, ≈
199 Chimes Tower Rd. (P.O. Box 216)
Avalon, CA 90704
☎510-0966 ou 800-3-PUEBLO
www.virtualcities.com

Zane Grey, the famous, prolific author of western novels, spend his sunset years in this unpretentious house, now converted into a hotel that bears his name. Grey undoubtedly sought inspiration from the magnificent panorama of Avalon Bay and the island's mountains when he chose to have his *pueblo* built here, on the mountainside. It's now the guests' turn to enjoy this enchanting setting, along with the outdoor swimming pool, large terrace and spacious lobby graced with a piano and fireplace. The 17 rooms, on the other hand, are considerably more rustic, with furnishings limited to the basics (no telephone or TV) and a decor of dubious taste. But, all in all, this is a suitable place with decent rates.

Seaport Village Inn
$$$
≡, *K*, ⊛
119 Maiden Lane (P.O. Box 2411)
Avalon, CA 90704
☎510-0344
☎800-2-CATALINA
⇆510-1156
raul@catalinacatalina.com

Located in a remote spot, on a lovely street that winds through the town's hills, the Seaport Village Inn is a fine choice. With its bright, simply furnished rooms facing the bay, the inn has undeniable charm. Also to its credit are the large, private balconies, with chaises longue for suntanning, and the smiles of the amiable staff, always ready to help.

Hotel Metropole
$$$$
≡, ⌂, ⊛
205 Crescent Ave.
Avalon, CA 90704
☎510-1884
☎(800) 541-8528
This romantic hotel could well be in the heart of New Orleans' French Quarter, but is fortunately available to visitors right here in Avalon. Some rooms feature charming balconies overlooking the shopping arcade, while others come with a fireplace and a whirlpool bath. Under no circumstances should you miss going up to the rooftop terrace, which offers a magnificent panorama of the town.

The Inn on Mt. Ada
$$$$$ fb
≡, ⊛, ℜ
398 Wrigley Rd.
Avalon, CA 90704
☎510-2030
☎800-608-7669
⇆510-2237
Overlooking Avalon and its emerald coast from a hill, this luxurious hotel was originally the home of the Wrigley family. The neo-Georgian-style house, built in 1921, displays the grandeur of a bygone era, with the most polished of decorative elements, delightful *objets d'art* and sumptuous furnishings. The full board offered here is simply exceptional. What is most amazing is that the hotel only has six rooms, all graced with stylish furnishings. Reservations required at least two months in advance.

Inland Orange County

See map on p 181.

Anaheim

Desert Inn
$$
≡, ≈, ⊛
1600 S. Harbor Blvd.
☎772-5050
☎800-433-5270
⇆778-2754
www.anaheimdesertinn.com
Right beside the park gates, the Desert Inn features large rooms, complete with a fridge and microwave. The indoor heated pool and hot tub are great on cloudy days, plus there is a terrific rooftop sundeck that is perfect for watching the fireworks show at Disneyland. Get a room above the ground floor as they are much more accessible. Two- or three-bedroom suites with separate living areas are also available and are ideal for families.

Tropicana Inn & Suites
$$
≡, ≈, ⊛
☎635-4082
☎800-828-4898
⇄635-1535
www.bei-hotels.com
The Tropicana is a motel-style property right at the gates of Disneyland. Rooms are rather generic with kitschy tropical art. The large heated pool and spa are a nice amenity at this budget establishment. Also on site is a guest laundry, convenience store and two take-out restaurants.

Holiday Inn at the Park
$$$
≡, ≈, ⊛, ⌚, ℜ
1221 S. Harbor Blvd.
☎758-0900
☎800-545-PARK
⇄917-0794
This five-storey Holiday Inn provides a convenient free shuttle service to the park. Rooms are comfortable and family oriented, with pull-out couches. A decent pool and spa area are open to guests 24hrs. As an added bonus, kids eat free all day, with up to four children allowed per adult.

Park Inn
$$$
≡, ≈, ⊛
1520 S. Harbor Blvd.
☎635-7275
☎800-828-4898
⇄800-828-4898
This Swiss-chalet style hotel is owned by the same company as the Tropicana but is slightly more upscale. The large rooms are furnished with care. Their heated pool and spa are on the fourth floor for a great night view of the park's fireworks show.

Mariott Fairfield Inn
$$$
≡,, ≈, *spa*, ℜ
460 S. Harbor Blvd.
☎772-6777
☎800-228-2800
⇄999-1727
The Marriot Fairfield goes out of its way to be kid-friendly: a magician entertains Monday, Wednesday and Friday; there's a large video arcade and McDonald's can be delivered right to your room. Their restaurant, Millie's, serves classic American fare and provides room service. The ample rooms feature a small fridge and pull-out couches.

The Hyatt Alicante
$$$$
≡, ≈, ⊛, ⌚, ℜ
100 Plaza Alicante
at Harbor and Chapman
☎750-1234
☎800-233-1234
⇄720-0465
www.hyatt.com
The Hyatt features a huge, 17-storey atrium that encloses the restaurant and bar, with towering live trees and fountains. Rooms are large and well laid out, with coffee makers, dataports and tasteful furnishings. On

the third floor there is a heated pool, hot tub and fitness area. The service is excellent and they provide shuttle service to Disneyland. Parking is extra.

Disneyland Hotel / Disneyland Pacific Hotel
$190-320
≡, ≈, ⊛, ℜ, ⊙
1150 W. Cerritos Ave.
☎778-6600
☎800-225-2024
⇄956-6508
www.disneyland.com
For the ultimate Disney experience, stay right beside the park at the one of the two Disney hotels. Though the warm, cozy rooms are decorated with classic Disney animation, guests will have little time to spend in them. The wonderfully landscaped grounds abound in fountains and waterfalls, with plenty of photo spots along the way. The recreation area is shared with the Pacific Hotel below, and includes a gigantic free-form pool with Captain Hook's ship in the centre. An additional pool and spa are located on the landscaped roof, offering perfect views of the nightly fireworks. Add to this the singing bellhops, live poolside shows and a variety of great restaurants and you'll easily be caught up in the magic of Disney.

Buena Park

Guest House International Inn at Buena Park
$$
≡, ≈, ℜ,
7878 Crescent Ave.
☎527-1515
☎888-782-9752
⇄527-2469
Directly across from Knott's Berry Farm, the Guest House offers clean, comfortable rooms equipped with a fridge and microwave. A large, square pool dominates the inner courtyard. Pet friendly.

Embassy Suites Buena Park
$$-$$$
≡, ≈, ⊛
7762 Beach Blvd.
☎739-5600
☎800-362-2779
⇄521-9560
The Embassy Suites features two room mini-suites, with a living room and private bedroom. Fridges, microwaves and coffee makers are also standard. A landscaped tropical courtyard gives way to the pool and spa. Extra amenities include a full, cooked-to-order breakfast and 2hrs of complimentary beverages each evening. A free shuttle service to Disneyland is provided.

Accommodations

Holiday Inn Buena Park
$$$-$$$$$
≡, ≈, ⊛, ◷, ℜ
7000 Beach Blvd.
☎*522-7000*
☎*800-HOLIDAY*
⇄*522-3230*
A recent multi-million dollar renovation is evident from the new fountains, updated decor and the enormous European-style lobby, with a polished granite floor and baby grand piano. Rooms are available for a variety of budgets, from standard doubles to the poolside terrace room with private courtyard. The fourth floor is business-oriented and offers an executive lounge, complimentary breakfast, late night snacks, and extra comfort.

Santa Ana

Quality Suites
$$-$$$$
≡, *tv*, ≈
2701 Hotel Terrace Dr.
☎*957-9200*
☎*800-228-5151*
⇄*641-8936*
www.hotelchoice.com
An excellent budget choice that is high on amenities. Two-room suites are standard and include a full breakfast, nightly happy hour and dinner Tuesday through Thursday. A shuttle service is provided to area attractions.

Costa Mesa

Residence Inn Costa Mesa
$$$$
≡, ≈, ⊛, ◷
881 Baker St.
☎*241-8800*
☎*800-331-3131*
⇄*546-4308*
www.residenceinn.com
Part of Marriott family, the Residence Inn is an all-suite hotel close to the South Coast Plaza district.
A choice of lodging includes studios, one bedroom/one bathroom and two bedroom/two bathrooms. All rooms feature fully equipped kitchens and some offer wood-burning fireplaces.

The Westin South Coast Plaza
$$$$
≡, ≈, ⊛, ◷, ℜ
686 Anton Blvd.
☎*540-2500 ou 800-WESTIN-1*
⇄*662-6608*
www.westin.com
The Westin is in a prime location in Costa Mesa, steps away from the South Coast Repertory and South Coast Plaza shopping center. The luxurious, elegant atmosphere extends to the rooms, which have incredibly comfortable beds and dark hardwood furniture. A full-service day spa is also available to guests. The Pinot Provence, an upscale Mediterranean bistro, is

conveniently located at the hotel.

The Beaches of Orange County

See map on p 181.

Seal Beach

Radisson Seal Beach
$$$-$$$$
≡, *P*, ⊛, ⏲, 🐕
600 Marina Dr.
☎***493-7501***
☎***800-333-3333***
⇄***596-3448***
www.radisson-seal.com
This lovely, three-storey Radisson is a short walk from the beach. The rooms are quite sterile, but all have balconies and most have a view of the water. An open atrium features a heated swimming pool and hot tub. The hotel also has a fleet of bicycles for rent. Small dogs are welcome.

Seal Beach Inn and Gardens
$$$-$$$$$ bkfst incl.
≡, *P*
212 Fifth St.
☎***493-2416***
☎***800-HIDEAWAY***
⇄***799-0483***
www.sealbeachinn.com
The Seal Beach Inn is an elegant bed and breakfast nestled in an idyllic garden setting one block from the beach. The gardens themselves bear special mention—a sea of fragrant flowers overflows into every nook and cranny. Each room is uniquely decorated and furnished with handpicked antiques and Victorian accents. Breakfast is a delight and tea is served in the lovely tea room.

Huntington Beach

Colonial Inn Hostel
$
sb, K
421 Eighth St.
☎***536-3315***
☎***536-9485***
www.colonialinnhostel.com
This pretty yellow hostel served as one of the few hotels in Huntington in the early 1900s. Today, it's the best deal in Huntington Beach with shared rooms for $16 and doubles for $18. Guests are welcome to use the large kitchen, T.V. room, laundry, garden and patio. An internet kiosk is also available. Toast and jam is served at breakfast and there is free coffee and tea all day. The beach is four blocks away.

Pacific View Motel
$
≡, *P*, ⊛
16220 Pacific Coast Hwy.
☎***592-4959***
☎***800-726-8586***
The Pacific View is north of downtown, on Bolsa Chica Beach. For those who want

to avoid the centre of town, this is a bargain. For an extra $20, guests can upgrade to one of the whirlpool suites, which have ocean views. The staff is friendly and the rooms are clean and comfortable.

Quality Inn
$$$
≡, ⊛, ℜ
800 Pacific Coast Hwy.
☎536-7500 ou 800-228-5151
⇄536-6846
www.hotelchoice.com
The Pacific Coast Highway is all that separates the Quality Inn from the beach. Rooms are a good value and range from modest to extravagant, as some of the suites have in-room spas and fireplaces. Unfortunately, the hotel lacks a pool, but there is an outdoor spa on the rooftop. Centrally located close to downtown.

Hilton Waterfront Beach Resort
$$$$-$$$$$
≡, ℜ, *P*, ⊛, ⏲
21100 Pacific Coast Hwy.
☎845- 8000 ou 800-822-7873
⇄845-8424
www.hilton.com
The Hilton Waterfront is just across the street from the beach and conveniently located downtown. Each of the 290 bright and comfortable rooms have ocean views from their private patios while a large, free-form pool area overlooks Huntington City Beach. The Palm Court restaurant specializes in Mediterranean-style cuisine. Hilton is expanding in the area and should have an additional 250 rooms open by late 2001.

Newport Beach

Newport Channel Inn
$$-$$$
≡
6030 W. Pacific Coast Hwy.
☎642-3030 ou 800-255-8614
www.newportchannelinn.com
The Newport Channel Inn is an excellent budget choice for a normally costly destination. Though it is short on amenities, the beach is just across the road, and the staff is very friendly. A variety of rooms are offered, with everything from king-sized beds to family-oriented oversized rooms that sleep up to seven. While the inn doesn't have a pool, there is a rooftop sundeck where you can catch some sun or watch the birds on the adjacent channel.

Newport Classic Inn
$$-$$$
≡, *P*, ⊛, ⏲, ℜ, ⌂
2300 W. Coast Hwy.
☎722-2999
☎800-633-3199
⇄631-5659
The Newport Classic is located right on Mariner's Mile, in the heart of the

restaurant and entertainment district. At first glance, the large glass and concrete structure resembles a shopping mall. The rooms are clean but rather kitschy and nondescript. For the price, however, this hotel is full of amenities such as a pool, hot tub, sauna and small gym. Above the lobby is a the Tsuru restaurant featuring a sushi bar and great Japanese/Chinese cuisine.

Balboa Bay Club
$$$$
≡, *P*, ⊛, ⏲, ⌂, ℜ
1221 W. Coast Hwy.
☎645-5000
☎800-882-6499
⇄642-6947
The Balboa Bay Club is a complete resort destination with 121 guest rooms and 14 suites on Newport Harbor. The list of amenities is impressive – two swimming pools, a private beach, men's and women's spas, indoor basketball and outdoor volleyball, racquetball and tennis courts. The guest rooms are equally impressive, bright and airy, with live plants and private balconies featuring ocean views. The Bay Club also has its own 140-slip private marina with guest- and charter-boat docking. The cheerful staff will help you arrange boat rentals or charters. The First Cabin restaurant serves fine fresh seafood while the Shell Bar and Lounge is ta great place for nightly entertainment.

Portofino Hotel
$$$$-$$$$$
≡, ⊛, ℜ
2306 W. Oceanfront
☎673-7030
☎800-571-8749
⇄723-4370
www.portofinobeachhotel.com
The Portofino offers sincere European hospitality in this charming oceanside bed and breakfast. The stunning rooms have been elegantly decorated with fine European antiques and many have exceptional views of the Pacific. Most rooms include in-room marble whirlpool tubs and all have private sundecks. Rates are negotiable for extended stays. True to their European atmosphere, English, French, German and Spanish are spoken.

Balboa Inn
$$$$-$$$$$
≡, *P*, ⊛, ℜ
105 Main St.
☎675-3412
☎877-225-2629
⇄673-4587
www.balboainn.com
The Balboa Inn is a beautiful Old World bed and breakfast conveniently located on the boardwalk in Balboa. The inn itself is a historical landmark. Built in 1929, Hollywood celebrities used to flock to the Balboa for dancing at the Rendezvous Ballroom. The historic

Accommodations

ambiance is alive and well today in the Balboa, and its location on the boardwalk makes for a multitude of shopping and dining possibilities. Standard rooms are warm and inviting, though they lack an ocean view. Their famous suites start at $295 and include a fireplace, jacuzzi tub and views of the ocean.

Doryman's Inn
$$$$-$$$$$
≡, ⊛, ℜ
2102 W. Oceanfront
☎675-7300

Doryman's is the place to go in Newport Beach for intimate, pampering service. Each of the 10 unique rooms features a fireplace, sunken Italian marble tub and luxurious American and French antiques surrounding the inviting canopy bed. A rooftop patio and sundeck overlook the ocean. The staff is extremely knowledgeable and all serve as concierges, ensuring your stay is worry-free. A full breakfast can be enjoyed in the parlour or on the ocean-view patio.

Four Seasons Hotel
$$$$$
≡, *P*, ⊛, ⊘, ℜ
690 Newport Center Dr.
☎759-0808
☎800-332-3442
⇄759-0809
www.fourseasons.com

For the most upscale experience in Newport Beach, many choose the Four Seasons Hotel, the only five-star establishment in Newport Beach. This oasis of casual elegance and impeccable service is adjacent to the Fashion Island shopping centre, nestled among majestic palms, sparkling pools and verdant gardens. Views from the upper floors of this 19-storey hotel are nothing short of breathtaking. Oversized guest rooms are comfortable and inviting while the Pavillion restaurant is one of the finest in Newport, overlooking a dense garden. Golfers will enjoy choice tee times and exclusive rates at the nearby Pelican Hill Golf Club.

Laguna Beach

Crescent Bay Inn
$$-$$$
≡,
1435 N. Pacific Coast Hwy.
☎494-2508
☎888-494-2508
⇄497-1708

This small, 29-room inn has ocean views and provides convenient access to Crescent Bay Park, Heisler Park, and the beach. The reasonable rates make this an attractive choice, though the beach is a short walk away and there is no swimming pool. The rooms are very clean and comfortable and half the rooms have kitchen facilities. Located about 1mi

(1.6km) north of downtown.

Tides Motel
$$-$$$$
≡, *K*, *P*
460 N. Coast Hwy.
☎494-2494
☎497-5209
The Tides is an intimate, 20-room hotel located a half-block from the beach just north of downtown. Ocean views and rooms with kitchens are available, some with patios. A colourful garden surrounds the barbeque, picnic and pool area.

Laguna Riviera
$$-$$$$
≡, *P*, ⊛, *K*
825 S. Pacific Coast Hwy.
☎494-1196
☎800-999-2089
⇄494-8421
www.laguna-riviera.com
The Laguna Riviera is a fabulous beachside hotel. Its rooms range from the budget-conscious street views, to the luxurious oceanfront suites. Whichever room you choose, the multi-tiered terraces are the perfect place to enjoy Californian surf and sun. The unique "tropical pavilion" houses a heated swimming pool, sauna bath and whirlpool under a partially retractable roof. The main lounge is the hub of the action with it's fireplace, grand piano and guest library. The Riviera is located in South Laguna, at the beginning of the shopping/gallery area.

Casa Laguna Inn
$$-$$$$$.
≡, *P*, *K*
2510 S. Coast Hwy.
☎494-2996
☎800-233-0449
⇄494-5009
The Casa Laguna is a lovely Spanish-style inn set on a terraced hillside in South Laguna. Guests have a choice of standard rooms, family suites with kitchens, or one of the two cottages with fireplaces. Each room is charming, with a mix of antique and contemporary furnishings. In addition to the scrumptious breakfast, afternoon tea, wine and snacks are provided in the library. Pet-friendly.

Hotel Laguna
$$$-$$$$$
≡, ≈, ℜ
425 S. Pacific Coast Hwy.
☎494-1151
☎800-524-2927
⇄497-2163
www.hotellaguna.com
The Hotel Laguna is the most historic hotel in Laguna Beach. With roots dating back to the late 1800s, the present Spanish-colonial-style building was constructed in 1931. Many of the rooms face the hotel's private beach, but unfortunately, none have balconies. The rooms are rather plain but neverthe-

less maintain some of their historic charm. The location is fantastic, however, right in the middle of downtown Laguna Beach. Three wonderful restaurants are in the hotel: Claes Seafood Etc. (see p 311), The Wine Cellar and the Terrace Café.

The Inn at Laguna Beach
$$$-$$$$$
≡, *P*, ⊛
211 N. Pacific Coast Hwy.
☎497-9722
☎800-544-4479
⇄497-9972
www.innatlagunabeach.com
This hotel has an enviable position on a bluff overlooking the Main Beach. The pool and spa area looks onto a bright patch of flowers and a short path winding down to the white-sand beach. Rooms are tastefully furnished with eclectic accents. A continental breakfast is served in-room, as it may be difficult to pull yourself out of the feather beds and duvets. Private balconies look out over the ocean from 52 rooms while the other 18 have a view of downtown Laguna Beach.

Laguna Brisas Spa Hotel
$$$-$$$$$
1600 S. Pacific Coast Hwy.
☎497-7272 ou 877-503-1466
⇄497-8306
www.lagunabrisas.com
Just across the Pacific Coast Highway from the beach, the Laguna Brisas Spa Hotel is a charming villa overlooking the Pacific in South Laguna. Each of the 64 attractive guest rooms has a wonderful marble spa for two as the main attraction, while wicker furniture and good-sized windows complete the decor. Not all rooms have a balcony, however, so be sure to ask.

Surf and Sand Hotel
$$$$$
≡, ℜ, *P*, ⊛, ⊘
1555 S. Pacific Coast Hwy.
☎497-4477
☎800-LAGUNA-1
⇄494-7653
The beautiful Surf & Sand Hotel has been family owned and operated for the past 50 years. All 157 rooms have fantastic ocean views. The rooms are bright, comfortable and cozy, with large glass doors opening out onto private balconies. Compact-disc players are an added bonus. A lovely pool area overlooks the pounding Pacific surf. Their two restaurants, Splashes and Towers, provide oceanfront dining ranging from casual to elegant, with Mediterranean and Pacific accents. Valet parking is extra and is required to park at the hotel.

Dana Point

The Best Western Marina Inn
$$$
≡, P, ⊙
24800 Dana Point Harbor Dr.
☎255-6843
☎800-255-6843
⇄248-0360
The Best Western is the only hotel located right at the marina on the beautiful Dana Point Harbor Drive. There is a small pool and the rooms are generic but comfortable. Within walking distance to the Marine Institute and Doheny State Beach.

Blue Lantern Inn
$$$$
≡,
34343 St. of the Blue Lantern
☎661-1304
☎800-950-236
⇄496-1483
This New England-style inn has a great location on a bluff overlooking the harbour. The main lobby features a large fireplace and stairs overflowing with stuffed animals. Each of the 29 airy, spacious rooms has a marble fireplace and whirlpool bath. A full buffet breakfast is provided every morning and wine and snacks are served in the afternoon. Even if you're not staying here, check out the great view from the adjacent lookout. Bikes are available for guests' use.

San Clemente

San Clemente Beach Hostel
$
sb, K
233 Avenida Granada
☎800-909-4776
☎492-2848
A member of Hostelling International, this seasonal hostel is open May 1 through October 31, when it's the best deal in town. Forty beds are available in either dorms or private rooms. There is a large kitchen and common room as well as two outdoor patios. The beach and the pier are five blocks away. A favourite with surfers and backpackers.

The Beachcomber Motel
$$$
≡, K
533 Avenida Victoria
☎492-5457
☎888-492-5457
⇄492-5476
www.beachcombermotel.com
The Beachcomber is a cute, *casita*-style motel overlooking the beach and San Clemente Pier. Barbecue grills and picnic tables can be found on the grassy grounds surrounding the motel. Each room is different, so take a look before you commit. The rooms are modest but the motel has a fun atmosphere and a beach-house feel.

Accommodations

San Clemente Inn
$$$$
≡, ≈, ⊛, ⌂, ⏲, *K*
2600 Avenida del Presidente
☎492-6103
⇄498-3014
www.sanclementeinn.com
From this resort, the beach is just a short walk through San Clemente State Park. Extra amenities include saunas for men and women, lit tennis courts and a children's play area. The rooms are modern and spacious and can accommodate up to six adults. Superb landscaping and the adjacent park make this a great choice.

Casa Tropicana
$$$-$$$$$
≡, ⊛, ℜ
610 Avenida Victoria
☎492-1234
☎800-492-1245
⇄492-2423
www.casatropicana.com
This lovely Spanish-style inn makes for an unforgettable stop in San Clemente. Choose one of their nine intricate theme rooms, such as the Emerald Forest with its vine ceiling or the Bali Hai with its mirrored bamboo canopy bed. Most rooms feature a spa and fireplace. The Tropicana Bar & Grill on the beach level serves Mexican and Californian favourites. Champagne and a full breakfast are also included.

San Juan Capistrano

Mission Inn
$$
≡, *P*
26891 Ortega Hwy.
☎493-1151
This small, 21-room motel, is designed after the mission itself. The affordable rooms are clean, comfortable, and within walking distance of the mission and downtown.

Best Western Capistrano Inn
$$$
≡, ≈, ⊛
27174 Ortega Hwy.
☎493-5661
☎800-441-9438
www.capoinn.com
This Best Western is located just two blocks from the mission, downtown and the Los Rios Historical district. Shuttle service is available to most other major attractions in the area. A variety of rooms are available, including some with kitchenettes.

Oceanside

Guesthouse Inn & Suites
$$-$$$
≡, ≈, ℜ
1103 N. Pacific Coast Hwy.
☎722-1904
☎800-914-2230
⇄722-1168
The Guesthouse is a modest inn overlooking a nearby estuary and the ocean from

a distance. The rooms are bland but clean, with decent balconies. The location is within walking distance of downtown, the harbor and Camp Pendleton. This is an excellent budget choice as rates can dip as low as $45 off-season.

Best Western Oceanside Inn
$$-$$$$
≡, ≈, ⊛, ⌚, *K*
1680 Oceanside Blvd.
☎722-1821
☎800-443-9995
⇄967-8969
www.bestwestern.com
This Best Western is well located, with lovely views of the ocean from its spacious rooms. A large pool and spa area is set among the palms and plants of the inner courtyard. Within walking distance to the beach, restaurants and shopping.

Oceanside Marina Inn
$$$$-$$$$$
≡, ≈, ⊛, *K*, ℜ
2008 Harbor Dr. N.
☎722-1561
☎800-252-2033
⇄439-9758
www.omihotel.com
The Marina Inn is in a wonderful secluded location that makes visitors feel as though they are staying on a small island in the middle of the Pacific. The one- or two-bedroom suites are spacious, with either marina or ocean views. A variety of rooms are available, with fireplaces, spas or kitchens. The friendly staff will help arrange any cruises or tours that may interest you. Sailboats and jet-skis are also available for rent.

Palm Springs

See map on p 213.

Motel 6
$$
≡, ≈, ⊛, *tv*
606 S. Palm Canyon Dr.
☎327-4200
The Motel 6 features clean, Spartan rooms for those on a tight budget. Reserve early as it's one of the cheapest hotels within walking distance of downtown. A pool and small hot tub are available.

The Royal Sun
$$ bkfst incl.
≡, ≈, ⊛, *K*
1700 S. Palm Canyon Dr.
☎(760) 327-1564
☎800-619-4SUN
⇄(760) 323-9092
Located just south of downtown, this family hotel has bright rooms furnished with a small desk, stove top, microwave and fridge. The pool and hot tub are ample and spotless. A full buffet breakfast is included. This is a definite bargain in Palm Springs.

Ramada Resort and Conference Center
$$$-$$$$
≡, ≈, ⊛, ℜ
1800 E. Palm Canyon Rd.
☎***323-1711***
☎***800-245-6907***
www.ramadapalmsprings.com

The balconies on the Ramada's 241 rooms surround a 2 acre (0.8ha) lawn and courtyard area with a large pool and hot tub. Rooms are spacious and cute, with natural wood furnishings, and feature either king-sized beds or two queen-sized beds.

Octillo Lodge
$$$-$$$$
≡, ≈, ⊛, ⊘
1111 E. Palm Canyon Dr.
☎***416-0678***

Daily weekly and monthly rates are available. While the hotel may not look like much from the outside, the suites are homey and well laid-out with a sofa, loveseat and full kitchen. There is no bath tub, however. They have an above average fitness room, plus two outdoor hot tubs and a heated pool.

Ballantine's Hotel
$$$$ bkfst incl.
ℝ
1420 N. Indian Canyon Dr.
☎***800-780-3464***
⇄***320-5308***
www.palmsprings.com/ballantines

Ballantine's has 14 theme rooms based on 1950s musicals, and 1950s France, complete with artwork by Léger and Miro. Every room features an authentic period fridge and a secluded patio. Try the all-pink Marilyn Monroe suite ($199) where she actually stayed at one point. Brat Pack music fills the air around the comfortable pool area. No children allowed.

L'Horizon Garden
$$$$
≡, *K*, ≈
1050 E. Palm Canyon Dr.
☎***(760) 323-1858***
☎***800-377-7855***

William Cody, a modernist architect of the 1950s, designed this two bedroom house and seven bungalows. Each open-concept studio bungalow includes a full kitchen plus king-sized bed. The unique showers face outside, but are protected from prying eyes by a wall and a bouquet of flowers. Marilyn Monroe refused to use these showers for fear of photogra phers coming over the fence. Rooms without a kitchen are $30 less. Two acres (0.8ha) of landscaped gardens surround a popular pool in the center. Nicky, the friendly owner, will be happy to fill you in on the history of the hotel and it's famous guests. No children allowed.

Hyatt Regency Suites
$$$$
≡, ≈, ⊛, ⌚, ℜ
285 N. Palm Canyon Dr.
☎322-9000
☎800-633-7313
⇄325-4027
www.hyatt.com
Each of the spacious, two-room suites at the Hyatt Regency features a private patio or balcony, marble bath and live plants. The elegant open-air atrium is rich in marble and brass and a half-block-long swimming pool is set among the impeccable landscaping. Located right in the heart of Palm Springs, the Hyatt is a step away from all the major downtown attractions. Ask for a mountain-view room, as they are quieter.

Ulysses's Favourite Restaurants

A downtown treasure, with an outdoor terrace:

Café Pinot (see p 278)

For atmosphere and panoramic views:

Yamashiro (see p 284)

For the cheerful atmosphere:

La Parrilla (see p 275)
ChaChaCha (see p 276)
Miceli's (see p 284)

For fine French cuisine:

Patina (see p 285)
La Cachette (see p 288)

For a California touch:

JiRaffe (see p 292)

For excellent vegetarian dishes:

Real Food Daily (see p 289)

For the terrace:

Figaro (see p 282)
Schatzi on Main (see p 292)
Casino Dock Cafe (see p 298)

For movie-star spotting:

Polo Lounge (see p 288)

For the romantic atmosphere:

The Raymond (see p 282)
La Poubelle (see p 283)
Ristorante Villa Portofino (see p 299)

For the view:

Encounter at LAX (see p 294)
Sky Room (see p 296)
Belmont Brewing Company (see p 295)

For the marvelous decor:

Traxx (see p 277)

For the desserts:

Schatzi on Main (see p 292)

Restaurants

Dining in a certain type of Los Angeles establishment is more about seeing and being seen than about friendly service and quality food. An entire subculture of Hollywood agents, scriptwriters and assorted wannabes seems to set great store by the table they get at some of these spots, if indeed they can obtain reservations without booking months in advance.

Sneering condescension by restaurant staff toward less-exalted patrons has been elevated to an art form at some eateries, with stratospheric prices demanded for dishes that are good but not exceptional.

Fortunately, most L.A. restaurants are entirely different from this all-too-real stereotype. Restaurants with cheerful staff and good value exist in abundance. Attitude problems do creep up occasionally, exemplified by staff at almost-empty restaurants shaking their heads sadly and promising to see what they can do for diners who arrive without reservations. However, this sort of approach seems to be going out of style.

Tips

Tipping is a touchy topic of conversation and is the subject of endless debates among those concerned. Customers and staff don't always seem to agree on the amount that should be left as a tip, and the situation in Los Angeles is no different. Good service means good tip. Waiters earn derisory wages and usually count on the generosity of tips to earn enough money to get by. As a rule, if you are able to afford a meal in a good restaurant, you are also able to afford leaving a corresponding tip: around 15% of the bill depending on the quality of service received. Be careful, however, before automatically leaving a tip, as some restaurants already include it in the bill total, leaving it to you to decide whether the service was exceptional enough to deserve more.

The diversified ethnic base of L.A. contributes enormously to the very evident variety in the local dining scene. This accounts, for example, for the profusion of fine Asian restaurants and the ready availability of good Mexican fare. Fine Italian cooking is also part of the scene. Although the local French population is smaller, French cuisine is far from absent. The "fusion cuisine" (sometimes referred to as "confusion cuisine"!) that was all the rage a few years ago, with cooking styles and ingredients from different continents blended holus-bolus, has mercifully passed its peak and now exists in more restrained form.

The emphasis in this chapter is on value. Not every establishment listed here is inexpensive, but an effort has been made to select restaurants that provide an enjoyable experience for the price, in various budget categories. Diners who are willing to put up with abuse in hopes of catching a glimpse of some Hollywood celebrity will have to look elsewhere for guidance.

As any visitor will quickly observe, the L.A. area is one of the world's great strongholds of fast-food culture, with a plethora of hamburger, pizza, taco and fried chicken joints. Among the various fast-food chains, the author's favourite is El Pollo Loco (literally, "The Crazy Chicken"), whose numerous branches offer Mexican-style grilled chicken served with tortillas, rice and a wide choice of condiments.

Unless otherwise indicated, the prices mentioned in the guide are for a meal for one person, not including taxes, drinks and tip.

$	$10 or less
$$$	$10 to $20
$$$$	$20 to $30
$$$$$	$30 to $40
$$$$$$	$40 or more

Downtown Los Angeles

See map on p 102.

Far more interesting than any bland modern food court is the Grand Central Market (*bound by Broadway, Third, Hill and Fourth sts.*), where the produce vendors and meat counters are joined by a small cluster of restaurants providing cheap and tasty dishes in atmospheric surroundings, from early morning to late afternoon. Among the favourites is **Maria's Pescado Frito *($)***, offering simple Mexican-style fish and seafood dishes, including *ceviches*.

Roast to Go
$
every day until 6pm
Central alley of Grand Central Market on Broadway Ave.
Grand Central Market, a block-long fruit and vegetable market, is lined with snack stands offering all kinds of Mexican delights. For authentic tacos, head to Roast to Go. Forget Tex-Mex; this restaurant's menu is in the purest popular tradition. Travellers pressed for time will love the *tacos al pastor* (braver souls can opt for tacos with brain, tongue and tripe) and the extremely nourishing burritos.

China Cafe
$
every day until 6pm
Central alley of Grand Central Market on Broadway Ave.

The China Cafe is also located in Grand Central Market, this time on the upper floor near the Hill Street exit. This is another small snack counter that people travelling on a tight budget will love. In fact, no dish on the menu costs more than $3. You'll especially get your money's worth with the enormous bowls of delicious, steaming-hot soup.

Original Pantry Café
$
every day 24hrs
877 S. Figueroa St. near Ninth St.

Almost a local landmark, this spot may appear a bit down at the heels, but it serves up old-time American favourites ranging from breakfast pancakes to a late-night steak at bargain prices.

The City Pier
$
Mon-Fri 10:30am to 3:30pm
333 S. Spring St., between Third and Fourth sts.
☎(213) 617-2489

This unpretentious spot, with indoor and outdoor seating areas, is popular with office workers and has a menu centred around sandwiches, including those made with fish or seafood.

Philippe the Original
$
every day 6am to 10pm
1001 N. Alameda St. at Ord St.
☎(213) 628-3781

Open since 1908, this is one of the oldest restaurants in town, serving a broad cross-section of local society. The owners claim this is where the "French dip" sandwich was invented. This style of sandwich, which is probably unfamiliar to anyone from France, involves placing slices of roasted meat (there are several to choose from) on a baguette that has been dipped in meat juices. Beef stew is another favourite. Food is served cafeteria style, with seating at long communal tables.

Langer's
$
Mon to Sat 8am to 4pm
704 S. Alvarado St. at Seventh St.
☎(213) 483-8050

This is a traditional Jewish delicatessen, with seating in booths and at a long counter. It is a popular spot despite its slightly seedy location. Many of the old favourites are available, including matzoh ball soup, pastrami (served several ways), and chopped-liver sandwiches.

La Parrilla
$
every day 8am to 11:30pm
2126 Cesar Chavez Ave., Boyle Heights
☎(213) 262-3434
This casual and cheerfully decorated spot, located in a largely Mexican neighbourhood east of downtown, offers authentic Mexican specialties in a festive atmosphere. Dishes include a variety of charcoal-grilled meats, seafood items such as shrimp in garlic sauce, *tamales* (cornmeal cakes with savoury stuffings), and *pozole* (a stew of large-grained corn with meat).

Shabu Shabu House
$$
Japanese Village Plaza
127 E. Second St. near Los Angeles St.
☎(213) 680-3890
This popular spot in Little Tokyo specializes in a variety of fondues, with meat and vegetables dipped into pots of boiling broth. Other items are also available.

Yang Chow
$$
every day 11:30am to 2:30pm and 5pm to 9:30pm, Fri to Sat until 10:30pm
819 N. Broadway near Alpine, Chinatown
☎(213) 625-0811
This old-style Chinatown favourite, with functional decor, offers a wide range of Mandarin and Szechuan dishes as well as some distinctive seafood specialties, including the popular fried "slippery shrimp" with a sweet-and-hot sauce. Steamed pork dumplings served on a bed of spinach are a signature appetizer.

Mon Kee
$$
every day 11:30am to 9:45pm, slightly later on weekends
679 N. Spring St., Chinatown
☎(213) 628-6717
This spot in the heart of Chinatown forsakes some of the trendy advances in decor, but offers a broad selection of Chinese seafood specialties, including soups. Main-course items include stir-fried scallops with ginger and fresh squid with garlic and pepper.

Empress Pavilion
$$
every day 9am to 10pm
988 N. Hill St., Chinatown
☎(213) 617-9898
Situated near the northern edge of Chinatown, this vast and modern upstairs Hong Kong-style eatery, with sliding dividers to create a greater sense of intimacy, offers an extensive *dim sum* selection earlier in

the day (with various sorts of dumplings and other small items served from roving trolleys) and a full traditional menu throughout the day with a special emphasis on fresh fish and seafood dishes.

ChaChaCha
$$
Sun to Thu 8am to 10:30pm
Fri to Sat 8am to 11:30pm
656 N. Virgil Ave., corner Melrose Ave., Silver Lake
☎(323) 664-7723
Empanadas, spicy seafood and other Caribbean specialties are on the menu at the lovely ChaChaCha. Classic Cuban, Puerto Rican, Jamaican and Haitian dishes also hold their own, much to the delight of guests in search of exotic cuisine. The reggae music and creative decor surely have something to do with this colourful restaurant's party-like atmosphere. However, this fiesta doesn't keep countless couples from enjoying an intimate dinner for two that is out of the ordinary, to say the least. Those who can't get enough can stop in for breakfast and enjoy ChaChaCha's unique omelettes, which combine bananas, yucca, onions and herbs with fresh *tomatillos* on a grilled tortilla: a delicious way to start the day!

Frying Fish
$$
every day 11am to 10pm
120 Japanese Village Plaza
☎(213) 680-0567
For delicious sushi at a reasonable price, head to the Frying Fish. Step 1: sit down on one of the 30 chairs around the rotating counter. Step 2: choose a dish from among the classic Japanese specialties that roll past your eyes on a small conveyor belt along the counter. This entertaining system ensures that all the dishes are fresh and lets you visually select what you'd like to eat. Finally, step 3: enjoy this delicious exotic cuisine, as you watch the head chef cook up a storm right in front of you.

Engine Company No. 28
$$-$$$
Mon to Fri 11:15am to 9pm,
Sat to Sun 5pm to 9pm
644 S. Figueroa St. between Sixth and Seventh sts.
☎(213) 624-6996
Modern versions of traditional American comfort foods like crabcakes, meatloaf and burgers fill the menu at this restored downtown fire station. The American wine list is interesting.

La Serenata de Garibaldi
$$-$$$
Tue to Sat 11am to 10:30pm, Sun 10am to 10pm
1842 E. First St., East L.A.
☎(213) 265-2887
This intriguing Mexican seafood restaurant comes as something of a surprise in a rather undistinguished neighbourhood. Dishes and decor reflect both modern and traditional tastes, with whole snappers and other fresh fish and seafood grilled and served on its own or with simple sauces.

Ciudad
$$$
Mon to Fri 11:30am to 10pm
Sat to Sun 5pm to 10pm
445 S. Figueroa St.
☎(213) 486-5171
It is to the initiative of chefs Mary Sue Milliken and Sue Feniger, who are famous for their restaurants, CityCafe and City Restaurant, that we owe the pleasure of Ibero-Southern American cuisine. With the help of chef Danielle Reed, they have developed their own versions of classic Central American, South American and Spanish dishes, but have also come up with new creations based on the same Latin ingredients. The menu features a Honduras *ceviche* that is served in a martini glass, Argentinian ribs stuffed with *jalapeño* pepper and garlic, and even chicken sautéed Cuban-style with Puerto Rican rice and fried bananas. However, the menu isn't the only thing that hits the spot; the decor will also delight your senses. Architect Josh Schweitzer created the inspired decor that makes you feel you're in the heart of Rio de Janeiro, rather than a dining room in a downtown office building. A sure bet.

Traxx
$$$
Mon to Fri 11:30am to 11pm
Sat 3:30pm to 11pm
800 N. Alameda St., inside Union Station
☎(213) 625-1999
This restaurant serves fine international dishes that meet at the crossraods of Asian, Italian and French cuisines. Chef Tara Thomas's innovation is no doubt the cornerstone of her success in harmoniously combining various cuisines. Curried lamb with almond couscous and currants; *romangioli* pasta with *porcini* mushrooms, Parmesan cheese and truffle oil; or even ginger chicken with green-tea noodles and *shiso* leaves—these are but a few examples of the dishes featured on the menu. Traxx not only features an array of cuisines, but attracts a mixed group of travellers as well, since the restaurant is located in the spectacular Union Station, built in 1939 (see p 105). To enjoy the

setting, opt for a table on the terrace in the train station, rather than confining yourself to the Santa Fe-style dining room. The restaurant's bar is also housed in the former public telephone room, which makes for an original place to have a drink (Scotch and tequila recommended).

Café Pinot
$$$-$$$$
Mon to Fri 11:30am to 2:30pm, every day 5pm to 9pm
700 W. Fifth St. at Hope St.
☎(213) 239-6500
This interesting spot, combining French and California cuisines, is located on the grounds of the Central Library, with both indoor and outdoor dining areas in a garden setting. Service includes free transport to the Music Center, making this a popular spot for pre-concert suppers. One of the favourite items here is rotisserie-grilled chicken in a three-mustard sauce, always available even though many menu items rotate through the seasons. Soups and desserts come recommended.

Cicada
$$$$
Mon to Fri 8:30am to 11pm
Sat 11am to 11pm
617 S. Olive St.
☎(323) 655-5559
It is advisable to make reservations if you hope to dine at Cicada, one of L.A.'s most popular Italian restaurants. Many consider this restaurant's most interesting feature to be its Art Deco decor, which includes large pannelled columns, a golden-leaf ceiling and murals that adorn the walls; the dining room is set around the vast hall of the Oviatt Building (built in 1928). Others might not consider the Roaring Twenties atmosphere to be the restaurant's focal point, but rather the culinary creations of chef Christian Shaffer. The thoughtfully elaborated menu features Northern Italian flavours, from appetizers to desserts: *foie gras* with strawberries and balsamic vinegar that has been aged 50 years; saffron *fettucine* with Santa Barbara mussels, leeks and sundried tomatoes are a few examples of what draws downtown businesspeople and professionals here. Impressive wine cellar and a bar on the balcony.

Pacific Dining Car
$$$$
every day, 24hrs/day
1310 W. Sixth St., corner Witmer St.
☎483-4000
L.A.'s oldest steak house, the Pacific Dining Car, is a great place to go any time of day. Well-prepared meat and fish dishes are served day and night in a perfectly relaxing and intimate setting. The breakfast *(1am to 11am)*, lunch *(11am to 4pm)* and dinner *(4pm to 1am)* menus all offer a choice of top-quality grilled delights. The restaurant's other specialties include grilled steak and daily specials such as the sautéed rabbit and grilled sole. The bar has a wine list that is particularly impressive. It is best to make reservations for dinner to avoid being disappointed.

Water Grill
$$$$
Mon to Fri 11:30am to 9:30pm
Sat to Sun 5pm to 10pm
544 S. Grand Ave., between Fifth St. and Sixth sts.
☎(213) 891-0900
Many consider the aptly named Water Grill to be L.A.'s ultimate seafood restaurant. A grand-style dining room, where the wood, leather and copper blend together marvellously, greets patrons who have come to enjoy the famous appetizers, fish and seafood that give this restaurant its reputation. Your best bet is to stick to these dishes to avoid disappointment. Guests, who consist of suit-and-tie businesspeople or even music lovers heading to the Music Center, seem to appreciate the bar's grandiose decor and liveliness that sets it apart from the rest. Reservations recommended.

Pasadena and Surroundings

See map on p 117.

Goldstein's Bagel Bakery
$
Sun to Thu 6am to 9pm
Fri to Sat 6am to 10:30pm
86 W. Colorado Blvd.
corner Delacey Ave.
☎(626) 79-BAGEL
What could be more enjoyable than to sit down and enjoy a coffee and bagel as you read the morning paper? Goldstein's Bagel Bakery, which offers a wide variety of bagels and cream cheese, is the perfect place to do just this. For lunch and dinner, the menu features sandwiches, delicatessen delights and light meals that are perfect for those pressed for time. This is a great place to mingle with the good people of Pasadena, as they go about their daily routines.

Rack Shack
$
58 E. Colorado Blvd.
☎(626) 405-1994
The Rack Shack appears to be a simple, narrow and banal hall, but the aroma of barbecued chicken titillates the tastebuds of passersby and convinces many to make a stop. The Cajun chicken is a must—seasoned with eye-popping spices and served with a scorching-hot sauce that could very well make you breathe fire! For something a little more moderate, try the beef ribs. All dishes come with a green salad, baked beans, yams or rice pilaf.

Old Town Bakery and Restaurant
$
every day 7:30am to 10pm, Fri to Sat until midnight
166 W. Colorado Blvd.
at Pasadena Ave.
☎(626) 792-7943
This cheerful bakery shop and café, set in a pleasant courtyard, offers an array of light dishes including sandwiches, salads and pastas, as well as pancakes and omelettes at breakfast.

All India Café
$-$$
Mon to Sat 11:30am to 10pm, Fri to Sat until 11pm
39 S. Fair Oaks Ave. near Colorado Ave., Pasadena
☎(626) 440-0309
This simple Old Pasadena café, enlivened by Indian tapestries, offers a broad range of Indian dishes, including vegetarian items, tandoori preparations, and several Bombay specialties like lamb frankie (pieces of seasoned lamb wrapped in a soft tortilla-like bread).

Kuala Lumpur
$$
Tue to Fri 11:30am to 2:30pm, Sat to Sun noon to 3:30pm, Tue to Sun 5:30pm to 10pm
69 W. Green St. near Fair Oaks Ave.
☎(626) 577-5175
As its name suggests, this bright and pleasantly decorated restaurant offers Malaysian cuisine, showing influences from Thailand, China and India. Items include a variety of noodle dishes as well as aromatic curry items, including vegetarian selections.

Mi Piace
$$-$$$
every day 11:30am to 11:30pm, until 12:30am Fri and Sat night
25 E. Colorado Blvd. near Fair Oaks Ave., Pasadena
☎(626) 795-3131
This popular Italian eatery offers a bright, high-ceilinged interior and a few

tables lining the sidewalk. Specialties include a sautéed chicken breast in a garlic and white wine sauce, mushroom capellini, veal *saltimbocca* with prosciutto, and risotto with seafood and ginger.

Twin Palms
$$-$$$
Mon to Sat 11:30am to 2:30pm, every day 5pm to 10:30pm
101 W. Green St. at De Lacey Ave.
☎(626) 577-2567
This vast but friendly outdoor restaurant (with a retractable tent for protection against rain; an indoor seating area is also available) is built around two enormous palm trees and includes a bandshell as well as a row of rotisserie spits. The menu focuses on California cuisine, which is to say a blend of Mediterranean, Asian and other influences. Dishes include pan-seared salmon with Asian vegetables, warm lamb salad with couscous and feta, and garlicky grilled chicken. Musical entertainment includes gospel singers during Sunday brunch.

Shiro
$$$
Tue to Sun 6pm to 10:30pm
1505 Mission St., corner Fair Oaks Ave.
☎(626) 799-4774
Anyone who becomes Orangerie's head chef and Wolfgang Puck's successor, can without hesitation lend his name to his own restaurant. And this is exactly what Hideo "Shiro" Yamashiro did. The Shiro restaurant blends French and Asian flavours to create a menu that features lambchops marinated with mint and garlic, as well as escalopes in a ginger and lime sauce and steamed salmon with capers. The catfish is also an excellent choice. Reservations are a must.

Yujean Kang's Gourmet Chinese Cuisine
$$$
67 N. Raymond Ave.
☎(626) 585-0855
Forget any preconceived notions you may have about what Chinese food should taste like: Kang serves up what is aptly named "new Chinese cuisine." Start with tender slices of lamb served on a bed of *enoki* mushrooms, topped with a mix of sautéed yams, or even sea perch drowned in a passion-fruit sauce. To finish your meal, choose the poached plums or frozen watermelon covered with white chocolate. The service is flawless and the decor can be described as Asian modernism.

The Raymond
$$$$
every day 11:30am to 9:30pm
1250 S. Fair Oaks Ave., corner Columbia St.
☎(626) 441-3136

Located at the heart of Pasadena's residential district, The Raymond is housed in a Craftsman-style cottage that was once associated with The Raymond Victorian hotel, from which the restaurant gets its name. Owner-chef Suzanne Bourg brings a romantic sensibility and an impeccable culinary instinct to her international dishes. The menu, which changes weekly, features soups, meat, poultry and inspired desserts. You have the choice of dining at one of the randomly set out tables inside or directly in the garden, which is a great idea on warm summer evenings.

Hollywood and Surroundings

See map on p 123.

Figaro
$
1804 N. Vermont Ave.
☎(323) 662-2874

Figaro's plesant terrace, which is shaded by lovely canopies, is almost a perfect replica of a Parisian café. Bistro tables and chairs, waiters dressed in black and white who speak with a slight French accent, authentic French bread—you'll find it all. This bakery-café attracts the neighbourhood's francophiles, who have come to enjoy a lunch-time sandwich, or simply to buy some delicious fresh bread.

Fred 62
$-$$
every day 24hrs
1854 N. Vermont Ave. near Franklin Ave., Los Feliz
☎(323) 667-0062

This ultra-hip diner, with a lime-green exterior and vinyl booths inside, offers a wide range of comfort foods to a diverse clientele. Some very original sandwiches, as well as burgers, noodles, salads and desserts, provide an intriguing selection. Service tends to be erratic.

Ita-Cho
$-$$
Mon to Sat 6:30pm to 11pm
6775 Santa Monica Blvd.
☎(323) 871-0236

Although it looks dingy and unappealing from the outside and not much better inside, the fresh fish and Japanese home-style cooking here have been winning followers from all across L.A. Most dishes are small, allowing diners to sample several items. Specialties include eggplant in ground shrimp, a selection of sashimi (raw fish), tofu in a soy and ginger sauce, and marinated pork.

Atch-Kotch
$-$$
Mon to Sat 11:30 to 10pm
1253 N. Vine St.
☎(323) 467-5537
With its black-lacquer decor, this snug Japanese spot offers an interesting variety of sushi, noodle dishes, and other specialities.

Jitlada
$-$$
Tue to Sun 11:30am to 3pm, 5pm to 10pm
5233 W. Sunset Blvd.
☎(323) 667-9809
Authentic Thai cuisine and two pleasant dining rooms covered with artwork form an agreeable contrast to the dreary mini-mall exterior. Spring rolls and lemongrass and seafood soup are among the openers. The main-course meat, seafood and noodle dishes are expertly sauced and seasoned.

Le Petit Bistro
$$
Mon to Fri 11:30am to 3pm, every day 5:30pm to 1am
631 N. La Cienega Blvd.
West Hollywood
☎289-9797
This atmospheric and inexpensive French bistro offers old-fashioned decor and some new and old favourites on the menu, including goat cheese salad and duck confit.

Hugo's
$$
every day 7:30am to 10:30pm
8401 Santa Monica Blvd.
West Hollywood
☎(323) 654-4088
This casual spot, with bright and rather plain decor as well as some tables on the sidewalk, offers an extensive selection of breakfasts and a lunch and dinner menu centred around pastas and other Italian dishes. This is augmented by health-food items such as vegetarian burgers.

Birds
$$
every day, noon to 11pm
5925 Franklin Ave.
☎(323) 465-0175
Birds rotisserie's ovens emit a mouthwatering roast-chicken aroma. Roasted, marinated, white or dark meat—chicken is served with all kinds of sauces and is prepared in every way imaginable (e.g. whole, burger, sandwich, salad). Regulars congregate at the bar, which remains lively late into the night.

La Poubelle
$$
every day 4pm to 11pm
5907 Franklin Ave.
☎(232) 465-0807
La Poubelle's name is quite misleading, as this small candlelit restaurant serves fine French and Italian food prepared with consummate

skill, as its loyal customers can attest.

Miceli's
$$
Mon to Thu 11:30am to 11pm
Fri 11:30am to midnight
Sat to Sun 4pm to 11pm
1646 N. Las Palmas
☎(213) 466-3438
Hollwood's oldest Italian restaurant (1949) has lost nothing of its original charm, which has no doubt contributed to its longevity. Its location near the ever-busy Hollywood Boulevard makes it popular with tourists. The atmosphere is extremely lively, thanks to the crowd that flocks here and the staff who make every effort to provide attentive service. Checkered tablecloths and a pannelled ceiling where hundreds of empty Chianti bottles are suspended, adorn the room. For a reasonable price, you can satisfy your appetite with thin-crust pizza or the *linguini pescatore*, a house specialty.

Yamashiro
$$$
Sun to Thu 5:30pm to 10pm, Fri and Sat 5:30pm to 11pm, bar open until 2am
1999 N. Sycamore Ave.
in the Hollywood Hills
☎(323) 466-5125
Although the food and service are good at this very romantic Japanese restaurant, the real reason to come here is for the extraordinary view of the city below. Finding the way isn't easy: the restaurant is reached via a narrow, twisting road up a hill, but it's worth the effort, especially if a window table is available. It is set in a replica of a Japanese palace, with elaborate gardens rounding out the atmosphere. Grilled tuna is a specialty, as are various sushi, sashimi and tempura dishes.

Pinot Hollywood
$$$
Mon to Fri 11:30am to 2:30pm, every day 6pm to 10:30pm
1448 N. Gower St.
☎(323) 461-8800
Popular with those who work in the middle echelons of the film industry, this sprawling but comfortable mid-Hollywood spot offers a selection of French and American dishes. Specialities include foie gras ravioli, lamb with goat cheese polenta, and chicken with mustard sauce.

Musso and Frank Grill
$$$
Tue to Sat 11am to 11pm
6667 Hollywood Blvd., corner Cahuenga Blvd.
☎(323) 467-7788
Musso and Frank Grill is Hollywood's oldest restaurant. Housed in a building dating back to 1919, its interior is decorated with dark wood pannelling, murals and red leather seats.

Its bar and open grill give it a private-club ambiance, which reflects the restaurant's long-standing tradition. Among the international dishes prepared here, the veal escalope, loin of lamb with mint jelly, sautéed lobster and a wide range of steaks and ribs, are all worth mentioning.

Campanile
$$$$
Mon to Fri 11:30am to 10pm
Sat 9:30am to 11pm
Sun 9:30am to 1:30pm
624 S. La Brea, north of Wilshire Blvd.
☎(323) 938-1447
You'll find one of L.A.'s best restaurants on La Brea Avenue—Campanile, a true gastronomical temple. Here owner-chefs Mark Peel and Nancy Silverton use only the richest ingredients in the complex creation of their dishes, which feature lobster, aïoli and mussels. The result is an exquisite cuisine with a thousand surprises and flavours. Mediterranean for some, Californian for others, the inspired cuisine of Campanile cannot be categorized. You'll enjoy this culinary experience amidst the grandiose decor of high ceilings and multiple floors and balconies. The restaurant is in fact housed in one of the private offices Charlie Chaplin built for himself in 1928. In addition to lunch and dinner, you have a choice between various types of meals: delicious breakfasts, delectable brunches served on weekends and a sampling menu every Monday night. It is wise to make reservations and wearing a jacket is recommended.

Patina
$$$$$
Sun to Thu 6pm to 9:30pm, Fri 6pm to 10:30pm, Sat 5:30pm to 10:30pm
5955 Melrose Ave. west of Cahuenga Blvd.
☎(323) 467-2208
Regarded by some as one of L.A.'s best restaurants, Patina is a warm, elegant and surprisingly low-key spot, noted for the French cooking of Joachim Splichal and his selected chefs. The decor is modern and subdued, the menu varies by season, and most dishes are inventive without going off the deep end.

Mid-Wilshire and Westside

See map on p 137.

Gumbo Pot
$
Mon to Sat 8:30am to 6:30pm, Sun 9am to 5pm
Farmer's Market, 6333 W. Third St. near Fairfax Ave.
☎(323) 933-0358
This is one of several self-service food counters at the bustling Farmer's Market in the Fairfax district. As its

Restaurants

name suggests, hearty chicken, sausage and shrimp gumbo is a specialty, along with other Louisiana items, including sandwiches, sweet-potato salad and beignets (doughnuts).

Asahi Ramen
$
Fri to Wed 11:30am to 9pm (closed Thu)
2027 Sawatelle Blvd., West L.A.
☎479-2231
This is a simple and delightful Japanese noodle house. Various noodle dishes and dumplings dominate the short menu.

Nam Kang
$$
every day 11:30am to 9:30pm
3055 W. Seventh St. near Vermont Ave., Koreatown
☎(323) 380-6606
The bland decor is not much to brag about, but the authentic Korean dishes, in particular some of the small side dishes, make it worth the trip. Savoury mixtures of meat, vegetables and rice, accompanied by spicy *jimchee* (marinated cabbage) are among the items available. Fish and seafood dishes also appear on the menu.

El Cholo
$$
Mon to Thu 11am to 10pm, Fri and Sat 11am to 11pm, Sun 11am to 9pm
1121 S. Western Ave. near Olympic Blvd.
☎(323) 734-2773
Open since 1927, this is one of the oldest Mexican restaurants outside Mexico. Located in a neighbourhood that is now largely Korean, this warm and cozy spot continues to appeal to a broad cross-section of L.A. society. The menu is vast and authentic, although the seasoning is toned down to appeal to American tastes.

Angeli Caffe
$$
Mon to Thu noon to 10:30pm, Fri and Sat noon to 11pm, Sun 5pm to 10pm
7274 Melrose Ave. between La Brea and Fairfax
☎(323) 936-9086
Part of the attraction here is the original architecture, with steel beams and simple furniture. The menu centres around pizzas, pastas, salads and grilled chicken. Fish soup is a specialty.

Authentic Café
$$
Mon to Thu 11am to 10pm, Fri 11am to midnight, Sat 8:30am to midnight, Sun 8:30am to 10pm
7605 Beverly Blvd. east of Fairfax
☎(323) 939-4626
This noisy and brightly decorated spot specializes in U.S. southwestern cuisine. Specialties include wood-grilled chicken and variations on tacos. A number of vegetarian items are available.

Mexica
$$
Mon to Fri noon to 2:30pm, every day 5pm to 10pm, Fri and Sat until 11pm
7313 Beverly Blvd. three blocks west of La Brea
☎(323) 933-7385
This spacious, artsy spot offers a version of nouvelle Mexican cuisine along with regional dishes such as *cochinita pibil* (Yucatan-style roast pork) and *mole poblano* (chicken with bitter, spicy chocolate sauce).

Bombay Café
$$
Tue to Thu 11:30am to 10pm, Fri 5pm to 11pm, Sat 4pm to 11pm, Sun 4pm to 10pm
12113 Santa Monica Blvd. near Bundy Dr., West L.A.
☎820-2070
Set in an unpromising location upstairs in one of L.A.'s countless mini-malls, this spot has built a reputation for creative Indian cuisine, with a constantly changing menu that includes excellent curries and tandoori items, as well as some interesting appetizers.

Maui Beach Café
$$
every day 11:30am to midnight, Fri and Sat until 1am
1019 Westwood Blvd., Westwood
☎ 209-0494
Popular with students from nearby UCLA and with assorted members of the Westwood crowd, this brassy and buoyant spot offers Hawaiian cuisine in its current manifestation as a blend of Asian and American dishes, running the gamut from sashimi to steak.

Le Colonial
$$-$$$
Mon to Fri 11:30am to 2:30pm, Sun to Thu 5:30pm to 11pm, Fri and Sat 5:30pm to midnight
8783 Beverly Blvd. near La Cienega, West Hollywood
☎289-0660
This charming spot aims to recreate the atmosphere of Vietnam during the French colonial period, with plenty of rattan, tiled floors, and old black-and-white photos of pre-war Vietnam. The menu offers a sophisticated range of Vietnamese dishes with a few French items or influences thrown in.

Louis XIV
$$-$$$
Mon to Sat 6pm to midnight
606 N. La Brea Ave. at Melrose
☎(323) 934-5102
Romantic, rustic decor provide an introduction to this simple, relaxed French bistro where typical menu choices include steak and *frites* or grilled salmon.

Chianti Cucina
$$-$$$
Mon to Thu 11:30am to 11:30pm, Fri and Sat 11:30am to midnight, Sun 4pm to 11pm
7383 Melrose Ave.
☎(323) 653-8333
This small, bright Italian spot is as good a place as any for a simple pasta dish or something a bit more elaborate. Specialties include beef carpaccio, linguine with seafood, and a grilled vegetable platter with polenta.

Mimosa
$$$
Mon to Sat 11:30am to 3pm and 5:30pm to 11pm, Fri and Sat until midnight
8009 Beverly Blvd. west of Fairfax
☎(323) 655-8895
This traditionally decorated bistro offers an authentic French menu that includes *cassoulet* (a bean stew with various meats) with duck confit, steamed mussels and roast pork.

La Cachette
$$$$
Mon to Fri 11:30am to 2:30pm, Mon to Thu 6pm to 10:30pm, Fri and Sat 5:30pm to 11pm, Sun 5:30pm to 9:30pm
10506 Santa Monica Blvd., West L.A.
☎470-4992
This is one of the top French restaurants in L.A., with a light California touch. Unappealing on the outside, it is all flowers, paintings and light on the inside, with banquette seating. According to the staff, some of the traditional French classics such as roast duck and *cassoulet* are prepared here in lower-fat versions. The menu ranges broadly and includes foie gras, *bouillabaisse* (Marseille-style fish soup), and *tarte tatin* (caramelized apple pie).

Polo Lounge
$$$$$
every day 6pm to 11pm
9641 Sunset Blvd., Beverly Hills
☎276-2251
The Polo Lounge is the legendary restaurant of the just-as-mythical Beverly Hills Hotel (see p 243) where a number of celebrities are seen regularly. Its rich decor, which includes painted wallpaper featuring banana-tree leaves, is of the utmost beauty. Its thoughtfully selected menu offers delicious meals. Jacket required.

Santa Monica and Surroundings

See map on p 149.

Jody Maroni's Sausage Kingdom
$
every day 9am to 6pm
2011 Ocean Front Walk, Venice Beach
☎822-5639
This is one of several snack stands along the Venice Beach boardwalk, but it stands out for the originality of its menu, consisting entirely of sausages served on crispy rolls. Selections include orange-garlic-cumin chicken and duck sausage, Bombay bangers (made with curried lamb) and Louisiana *boudin* hot links. Jody Maroni's is expanding into a chain, though this outlet is where it all began. Outdoor picnic-style seating nearby.

Polly's Pies
$
Mon to Thu 6:30am to 11pm, Fri 6:30am to midnight, Sat 7am to midnight, Sun 7am to 11pm
501 Wilshire Blvd. at Fifth St., Santa Monica
☎394-9721
This traditional American diner is not the least bit trendy, unless the attached outdoor terrace qualifies. Nonetheless, it offers large, wholesome breakfasts and, later in the day, sandwiches, burgers, fried or grilled chicken, salads and, as the name suggests, a wide variety of pies.

Real Food Daily
$-$$
Mon to Sat 11:30am to 10pm
514 Santa Monica Blvd. near Fifth St., Santa Monica
☎451-7544
This has to rank as one of the top vegetarian restaurants in California. The menu is strictly vegan, with no dairy or egg products used (for example, the Parmesan-style dressing on the Caesar salad is soy-based), and great care is taken to provide good nutritional balance. The main menu selections offer various combinations of beans, grains and vegetables.

Reel Inn
$-$$
Sun to Thu 11am to 10pm, Fri to Sat 11am to 11pm
1220 Third St. near Wilshire Blvd.
☎395-5538
Located along the Third Street Promenade, this big barn of a place has seating at long benches as well as a small outdoor terrace. On offer are a very substantial variety of fresh fish and seafood, including some Mexican-accented items.

Beach Front Café
$-$$
every day 6:30am to 6pm
17th Ave. at Speedway, Venice Beach
☎399-6558
This casual spot, located half a block from the Mus-

Restaurants

cle Beach area of Venice Beach, offers big portions and what it bills as "body-builder specials." The menu includes simple items such as pork chops, grilled fish and fried noodles, along with salads and other vegetarian dishes.

The Terrace
$-$$
Mon to Fri 11am to 11pm, Sat and Sun 9am to 11pm, bar open later
7 Washington Blvd. at Ocean Front Walk
☎578-1530
Bordering the south end of Venice Beach, this casual spot has a bright, pleasant dining room and a small terrace outside. The menu focuses on sandwiches, pizza, pasta and salads but also offers a number of interesting seafood appetizers.

Neptune's Net
$-$$
Mon to Thu 9am to 8pm, Fri and Sat 9am to 9pm, Sun 9am to 8:30pm
42505 Pacific Coast Hwy., Malibu
☎457-3095
Located across the highway from the beach at the western edge of Malibu not far from the border of Ventura County, this extremely casual self-service shack-like establishment makes up in value what it lacks in finesse. Clam chowder is a favourite. Steamed fresh seafood is remarkably inexpensive.

Gate of India
$-$$
every day 11:30am to 11pm
115 Santa Monica Blvd. near Ocean Ave., Santa Monica
☎656-1664
This very welcoming spot is tastefully decorated with Indian fabrics and art and features a copious lunch buffet until 3pm. The menu items include a broad range of curries, as well as tandoori dishes.

Fritto Misto
$$
Mon to Thu 11:30am to 10pm, Fri and Sat 11:30am to 10:30pm, Sun 5pm to 9:30pm
601 Colorado Ave. at Sixth St., Santa Monica
☎458-2829
This simple Italian restaurant offers basic decor, a friendly atmosphere, and a menu that ranges from a mix-and-match selection of pastas and sauces to more interesting meat or seafood items, including the restaurant's namesake dish prepared here with shrimp, calamari and vegetables.

Crocodile Café
$$
Sun to Thu 11am to 10pm, Fri and Sat 11am to 11pm
101 Santa Monica Blvd. at Ocean Ave., Santa Monica
☎394-4783
This casual yet comfortable spot offers the archetypal California eating experience, with touches of Asia, Mexico, New Mexico and

Italy. The menu ranges from pizzas (from a wood-burning oven) to chilis to burgers to moo shu chicken calzone and tostada salad with corn, black beans and chicken. Somehow, it all seems to work.

Venice Whaler Bar and Grill
$$-$$$
every day 11am to 2am
10 Washington Blvd. at Ocean Front Walk
☎ ***821-8737***
With a breezy dining room overlooking the southern end of Venice Beach, this attractive spot offers a varied menu centring around sandwiches, pizzas, salads and meat dishes, but also includes more elaborate items such as shrimp Alfredo and fresh albacore tuna with pear sauce.

Mercedes Grill
$$-$$$
Mon to Thu 7:30am to 10:30pm, Fri and Sat 8:30am to 11:30pm, Sun 8:30am to 9:30pm
14 Washington Blvd. near Ocean Front Walk
☎ ***827-6209***
Located near the southern end of Venice Beach, this restaurant bills itself as Cuban-Californian. The dining room is bright and open, with big skylights. The menu offers an imaginative selection of starters and salads, as well as several vegetarian dishes. Feature items include cilantro papaya chicken, shrimp Florentine enchiladas and mango-almond halibut. Full breakfast menu also available.

Restaurant Hama
$$-$$$
Mon to Fri 11:30am to 2:30pm, Mon to Thu 6pm to 11pm, Fri and Sat 6pm to 11:30pm
213 Windward Ave., Venice Beach
☎***396-8783***
Facing the small traffic circle across from the Venice Beach post office, this friendly, casual spot specializes in sushi. Seating is in two attractive rooms with tables and a long sushi bar. The sushi list changes daily. The menu also includes tempura and teriyaki items.

72 Market Street
$$$-$$$$
Mon to Fri 11:30am to 3pm, Mon to Thu 6pm to 10pm, Fri and Sat 6pm to 11pm
72 Market St., Venice Beach
☎***392-8720***
This is one of the more elegant spots at Venice Beach, but it still manages to maintain a casual air, with an attractive dining room and above-average background music. Appetizers include selections of sushi and oysters, as well as other items like lobster cakes. Main courses include wild mushroom risotto, pan-roasted lamb loin and jerk chicken.

JiRaffe
$$$-$$$$
Tue to Fri noon to 2pm and 6pm to 11pm, Sat 5:30pm to 11pm, Sun 5:30pm to 9pm
502 Santa Monica Blvd. at Fifth St., Santa Monica
☎917-6671
Decorated like a French bistro and offering a blend of traditional French and new American cooking, this spot appears to have developed a large and loyal clientele, meaning it can be noisy and cramped, but local food critics give it high marks. The menu changes frequently according to season and the quality of fresh ingredients. Recent selections have included spiced whitefish with ginger-carrot sauce and rabbit with polenta gnocchi and baked tomatoes.

Schatzi on Main
$$$$
every day 9am to 11pm
3110 Main St., Santa Monica
☎399-4800
In the past few years, it has become trendy for Hollywood celebrities to open their own restaurant, and Arnold Schwarzenegger probably became one of the instigators of this trend when he founded Schatzi on Main in 1991. Offering Austrian cuisine, this establishment is both elegant and charming, featuring a long dining room with an arched ceiling inspired from the famous *Orient Express*, walls plastered with photographs of its famous founder, and a quaint terrace. On the menu you will find typical Austrian dishes such as *Wienerschnitzel*, *Zwiebelröstbraten* and Arnold's favourite dessert, *Kaiserschmarrn* (caramelized, raisin-stuffed crepes topped with apple sauce). "Schatzi's Austrian Menu," "Dinner Under the Stars" and "Monte Carlo Buffet" are a few of the many fixed-price menus (four courses) available. The steak tartare is simply delicious. Those who hope to meet Schwarzenegger in person should stop by on the first Monday of the month, which is Cigar Night, the Terminator's favourite.

South Bay and Surroundings

See map on p 159.

Fun Fish Market
$
121 International Boardwalk, Redondo Beach
Among the array of inexpensive restaurants available to Redondo Beach excursionists, the Fun Fish Market, located in Redondo Beach's Fisherman's Wharf, is the best option. Seafood and fish are served without much ceremony, granted,

but are always fresh, which is the most important thing when it comes to seafood. During lobster season, it only costs $10 to sample this delicious crustacean, and the same goes for fried fish and snow crab.

Good Stuff
$
every day 7am to 10pm
1300 Highland Ave. at 13th St., Manhattan Beach
☎545-4775
1286 The Strand, Hermosa Beach
☎374-2334
1617 Pacific Coast Hwy., Redondo Beach's Riviera Village
☎316-0262
In a decor that evokes the world of lifeguards, the three Good Stuff restaurants of South Bay are a good place to refuel after a day at the beach. They offer an interesting choice of pasta and sandwiches, as well as a surprising selection of Mexican dishes. You can partake of all this in the dining room or on the terrace, if you prefer to fully enjoy the California sun.

The Kettle
$-$$
every day 24hrs
1138 Highland Ave., Manhattan Beach
☎545-8511
This friendly spot carries the American coffee shop concept to a new level, with a good assortment of sandwiches, salads and burgers served in a nondescript indoor dining room and a much more appealing outdoor terrace.

Reed's
$$-$$$
Mon to Fri 11:30am to 2:30pm, Mon to Sat 5:30pm to 10:30pm
2640 N. Sepulveda Blvd., Manhattan Beach
☎546-3299
Despite its shopping mall location, this spot is elegant inside, with high windows and pale wooden walls. The menu changes regularly and recently offered new American dishes such as tuna tartare, smoked salmon ravioli and an interesting take on chicken pot pie.

Tony's
$$
Mon to Fri 5pm to 11pm
Sat and Sun 11am to 11pm
112 and 210 Pier Plaza, Redondo Beach's Fisherman's Wharf
☎376-6223
Tony's, located on Pier Plaza in Redondo's Fisherman's Wharf, suffers from a split personality due to its two side-by-side locales. Indeed, at number 210, Tony's (open since 1952) offers its traditional formula to patrons who can either dine near the panoramic windows that provide a magnificent view, or simply sit around the fireplace on chilly winter nights. At number 112, the new Tony's has adopted a con-

temporary decor to distinguish itself from its older brother. Aside from this, both establishments are very similar, offering generous portions of excellent seafood and meat dishes prepared according to the best Italian recipes. Note that on the second floor, the "210" features an unusual UFO-shaped bar which attracts its own clientele thanks to the restaurant's famous cocktails.

Le Beaujolais
$$$
522 S. Pacific Coast Hwy., Redondo Beach
☎543-5100
The French culinary embassy in Redondo Beach is Le Beaujolais, which has been serving classic French cuisine since 1983. The savoury loin of lamb, with just the right amount of spices, and the fresh halibut are the best choices from the establishment's many selections. The old-style, candlelit dining room will certainly please couples looking for a romantic evening. In addition, a copious brunch is served on Sunday mornings for as little as $14, including freshly squeezed orange juice and two glasses of champagne.

Encounter at LAX
$$$
every day 10:30am to 10pm
209 World Way, inside the Theme Building, LAX
☎215-5151
Encounter at LAX, located in the Theme Building, a structure whose daring architectural style has made it the airport's symbol since its construction in 1961, seems to be the airport's most famous restaurant. Its menu features Californian cuisine, with such favourites as grilled chicken breast with Gorgonzola and *prosciutto*, radish-wrapped salmon and tuna sashimi with Japanese cucumber salad. To create a futuristic atmosphere in the dining room, the owners called upon the Walt Disney Imagineering firm to design a decor inspired by the movie *The Jetsons*, complete with intergalactic objects and a crater-shaped bar. A splendid view of the ocean and mountains can be seen from the window seats. Reservations are recommended.

Kincaid's Bay House
$$$-$$$$
Mon to Thu 11am to 10pm, Fri and Sat 11:30am to 11pm, Sun 10am to 10pm
500 Fisherman's Wharf at Harbor Dr., Redondo Beach
☎318-6080
The sedate atmosphere and soothing ocean views at this classy spot along the rejuve-

nated Redondo Beach pier are a good introduction to the nouveau Hawaiian-influenced menu, which includes items like marinated pork brochettes grilled over apple wood, crab-and-shrimp hash with sherry cream sauce, and simpler fresh fish dishes.

Long Beach and Surroundings

See map on p 163.

Dragon House Restaurant
$-$$
every day 11am to 1am
101 Alamitos Ave. at First St., Long Beach
☎(562) 437-3303
This great cavernous place, with a brighter area facing the street, offers a wide variety of Chinese and Thai dishes. Excellent value.

Shenandoah Café
$$-$$$
every day 5pm to 9pm or later (hours vary), Sun brunch 10am to 2pm
4722 E. Second St., Long Beach
☎(562) 434-3469
Decorated New Orleans style, this friendly spot offers Louisiana specialties such as blackened fish, shrimp in beer batter, and specially seasoned steaks.

Taco Company
$
Corner Fifth and Gaffey sts.
☎514-2808
For a quick lunch, Mexican tacos are always a safe bet. Taco Company, a tiny but highly popular stand located at the corner of Fifth and Gaffey streets, serves them up in a truly authentic style. The fish tacos (grilled or fried) are especially delicious.

Belmont Brewery Company
$$
25 29th Place, Long Beach
☎433-3891
One of the first microbreweries in Long Beach, the Belmont Brewing Company offers ales, seasonal beers and one dark porter, the Long Beach Crude, which looks a little like the black gold that gushes out from the nearby wells. Salads, sandwiches, pasta, meat and fish dishes are served in the dining room, at the bar or on the terrace, where you can enjoy a great view of Palos Verdes and Catalina Island.

Alegria Cocina Latina
$$-$$$
115 Pine Ave., Long Beach
☎(562) 436-3388
Alegria Cocina Latina is an ideal spot for amateurs of Latin, Iberian Peninsula and Latin American cuisine. The floor's bold colours, Art Nouveau bar and *trompe-l'œil* murals create a dy-

namic and friendly ambiance which seems to be appreciated by the youthful, hip clientele. The establishment features the best of Latin dishes, from *ceviche* to *molcajete* to paella. The latter alone is worth the detour. At dinner, the atmosphere is enhanced by guitarists who love to play, among other things, passionate flamencos.

Sky Room
$$$$
Wed to Mon 5pm to midnight
40 S. Locust Ave., Locust Beach
☎(562) 983-2703
True, you will have to loosen your purse strings if you want to dine at the Sky Room, but the experience is well worth it. At the entrance of the historic Breakers building, take the red carpet that leads to the elevator, where you will be escorted to the 15th floor by a tuxedoed attendant. There, you will discover an elegant dining room with hints of Art Deco and a beautiful 360° view of Los Angeles. This is a great place that is certain to leave you with a lasting impression.

The San Fernando Valley

See map on p 169.

Ventura Boulevard, one of California's best restaurant zones, stretches along several miles at the southern border of San Fernando Valley and features many good addresses.

Art's Delicatessen
$
12224 Ventura Blvd.
☎(818) 762-1221
Art's Delicatessen is without a doubt one of the best Jewish delis in town, and a very friendly restaurant to boot. Big salted beef and pastrami sandwiches are favourites among regulars, but it's the matzo-ball and cabbage soups that are the chef's specialties. The choice is yours.

Law Dogs
$
Mon, Tue and Thu 10am to 5pm
Wed and Fri 10am to 9pm
Sat 10am to 8pm
14114 Sherman Way near Hazeltine, Van Nuys
☎(818) 989-2220
For an L.A.-style hot dog, you must stop by Law Dogs, which is actually only a small counter. Ask for a Judge Dog with mustard, onions and chili; you'll get your money's worth. What

sets it apart from other fast-food joints is the fact that here, you can get legal advice (!), hence the name. Credit cards are not accepted.

Du-par's Restaurant
$-$$
Sun to Thu 6am to 1pm
Fri and Sat 6am to 4am
12036 Ventura Blvd., Studio City
☎(818) 766-4437
Du-par's Restaurant's stainless-steel exterior leaves nothing to the imagination: this is an authentic diner, with the same chrome look it had when it opened in 1948. The waiters and waitresses are dressed in fashions of that era, and occasionally dance to the rock n' roll tunes emanating from the jukebox. The menu features burgers, club sandwiches, cherry Coke and milkshakes, but what makes this place famous are its huge breakfasts. Ideal for families.

Paty's
$$
10001 Riverside Dr., Toluca Lake
☎(818) 761-9126
If your stomach is growling after a visit to the Warner Bros. or NBC studios, stop by Paty's. Whether it's for lunch or dinner, steak or stew, the portions are always generous. In a hurry? Call ahead to order and they will deliver to your car.

Talésai
$$
Mon to Fri 11:30am to 10:30pm
Sat and Sun 5:30pm to 10:30pm
11744 Ventura Blvd. at Colfax
Studio City
☎(818) 753-1001
At Talésai, Thai cuisine gets top billing. Forget Thai counters that all serve the same noodles: here, discover exotic fine cuisine with hints of curry, mint and coconut milk (chicken, vegetarian dishes, rice, salads, noodles). Sublime! The decor is minimalist, while the service is discreet and courteous.

Mistral
$$$
Mon to Fri 11am to 11pm
Sat 4pm to 11pm
13422 Ventura Blvd. at Sherman Oaks
☎(818) 981-6650
Mistral is a bistro featuring cuisine from the south of France, so expect dishes that are high in olive oil, garlic and herbs from the region. But the establishment's menu also offers international fare, with the traditional steak and seafood. In any case, visitors in search of an exotic experience will be able to, with lots of imagination, pretend they're dining in France.

Paul's Cafe
$$$
Mon to Fri 11:30am to 11pm
Sat and Sun 5pm to 11pm
13456 Ventura Blvd. between Dixie Canyon Ave. and Wordman Ave.
☎(818) 789-3575

Paul's Cafe became extremely popular when it first opened in 1999. The quality of its French-Californian dishes continues to seduce one and all, making it a successful, busy establishment where it is best to reserve ahead. Here, the menu consists of generous appetizers, deliciously prepared seafood and red-meat dishes that will surely satisfy the carnivore in you. In addition to this, the key to its success is its great price/quality ratio.

Pinot Bistro
$$$$
Mon to Fri 11am to 10pm
Sat 6pm to 10pm
12969 Ventura Blvd. west of Coldwater Canyon Ave., Studio City
☎(818) 990-0500

Facing the Mistral (see above), you will find another replica of a French bistro, this time more authentic: the Pinot Bistro. Its multiple rooms with different decors that evoke, in turn, a family restaurant, a café and a large dining room with fireplace, attract a chic clientele. The establishment's chef is very proud of his French-Californian specialties, such as fresh oysters, sautéed *foie gras* with caramelized apples and Basque bouillabaisse. The chocolate-based desserts are also a must. This is one of our favourites in Los Angeles.

Catalina Island

See map on p 173.

As with hotels, there are many things to consider when choosing a restaurant, starting with prices. In Catalina Island, they are higher, and all restaurants, with a few exceptions, are located in Avalon. Since commercial activity on the island is seasonal, opening hours can vary quite a bit: in summer, most establishments serve three meals a day, while in winter, only dinner is served. It is best to inquire ahead.

Casino Dock Cafe
$
Mon to Sun 7am to 6pm
Closed Tue in Dec
2 Casino Way, Avalon
☎510-2755

The Casino Dock Cafe, located at the end of Casino Way next to the Avalon Casino, is a welcomed halt for beach-goers. Here, you will find simple dishes and refreshing beverages at reasonable prices.

Pancake Cottage
$
every day 6:30am to 2pm
118 Catalina St., Avalon
☎510-0726
For a generous breakfast or lunch, head to the Pancake Cottage. Not only will you pay next to nothing, but you will walk away full enough to last for three days, after feasting on crepes, waffles, eggs, omelets, muffins, fresh fruit, and so on .

Busy Bee Cafe
$$
every day 8am to 10pm
30 Crescent Ave., Avalon
☎510-1983
The Busy Bee Cafe is a victim of its own success. Located in the heart of the pier, this café easily attracts many vacationers with its lovely terrace looking out on the harbour. However, once you're comfortably seated under blue parasols with the seagulls and pigeons (quite unpleasant dinner companions), you will quickly realize that this is not the most refined place. Rather, the meals are hearty, so it's best to come when you have a craving for burgers, giant seafood plates and gargantuan breakfasts.

Mi Casita
$$
every day 11am to 10pm
Clarissa Ave., Avalon
☎510-1772
At the corner of Clarissa Avenue and Third Street you will find a small, beige house with brown awnings and a red roof. That's the Mexican restaurant Mi Casita. The decor is reminiscent of a colonial hacienda and the casual atmosphere is authentically evocative of Mexico. The chicken enchiladas, *carne asada* and fajitas will convince you that you're not dreaming: this is a real vacation under the sun.

Ristorante Villa Portofino
$$-$$$
101 Crescent Ave., Avalon
☎510-0508
The romantic setting of Ristorante Villa Portofino, which features Italian cuisine, is perfect for a cozy *tête-à-tête*. The black baby grand piano, the pink stucco walls, the softly candlelit tables, the sensual Art Deco curves and the reproductions of masterpieces… everything here creates a warm, pleasant atmosphere. The menu offers a number of veal dishes as well as the traditional scampi, filet mignon, swordfish and pasta.

Cafe Prego
$$$
603 Crescent Ave., Avalon
☎510-1218
People line up for the privilege of eating at Cafe Prego, a typical Italian bistro with waxed tablecloths and stucco arches. Seafood and pasta are the house specialties, including swordfish, bass and halibut, and manicotti, rigatoni, fettuccine and lasagna, all served in a charming seaside setting.

Channel House
$$$$
205 Crescent Ave., Avalon
☎510-1617
With its lovely terrace overlooking Avalon Bay, comfortable dining room and animated Irish bar, Channel House is a friendly establishment whose recipes have been handed down for generations. The coq au vin, pepper steak and Catalina swordfish are among the top selections.

The Clubhouse
$$$$
every day 11am to 9pm
Catalina Country Club Building, Avalon
☎510-7404
Recently reopened, the Catalina Country Club's restaurant is one of the island's most distinguished establishments and one of the best places to dine. The large dining room evokes splendour and luxury with a fireplace and chandeliers, and there is a quaint terrace that's just as luxurious as the interior. The California-style menu features a number of grilled dishes and refreshing salads. Brunch is served on Sundays, cocktails every night.

Inland Orange County

See map on p 181.

Anaheim

Spire's
$
990 S. Euclid St. at Ball Rd.
☎635-5730
Spire's is a family-style restaurant offering traditional American food. Six breakfast specials under $3 and daily dinner specials are perfect for those on a budget.

Millie's Restaurant
$-$$
1480 S. Harbor Blvd.
☎535-6892
Located just across from the park gates, Millie's is a great inexpensive way to feed an army of kids. Classic diner fare is available as well as a decent breakfast or dinner buffet.

The Spaghetti Station
$-$$
999 West Ball Rd.
☎956-3250
In an old rustic building two blocks north of Disneyland, a stagecoach and life-sized horses sit on the roof of this Wild West restaurant. Choose from steaks, ribs, or 14 kinds of spaghetti as you examine the vast collection of antique art and mining memorabilia of the Old West that covers the walls. Live entertainment is offered most nights of the week.

Breakfast with Minnie and Friends
$$
1717 S. West Ave.
☎956-6755
Head to the Disneyland Pacific Hotel before going into the park, to have an all-you-can-eat breakfast with Minnie and her friend Merlin the Wizard. The interactive show is full of song and dance, sure to start off a great day at Disneyland.

J.T. Schmid's Brewhouse and Eatery
$$-$$$
2610 E. Katella Ave.
☎634-9200
Across from the Pond and Edison Field, J.T. Schmid's gets packed before and after a game. A brewery is on site, offering a selection of ales and lagers to accompany the California cuisine. The giant display kitchen serves up wood-fired pizza, Angus steaks, seafood and pasta in a fun, open-concept dining room. After dinner, relax in their comfortable bar.

Cuban Pete's
$$-$$$
1050 W. Ball Rd.
☎490-2020
Authentic Cuban and Caribbean cuisine is served in a 1940s Havana decor. Live music is featured every day but Monday, with everything from jazz to salsa. Flamenco shows accompany dinner on weekends with two performances on Saturdays at 6pm and 8pm. Reservations are recommended.

Charley Browns Steakhouse
$$$
1751 S. State College Blvd.
☎634-2211
Here, steaks and tender prime rib are complimented by an amazing selection of soups and salads. Steps away from Anaheim Stadium and the Pond. They also have a cozy little bar area that spills out onto a shaded patio.

The Anaheim White House Restaurant
$$$$
887 S. Anaheim Blvd.
☎722-1381
This restored 1909 Victorian home has consistently been ranked among the best res-

Restaurants

taurants in Orange County for its scrumptious Italian specialties and seafood. Eight different dining rooms feature crackling fireplaces, romantic lighting and elegant Victorian decor. Every choice on the menu is a winner, artistically arranged and flawlessly served. Reservations are highly recommended and a jacket and tie is suggested, but not required.

Orange

Gameworks
$$
The Block in Orange - City Dr.
☎ ***939-9690***
Gameworks is the kind of place where you are encouraged to play with your food. American classic cuisine is served, and usually gulped down in a rush to get to the numerous pool tables and extensive video arcade.

The Lotus Cafe
$$
1515 W. Chapman Ave.
☎ ***385-1233***
The Lotus Cafe offers authentic Chinese vegetarian cuisine. There's not a trace of meat in the place, but some of the favourites include decent approximations of meatballs, pork dim sum and hot wok beef. Health-conscious cooking is combined with fresh ingredients and served with a smile.

Café TuTu Tango
$$-$$$
The Block in Orange- 20 City Dr.
☎ ***769-2222***
www.cafetututango.com
The brick interior and artwork seemingly displayed at random make this the perfect artist's café. A large patio is usually full of beautiful people watching the crowd go by. Try one of their "starving artist" specials, the fried alligator or barbecue salmon spears.

Wolfgang Puck
$$-$$$
The Block in Orange - 20 City Dr.
☎ ***546-9653***
Wolfgang Puck offers Asian-fusion cuisine as well as pizza, steaks and sushi—something to please almost anyone. The busy mosaic tile-motif walls preside over comfortable booths. Try their signature grilled tuna burger.

PJ's Abbey
$$$
182 S. Orange St.
☎ ***771-8556***
PJ's Abbey is housed in a centennial Victorian church with vaulted ceilings, rich woodwork and beautiful stained-glass windows. Hand-cut filet mignon with tiger shrimp, chicken cordon bleu and a marinated rack of lamb are just a few of the highlights. Friday and

Saturday nights feature jazz from 6pm to 9pm.

Buena Park

Bernie's Diner
$
6086 Beach Blvd.
☎739-4504
Bernie's is an inexpensive option along the "entertainment corridor" of Buena Park. The classic diner-style menu is offered from 5am to 3am daily.

The Train McDonald's
$
7861 Beach Blvd.
☎521-2303
The McDonald's restaurant in Buena Park merits special mention. Inside the early 20th-century exterior is the first high-tech amusement ride in a McDonald's. The McThriller simulates roller-coaster rides, jet-fighter acrobatics or downhill skiing. There are also five trains that make their way throughout the establishment, the largest McDonald's in America.

PoFolks
$-$$
7701 Beach Blvd.
☎521-8955
This friendly home-style restaurant serves generous helpings of classic American fare. A 500ft (160m) model railroad chugs its way through the restaurant.

Santa Ana

Ruby's Diner
$-$$
2800 N. Main St.
☎836-7829
This 1940s style diner has everything you could ever want in the way of burgers, fries and shakes. For an authentic experience, pop a quarter in the jukebox and settle into one of the vinyl booths.

Jerry's Famous Deli
$$
3210 Park Centre Rd.
☎662-3363
Located a half-block from the Orange County Performing Arts Centre, Jerry's Deli boasts a menu of over 600 items, ranging from traditional deli-style to Californian Cuisine. Just about anything you can imagine is on the menu, including a large kosher selection.

Shelley's Courthouse Bistro
$$-$$$
Mon to Fri 11am to 4pm
Thu to Sat 5pm to 9pm
400 Fourth St.
☎543-9821
Shelley's offers Cajun cuisine in a charming, bistro-style atmosphere. Try the signature alligator or the spicy seafood gumbo.

The Bluewater Grill
$$-$$$
1621 W. Sunflower Ave. Suite D-50
☎546-3472
The Bluewater Grill is reminiscent of casual New England seafood restaurants with it's wood decor and paper placemats. More than 20 varieties of fresh fish can be enjoyed either inside or on the patio. The oyster bar is also quite popular.

Costa Mesa

The Gypsy Den Cafe
$$
2930 Bristol St.
☎549-7012
Located in the Anti-mall shopping centre, the Gypsy Den is a perfectly eclectic spot where thrift-store paintings line the walls and the furniture has been scrounged from garage sales. They offer a great selection of giant sandwiches, vegetarian delights, and their famous gooey lasagna.

Memphis Soul Cafe & Bar
$$-$$$
2920 Bristol St.
☎432-7685
The Memphis Soul Cafe offers a casual, funky atmosphere and a menu featuring Southern-style meatloaf, Cajun gumbo, Creole shrimp and other inspiring dishes. The presentation is wonderful and the cozy bar is great for an after-dinner drink.

Antonello Ristorante
$$$$
1611 W. Sunflower Ave.
☎751-7153
Fantastic, well-presented northern Italian specialties are accompanied by an award-winning wine list of 300 foreign and domestic labels. Guests dine amidst frescoes of hanging vines and fine art. Former President Clinton dined at Antonello during a recent visit, and the restaurant is often filled with famous personalities.

The Beaches of Orange County

See map on p 181.

Seal Beach

Hennessey's Tavern
$
143 Main St.
☎598-6456
Inside this lovely stone building is a pub-style restaurant/bar, a great spot for a beer on a hot day. The restaurant serves classic yet uninspired pub grub, including a good selection of sandwiches and burgers. The bar heats up after dark and is open for breakfast as well.

BJ's Pizza & Grill
$
209 Main St.
☎***594-9310***
This open-air pizza joint features deep-dish pizza, hot subs, burgers and pasta. Try the honey-crisp chicken salad and the chunky vegetarian deep-dish pizza.

Finbars Italian Kitchen
$-$$
550 Pacific Coast Hwy. #111
☎***430-4303***
Swing and big band music plays in the background of this lovely family restaurant. Daily specials compliment the Italian-American fare of pasta, pizza, shrimp, chicken and salads. Try the chicken tequila fusilli or design your own pizza.

"Kinda" Lahaina Broiler
$$-$$$
901 Ocean Dr.
☎***596-3864***
The "Kinda" Lahaina Broiler has a wonderful seaside location overlooking Seal Beach. Its extensive menu features a wide selection of fresh seafood, but also offers Angus beef, pasta and salads. Breakfast is served until 2:30pm, with incredible omelettes, fresh fruit and seafood.

Bayou St. John
$$-$$$
dinner only
320 Main St.
☎***431-2298***
Bayou St. John is famous in Seal Beach for its Creole and Louisiana cuisine. A definite break from the ordinary, try the spicy jambalaya, blackened redfish or prime rib. The service is friendly and the atmosphere is comfortable.

The Glide'er Inn
$$$
1400 Pacific Coast Hwy.
☎***431-3022***
The Glide'er Inn combines fresh seafood with a taste of history. First established in 1930, this restaurant borders the local airstrip and used to be a popular hangout for the area's pilots. Fresh clam chowder, local seafood and thick, juicy steaks highlight the menu. Over 100 model airplanes hang from the ceiling and hundreds of historical photos line the walls.

Huntington Beach

The Longboard Restaurant and Pub
$
217 Main St.
☎***714-960-1896***
www.longboard-pub.com
A true salute to the surf heritage of Huntington Beach, the Longboard serves a great variety of

salads, sandwiches and seafood in a bar that looks like it's "in the trough of the wave," decorated with surfboards and old surf photos. It also has an outdoor patio and happy hour from 3pm to 7pm.

Ruby's Surf City Diner
$
End of the Huntington Beach Pier
☎969-7829
After you've walked all the way to the end of the pier, some refreshments may be in order. Ruby's is a1950s-style diner that serves up a giant burger with a thick milkshake and slice of pie. Many come for the view alone, through the glass wall that looks out onto the Pacific.

Huntington Brewery
$$
201E. Main St. second floor
☎960-5343
The Huntington Brewery serves pasta, pizza, burgers, and of course, beer! Try their own brews, made in the stainless kettles right behind the bar. $1 "tasters" of their 10 on-tap selections are available. Exposed brick inside gives way to the beach–view patio. Also try the Cajun jambalaya and grilled salmon with dill sauce.

Louise's Trattoria
$$$
300 Pacific Coast Hwy.
☎714-960-0996
Louise's offers Italian specialties, including pizza and pasta, in a perfect location overlooking the ocean. Dine on the beautiful open patio or in one of the comfy booths. The Sunday brunch will start off the day in style with champagne and an expansive buffet.

Chimayo
$$-$$$
317 Pacific Coast Hwy.
☎374-7273
Chimayo offers fine Mexican food, imaginatively prepared and presented, with incredible ocean views to match. Located below Duke's, the menu ranges from traditional Mexican specialties like *queso fundido* (Mexican cheese, chicken sausage and chiles served in a skillet) to sage-crusted sea bass and grilled proscuitto. At night, guests sip a margarita and gather around a cozy beach fire pit. Impeccable service.

Duke's of Hawaii
$$$
317 Pacific Coast Hwy.
☎374-6446
Duke's is right on the beach with grand, panoramic views of the ocean. The decor is fun and interesting with koa-wood walls, tropical plants, Hawaiian artifacts and Huntington Beach

memorabilia. Dine outside on one of their two dining areas or have a drink at the palapa-covered beach bar. In addition to the Hawaiian-inspired steaks, pastas and seafood, try the *huli-huli* chicken or a generous fillet of mahi mahi.

Newport Beach

Alta Coffee
$
506 31st St.
☎675-0233
Alta Coffee is a good place to take a quick break with a coffee and pastry or a light meal. Live impromptu entertainment is often supplied by local artists, poets and musicians.

Veg A Go-Go
$
401 Newport Center Dr.
☎721-4088
A fantastic vegetarian restaurant where even carnivores won't mind dining. The trendy decor highlights tasty veggie burgers, intriguing salad combinations and some tofu delights.

Alysia 101
$-$$
Newport Beach2901 W. Pacific Coast Hwy.
☎722-4128
A variety of tempting Asian tastes is available at Alysia 101 in its many themed dining rooms. Choose from 1930s Shanghai, the Java or Bali Terraces or sip some saki at the Tiger or Dragon Bars. Sushi and sashimi are available at the Yuyake Sushi Bar. Prices are very reasonable, and the restaurant offers panoramic views of Newport Harbor.

The Blue Beet Cafe
$-$$
107 21st Place
☎675-BEET
The Blue Beet is a local favourite for thick, juicy steaks. Built in 1912, this is also the oldest commercial structure in Newport. Live music can be enjoyed nightly, as it has for the past several decades. For the quality of food and entertainment, the Blue Beet is ridiculously underpriced.

The Tale of the Whale
$$
400 Main St, Balboa Peninsula
☎673-4633
The Tale of the Whale is located in the historic Balboa Pavilion overlooking Newport Harbor. This family-style restaurant has a wide variety of seafood dishes prepared just about any way you like it. The lunch menu has a good selection of wraps and sandwiches to eat in or take out on one of the harbour cruises departing from the pavilion.

The Riverboat Restaurant
$$-$$$
closed Mon and Tue
151 E. Pacific Coast Hwy.
☎673-3425
Dine aboard an actual riverboat in Newport Harbor at this unique Louisiana-inspired restaurant. Try the macadamia-nut crusted, mahi mahi southern fried catfish or the "Dr. Voodoo" jambalaya while enjoying views of the harbour. Live entertainment and brunch is provided on weekends. After lunch you can also explore the Newport Maritime Museum, also on board.

Tutto Mare Ristorante
$$-$$$
545 Newport Center Dr.
☎640-6333
Meaning "everything from the sea," Tutto Mare specializes in coastal Italian seafood. The exhibition kitchen produces succulent fish and pasta baked in a wood-fire oven. Chicken and beef are roasted over a mesquite grill. Eat inside or, preferably, on the garden patio. Sunday brunch features classical guitar. Reservations are highly recommended.

The Chart House
$$-$$$
dinner only
2801 W. Pacific Coast Hwy.
☎548-5889
Deep wood accents and comfortable booths compliment panoramic harbour views at the Chart House. The restaurant is built over the water, with boat parking available underneath. Inside, enjoy the teriyaki beef medallions, pan-fried sea scallops or choose your meal from the oyster and salad bars.

The Spaghetti Bender
$$$
dinner only
6204 W. Pacific Coast Hwy.
☎645-0651
Having a meal at the Spaghetti Bender is like visiting an old Italian home, with its many small rooms accented by dark carpeting, myriad candles and slightly kitschy floral wallpaper. Their gnocchi, which is handmade on the premises, has developed an almost religious following in the city over the past 30 years. Combination platters are also available, featuring veal, chicken and beef dishes accompanied with pasta and salad. The kids can choose anything on the menu with half portions for half price.

Roy's Newport Beach
$$$
453 Newport Center Dr.
☎640-7697
Roy's caused quite a stir when it landed in Newport. The menu was created by Roy Yamaguchi, who made this restaurant nationally famous in Hawaii. His

unique fusion of fresh seafood, classic French sauces and Asian seasonings is given a Hawaiian twist and then artfully delivered to your plate. The casual upscale environment, near-perfect service and an extensive wine list compliment the meal. Reservations are usually necessary.

Hornblower Cruises
$$$$$
Fri to Sun
2431 W. Pacific Coast Hwy.
☎646-0155
Perhaps one of the best ways to spend an evening in Newport Beach is to go on a dinner-and-dancing cruise out into the ocean. Hornblower offers fixed-menu dinner cruises ($58 for 2.5hrs),that feature three-course meals with dancing to follow. Sunday champagne brunch cruises ($40 for 2hrs) offer a full buffet and a chance to admire the coastline. Reservations must be made in advance.

Laguna Beach

Wahoo's Fish Tacos
$
1133 S. Pacific Coast Hwy.
☎497-0033
www.wahoos.com
Wahoo's has become a Californian institution for semi-healthy fast-food. Choose from one of their many fish tacos, from tuna to mahi mahi.

Gina's Pizza
$
217 Broadway
Gina's looks a little like a dive but serves generous portions of pizza and pasta that definitely won't break the bank. Vegetarian to "meatsa" pizza is offered as well as lasagna, manicotti and a selection of sandwiches and salads.

Madison Square & Garden Cafe
$
320 N. Pacific Coast Hwy.
☎494-0137
This lovely floral café is a great stop for a pastry and a cappuccino while strolling through the shops at Madison square.

Ruby's Auto Diner
$
30622 S. Pacific Coast Hwy.
☎497-7829
One of a chain of diners in California, this is a great place to travel back to the 1950s and enjoy a burger and a malt. Play some tunes on the jukebox or relax on the sunny, ocean-view patio.

Goko Cafe & Deli
$-$$
907 S. Pacific Coast Hwy.
☎494-4880
The Goko Cafe is a vegetarian- and vegan-friendly stop in South Laguna. Choose from one

of its many soups, salads and sandwiches.

Nature's Oven II
$$
1100 S. Pacific Coast Hwy.
☎376-2026
Nature's Oven is another great spot to find high-quality vegetarian dining in a comfortable setting.

230 Forest
$$
230 Forest Ave.
☎494-2545
Right in downtown Laguna, this sidewalk café is one of the trendiest spots in town. Contemporary Californian cuisine is complimented by a well-chosen selection of California wines.

Romeo Cucina
$$
294 Broadway St.
☎497-6627
Romeo Cucina features 16 different pastas and 15 wood-fired pizzas at reasonable prices. Live music fills the restaurant every night but Sunday. Watch the open kitchen prepare authentic carpacio and wonderful *frittura mista* (deep fried calamari, shrimp, tuna and swordfish).

Bombay Duck Bistro & Grill
$$-$$$
231 Ocean Dr.
☎497-7307
The Bombay Duck serves fine Indian cuisine inside their tiny, intimate restaurant, or on their two-table patio. Try the whole turkey *($40)* which serves at least six. The smoked baby back ribs are delightful as are their tandoori specialties.

The White House
$$$
340 S. Coast Hwy.
☎494-8088
The White House is a landmark in Laguna Beach, built in 1918 and once popular with the "in" Hollywood crowd. Today, the menu offers a funky combination of giant Californian salads, pasta and sandwiches for lunch. Dinner features well presented meats and seafood with a Californian twist. At night, the White House provides live entertainment and dancing. Breakfast is available on weekends.

C'est La Vie
$$$
373 S. Coast Hwy.
☎497-5100
Imaginative French cuisine is served indoors or outside on the award-winning patio overlooking the ocean. There is also a French bakery on site to pick up some picnic supplies. Extensive wine list.

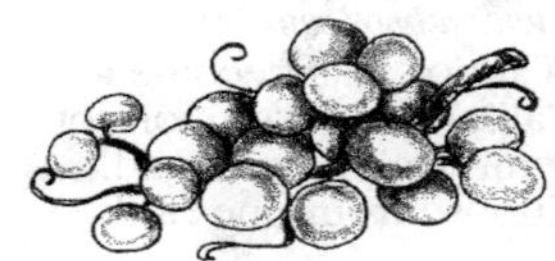

Claes Seafood Etc.
$$$
425 S. Coast Hwy.
☎376-9283
Located in the Hotel Laguna, Claes offers creative seafood selections with international accents. Though seafood is the main attraction, it also features lamb chops and steaks from the grill. Over 250 vintages of wine are available to accompany your meal, and the intimate "Wine Cellar" caters to groups of 10 or less. Panoramic views of the ocean are included at no extra charge.

Tivoli Terrace
$$$
650 Laguna Canyon Rd.
☎494-9650
The Tivoli Terrace is located on the Festival of Arts grounds, making it a convenient but overcrowded choice during the festival. Reserve in advance, however, and enjoy Cornish hen, tenderloin beef brochettes, or an extensive brunch menu in a beautiful French garden setting.

Aegean Cafe
$$$
closed Mon
540 S. Pacific Coast Hwy.
☎494-5001
The Aegean Cafe features authentic Greek classics such as mousaka and chicken souvlaki in a lively Mediterranean environment. Belly dancers wander about the tables, waiters spontaneously break into dance, and there is live entertainment nightly. Fridays and Saturdays have a $20 minimum per person, which you'll have no problem reaching.

French 75
$$$-$$$$
1464 S. Coast Hwy.
☎494-8444
A fireplace accents the giant leather booths and the moody interior of French 75. This French bistro and champagne bar tries to recreate an ambiance of Paris in the 1940s, with some success. Reservations recommended.

Dana Point

The Inca Amazon Grill
$-$$
closed Mon
25001 Dana Point Harbor Dr.
☎489-1900
This small Peruvian restaurant has a slightly kitschy decor with leopard-skin accents on the booths and chairs. Spicy selections are available in chicken, pasta, beef and seafood. You should also try the fresh ceviche. Live Spanish music on Saturday and Sunday nights.

Yama Teppan House
$$-$$$
5pm-10pm
24961 Dana Harbor Rd.
☎***240-6610***
Sizzling teriyaki and teppan specialties are cooked right before your eyes and the large, communal tables make for a friendly, sociable atmosphere. You can also enjoy sushi, chicken and steak delicacies either indoors or out on their patio. Karaoke "entertainment" is available on weekends.

Ristorante Ferrantelli
$$-$$$
25001 Dana Harbor Rd.
☎***493-1401***
This beautiful Italian restaurant is accented with classical busts and pillars. Chef Ligi Mazzaro serves up authentic cuisine amid the live operatic arias and songs in Italian, French, Spanish and English each evening. Try the amazing *cartoccio di mare* which combines a sampling of lobster, scallops, mussels, shrimp and fish of the day in a saffron, garlic and wine sauce.

The Chart House
$$-$$$
34442 Green Lantern St.
☎***492-1183***
A beautiful panoramic view of the harbour is the main attraction of this restaurant, perched atop a promontory overlooking the ocean. Inside, comfy booths are surrounded by a naval motif with copper accents. Try a thick-cut steak or fresh seafood.

San Clemente

Beach Garden Cafe
$
Mon to Fri 7am to 2pm, Weekends 7am to 3pm
618 ½ Avenida Victoria
☎***498-8145***
This is a great place for breakfast or lunch across from the San Clemente Pier. During the summer, hours are extended for sunset dining. Inside, sidewalk and patio dining are available. Reasonable prices make this a good stop to grab some take-out for the pier.

The Shore House Cafe
$-$$
201 Avenida del Mar
☎***498-3936***
So you're hungry for meatloaf at 5am? No problem. Bacon and eggs for dinner? Sure thing. The Shore House Cafe offers 24hr service and an 11-page diner-style menu. Comfortable booths and high-back stools invite you to stay all day. There's something for everyone here, including a decent vegetarian section.

The Tropicana Grill
$$
610 Avenida Victoria
☎***498-8767***
The panoramic ocean views are the major draw of the

Tropicana. The menu features Mexican selections, Californian-style fare, seafood and ribs. The restaurant is fun and lively, with its bamboo ceiling and bright tropical-colour scheme. Reservations are suggested, especially in the summer.

Vintage Restaurant & Bar
$$-$$$
110 N. El Camino Real
☎492-3236
Elegant surroundings are complimented by affordable prices at Vintage. Wraparound leather booths hug white tablecloths under soft lighting. The daily specials include prime rib, braised lamb or veal, served with ample side dishes. Dine inside or out on the garden patio.

Carbonara
$$-$$$
111 Avenida Del Mar
☎366-1040
"It's not a table without bread and wine" is the motto at Carbonara Trattoria Italiana. With an extensive (and affordable) wine list and freshly baked focaccia bread upon arrival, very few tables are without bread and wine. The atmosphere is casual and family oriented, but there are still some cozy corners available. The menu features authentic northern and southern Italian pasta, veal and seafood. Reservations are suggested, especially on weekends.

San Juan Capistrano

Mollies Famous Cafe
$
32033 Camino Capistrano
☎240-9261
With over 150 items on the menu to choose from, deciding is the hardest thing to do here. Try their enormous breakfast specials, all priced at $3.75, or stop in for a soup and sandwich at lunch. The patio, unfortunately, is a little too close to the parking lot, but the food makes up for the view.

The Tea House on Los Rios
$-$$$
Wed to Sun
31731 Los Rios St.
☎443-3914
The Tea House on Los Rios is a true gem, full of lace, and crammed with more antiques than is truly necessary. With the staff in proper 19th-century attire and light classical music in the background, the illusion is almost complete. Enjoy world-class Herney loose-leaf tea, delicious scones and assorted finger sandwiches. For more substantial fare, classics like shepherds' pie and prime rib with Yorkshire pudding will not disappoint. The last seating is at 4pm, so make

it a point to get there early to enjoy the ambiance.

Sarducci's
$$-$$$
7am to 9pm daily
26701 Verdugo St.
☎493-9593
Sarducci's offers contemporary Californian cuisine in the historic Capistrano Depot, across from the mission. Live jazz fills the restaurant Thursday through Saturday evenings. The menu offers a delicious variety from breakfast through dinner, with seafood omelettes, cobb salads, rich cream pastas and seared *ahi* tuna. Dine inside or on the patio.

L'Hirondelle
$$$
closed Mon
31631 Camino Capistrano
☎661-0425
Pink bougainvillea caress the walls of this lovely adobe-style restaurant. Inside, French and Belgian specialties are served in a lovely patio garden within view of the mission. Enjoy braised duckling in a green peppercorn sauce, fresh bouillabaisse or veal medallions *aux champignons*, all beautifully presented with impeccable service.

Oceanside

The 101 Cafe
$
631 S. Pacific Coast Hwy.
☎722-5220
The 101 Cafe is the oldest restaurant in Oceanside, built in 1928 and last remodeled in the 1950s. Old photos of the area and a well-stocked jukebox provide the entertainment. Full menu, diner-style food is available from 6:30am to midnight every day. The staff is incredibly knowledgeable about the town and will be happy to give you some suggestions and even some tourist pamphlets on area attractions. Try a classic burger, shake and fruit cobbler, but leave your credit card at home since it's cash only.

The Longboarder Cafe
$-$$
228 N. Pacific Coast Hwy.
☎721-6776
The Longboarder is in the middle of downtown, just a few blocks from the beach. It has a fun, friendly atmosphere with its muraled walls and surfboards hanging from the rafters. Try it for breakfast, lunch or dinner, with huge omelettes, salads and black Angus beef.

La Mission
$-$$
3232 Mission Ave.
☎***760-435-9977***
La Mission is a local favourite for authentic Mexican food but also serves American classics for those who aren't so bold. Live mariachi music accompanies the meal and a champagne brunch is served on Sundays.

Harbor Fish & Chips
$$
276-A Harbor Dr. S.
☎***722-4977***
This family-owned and operated restaurant is also home to the largest display of mounted fish in the county. This is a great place to enjoy a generous helping of beer-battered fish while enjoying views of the harbour.

The Caribbean Grill
$$
311 N. Tremont
☎***722-3334***
Owner Mark Cameron serves up gigantic plates of soul-pleasing Jamaican and Cajun cooking. The walls of this casual restaurant are covered by his original works of art, and jazz and reggae play in the background. Try the jerk chicken, tender ribs and spicy combination platters.

Chart House
$$$
dinner only
314 Harbor Dr. S.
☎***722-1345***
Beef, pasta, fresh fish and seafood dishes are accompanied by wonderful views of the ocean and harbour. This is a great place to slip into a comfy booth and watch the sun go down over the water with a bottle of wine. Brunch is offered on Sundays.

Palm Springs

See map on p 213.

Jamba Juice
$
111 S. Palm Canyon Rd.
Jamba Juice has over 20 fruit smoothies with a huge selection of fresh ingredients that are meals in themselves. Various "boosts" are available to increase the vitamin and protein content. They also offer a selection of fresh juices including citrus, wheatgrass, carrot and any mix in-between. Vegetarian salads and soups are available as well as a selection of energy bars and health foods.

LalaJava
$
300 N. Palm Canyon Dr.
☎***325-3484***
Lalajava is a trendy corner coffee shop with a popular street side patio. Stop in for

the organic coffee or a frozen mochaccino and a quick bite.

Sherman's Deli and Bakery
$-$$
401 Tahquitz Canyon
☎325-1199
Sherman's is an all-kosher, premium-quality deli in the heart of Palm Springs. They have an incredible array of soups, sandwiches, pastries and desserts all served with their famous dill pickles and sauerkraut. The patio is always busy.

Village Pub
$-$$
226 S. Palm Canyon
☎323-3265
The Village pub features live daily music on the patio all day on weekends and at 9pm during the week. Their internationally-inspired pub menu does credit to the countries where their sandwiches, pastas and salads originated. The heat of the patio is somewhat moderated by the great volumes of mist that characterize the outdoor patios of Palm Springs. The interior is decorated with cheesy art and dollar bills from customers gone-by.

Peabody's Coffee Bar and Music Studio
$-$$
134 S. Palm Canyon Dr.
☎322-1877
Peabody's is the place for breakfast. Try their "eggs benny," which are the best in the city. Live local jazz and blues is presented Thursday to Sunday, accompanied by snacks, desserts and alcohol-laden coffees. They also have an impromptu gallery that changes every month, showcasing local artistic talent.

The Rock Garden Café
$-$$
777 S. Palm Canyon Dr.
☎(760) 327-8840
Just south of downtown, the Rock Garden Café has a rock-walled patio enclosing many fountains, flowers, fruit and palm trees. The rock motif continues inside, where the casual dining room is bounded by stone walls. The menu is varied, from moussaka to shrimp fajitas with chicken marsala and burgers in between. They also have a small bakery providing the freshly baked breads and desserts.

Capra's
$-$$
204 N. Palm Canyon Dr.
☎325-7073
Capra's bills itself as "a wonderful Italian ristorante and deli" and is owned by Tom Capra, son of legend-

ary director Frank Capra. Inside is a 1940s movie star motif, with Capra posters adorning the walls and an actual academy award. Capra's offers a wide array of sandwiches and salads in addition to their extensive daily specials. The patio is misted to ward off the desert heat.

Las Casuelas Terraza
$$
225 S. Palm Canyon Dr.
☎***325-2794***
Las Casuelas is a wonderful Mexican restaurant with a palapa covered bar and heated patio. They serve grilled steak, chicken, and shrimp meals in an authentic Mexican style. Choose their spicy *camarones diablos*, a simple burrito or one of their combination platters. The margaritas are legendary, and this place gets packed every night of the week. Wandering mariachis provide impromptu entertainment. They also have the largest selection of tequilas in the desert valley.

Kiyosaku
$$
closed Wed
5:30pm to 10:30pm
1418 N. Palm Canyon Dr.
☎ ***327-6601***
Kiyosaku is an authentic and unpretentious Japanese tepanyaki and sushi restaurant with a classic Japanese decor.

The Delhi Palace
$$
11:30am to 2:30pm, 5pm to 10pm
1422 N. Palm Canyon Dr.
☎***325-3411***
Inexpensive and cheerful, this place may not look like much, but it is rumored to have the finest Indian cuisine in Palm Springs.

The Kaiser Grill
$$-$$$
205 S. Palm Canyon Dr.
☎***779-1988***
The Kaiser Grill has an almost overwhelming metallic-red interior that becomes more subtle as the evening progresses. Their specialty is anything and everything that comes out of their wood-burning ovens or off of their mesquite grill, from fresh fish to marinated chicken and thick, juicy steaks. The heated patio is alive with greenery that separates diners from the busy street. Get a seat near the kitchen to watch you meal prepared through the glass, indoor fountain.

Sorrentino's Seafood House
$$$
1032 N. Palm Canyon Dr.
☎***325-2944***
The dark, Italian-style interior of Sorrentino's was a favourite of Sinatra and the Brat Pack. The historic piano bar was the sight of many impromptu performances over the years. Settle into one of the leather

booths and enjoy fantastic steaks and seafood.

Muriel's Supper Club
$$$-$$$$
210 S. Palm Canyon Dr.
☎325-8839
Muriel's is *the* place in Palm Springs for fine dining in a fun and interesting atmosphere. The menu is created from scratch every evening and has featured such delicacies as braised venison shank over wild mushroom and truffle crepes, pan seared rare ahi tuna and roasted quail. The interior is Art Deco in its styling and features high-quality live entertainment from salsa to blues every evening. The patio is the hip place to see and be seen at night.

Entertainment

As might be expected in the home of the entertainment industry, Los Angeles is a leading centre for popular music as well as for various alternative styles ranging from blues to techno.

The city has an extremely lively club scene that caters to a wide variety of tastes. Some clubs seem to be perennial favourites, while others move in and out of trendy acceptance with bewildering speed. We hesitate to venture opinions as to what's hot at any given moment, and thus provide only general guidance here, along with suggestions (two paragraphs below) as to where to look for more detailed and up-to-the-minute information.

In addition to its unique local scene, including live theatre and a number of comedy clubs, L.A. also offers more run-of-the-mill entertainment. The area is dotted with multi-screen cinema complexes showing recent Hollywood releases as well as a few repertory or art cinemas. (Again, the sources indicated below provide detailed listings.) Spectator sports provide an additional option for an evening (or afternoon) outing.

Contrary to the image it sometimes conveys, Los Angeles is also home to what some would consider more serious forms of cultural endeavour, including live theatre, classical music, jazz, and ballet or modern dance. Although these tend to attract less attention than popular music and some of its newer variants, they do exist in abundance.

Helpful sources of information on the L.A. entertainment scene include the *Los Angeles Times* daily newspaper, which publishes movie and cultural listings in its Calendar section. Comprehensive listings for the coming week appear in its Sunday edition and for the following weekend in its Thursday edition. Other excellent sources of listings and suggestions are two weekly papers, the *L.A. Weekly* and the slimmer but more informative *New Times*. Both are distributed free from racks near the entrances to various stores, restaurants and public buildings, as well as from some street boxes. For visitors with Internet access, useful sources of entertainment information include the *L.A. Times'* www.calendarlive.com and the rival www.at-la.com.

In Los Angeles, as elsewhere in California, smoking is allowed only in outdoor areas at bars and clubs, and last call for alcohol is at 2am. Bars with live entertainment often have a cover charge, which may vary according to the day of the week, with higher prices on weekends. As in most cities, ticket prices for movies are often lower in the afternoon than in the evening.

Downtown Los Angeles

Many downtown L.A. streets become nearly deserted by early evening, creating an almost eerie atmosphere that seems anything but conducive to enjoyable night life. Even so, the variety of things to do is quite surprising, from spectator sports to classical concerts to theatre.

Music Venues and Theatres

The Music Center
Grand Ave. between First and Temple sts., across from the Civic Center
The Music Center is L.A.'s most important venue for classical music as well as other types of musical performance and theatre. This multi-hall complex comprises the Dorothy Chandler Pavilion, home to the Los Angeles Philharmonic *(☎213-850-2000, www.laphil.org)*, along with the Ahmanson Theater and the more intimate Mark Tapper Forum, each the scene of numerous theatrical productions.

The Japan Cultural Arts Center
244 S. San Pedro St. between Second and Third sts., Little Tokyo
☎(213) 628-2725
The Japan Cultural Arts Center hosts both Japanese and non-Japanese ensembles that include children's theatre groups, dance troupes and the Los Angeles Chamber Orchestra.

Bars

Al's Bar
305 S. Hewitt St. at Third St., two blocks east of Alameda
☎(213) 625-9703
For jazz and lighter music, several of the larger hotels offer live bands most evenings, though audiences tend mostly to be hotel guests. One long-surviving independent club downtown is Al's Bar in a somewhat grungy neighbourhood favoured by artists. This dark, graffiti-covered spot attracts bands (and audiences) that seem to have a knack for zeroing in on the next trend.

La Plata
1026 Grand Ave.
☎(213) 747-8561
La Plata will delight lovers of cigars made as only Cubans know how. This is, in fact, the only cigar factory in Los Angeles where Churchill's favourite stogies

are still made by hand. Catering to California's fine connoisseurs, these premium hand-rolled cigars have been featured in scores of Hollywood movies. They can also be smoked on the premises since, in addition to being an impressive factory, La Plata has an appealing cigar room redolent of tobacco.

Red Lion Tavern
2366 Glendale Blvd., Silver City
☎*(323) 662-5337*
The pleasant Red Lion Tavern will undoubtedly satisfy fans of German beer. Indeed, barley beers such as Warsteiner, Becks and Bitburger seem to flow like water here. A good mix of German expats, downtown yuppies and the local working class regularly come as they are, paying no attention to the surrounding kitschy decor. German-style light fare available.

Fais Do-Do
cover charge
every day 7pm to 2am
5257 W. Adams Blvd.
☎*(323) 954-8080*
In another somewhat remote area of the city is one of LA's prominent nightclubs, Fais Do-Do. Brilliantly laid out in what was once a stately bank, the establishment is particularly noteworthy for its warm, New Orleans-like ambiance. For that matter, good Cajun cuisine is offered along with drinks and music all night long. Music-wise, blues, jazz and 1960s and '70s rock get top billing.

Pasadena

The Pasadena Playhouse
39 S. El Molino Ave. near Green St.
☎*(626) 356-7529*
The Pasadena Playhouse, built in 1924 and refurbished in the 1980s, is one of California's top theatrical venues. Registered as a national landmark, it has also built a reputation for the high quality of its productions. Several multiscreen **cinemas** are clustered along Colorado Boulevard in Old Pasadena, with restaurants close by, making this a favoured area for an evening out.

Hollywood and Surroundings

Cinemas

Hollywood is synonymous with entertainment and it certainly lives up to its reputation. Several of the major **film studios** offer tours (see page 128 in the "Exploring" section), and some of their wares can be seen at historical venues that are landmarks in themselves.

These include Mann's Chinese Theater and the Egyptian Theater along Hollywood Boulevard (see page 121), where current films can be seen amid lavish decor that evokes the splendour of Hollywood's golden era. In a rather different style, Universal City Walk in North Hollywood is the setting for a gigantic 18-screen cinema and entertainment complex.

Theatres

Pantages Theatre
6233 Hollywood Blvd. near Vine St.
☎(323) 468-1770
Needless to say, Hollywood is much more than cinema. Local actors also work in live theatre. The newly refurbished Pantages Theater is a massive Art Deco classic that's often used to stage Broadway-style musicals.

A stretch of Santa Monica Boulevard running west from Vine Street is home to several smaller theatres, including the **Actor's Gang Theater** *(6201 Santa Monica Blvd. near Vine St., ☎323-465-0566)* and the **Hudson Avenue Theater** *(6539 Santa Monica Blvd. near Wilcox Ave., ☎323-856-7012)*, which is divided into several small venues. **The James A. Doolittle Theater** *(1615 Vine St. between Hollywood and Sunset blvds., ☎323-462-6666)*, operated by UCLA, has showcased several top productions. Several other theaters are located in West Hollywood and in the Los Feliz area.

The **Hollywood Bowl** *(2301 N. Highland Ave., off the Hollywood Fwy, ☎323-850-2000, www.hollywoodbowl. org)* is a giant outdoor amphitheatre nestled in a canyon in the Hollywood Hills. Built in the early 1920s, it remains a popular venue for classical, jazz or popular concerts and serves as the summer home of the Los Angeles Philharmonic. The grounds outside the amphitheatre are ideal for a pre-concert picnic, a fine local tradition.

Bars and Clubs

The ever-changing **club scene** in Hollywood remains very active, both in central Hollywood and outlying areas, with offerings ranging from traditional jazz in a dinner club setting to underground dance rhythms in what look like abandoned garages.

West Hollywood has become known for its **comedy clubs**, including the Comedy

Store *(8433 Sunset Blvd., ☎323-656-6225, www.comedystore.com)*, featuring a range of stand-up comics, and the **Groundling Theater** *(7307 Melrose Ave., ☎323-934-9700)*, noted for improvisation and biting satire.

Hollywood Palace
Thu to Sun
1735 N. Vine St.
☎(323) 462-3000
www.hollywoodpalace.co
Among Hollywood's wide choice of night spots are several hot nightclubs, including the Palace, where a lively crowd of young students (18 and over) whoops it up until the wee hours of the morning. But the legendary venue is primarily known for its weekly rock shows, which have included the likes of Nirvana, Green Day, the Smashing Pumpkins and Nine Inch Nails.

Hot House Cafe
12123 Riverside Dr.
☎(626) 564-8656
The Hot House Cafe is located in the heart of the lively NoHo District, LA's answer to New York's and London's trendy SoHo districts. This is just the place to get together with friends for a confab, and the local young jet set seem to have adopted it as their own. But the real star attraction here is the coffee: the selection of flavours, coffee beans and concoctions is particularly interesting.

Cyber Java
7080 Hollywood Blvd.
☎(323) 466-5600
You can surf the Net to your heart's content at Cyber Java, located on Hollywood Boulevard. In addition to snacks and a charming decor marked by pastel shades, the place offers 12 computers on which to navigate the World Wide Web or simply check your e-mail. Rates: $2.50/15min, $9/hr.

Catalina Bar & Grill
cover charge
1640 N. Cahuenga Blvd.
☎(323) 466-2210
Located in the heart of Hollywood, the Catalina Bar & Grill is the place to go if you're in the mood to listen to good live jazz until the wee hours of the morning. Downtown Hollywood's decline doesn't seem to have affected this bar, which continues to draw some of the biggest names in modern jazz. What's more, the supper club has comfortable seating and great acoustics.

Cinegrill
cover charge
7000 Hollywood Blvd.
☎(323) 466-7000
Cinegrill is the renowned nightclub of the no-less-renowned Hollywood Roosevelt Hotel (see p 131,

241). Set up in a room adjacent to the hotel's superb Art Deco-inspired lobby, it's worth checking out to hear quality jazz and country-pop acts.

The Derby
4500 Los Feliz Blvd.
☎(323) 663-8979
Largely responsible for the resurgence of swing, the Derby offers live swing bands and free dance lessons for beginners on Sundays and Thursdays. Note that swing is enjoying a real upsurge in popularity in L.A. and scores of nightclubs host a swing night at least once a week (info: www.swingset.net).

Daddy's Lounge
110 N. Vine St.
☎(323) 463-7777
To escape from the teeming crowds that overrun the city's bars, you can always find refuge at Daddy's Lounge, a swanky wood-panelled pub located one block from Hollywood Boulevard. Subdued lighting favours intimate conversation, the drink selection is highly varied and bartender Paul O'Neill proves to be the preferred authority on what to order. Try his "Hat Trick," a nice mix of three kinds of vodka and passion-fruit juice.

Bourgeois Pig
every day 9pm to 2am
5931 Franklin Ave.
☎(213) 962-6366
Los Angeles's coffeehouses, very much in vogue, have the advantage of being open to those under 21 years of age. Among them, the Bourgeois Pig is a good choice. The black walls, black lights and red-lined pool table successfully manage to create a dark and appealing atmosphere, in keeping with star-studded Hollywood.

Mid-Wilshire and Westside

Westwood Village, in particular a short stretch of Westwood Boulevard near Wilshire Boulevard a few short blocks south of the UCLA campus, is a popular evening hangout among a younger crowd, with numerous multi-screen **cinemas**, a multitude of fast-food restaurants (along with a few sit-down places) and a generally boisterous atmosphere. The **Geffen Playhouse** *(10886 Le Comte Ave. near Westwood Blvd., Westwood Village, ☎208-6500)*, noted for excellent acoustics and sight lines, is a top theatrical venue. It's run by UCLA, although it's not on the campus.

Coconut Club
cover charge
Fri and Sat
9876 Wilshire Blvd., Beverly Hills
☎285-1358
At the Beverly Hilton, people gather at the Coconut Club to dance. Owned by entertainment mogul Merv Griffin, this modern version of the famous Cocoanut Grove Club attempts to revive the golden years of Hollywood. Mission accomplished, if one goes by the crowd that flocks here every Friday and Saturday night, when the 900sq-ft (300m²) dance floor becomes packed with people dancing the night away to Latin rhythms or Big Band swing. What's more, the cover charge provides access to the **Chimps Cigar Club**, owned by none other than Chuck Norris and Jim Belushi, as well as the **Mango Lounge**, both adjacent to the dance club.

Conga Room
cover charge
534 Wilshire Blvd.
☎(323) 938-1696
www.congaroom.com
For a night of dancing to mambo, salsa, merengue and other hot Latin rhythms, head to the Conga Room. Located on Wilshire Boulevard, in the heart of Miracle Mile, this new dance club draws crowds of people, from West L.A. to downtown. And for good reason: the place presents great shows by the best Latino musical acts in town. Note that, on Thursday and Saturday nights, the club offers dance lessons for neophytes who wish to perfect their dance moves.

Viper Room
cover charge
8852 Sunset Blvd.
☎358-1880
www.viperroom.com
If there's a place that has contributed to the ever-growing popularity of the very fashionable Sunset Strip, it's definitely the Viper Room. This world-famous nightclub has been at the forefront of the club scene since 1993, the year of its opening by co-owners Johnny Depp and Sal Jenco. With its intensely eclectic decor, the Viper Room has played host to a long and impressive list of big-name acts (including Johnny Cash, Tom Petty, Everclear and Nancy Sinatra), many of whom have made surprise appearances.

Sky Bar
8440 Sunset Blvd.
☎(323) 650-8999
LA's top male and female models, and especially their fans and emulators, gather at the Sky Bar, the Mondrian Hotel's high-class club. These "beautiful people" shake their booties in front of picture windows that offer a spectacular view of the L.A. skyline. Dress to

impress if you hope to get in, given the club's highly selective, very strict door policy.

Two long-established live-music venues have also been instrumental in making the Sunset Strip a household name. **Whiskey à Go Go** *(cover charge; 8901 Sunset Blvd., ☎652-4202)* showcases rock bands every night, while **The Roxy** *(cover charge; 9009 Sunset Blvd., ☎276-2272)* hosts well-known rock'n'roll and alternative rock bands in a space with Art Deco features. **(Doug Weston's) Troubadour** *(cover charge; 9081 Santa Monica Blvd., ☎276-6168)* specializes in live heavy-metal music.

360º
6920 Sunset Blvd.
☎(323) 871-2995
Another sophisticated bar, with a spectacular view of the city as well as the giant white letters of the Hollywood sign, 360° is perched on the top floor of an office building at Sunset and Vine. This club is sure to be a unanimous favourite: guests can strut their stuff to R&B or house music, or simply cozy up to the bar to better admire their lovely fellow night owls. Reservations recommended.

House of Blues
cover charge
8430 Sunset Blvd.
☎(323) 848-5100
One of the Sunset Strip's trademark nightspots is unquestionably the House of Blues, a nightclub that doubles as a restaurant. This veritable temple of music is easily recognizable by its Southern Delta-style "tin-shack" exterior. With regard to the music, the establishment's name is somewhat misleading, as jazz, R&B and even hip-hop bands often perform in addition to blues. Duran Duran, Cheap Trick, Joe Cocker, Etta James and The Commodores are just some of the big-name acts that have graced the club's stage. What's more, the place features a rousing gospel brunch every Sunday.

Luna Park
cover charge
665 N. Robertson Blvd.
☎652-0611
The city's most famous drag queens perform and manage to draw an impressive mixed crowd at Luna Park. The nightclub is spread over two levels: the main floor offers a relaxing, intimate ambiance, while upstairs is party central, with revellers grooving to the sounds of varied international music in front of the stage.

Groundling Theater
cover charge
7307 Melrose Ave.
☎*(323) 934-9700*
Satire, improv and music have been the ingredients of a winning recipe for over 20 years at the Groundling Theater, a small showroom that features stand-up comics guaranteed to tickle your funny bone from Thursday to Sunday. The club is widely considered to be the launchpad for Saturday Night Live players, and Los Angeles's cut-ups have no trouble generating laughs and smiles here, most notably by deriding Chicago, L.A.'s perennial rival.

La Masia
cover charge
9077 Santa Monica Blvd.
☎*(323) 272-3502*
If you feel up to dancing all night to wild Latin rhythms, make a beeline for La Masia. Salsa bands fire up the mature, well-heeled crowd, here to cut loose or perhaps even meet their soul mate.

Palm Tree L.A.
3240 Wilshire Blvd., 4th floor
☎*(213) 381-3388*
Mid-Wilshire's sombre office buildings are not generally known as being very fashionable, but that which houses the swanky Palm Tree L.A. can prove to be one of best choices for a night out in the area. While the chef prepares *kimchis* and delicious coconut shrimp for you, young go-getters hang out around the pool table with an imported beer in hand, while others tear up the booming dance floor amidst constant flashing green and yellow lights.

Hard Rock Cafe
every day 11am to 1am
Beverly Center, 8600 Beverly Blvd., corner San Vicente Blvd.
☎*276-7605*
Universal City Walk, Universal Center Dr. Exit off US Hwy. 101
☎*(818) 622-7625*
You'll have no trouble finding either of L.A.'s two Hard Rock Cafes, the international chain of bar-restaurants devoted to rock'n'roll memorabilia. At the exit, a gift shop reminds you how very popular the place is with tourists.

Gypsy Cafe
940 Broxton Ave., Westwood
☎*824-2119*
On arriving at the Gypsy Cafe on a Friday or Saturday night, the astonishing sight of a dozen students from nearby UCLA seated on the terrace and smoking hookahs will meet your eyes. Not to worry though, as the smoke emanating from these hookahs doesn't come from illegal substances, but from fruit-flavoured tobacco. Apple is the most popular flavour, with cherry as a close second. The café rents out

hookahs ($10), which are shared.

Santa Monica and Surroundings

The car-free **Third Street Promenade** in downtown Santa Monica is one of the L.A. area's liveliest and most pleasant places to be after work hours, with its numerous **cinemas**, restaurants, cafés, bookshops and other establishments that attract large and generally well-behaved crowds late into the evening. Street entertainers add to the atmosphere and many people come here just for a stroll. A mile or so to the south, the boardwalk at **Venice Beach** remains spirited after dark, retaining its younger, funkier ambiance. A selection of casual restaurants, bars and cafés keep the area around Windward Avenue near the beach hopping well into the night.

Santa Monica Playhouse
1211 Fourth St. at Wilshire Blvd.
☎(310) 394-9779
The tiny Santa Monica Playhouse offers varied programs and a cozy atmosphere. Several small **clubs** nearby (check the newspaper listings) help round out the Santa Monica night life scene.

Harbor Room
195 Culver Blvd.
☎821-6550
The Harbor Room is just the place for those who like crowded bars with a friendly, laid-back vibe. In fact, you'll soon be getting up close and personal with your fellow barflies, as the place is known to be the smallest bar in the City of Angels.

Gotham Hall
every day 5pm to 2am
1431 Third St. Promenade, Santa Monica
☎394-8865
www.gothamhall.com
Gotham Hall is a veritable entertainment playground, with its 14 pool tables, three dance floors and a musical repertoire that changes every night of the week. Salsa is offered on Sundays, 1970s and 1980s music gets top billing on Tuesdays, techno holds sway on Wednesdays, as does hip hop on Thursdays, while the resident DJ lets his imagination run wild on Friday and Saturday nights.

Yankee Doodles – Santa Monica
1410 Third St. Promenade, Santa Monica
☎394-4632
Yankee Doodles – Marina del Rey
300 Washington Blvd., Marina del Rey
☎574-6868
Both branches of the Yankee Doodles sports bars allow their high-spirited

patrons to watch their favourite sports matches. The place encompasses a large bar-restaurant, several pool tables and scores of big-screen TVs that broadcast the exploits of the Dodgers, Lakers or Raiders.

South Bay

Hermosa Beach's oceanfront walk and the adjacent Pier Plaza have become known for a lively bar scene that draws a young and sometimes rowdy crowd, reaching a crescendo on summer weekends. The Fishermen's Wharf area of Redondo Beach provides an alternative; a couple of the bars here provide live music on weekends.

Redondo Beach Performing Arts Center
1935 Manhattan Beach Blvd., Redondo Beach
☎ *372-4477*
The Redondo Beach Performing Arts Center is the South Bay area's major venue for theatrical and musical presentations.

Lighthouse Cafe
cover charge
30 Pier Ave., Hermosa Beach
☎*372-6911*
If you happen to be in Hermosa Beach after sundown, swing by this bar, which offers good blues, rock and reggae shows. Live music kicks off at 9pm every night of the week. Karaoke every Monday.

Long Beach

On Pine Avenue near Broadway in downtown Long Beach lies the epicentre of what passes for evening activity in this very sedate community. Pine Avenue has a restaurant row with establishments catering to a variety of tastes, interspersed with a few bars and cafés.

Observation Bar
every day 12:30pm to 1am
Queen Mary Seaport
1126 Queen's Hwy., Long Beach
☎*(562) 435-3511*
Long Beach's other bars and nightclubs can't hope to rival the elegance of the Observation Bar, aboard the *Queen Mary*. Once reserved for first-class passengers, the lounge looks out on the ocean liner's prow and downtown L.A.'s skyscrapers. The rare-wood panelling, magnificent mural painting and Art Deco features create a most refined setting. Light rock and soft ballads are offered on weekends; **Sir Winston's Piano Bar**, also on board, is patronized by those in search of a quieter, more intimate ambiance. Former British prime-minister Winston Churchill is honoured here with a collection

of photographs and period objects.

San Fernando Valley

Crazy Jack's
4311 W. Magnolia Blvd., Burbank
☎(818) 845-1121
What would an American city be without a few country-music bars, the most popular music in the United States, in case anyone needs a reminder. Enjoy nightly entertainment and try your hand (or feet) at line dancing. Just the place to come as you are and quench your thirst.

Without wanting to compete with downtown's big theatre companies, small playhouses in the San Fernando Valley have managed to carve out a place for themselves on the stages of Los Angeles. The **Group Repertory Theatre** *(10900 Burbank Blvd., ☎818-769-7529)* has been a brilliant leading player in the development of the Valley's theatre scene, presenting a varied repertoire of plays, from experimental theatre to the classics of the stage.

In Glendale, **A Noise Within** *(234 S. Brand Blvd., Glendale, ☎818-546-1924)* mainly offers classical plays, notably those of Shakespeare and Molière. Moreover, a host of small theatre companies have cropped up in the new NoHo District. **Actor's Alley** *(5269 Lankershim Blvd., North Hollywood, ☎818-508-4200)* has set up shop in the historic El Portal Theater in order to present comedies, dramas or its own productions, while the **Actors Workout Studio** *(4735 Lankershim Blvd., ☎818-506-3903)* troupe regularly stages "one-man shows" in a small space.

Catalina Island

Marlin Club
every day 10pm to 2am
108 Catalina Ave.
☎510-0044
www.marlinclub.com
Although Catalina Island isn't known for its vibrant nightlife, there are nevertheless a few small bars where you can sip an aperitif or knock back a few beers. Among them, the Marlin Club is considered a pioneer as it has been entertaining visitors and islanders since 1946—something amply evidenced by the decor that has remained unchanged since that time.

Luau Larry's
509 Crescent Ave.
☎510-1919
"Where the bar meets the bay" is the motto of Luau Larry's, a bar offering a lovely view of Avalon Bay. Patrons here can quench their thirst with a "Wicky Wacker," the house drink,

or a home-brewed Garibaldi Lager.

El Galleon
411 Crescent Ave.
☎*510-1188*
Hot summer days prove to be the perfect time to take advantage of "happy hour" at El Galleon, located on very popular Crescent Avenue. Vacationers run aground here every day of the week until late at night to sample the bar's selection of microbrews and draught beers. Karaoke nights.

Inland Orange County

Anaheim

Sun Theatre
2200 E. Katella Ave.
☎*712-2700*
The Sun Theatre offers an intimate venue to catch some of the top names in the music industry. Dinner and show tickets are available which include a full three-course meal and the show.

Good Ol' Boys Saloon & Sports Bar
10624 Katella Ave.
☎*535-4355*
At the Good Ol' Boys Saloon & Sports Bar you'll be equally comfortable in cowboy boots or a ball cap as you catch a game on one of the big-screen TVs. Drink specials and a happy hour make this a popular spot.

Linda's Doll Hut
107 S. Adams
☎*879-8699*
Linda's Doll Hut is one of the most crowded clubs in Orange County. The size of a small apartment and with no stage, Linda's has had bands such as The Offspring, Weezer and Brian Setzer play in the corner of the bar.

Alcatraz Brewing Company
20 City Dr., Block in Orange
☎*939-8686*
The Alcatraz Brewing Company has a prison motif and a fun bar atmosphere with its many micro-brewed beers. Live blues and jazz are presented on the weekends.

Dave and Buster's
20 City Dr., Block in Orange
☎*769-1515*
Dave and Buster's is a combination restaurant, bar and arcade. Try one of their golf simulators, 150 video games or shoot some pool.

Crooner's Lounge
12911 Main St., Garden Grove
☎*638-3790*
Elvis fans will have to stop by the Crooner's Lounge in the Azteca Mexican Restaurant. The walls are covered with photos and memorabilia of the King himself,

and the music, of course, suits the decor. A fun place for a night out, but get here early to avoid a lineup.

El Calor
2916 W. Lincoln Ave.
☎*527-8873*
El Calor is a Latin dance favourite and tends to get crowded on Wednesday, which is gay night, when a fun drag show is presented.

Buena Park

Wild Bill's Wild West Dinner Extravaganza
7600 Beach Blvd.
☎*522-6414*
Wild Bill's Wild West Dinner Extravaganza offers a 2hr show nightly that features Western-style singing, dancing and even a comical magician. The price of admission includes the show plus an all-you-can-eat chicken and rib dinner including beer, wine and all the fixin's. Yeehaw! Reservations are required.

The Medieval Times Dinner & Tournament
7662 Beach Blvd.
☎*521-4740*
The Medieval Times Dinner & Tournament is a unique experience. Inside an 11th-century European-style castle, guests are encouraged to eat with their hands and cheer on the jousting and sword-fighting knights as they battle in the centre arena. One price includes a veritable feast of ribs and chicken, plus two rounds of beer, wine or soft drinks, and the show. Dinner shows take place nightly, and there is also a Sunday matinee. Reservations are required.

The Ozz
6231 Manchester Blvd.
☎*522-1542*
The Ozz is a high-quality gay club in Buena Park that offers fantastic dancing and a live cabaret show.

Costa Mesa

Orange County Performing Arts Center
600 Town Center Dr.
☎*556-2787*
Orange County Performing Arts Center features national and international selections of ballet, opera ballet, opera, musical theatre, classical music, and jazz throughout the year.

South Coast Repertory
655 Town Center Dr.
☎*708-5500*
The Tony-Award-winning South Coast Repertory provides creative new and classic drama and has drawn national attention for productions such as David Henry Hwang's *Golden Child*, first produced at South Coast Repertory and now on Broadway. Same day, half-price tickets can

be purchased at the box office.

Yard House
1875 Newport Ave.
☎***642-0090***
The Yard House has an incredible 250 beers on tap and a dark and inviting bar. Classic rock fills the bar, but not to the point that it drowns out conversation.

Shark Club
841 Baker St.
☎***751-6428***
The Shark Club is a beautiful club whose most striking feature is a 2,000-gallon (8,000L) shark tank in the middle of the 27 pool tables downstairs. A small, ambiance-filled room behind the bar spins techno beats. Happy hour Thursday and Friday.

Chester Drawers' Inn
179 E. 17th St.
☎***631-4277***
The Chester Drawers' Inn is a fun place to dance, with a friendly, energetic crowd and a relaxed dress code. Things get started pretty late, with the DJs spinning everything from alternative to dance and disco.

Santa Ana

Crazy Horse Saloon
1580 Brookhollow Dr.
☎***549-1512***
The Crazy Horse Saloon features live shows nightly by some up-and-coming and established country music acts.

The Beaches of Orange County

Seal Beach

Besides a few taverns like **Henessey's** *(143 Main St.; ☎598-6456)* and **O'Malley's** *(140 Main St.; ☎598-0843)*, most of the nightlife is found in Long Beach to the north or Newport Beach to the south.

Huntington Beach

Huntington Beach Playhouse
$13-15
Thu to Sat 8pm, Sun 2pm
7111 Talbert Ave.
☎***375-0696***
Huntington Beach Playhouse, has been entertaining Southern Californians since 1963 with itswide repertoire of musicals, dramas and comedy. Aside from stage shows, the company also presents Shakespeare in the Park,

weekends at 2pm *($7)* throughout the summer.

Gallagher's
300 Pacific Coast Hwy., Ste. 113
☎536-2422
In the mood for a laugh? Check out Gallagher's on Thursday nights for their comedy show. Admission is free before 8:30pm and $3 after.

Rhino Room
7979 Center Ave.
☎892-3316
For an entertaining night out, try the Rhino Room on Wednesdays with a full orchestra and free swing lessons. When your feet get sore, relax in the Martini Lounge upstairs.

Gecko's
7887 Center Dr.
☎892-0294
Fridays are big at Gecko's, with a high-energy, unpretentious crowd. A little bit of everything gets spun by the DJ, from Top 40 to brand-new alternative. Minors (18+) are admitted but can't drink.

Newport Beach

Newport Beach International Jazz Festival
☎650-LIVE
The Newport Beach International Jazz Festival takes place in May at selected venues around the city including the Hard Rock Cafe and Fashion Island. The week long festival attracts acts from around the world.

Newport Theater Arts Center
2501 Cliff Dr.
☎631-0288
The Newport Theater Arts Center is known as the "theatre on the cliff" due to its envious position. Community theatre productions run throughout the year.

Newport Beach Brewing Company
2920 Newport Blvd.
☎675-8449
www.nbbrewco.com
The Newport Beach Brewing Company is the only micro-brewery in Newport Beach and offers a selection of homemade beers to enjoy inside or out in the gardens. A decent menu accompanies the original brews.

Margaritaville
2332 W. Coast Hwy.
☎631-4110
Margaritaville offers award-winning margaritas and live entertainment on Mariners Row.

The Blue Beet
107 21st Pl.
☎675-BEET
The Blue Beet is a favourite jazz and blues club near the Newport Pier. A lively mix of tourists and locals pack the club most nights of the week.

Woody's Wharf
2318 W. Newport Blvd.
☎675-0474
For live rock'n'roll, try Woody's Wharf with its great waterfront location.

Laguna Beach

Laguna Playhouse
$30-$40
606 Laguna Canyon Rd.
☎497-ARTS
www.lagunaplayhouse.com
The oldest continuously running theatre on the West Coast is the Laguna Playhouse, founded in 1920. This award-winning professional theatre company claims such alumni as Harrison Ford and has performances every night except Monday at 8pm, with two shows on the weekend at 2pm and 8pm. Dinner and brunch packages are available.

Ocean Brewing Company
237 Ocean Ave.
☎497-3381
The Ocean Brewing Company beside the Bombay Duck is a great place for after-dinner drinks. An enormous copper kettle dominates the bar area while a small fireplace gives it a slightly homey glow. They have a fine selection of local micro brews and are quite busy on weekends.

Laguna Beach Brewery
$6-$10
422 S. Coast Hwy.
☎499-BEER
The Laguna Beach Brewery is a second-floor brewpub right across from the Hotel Laguna. If you choose the right seat you can even get a good view of the ocean. Try the Thai chicken pizza and the artichoke chicken pasta. Burgers are available in beef, turkey and vegetarian. Try the sampler of their seven beers brewed on site.

Sandpiper Lounge
1183 S. Pacific Coast Hwy.
☎494-4694
The Sandpiper Lounge is a popular place with locals and gets jammed with gyrating locals on Tuesday, Thursday and Saturday.

Dana Point

Renaissance
24701 Del Prado Ave.
☎661-6003
For the best in jazz and blues, stop by the Renaissance, which has live shows seven nights a week with little or no cover charge. Shows start at 8pm, but on weekends get there early as it can get packed.

Hennessey's Tavern
34111 La Plaza
☎488-0121
Hennessey's Tavern has a familiar pub-style atmo-

sphere and some imported beers on tap.

San Clemente

China Beach Canteen
2371 S. El Camino Real
☎ ***492-6228***
The China Beach Canteen offers a casual night out with live music, dancing and a fun atmosphere.

Jonny James Steakhouse and Lounge
301 N. El Camino Real
☎ ***492-5666***
In addition to fine cuts of meat, the Jonny James Steakhouse and Lounge, offers jazz, swing and blues Wednesday through Saturday.

Cabrillo Playhouse
$12
202 Avenida Cabrillo
☎ ***492-0465***
For community theatre, check out what's happening at the Cabrillo Playhouse. The playhouse itself is in a historic 1926 white stucco house with a Spanish tile roof.

San Juan Capistrano

The Swallows Inn
31786 Camino Capistrano
☎ ***493-3188***
The Swallows Inn is a cowboy saloon that features live music and dancing six nights a week. Grab your boots and head in for some line dancing and cheap beer. Happy hour 4pm to 6pm.

Freight House Saloon
26701 Verdugo St.
☎ ***493-9593***
The Freight House Saloon is a comfortable bar located in the historic train depot. Live music is provided most nights of the week. Note the restored mural depicting life in San Juan.

Coach House Concert Theatre
33157 Camino Capistrano
☎ ***496-8930***
The Coach House Concert Theatre hosts a variety of live events from jazz and blues to rock and reggae. B.B. King and Chris Isaak have graced this intimate venue in the past. A full bar and dinner service are also available. Call to find out the latest events.

Oceanside

Oceans 11 Casino
121 Brooks St.
☎ ***439-6988***
If you're feeling lucky, you might want to try out the Oceans 11 Casino with an assortment of card games, from blackjack to seven card stud. Live entertainment and a full meal service is available in the Rat Pack Lounge.

La Mission
3232 Mission Ave.
☎*435-9977*
In addition to its authentic Mexican food, La Mission is also home to the Las Fuentes Cantina, with Spanish music and dancing, as well as top dance hits until 2am.

Strand Bar
608 N. Pacific Coast Hwy.
☎*722-7831*
The Strand Bar is a popular watering hole in Oceanside with pool tables, live rock and roll on weekends and an omnipresent jukebox.

Palm Springs

Casinos

Spa Hotel and Casino
24hrs
100 N. Indian Canyon Dr.
☎*325-1461*
At the Spa Hotel and Casino you can try your luck at the one of the 1,100 slot machines or sit in on a hand of poker or blackjack.

Theatre

Palm Canyon Theatre
538 N. Palm Canyon Dr.
☎*323-5123*
The Palm Canyon Theatre is the only professional theatre company in the Coachella Valley. Check out one of their Broadway-style plays or musicals.

Annenberg Theater
1101 Museum Dr.
☎*325-4490*
The Annenberg Theater in the Desert Museum presents ballet, opera and classical music in a 450-seat, state-of-the-art theatre facility.

Plaza Theater
128 S. Palm Canyon Dr.
☎*327-0225*
The Plaza Theater is home to the critically acclaimed Palm Springs International Film Festival.

Bars and Nightclubs

Hair of the Dog
238 N. Palm Canyon Rd.
☎*323-9890*
The Hair of the Dog is a little hole-in-the-wall English pub across from the Hyatt Downtown. They have plenty of international bottled beers and great happy-hour specials.

Zeldaz
169 N. Indian Canyon Dr.
☎*325-2375*
Zeldaz may not look like much from the outside, but has been a local hotspot for

the past 22 years. Dancing, comedy and live entertainment are presented.

Banana'z
72291 Hwy. 111, Palm Desert
☎ ***776-4333***
Banana'z is a sports bar during the day with over 40 TVs catching all the action. At night it's a lively dance bar.

Blue Guitar
125 E. Tahquitz Canyon Way
☎ ***327-1549***
The Blue Guitar is an intimate concert nightclub that presents local and international blues and jazz artists. The balcony on the second floor is perfect for people watching.

Peabody's Coffee Bar
134 S. Palm Canyon Dr.
☎ ***322-1877***
Peabody's Coffee Bar offers java and jazz in a comfortable lounge setting.

The Gay Scene

Los Angeles is home to a large and vibrant gay population. Several establishments therefore cater to this crowd, mostly in West Hollywood, Venice and Santa Monica.

Every year, in late June, Los Angeles's gay community fills the streets of West Hollywood for the **Los Angeles Gay and Lesbian Pride Celebration**, an exuberant parade and festival that stretches over two days.

There's also Halloween on October 31, a day during which the gay community joins in the wild costume party on Santa Monica Blvd., dressing in the most outrageous disguises.

Bars

Beige
6290 Sunset Blvd.
☎ ***(323) 871-2995***
The smart set congregates at the convivial Beige, a weekly dance night at 360° (see p 327).

Circus Disco and Arena
6655 Santa Monica Blvd.
☎ ***(323) 462-1291***
You can dance up a storm at the Circus Disco and Arena, which draws both a gay and "straight" crowd. Rock and techno beats get top billing.

Club 7969
7969 Santa Monica Blvd.
☎ ***(323) 654-0280***
Club 7969 offers drag shows and live rock music. Gays, lesbians and heteros mingle on the large dance floor, at the two bars and around the pool table.

Girl Bar
652 N. La Peer Dr.
☎659-4551
One of the hottest lesbian bars in town is Girl Bar, which caters to those looking to see and be seen. A few West Hollywood hotels host the club on various nights.

Jewel's Catch One
4067 W. Pico Blvd., Mid-Wilshire
☎(323) 734-8849
Though somewhat removed from West Hollywood's gay scene, Jewel's Catch One is worth considering for the diversity of its clientele. Gays and "straights" gather here to cut loose until late into the night (closing time: 4am Fri and Sat).

Rage
8911 Santa Monica Blvd.
☎652-7055
The Rage dance club is a longstanding favourite with the all-muscle crowd. DJs spin different music every night, including house, dance remix and keraoke. Snacks available.

Sports

Perhaps a bit surprisingly for a city as decentralized as Los Angeles, the major **professional sport** venues are concentrated near the downtown area. **Dodger Stadium**, set atop a panoramic but isolated ravine about 1mi 1.6km north of downtown L.A., is one of the great temples of major league **baseball** and home to the National League's legendary Dodgers since soon after the team's controversial move from Brooklyn in 1957. More than four decades after its construction, this magnificent 56,000-seat open-air stadium is still regarded as one of the finest baseball venues in the land.

The six-month regular season opens in early April. At the time of writing, no game here had ever been postponed because of rain, a great tribute Southern California's climate. (The Los Angeles area's other major league baseball team, the Angels of the American League, play at Anaheim Stadium in Orange County.) Dodger Stadium is easy to reach by car and is surrounded by many acres of free parking. (In a less flattering reflection of Southern California, it's not served by public transit. The nearest bus stop is at the corner of Sunset Boulevard and Elysian Park Avenue, about a 10min walk from the stadium. Taxis are usually available after each game directly behind the centre field wall.) Tickets are easy to obtain for most games *(information: ☎323-224-1400, www.dodgers.com).*

Two professional **basketball** teams (the Lakers and Clippers) and one professional **hockey** team (the Kings) share the gleaming new 19,300-seat indoor **Staples Center** *(Figueroa St. at 11th St., adjacent to the Convention Center)*. Named after an office-supply retailer that paid a sponsorship fee, the Staples Center opened in 1999. The regular season in both the National Basketball Association and the National Hockey League begins in early October and runs until April, followed by interminable playoff series. For schedule and ticket information, contact the Lakers *(☎213-480-3232, www.nba.com/lakers)*, the Clippers *(☎213-742-7555, www.nba.com/clippers)*, or the Kings *☎888-546-4752, www.lakings.com)*.

The L.A. area is home to vast numbers of football fans, but for some strange reason its two National Football League teams both departed in 1995 and nobody rushed in to fill the vacuum. That leaves **college football**, which has a very wide following. The top venue is the venerable **Los Angeles Coliseum** in Exposition Park, home to the University of Southern California Bruins and their heated rivalry with the Trojans of the University of California at Los Angeles (UCLA).

Staples Center

Shopping

Like almost every other aspect of life in Los Angeles, shopping follows the dictates of a very decentralized geography, and the often neglected downtown area is not necessarily where the action is, especially now that the grand old department stores are all gone.

The big suburban malls, as well as some of the upscale shopping streets in districts like Beverly Hills and Hollywood, account for larger shares of consumer spending, particularly for trendy or fashionable items. But wherever you decide to shop, you're sure to amass some great souvenirs of the L.A. experience!

Downtown Los Angeles

Even if downtown L.A. is not the region's top shopping destination, it does offer quirky and original experiences that should not be neglected, especially by bargain-hunters and seekers of the exotic.

A shopping tour could begin in the southeast corner of downtown L.A., in the extensive **garment district**, whose promoters call it the **Fashion District**, though the emphasis is more on everyday, down-to-earth items than on pricier fashions.

Hundreds of shops—some independently run, others operated as outlets for nearby factories—offer a broad range of name-brand and generic goods, often at substantial savings compared to the big chain stores.

The garment district covers much of an often grimy area seven blocks wide and eight blocks long, bound by Broadway Avenue on the west, Seventh Street on the north, Wall Street on the east, and Pico Boulevard on the south. What you find here is miles removed from your average shopping mall environment and light years distant from the sunny Southern California stereotypes. Many shops operate on a cash-and-carry basis, with no credit cards accepted and no returns or exchanges. Some specialize in overruns or in goods that are slightly flawed—it's important to pay attention. Dressing rooms are often rudimentary or nonexistent. And haggling over price may sometimes be part of the experience, particularly in the outdoor bazaar known as Santee Alley near Olympic Boulevard and 12th Street. Elsewhere, certain establishments cater exclusively to the wholesale trade.

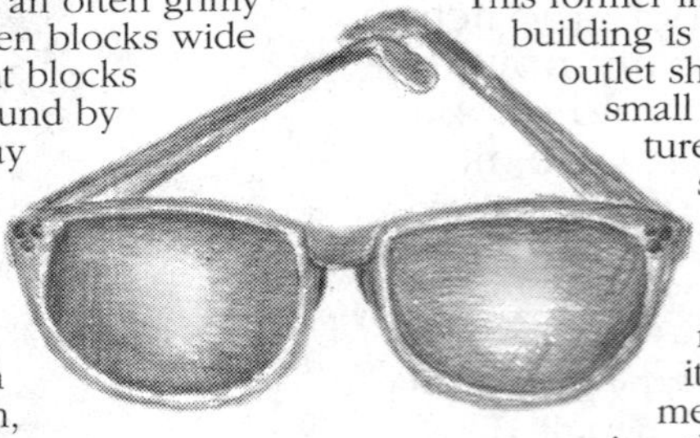

For the less adventurous, a good place to look for women's clothing is the eight-storey Cooper Building at the corner of Ninth and Los Angeles streets. This former industrial building is filled with outlet shops for small manufacturers, with some shops selling brand-name items. For men's clothing, there is a cluster of shops along Los Angeles Street between Seventh and Ninth. Wall Street offers selections of fabrics as well as over-size and children's clothing.

Another specialized shopping area downtown is the **jewellery district**, centred around Hill Street between Sixth and Seventh streets. Many dozens of small establishments offer a vast selection of jewellery and watches at often cut-rate prices, some produced locally and others imported from Asia. Prices and quality tend to be lower to middle range. Some shops face the street directly, but many others are hidden away along indoor passageways between several buildings in the immediate area. Signs posted at the entrances make these buildings easy to spot.

Broadway lies at the heart of downtown L.A's historic shopping district. Its character has changed immensely over the decades, and the ornate stone facades of many buildings pay homage to an earlier, more prosperous era. Today, the street has recovered much of its former vitality, although the dominant language is Spanish rather than English. Many of the businesses cater to L.A.'s large Mexican and Central American immigrant communities, particularly along an extremely vibrant stretch between Third and Ninth streets. This is a good place to look for low-end electronic goods, assorted luggage, and cheaper items of clothing and footwear. The **Grand Central Market** (also described on p 110), bordering Broadway between Third and Fourth streets offers a variety of food, ranging from bulk produce to freshly cut meat to cheap and satisfying sit-down or take-out meals.

Downtown L.A. also offers a range of ethnic shopping experiences that straddle the divide between the authentic and the touristy. **Olvera Street**, located at the northern edge of the El Pueblo de Los Angeles historic district between the Civic Center and Union Station, is a block-long pedestrian-only street lined with **Mexican** handicraft stalls and restaurants. Interesting selections of leather items, textiles, clothing, jewellery, paintings and carvings are available. **Little Tokyo** features dozens of shops, with the biggest concentration found in the **Japanese Village Plaza** covering part of the block bound by First Street, San Pedro Street, Second Street and Central Avenue. Items include Japanese crafts, toys and clothing. **Chinatown**, north of the Civic Center, is dotted with shops selling items ranging from heavy porcelain planters to light silk scarves. There are also many food shops.

More recent additions to the shopping scene, located toward the western edge of the downtown area, include the attractive open-air **Seventh Market Place**, at Seventh and Figueroa streets, built around a distinctive three-storey circular atrium, with two department stores among its approximately 50 retail establishments. **Macy's Plaza**, a block away at Seventh Street and Flower Street, contains a branch of the namesake department store chain and about 30 other shops. These outlets, however, hardly compare in scale to the grand downtown department stores they replaced.

Gifts and Souvenirs

Dalmatian's Fire House
2900 W. Temple St.
☎*(213) 380-2900, ext. 264*
The Los Angeles Fire Department opens its doors to the public to liquidate its surplus of goods, including T-shirts, pieces that need mending, unused accessories and other finds.

Galco's Old World Grocery
5702 York Blvd.
☎*(323) 255-7115*
Galco's Old World Grocery is a small family grocery store in Highland Park that specializes in the hard-to-find soft drinks and beers of yesteryear. Soft-drink lovers can enjoy Grapett, Nehi and even Delaware Punch, while beer connoisseurs will delight in the vast selection of beers brewed around the world.

Carol and Barry Kaye Museum of Miniatures
5900 Wilshire Blvd., East Wing
☎*(323) 937-6464*
For a different gift idea, visit the Carol and Barry Kaye Museum of Miniatures, which offers miniature crafts, each more original than the next.

Antiques

BPA Collectibles
Mon-Fri 9am to 5pm
1315 W. Pico Blvd.
☎*(213) 749-7145*
BPA Collectibles is a warehouse antique store, where you can find treasures from Asia, Africa and India, as long as you are willing to pay the price.

Luggage

Richard's Luggage
Seventh + FIG Shopping Center, 735 S. Figueroa St., Suite 221
☎*(213) 622-3519*
You'll find suitcases, handbags and all kinds of travel items at Richard's Luggage.

Pasadena

Old Pasadena has been revived and gentrified. A pleasant area for strolling and shopping, it's characterized by an eclectic mix of shops selling books, home furnishings, crafts, clothing, and a wide range of other items. Many are original one-of-a-kind shops, although some of the national chains have begun to intrude. The main shopping streets are Colorado Boulevard over a seven-block stretch between Pasadena Avenue and Los Robles Avenue, parallel portions of Green Street one block south, and a four-block section of South Lake Avenue running south from Colorado Boulevard, portions of it lined with London-style arcades.

The **Rose Bowl Flea Market** *($6 after 9am, $10-$15 before 9am; 6am to 3pm, 991 Rosemont Ave., Pasadena, ☎323-560-7469)* is held the second Sunday of each month at the namesake football stadium and bills itself as the biggest flea market in the U.S., with more than 1,500 vendors offering antique furnishings, clothing, assorted knick-knacks and more. **The Pasadena Antique Mall** *(free, Mon 10am to 5pm Tue- Sun 10am to 9pm, 35 S. Raymond St. between Colorado Blvd. and Green St., ☎626-304-9886)* has about 50 exhibitors offering a wide range of antiques.

Florists

Flowers by Piccolo at The Ritz-Carlton Hotel
1401 S. Oak Knoll Ave., Pasadena
☎(626) 577-7400
☎800-331-2100
Flowers by Piccolo at The Ritz-Carlton Hotel is an extremely renowned florist shop that offers a lovely selection of flowers and floral-design creations.

Accessories

Old Focals
40 W. Green St., Pasadena
☎(626) 793-7073
Old Focals offers a dazzling selection of eyeglasses (more than 50,000 pairs), especially in the retro style of the 1950s and 1960s.

Hollywood and Surroundings

Hollywood Boulevard, the central artery in a district synonymous with the film industry, is going through a difficult period of revival following decades of decline. Still, amid the garishness and tackiness that have come to characterize parts of the area are several first-rate shops offering posters, books, scripts, videos, tasteful souvenirs and assorted memorabilia. The stretch between Gower Street and La Brea Avenue is the main shopping area.

Melrose Avenue between Fairfax and La Brea Avenues has developed a reputation for cutting-edge fashion. The street is lined with hundreds of boutiques and restaurants appealing to an upscale crowd but also to people with an eye for some of the hipper trends in clothing and jewellery. It's also fun just for a stroll.

The **Los Felix-Silver Lake** area at the eastern edge of Hollywood has emerged as a leading centre of Bohemian life, with numerous cafés, nightclubs and funky shops scattered over a vast area. Some shops are clustered in smaller areas, in particular along Vermont Avenue between Hollywood Boulevard and Franklin Avenue and nearby along Sunset Avenue between Vermont and Hillhurst avenues. This is where to look for vintage clothing, trendy modern clothing, strange items of furniture and household accessories (for example, a store named Plastica, 4685 Hollywood Boulevard east of Vermont Avenue, focuses on plastic objects from the 1950s), and music shops appealing to specialized tastes in CDs and vinyl.

The **Sunset Strip** in West Hollywood has achieved fame for the eccentric character of some of its denizens and commercial establishments, but this long stretch of Sunset Avenue between La Cienega Boulevard and Doheny Drive is also home to the two largest mainstream record shops in L.A., Tower Records *(8801 W. Sunset Blvd.)* and Virgin Megastore *(8000 W. Sunset Blvd.)*. A varied selection of shops offer clothing, jewellery, books, stage props and diverse other items.

On a completely different note, **Universal City Walk** in North Hollywood, adjacent to the Universal Studios theme park, is a sanitized recreation of a traditional shopping street for people who want to escape from the modern mall environment without exposing themselves to some of the harsher realities of urban life. Nonetheless, among its several dozen shops are a few selling original Native American crafts, antique toys, ecologically sensitive gifts and science fiction memorabilia.

Video Rentals

Eddie Brant's Film Store
5006 Vineland Ave., North Hollywood
☎ ***(818) 506-4242***
Real movie buffs will not want to miss this video store, which offers no fewer than 45,000 videos, most of which are hard to come by. Here, you're likely to find 20th-century movie and TV productions, especially

silent movies, animation and foreign films.

Art Galleries

Mordechai's North Hollywood Studio
12414 Burbank Blvd., North Hollywood
☎*(818) 980-9026*
www.jewishartbymh.com
For something exclusive, head to Mordechai's North Hollywood Studio, a remarkable gallery featuring Jewish art. The handmade painted-porcelain pieces are a great gift idea.

Men's and Women's Clothing

Reel Clothes & Props
12132 Ventura Blvd., Studio City
☎*(818) 508-7762*
www.reelclothes.com
Reel Clothes & Props is a second-hand clothes shop that sells clothing from TV and movie sets. You can buy dresses, jackets or pants that have been worn in movies or TV series. Extremely popular in Los Angeles.

Westside and Mid-Wilshire

Rodeo Drive in Beverly Hills is one of the best-known and most elegant shopping streets in the United States. Many of the famous names—Tiffany, Louis Vuitton, Giorgio, Hermès, Gucci, Ralph Lauren—along with others that are less famous but no less classy are clustered along a short three-block stretch between Wilshire and Santa Monica boulevards. The street runs through the heart of what has become known as the **Beverly Hills Golden Triangle**, bound by the above two boulevards and Crescent Drive, with Beverly Hills City Hall at its apex. This small triangular area forms a shopping district for the seriously wealthy and the seriously pretentious, but also for ordinary folk out on a splurge.

Beverly Hills is flanked by two major malls located outside its municipal limits. The **Century City Shopping Center** *(10250 Santa Monica Blvd. in Century City just west of Beverly Hills)* is a generally upscale mall open to the outdoors, with two department stores and a multi-screen cinema complex. The **Beverly Center** *(Beverly Blvd. and La Cienega Ave., a short distance east of Beverly Hills)* is a high-end, multi-storey mall that also includes two department stores and a multi-screen cinema complex as well as a food court. With about 160 stores, it differs from most other L.A.-area malls with its vertical structure and multiple layers of indoor parking.

A little further east, at Fairfax Avenue and Third Street, is the partly open-air **Farmers Market** with numerous stalls selling fresh produce, meat and seafood, as well as various prepared dishes or gift items.

Music

Weisshaar Hans
627 N. Larchemont Blvd.
☎ ***(213) 466-6293***
Since 1947, the stringed-instrument makers of this tiny workshop have repaired the violins and cellos of L.A.'s great musicians, including those of the Los Angeles Philharmonic and the Hollywood Bowl Orchestra. Weisshaar Hans also sells precious instruments and counts virtuosos Isaac Stern and Mstislav Rostropovich among its customers.

Rhino Records
1720 Westwood Blvd.
☎ ***474-8685***
Rhino Records sells a vast selection of new and second-hand recordings, in all formats: cassette, CD, vinyl. The staff's expertise makes Rhino Records popular with all music lovers.

For music, the two biggest mainstream CD shops are located a flew blocks apart on the Sunset Strip, **Tower Records** *(8801 W. Sunset Blvd.)* and **Virgin Megastore** *(8000 W. Sunset Blvd.)* **Rhino Record** *(1720 Westwood Blvd., north of Santa Monica Blvd.)* is something of a local institution and is noted for its selection of independent music. It also has a second-hand section.

Children's Clothing

Harry Harris Shoes for Children
409 N. Canyon Dr.
☎ ***274-8481***
Harry Harris Shoes for Children has a large selection of leather and sport shoes for kids.

Tartine et Chocolat
316 N. Beverly Dr.
☎ ***786-7882***
Tartine et Chocolat is a chic boutique that sell children's clothing and accessories imported from France.

Men's Clothing

Hugo Boss
Beverly Center, 8500 N. La Cienega Blvd.
☎ *659-6675*
Men's fashion is always done justice at Hugo Boss, which offers stylish designers suits, as well as just as fashionable ready-to-wear clothing.

Men's and Women's Clothing

Emporio Armani Boutique
9533 Brighton Way
☎ *271-7790*
The master Italian designer is well represented in Los Angeles with his three-storey boutique featuring sports clothes, audacious and elegant accessories, and a perfume counter selling Armani fragrances.

NikeTown
9560 Wilshire Blvd.
☎ *275-9998*
The screens that continuously display sporting events make Nike Town a fun place to shop for sports clothes and accessories.

Department stores

Barneys New York
9570 Wilshire Blvd.
☎*276-4400*
The West Coast branch of this stylish New York department store offers clothes for men and women, jewellery and designer shoes.

Saks Fifth Avenue
9600 Wilshire Blvd.
☎ *275-4211*
Saks Fifth Avenue is another U.S. retail and fashion giant.

Candies and Chocolates

See's Candies
3423 S. La Cienega Blvd.
☎ *559-4911*
Chocolate holds a dear place in the hearts of connoisseurs, and this is precisely why See's Candies's creations are so appreciated by lovers of its delicious chocolate and other sweets.

Jewellery

Cartier
370 N. Rodeo Dr.
☎ *275-4272*
220 N. Rodeo Dr.
☎*275-5155*
The highly renowned French jeweller has two locations on Rodeo Drive,

but both stores offer the same high quality for luxurious gifts and sumptuous jewellery.

Santa Monica and Surroundings

Santa Monica's **Third Street Promenade** is one of North America's most successful pedestrian-only shopping streets. It succeeds because it contains a mixture of businesses that include many restaurants, cafés, cinemas, bookshops, music stores and other establishments that draw large crowds until late in the evening. It also has many clothing stores. Covering three long blocks from Broadway to Wilshire Boulevard, the Third Street Promenade is designed with small kiosks, benches and other installations that ease pedestrian movement without creating feelings of agoraphobia. Large directories at each corner can help shoppers find their way. Musicians and other street performers contribute to the lively atmosphere. This is justifiably one of the most popular streets in California. At its southern end is the stylish Santa Monica Place indoor shopping mall.

Another popular shopping street in Santa Monica is **Montana Avenue**, where a 10-block stretch from Seventh to 17th streets is home to many original boutiques offering interesting selections of home furnishings, as well as clothing, jewellery, items for children and other merchandise. A long section of **Main Street**, stretching from Pacific Street in Santa Monica to Rose Avenue in Venice, is sprinkled with art galleries, funky boutiques, small cafés and restaurants, antique shops and stores selling beach supplies ranging from surfboards to swimsuits.

Ocean Front Walk, running alongside Venice Beach, gives new meaning to "hip." If you ever need tie-dyed T-shirts, weird sunglasses, leather bikinis, or almost any sort of personal ornament that tickles your sense of the outrageous, this is where to come, especially on weekends.

Gifts and souvenirs

Discovery Channel Store
Third St. Promenade, corner Arizona St., Santa Monica
☎ ***899-9021***
The famous TV channel's boutique sells related items, at the heart of Santa Monica.

Art Galleries

Bergamot Station
2525 Michigan Ave., B-1, Santa Monica
☎*453-7535*
Bergamot Station houses several contemporary art galleries under the same roof. This cultural centre is perfect for contemporary-art lovers who enjoying browsing, and admiring countless works of art.

Car Wash

Santa Palm Car Wash
8787 Santa Monica Blvd.
☎*(310) 659-7888*
You will surely have noticed that Los Angeles has a countless number of car washes to keep its cars clean and shiny. In addition to marvellously serving its purpose, the Santa Palm Car Wash has a terrific ambience that helps exhausted drivers relax. All you have to do is sit down in an automated massage chair to enjoy a 5min Swedish or Shiatsu massage.

Shoes

Step Shoes
1004 Montana Ave., Santa Monica
☎ *899-4409*
Step Shoes offers a vast array of shoes, in all sizes and styles, for men, women and children.

Posters

Jason Vass Gallery
1210-A Montana Ave., Santa Monica
☎ *395-2048*
Those who love reproductions, posters and prints will be in heaven at the Jason Vass Gallery in Santa Monica, which sells original Edwardian-style, Art Nouveau and Art Deco, propaganda and movie (1880-1950) signs and posters.

Children's Clothing

Baby Boomers
1607 Montana Ave., Santa Monica
☎ *434-9902*
Baby Boomers sells all kinds of clothes, accessories and gifts for children, in all price ranges.

Women's Clothing

BCBG Max Azria
10250 Santa Monica Blvd.
☎ *553-2281*
8634 W. Sunset Blvd.
☎ *360-0946*
At BCBG Max Azria, you will find exquisite, stylish women's fashions that are all the rage on the West Coast.

Lisa Norman
1134 Montana Ave., Santa Monica
☎*(310) 451-2026*
Lisa Norman sells suggestive and elegant women's lingerie.

Sports Equipment

ZJ Boarding House
2619 Main St., Santa Monica
☎*(310) 392-56469*
www.zjboardinghouse.com
Surfing, snowboarding and skateboarding all require a little talent, but good equipment is essential. Head to ZJ Boarding House for boards, clothes and accessories.

Home Decor

Restoration Hardware
10250 Santa Monica Blvd., Century City Shopping Center
☎*551-4995*
A short visit to Restoration Hardware will surely give you tons of original ideas to decorate your home, whether you are looking for lovely utensils, innovative furniture or original accessories.

South Bay

Hermosa Beach Pier Strand, along Pier Avenue between Hermosa Avenue and the pier in Hermosa Beach, has been spruced up and converted to an attractive palm-lined walkway with shops and restaurants. Although serious shoppers may not find the selection of fashions and other items especially interesting, the setting is distinctive.

Long Beach

Women's Clothing

Annie's Closet
4554 Atlantic Ave., Long Beach
☎*428-7330*
Women will surely find a little something to treat themselves at Annie's Closet. The boutique abounds in a vast array of beautiful clothing.

Catalina Island

One of the favourite activities of vacationers on Catalina Island is no doubt strolling through the village and buying a few things in its boutiques. Avalon has several shops, all of which are located near Crescent Avenue. The **Metropole Market Place** *(entrance on Metropole Ave., corner Crescent)* is a charming, French-style, commercial street that has several gift shops, craft, T-shirt and sports stores. The lovely **Art, Caps'n Designs** *(Metropole Market Place, ☎510-2620)* souvenir shop, the **Bay of the Seven Moons** *(☎510-1450)* craft store and finally, if you're looking for a romantic gift, **First Comes Love...** *(☎510-2199, www.catalinatoday.com/weddings)* are all worth mentioning.

El Encantor, another commercial street, is located at the end of Crescent Avenue, on the way to the casino. It features art stores and beachwear, as well as a jewellery store.

Avalon Bay Company
407 Crescent Ave.
☎*510-0178*
www.avalonbaycompany.com
The Avalon Bay Company has the island's widest selection of women's clothing, shoes and accessories.

Moondance Jewelry Gallery
1530 Montana Ave.
☎ *395-5516*
The elegant Moondance Jewelry Gallery offers a lovely selection of admittedly expensive, but extremely flamboyant jewellery. No fewer than 70 artisan-jewellers work to create these gems.

Inland Orange County

Anaheim

Anaheim Plaza
530 N. Euclid St.
☎*429-3002*
The Anaheim Plaza is an open-air shopping centre located a few minutes north of Disneyland at the I-5 Freeway and Euclid Street. Major department stores are represented, as well as a few specialty shops.

Hobby City
1238 S. Beach Blvd.
☎*527-2323*
Hobby City is 6 acres (3ha) of hobby, collector and craft shops located beside Adventure City.

Orange

The Block at Orange
City Dr. at I-5
☎*769-4001*
Just a few minutes to the east of Anaheim is the city of Orange and its multitude of shopping possibilities. The Block at Orange is Orange County's newest outdoor mall. Amid the neon lights, The Block is an attraction in itself, with a full city block of restaurants, cafés, shopping and entertainment. The open air concept takes advantage of California's sunny climate.

Old Town Plaza Heritage District
At Chapman Ave. and Glassel St.
For a more nostalgic experience, the Old Town Plaza Heritage District is home to the largest block of buildings on the National Register of Historic Places. These late 19th- and early 20th-century buildings are home to more than 40 antique stores.

Santa Ana

MainPlace
2800 N. Main St.
☎***547-7800***
MainPlace is Santa Ana's main shopping centre and home to 190 stores, a six-plex theatre and four restaurants. A free shuttle service is available by contacting the front desk of your hotel.

Costa Mesa

South Coast Plaza
3333 Bristol St.
☎***435-2000***
The South Coast Plaza is visited by 23 million people every year. Hundreds of stores in this beautiful, modern shopping centre are complimented by excellent dining choices. It is also home to the Discovery Launch Pad, a preview of the Discovery Science Centre (see "Exploring," p 187). Located in the Orange County Theatre District.

Lab Anti-Mall
2930 Bristol St.
☎***996-6660***
If you're not looking for the Lab Anti-Mall, you'll probably miss it. The one-storey, renovated factory is an eclectic mix of 16 second-hand boutiques, funky clothing stores and intimate cafés.

Farmers Market
Thu 8:30am to 1pm
88 Fair Dr.
☎***723-6616***
The grounds of the Orange County Fair & Exposition Center hosts a Farmers Market every Thursday with a selection of locally grown produce as well as crafts.

The Beaches of Orange County

Laguna Beach

Laguna is famous for its art galleries, boutiques and local craft stores which can all be found along the Pacific Coast Highway. The main areas are in the 300-400 north block and from 900 to 1800 south.

Huntington Beach

The **Farmers Market** and **Art A-Faire Street Faire** takes place Fridays from noon to dusk at Pier Plaza, beside the Huntington Pier. In addition to the local produce, there is also a great selection of handmade art and collectibles.

Loehmann's Five Points Plaza
18593 Main St.
☎***841-0036***
Loehmann's Five Points Plaza has a collection of fashion and specialty stores

including the full spectrum of Gap stores, Bath & Body Works and Old Navy.

Newport Beach

The stretch of Pacific Coast Highway between Newport Boulevard and Dover Drive is known as **Mariners Mile**. Along this mile is a great collection of shops and galleries that all share a common nautical theme.

Fashion Island
Mon - Fri 10am to 9pm, Sat 10am to 7pm, Sun 11am to 6pm
☎800-495-4753
www.fashionisland-nb.com
Fashion Island can be reached by Newport Center Drive from the Pacific Coast Highway. A unique upscale American shopping centre, Fashion Island is a collection of over 200 specialty shops and department stores, and over 40 cafés and restaurants. There is also a farmers market in the main plaza and plenty to keep the kids occupied. The open-air plazas and Mediterranean ambiance make for a wallet-draining experience.

Dana Point

The harbour in Dana Point is home to a variety of small boutiques, galleries and specialty stores all within a short walk.

San Clemente

Posh Peasant
220 Avenida del Mar
☎498-7813
The Posh Peasant is a charming antique and collectible store. While you're there, stop for a break in the tea room.

San Juan Capistrano

Downtown San Juan Capistrano features antique, craft and collectible shopping in many of the old historic buildings that surround the mission.

Palm Springs

Desert Walk
123 N. Canyon Dr.
☎320-8282
The Desert Walk shopping center features some of the most upscale fashion stores in Palm Springs including a Saks Fifth Avenue. There are also several restaurants to choose from.

Modern Way Mid-Century Furniture
Tue and Wed
by appointment only
1426 N. Palm Canyon Dr.
☎320-5455
Modern Way Mid-Century Furniture has everything to

suit your retro and Art Deco furnishing needs. They were also instrumental in furnishing the retro-styled Ballantine's Hotel. (see p 268)

Adagio Galleries
closed Wed and Thu
193 S. Palm Canyon Dr.
☎320-2230
The Adagio Galleries has a wonderful collection of Southwest, Californian, and Native American art on display and for sale.

G. Wm. Craig Bookseller
33 N. Palm Canyon Dr.
☎323-7379
G. Wm. Craig Bookseller is a small bookstore that deals in used but also rare and first edition books.

Dazzles
1414 N. Palm Canyon Dr.
☎327-1446
Dazzles sells 1950s furniture, antiques and decorations.

Natures RX
555 S. Sunrise Way
☎323-9487
Natures RX has a wide selection of natural and homeopathic vitamins, herbs and health food.

Outlaw Lingerie
245 S. Calm Canyon Dr.
☎322-1675
Outlaw Lingerie has a wide assortment of things to get a little more (or less) comfortable in.

Bookstores in Los Angeles and Surroundings

Some L.A. residents recently arrived from New York or Boston have been known to complain that the city has a paucity of serious bookshops for a place its size, but visiting bibliophiles should have little trouble finding something to whet their appetites.

One of the better parts of town to look for books is the Third Street Promenade in Santa Monica which, besides large outlets of national chains **Borders** and **Barnes & Noble**, has several well-stocked independent bookshops, among them **Midnight Special Bookstore**, with many authors readings on site and an obvious sense of political commitment, and **Hennessy & Ingalls**, specializing in books on art, design and architecture. All are just a couple of blocks apart.

Two of the most noted independent bookshops in L.A. are **Book Soup** *(8818 W. Sunset Blvd., West Hollywood)* and **Dutton's Brentwood Books** (*11975 San Vicente Blvd. in Brentwood, west of Montana Ave.)*. Both have very extensive collections and knowledgeable staff.

For travel guidebooks and maps, places to look include **Thomas Bros. Books and Maps downtown** *(521 W. Sixth St. near Grand Ave.)* and **Traveler's Bookcase** on the west side *(8375 W. Third St. near La Cienega).* The latter also offers a selection of travel narratives.

Two of the biggest second-hand bookshops, both with immense selections, are **Acres of Books** in Long Beach *(240 Long Beach Blvd.)* and Book City in Hollywood.

Book City Collectables
6631 Hollywood Blvd.
☎ ***(323) 962-6242***
www.hollywoodbookcity.com
Book City Collectibles is a stunning bookstore that sells Hollywood screenplays. From great classics to the latest commercial blockbusters, Book City offers 2,000 screenplays and Hollywood productions for only a few bucks apiece. Scripts are generally sold for $15 but very long movies such as *Gone with the Wind* can go for $20.

UCLA Store
UCLA, Ackerman Union, 308 Westwood Plaza
☎ ***824-6064***
The UCLA Store is a complete university bookstore where you can also pick up sportswear featuring the UCLA logo.

Vroman's Bookstore
695 E. Colorado Blvd., Pasadena
☎ ***(626) 449-5320***
Vroman's Bookstore is Southern California's biggest and oldest independent bookstore and is a great place to discover the latest novel or even a limited-edition specialized work.

Mexican craft

index

Index

Travel Notes

Travel Notes

Order Form

Ulysses Travel Guides

- ☐ Acapulco . . . . . $14.95 CAN $9.95 US
- ☐ Alberta's Best Hotels and Restaurants . . . $14.95 CAN $12.95 US
- ☐ Atlantic Canada $24.95 CAN $17.95 US
- ☐ Beaches of Maine $12.95 CAN $9.95 US
- ☐ Inns and Bed & Breakfasts in Québec . . . . $14.95 CAN $10.95 US
- ☐ Belize . . . . $16.95 CAN $12.95 US
- ☐ British Columbia's Best Hotels and Restaurants . . . $14.95 CAN $12.95 US
- ☐ Calgary . . . . . . $17.95 CAN $12.95 US
- ☐ California . . . . . $29.95 CAN $21.95 US
- ☐ Canada . . . . $29.95 CAN $21.95 US
- ☐ Cancún & Riviera Maya . . . . . $19.95 CAN $14.95 US
- ☐ Cartagena (Colombia) . . . . . $12.95 CAN $9.95 US
- ☐ Chicago . . . . . . $19.95 CAN $14.95 US
- ☐ Chile . . . . $27.95 CAN $17.95 US
- ☐ Colombia . . . . . $29.95 CAN $21.95 US
- ☐ Costa Rica . . . . $27.95 CAN $19.95 US
- ☐ Cuba . . . . $24.95 CAN $17.95 US
- ☐ Dominican Republic . . . . $24.95 CAN $17.95 US
- ☐ Ecuador and Galápagos Islands . . $24.95 CAN $17.95 US
- ☐ El Salvador . . . . $22.95 CAN $14.95 US
- ☐ Guadalajara . . . $17.95 CAN $12.95 US
- ☐ Guadeloupe . . . $24.95 CAN $17.95 US
- ☐ Guatemala . . . . $24.95 CAN $17.95 US
- ☐ Havana . . . . . . $16.95 CAN $12.95 US
- ☐ Hawaii . . . . $29.95 CAN $21.95 US
- ☐ Honduras . . . . . $24.95 CAN $17.95 US
- ☐ Huatulco– Puerto Escondido . . . . $17.95 CAN $12.95 US
- ☐ Inns and Bed & Breakfasts in Québec . . . . $14.95 CAN $10.95 US
- ☐ Islands of the Bahamas . . $24.95 CAN $17.95 US
- ☐ Las Vegas . . . . . $17.95 CAN $12.95 US
- ☐ Lisbon . . . . $18.95 CAN $13.95 US
- ☐ Los Cabos and La Paz . . . . $14.95 CAN $10.95 US
- ☐ Louisiana . . . . . $29.95 CAN $21.95 US
- ☐ Martinique . . . . $24.95 CAN $17.95 US
- ☐ Miami . . . . $9.95 CAN $12.95 US
- ☐ Montréal . . . . . $19.95 CAN $14.95 US
- ☐ New Orleans . . $17.95 CAN $12.95 US
- ☐ New York City . $19.95 CAN $14.95 US
- ☐ Nicaragua . . . . . $24.95 CAN $16.95 US
- ☐ Ontario . . . . . . $27.95 CAN $19.95US
- ☐ Ontario's Best Hotels and Restaurants . . . $27.95 CAN $19.95US
- ☐ Ottawa–Hull . . . $17.95 CAN $12.95 US
- ☐ Panamá . . . . . . $24.95 CAN $17.95 US
- ☐ Peru . . . . $27.95 CAN $19.95 US
- ☐ Phoenix . . . . . . $16.95 CAN $12.95 US

Title	Qty	Price	Total
Name:		Subtotal	
		Shipping	$4 CAN $3 US
Address:		Subtotal	
		GST in Canada 7%	
		Total	

Tel: Fax:

E-mail:

Payment: ☐ Cheque ☐ Visa ☐ MasterCard

Card number__________________________

Expiry date________________

Signature____

ULYSSES TRAVEL GUIDES

4176 Saint-Denis,
Montréal, Québec,
H2W 2M5
☎(514) 843-9447
Fax: (514) 843-9448

305 Madison Avenue,
Suite 1166,
New York, NY 10165

Toll-free: 1-877-542-7247
Info@ulysses.ca
www.ulyssesguides.com

☐ Portugal . . . . . . $24.95 CAN $16.95 US
☐ Provence & the Côte d'Azur $29.95 CAN $21.95US
☐ Puerto Plata–Sosua . . $14.95 CAN $9.95 US
☐ Puerto Rico . . . $24.95 CAN $17.95 US
☐ Puerto Vallarta . $14.95 CAN $9.95 US
☐ Québec . . . . . . $29.95 CAN $21.95 US
☐ Québec City . . . $17.95 CAN $12.95 US
☐ Québec and Ontario with Via . . . . $9.95 CAN $7.95 US
☐ San Francisco . . $17.95 CAN $12.95 US
☐ Seattle . . . . $17.95 CAN $12.95 US
☐ St. Martin and St. Barts . . . . . $16.95 CAN $12.95 US
☐ Toronto . . . . . . $18.95 CAN $13.95 US
☐ Tunisia . . . . $27.95 CAN $19.95 US
☐ Vancouver . . . . $17.95 CAN $12.95 US
☐ Washington D.C. $18.95 CAN $13.95 US
☐ Western Canada $29.95 CAN $21.95 US

budget.zone

☐ Central America $14.95 CAN $10.95 US
☐ Western Canada $14.95 CAN $10.95 US

Ulysses Travel Journals

☐ Ulysses Travel Journal (Blue, Red, Green, Yellow, Sextant) . . . . $9.95 CAN $7.95 US
☐ Ulysses Travel Journal (80 Days) . . . . . $14.95 CAN $9.95 US

Ulysses Green Escapes

☐ Cycling in France $22.95 CAN $16.95 US
☐ Cycling in Ontario . . . . . $22.95 CAN $16.95 US
☐ Hiking in the Northeastern U.S. . . $19.95 CAN $13.95 US
☐ Hiking in Québec . . . . . $19.95 CAN $13.95 US

Ulysses Conversation Guides

☐ French for Better Travel . . . . $9.95 CAN $6.50 US
☐ Spanish for Better Travel in in Latin America $9.95 CAN $6.50 US